Other Works in English by Norman Manea

The Black Envelope

Compulsory Happiness

On Clowns: The Dictator and the Artist

October, Eight o'Clock

The Hooligan's Return

The Hooligan's Return

A MEMOIR

Norman Manea

Translated by Angela Jianu

Farrar, Straus and Giroux   New York

Farrar, Straus and Giroux
19 Union Square West, New York 10003

Copyright © 2003 by Norman Manea
Translation copyright © 2003 by Farrar, Straus and Giroux, LLC
All rights reserved
Distributed in Canada by Douglas & McIntyre Ltd.
Printed in the United States of America
First edition, 2003

Library of Congress Cataloging-in-Publication Data

Manea, Norman.
    The hooligan's return ; a memoir / Norman Manea ; translated by
Angela Jianu.
        p.   cm.
    ISBN 0-374-28256-0
    1. Manea, Norman.   2. Manea, Norman—Childhood and youth.
3. Manea, Norman—Journeys—Romania.   4. Novelists, Romanian—20th
century—Biography.   5. Romania—Description and travel.   6. Romanian
Americans—Biography.   7. Concentration camps—Romania.   I. Title.

PC840.23.A47Z466 2003
859'.334—dc21
[B]

                                                            2003044068

Designed by Cassandra J. Pappas

www.fsgbooks.com

10 9 8 7 6 5 4 3 2 1

For Cella

Contents

Preliminaries

Barney Greengrass

The bright spring light, like an emanation from Paradise, streams through the large picture window wide as the room itself. There is a man in the room, looking down from his tenth-floor apartment at the hubbub below, at the buildings, the shop signs, the pedestrians. In Paradise, he must remind himself again this morning, one is better off than anywhere else.

Across the street is a massive red-brick building. His eye catches groups of children going through their paces in dance and gym classes. Yellow lines of taxicabs, stuck in traffic at the juncture of Broadway and Amsterdam Avenue, are screaming, driven mad by the morning's hysterical metronome. The observer, however, is now oblivious to the tumult below, as he scrutinizes the sky, a broad expanse of desert across which drift, like desert beasts, slow-moving clouds.

Half an hour later, he stands on the street corner in front of the forty-two-story building where he lives, a stark structure, no ornamentation, a simple shelter, nothing less, or more, than an assemblage of boxes for human habitation. A Stalin-era apartment block, he thinks. But no Stalinist building ever reached such heights. Stalinist nonetheless, he repeats to himself, defying the stage set of his afterlife. Will he become, this morning, the man he was nine years ago, when he first arrived here, bewildered now, as he was then, by the novelty of life after death? Nine years, like nine months brimming with novel life in the womb of the adventure giving birth to this brand-new morning, like the beginning before all beginnings.

On the left, the drugstore where he regularly buys his medicines. He is idly looking at the store's sign—RITE AID PHARMACY, spelled out in white letters on a blue background—where suddenly five fire engines, like metallic fortresses, advance on the street in a screech of sirens and horns. Hell's fires can rage in Paradise, too.

But it is nothing serious, and in an instant everything is back in place—the photo shop where he is having the photo for his new ID processed; the neighborhood diner; the local Starbucks; and, of course, a McDonald's, its entrance graced by a pair of panhandlers. Next come the Pakistani newsstand, the Indian tobacconist, the Mexican restaurant, the ladies' dress shop, and the Korean grocery, with its large bunches of flowers and displays of yellow and green watermelons, black and red and green plums, mangoes from Mexico and Haiti, white and pink grapefruit, grapes, carrots, cherries, bananas, Fuji and Granny Smith apples, roses, tulips, carnations, lilies, chrysanthemums. He walks past small buildings and tall buildings, a mixture of styles and proportions and destinies, the Babylon of the New World, and of the Old World, too. There is a population to match—the tiny Japanese man in a red shirt and cap, swaying between two heavy loads of packages; the fair-haired, bearded, pipe-smoking man in shorts, walking between two big blond female companions in pink shorts and dark sunglasses; the tall, slim barefoot girl, with cropped red hair, skimpy T-shirt, and shorts the size of a fig leaf; the heavy, bald man with two children in his arms; the short fat man with a black mustache and a gold chain dangling down his chest; beggars and policemen and tourists as well, and none seem irreplaceable.

He crosses to Amsterdam Avenue at Seventy-second Street and is now in front of a small park, Verdi Square, a triangle of grass bordered on three sides by metal railings and presided over by a statue of Giuseppe Verdi, dressed in a tailcoat, necktie, and hat, surrounded by a bevy of characters from his operas on which the placid pigeons of Paradise have come to rest. A scattering of neighborhood denizens sit on the nearby benches, the pensioners, the disabled, the bums swapping stories and picking at their bags of potato chips and slices of pizza.

There is nothing lacking in Paradise—food and clothing and newspapers, mattresses, umbrellas, computers, footwear, furniture, wine, jewelry, flowers, sunglasses, CDs, lamps, candles, padlocks, dogs, cars, prostheses, exotic birds, and tropical fish. And wave after wave of salesmen, policemen, hairdressers, shoeshine boys, accountants, whores, beggars. All the varieties of human faces and languages and ages and heights and weights people that unlikely morning, on which the survivor is celebrating the nine years of his new life. In this new Afterlife world, all the distances and interdictions have been abolished, the fruit of the tree of knowledge is available on computer screens, the Tree of Eternal Life offers its pickings in all the pharmacies, while life rushes at breakneck speed and what really matters is the present moment.

Suddenly hell's alarm bells break out again. No fire this time, but a white, roaring juggernaut leaving behind the blur of a blood-red circle with a red cross and red letters reading AMBULANCE.

No, nothing is missing in this life-after-death, nothing at all. He raises his eyes toward the heavens that allowed this miracle to happen. An amputated firmament it is, for the concrete rectangles of the buildings narrow the prospect to a chink of blue sky. The façade on the right, blocking the view, is formed by a brownish wall flanked by a waste pipe; on the left, a yellow wall. Against this golden background, spelled out in iridescent blue, is the message DEPRESSION IS A FLAW IN CHEMISTRY NOT IN CHARACTER. Warning, or mere information—hard to tell. DEPRESSION IS A FLAW IN CHEMISTRY NOT IN CHARACTER, displayed on five separate lines, one after the other.

He stares at the lines of sacred text, his head tilted backward. Jolted out of his reverie, he steps back and finds himself walking along Amsterdam Avenue again. There is an advantage to his new life—immunity. You are no longer chained to all the trivia, as in the previous life, you can walk on in indifference. He heads toward the restaurant/delicatessen Barney Greengrass, famous for its smoked fish. "The place will remind you of your previous life," his friend has promised.

The buildings along Amsterdam Avenue have been reclaimed from the past, old houses, reddish, brown, smoke-gray, four-five-six stories, iron balconies, fire escapes blackened by time. These streets of the Upper West Side, when he first encountered them, reminded him of the Old World. However, over the nine—or is it ninety?—years since he moved into the neighborhood, the tall buildings have multiplied, dwarfing even the forty-two stories of his apartment building to the proportions of a paltry Stalinist construction—there is that insidious adjective again.

On the ground floor of the building, the old shops, as before—Full Service Jewelers, Utopia Restaurant, Amaryllis Florist, Shoe Store, Adult Video, Chinese Dry Cleaning, Nail Salon, Roma Frame Art, and, at the corner of Seventy-sixth Street, Riverside Memorial Chapel. A young girl with thick legs and long dark hair, wearing a black short-sleeved dress, black stockings, and thick, dark sunglasses, comes out of the building. Three long black cars with darkened windows, like huge coffins, are parked at the curb. Out of them step smartly dressed gentlemen in black suits and black hats, elegant ladies in black dresses and black hats, teenagers in sober dress. Once more the metronome has struck the hour of eternity for some poor soul. Life is movement, he has not forgotten, and he hurries away. One step, two, and he is out of danger.

On the sidewalk in front of the venerable Ottomanelli Bros. meat market (SINCE 1900, a sign proclaims) are two wooden benches. An old woman sits on the one on the right. He collapses onto the other, keeping an eye on her. She stares vacantly into space, but he feels she is observing him. They seem to recognize each other. Her presence is familiar, as if he has felt it before on certain evenings, in certain rooms suddenly charged with a protective silence that would envelop him. Never has he felt this way in broad daylight amid the hubbub of the workaday world.

The old lady gets up from the bench. He waits for her to take a few steps, then follows her. He walks behind her in the slow rhythm of the past. He observes her thin legs, fine ankles, sensible shoes, cropped white hair, bony shoulders bent forward, her sleeveless, waistless dress, made of a light material in red and orange checks on a blue background. In her left hand, as in time before, she carries a shopping bag. In her right hand, as in time before, she holds a folded gray sweater. He overtakes her and makes a sudden turn. She gives a start. She probably recognizes the unknown man who had collapsed, exhausted, on the other bench at Otto-manelli's. They look at each other, startled. A ghost, out of the blue, on a bench, on a city sidewalk.

All is familiar—the gait, the dress, the sweater, the cropped white hair, the face half-seen in a fraction of a second. The forehead and the eyebrows and the eyes and the ears and the chin are all as before, only the mouth has lost its full contour and is now just a line, the lips too long, lacking shape; and the nose has widened. The neck sags, with wrinkled skin.

Enough, enough . . . He turns around and follows her from a distance. Her silhouette, the way she walks, her whole demeanor. You do not need any distinguishing marks, you always carry everything with you, well-known, immutable; you have no reason to follow a shadow down the street. He slows down, lost in thought, and the vision, as he had wished, vanishes.

Finally, at Eighty-sixth Street, he reaches his destination: Barney Greengrass. Next to the window, the owner sits sprawled in a chair, his hunched back and big belly enveloped in a loose white shirt with long sleeves and gold buttons. The neck is missing; the head, topped by a rich mane of white hair, is ample, the nose, mouth, forehead, and ears firmly drawn. On the left, behind the salami-halvah counter, stands a worker in a white coat. Another counterman tends the bread-bagels-buns-cakes section.

He greets the owner and the young man standing next to him, who has a telephone glued to each ear. Then he walks into the room on the left, the restaurant area. At the table next to the wall a tall, thin man with gold-rimmed spectacles raises his eyes from his newspaper and calls out the customary greeting: "How're you doing, kid?" A familiar face, a familiar voice. Exiles are always grateful for such moments. "What's up?"

"Not much. 'The social system is stable and the rulers are wise,'" as our colleague Zbigniew Herbert says. "'In Paradise one is better off than anywhere else.'" The novelist, to whom these quotations are directed, is not keen on poetry, but luckily, it sounds more like prose.

"How are you? Tell me the latest. News from here, not from Warsaw."

"Well, I'm celebrating nine years of life in Paradise. On March 9, 1988, I was shipwrecked on the shore of the New World."

"Children love anniversaries, and Barney Greengrass's is the ideal place for such things. It has all the memories of the ghetto, pure cholesterol, *Oy mein Yiddishe mame.* The old world and the old life."

He hands me the plastic-covered menu. Yes, the temptations of the ghetto are all here: pickled herring in cream sauce, fillet of schmaltz herring (very salty), corned beef and eggs, tongue and eggs, pastrami and eggs, salami and eggs, homemade chopped chicken liver, gefilte fish with horseradish. The chicken liver is no pâté de foie gras, nor are incubator-bred American chickens East European chickens. The fish isn't like the fish of the Old World, the eggs aren't like the eggs we used to know. But people keep trying, and so here are the substitutes for the past. Russian dressing with everything, with roast beef, turkey . . . Yes, the myth of identity, the surrogates of memories translated into the language of survival.

A handsome young waiter approaches. He recognizes the famous novelist and says to him, "I've read your latest book, sir." Philip seems neither flattered nor upset by this greeting. "Indeed? And did you enjoy it?" He had, the waiter avowed, but not as much as the previous book, much sexier.

"Good, good," the novelist says, without raising his eyes from the menu. "I'll have the scrambled eggs with smoked salmon and orange juice. Only the whites, no yolks." The waiter turns to the customer's unknown companion. "What about you, sir?"

"I'll have the same," I hear myself mumbling.

Barney Greengrass offers acceptable surrogates of East European Jewish cuisine, but it is not enough to add fried onions or to affix bagels and knishes to the menu to produce a taste of the past.

"So, how did you like Barney's cuisine?"

No reply.

"Okay, you don't have to answer that. Are you going to go back to Romania or not, what have you decided?"

"I haven't decided anything yet."

"Are you afraid? Are you thinking of that murder in Chicago? That professor . . . what was his name? The professor from Chicago."

"Culianu, Ioan Petru Culianu. No, I'm not in the least like Culianu. I am not a student of the occult like Culianu, nor, like him, have I betrayed the master, nor, like him, am I a Christian in love with a Jewish woman and about to convert to Judaism. I'm just a humble nomad, not a renegade. The renegade has to be punished, while I . . . I am just an old nuisance. I cannot surprise anybody."

"I don't know about surprises, but you've been quite a nuisance occasionally. A suspect, becoming more suspicious. This is not to your advantage."

Professor Ioan Petru Culianu had been assassinated on the twenty-first of May 1991, in broad daylight, in one of the buildings of the University of Chicago. A perfect murder, apparently—a single bullet, shot from an adjacent stall, straight into the professor's head, as he sat on the plastic seat in the staff toilets of the Divinity School. The unsolved mystery of the assassination had, naturally, encouraged speculation—the relations between the young Culianu and his mentor, the noted Romanian scholar of religion Mircea Eliade, with whose help he had been brought to America; his relations with the Romanian community of Chicago, with Romania's exiled King, his interest in parapsychology. There was, in addition, the Iron Guard connection, that movement of extreme-right-wing nationalists whose members were known as *legionari*, the Legionnaires. The Iron Guard, which Mircea Eliade had supported in the 1930s, still had adherents among the Romanian expatriates of Chicago. It was said that Culianu was on the verge of a major reassessment of his mentor's political past.

The Chicago murder, it was true, coincided with the publication of my own article about Eliade's Legionnaire past, in *The New Republic*, in

1991. I had been warned by the FBI to be cautious in my dealings with my compatriots, and not only with them. It was not the first time I had talked about this with my American friend. Culianu, Eliade, Mihail Sebastian—Eliade's Jewish friend—these names had come up frequently in our conversations over the previous months.

As the date of my departure for Bucharest approached, Philip insisted that I articulate the nature of my anxieties. I kept failing. My anxieties were ambiguous. I did not know if I feared meeting my old self there, or if I feared bringing back my new image, complete with the expatriate's laurels and the homeland's curses.

"I can understand some of your reasons," Philip says. "There must be others, probably. But this trip could cure you, finally, of the East European syndrome."

"Perhaps. But I'm not ready yet for the return. I am not yet indifferent enough to my past."

"Exactly! After this trip, you will be. Those who come back, come back healed."

We have reached the same old dead end. But this time, he persists.

"What about seeing a few old friends? A few old places? You did say you would be willing to see some of them, despite not being quite ready for it. Last week, you said something about going to the cemetery to visit your mother's grave."

A long pause follows. "I saw her again," I finally say. "This morning, half an hour ago. I was on my way here, and suddenly there she was, seated on this bench, on Amsterdam Avenue, in front of Ottomanelli's."

We fall silent again. When we leave Barney Greengrass's, our conversation returns to familiar topics and resumes its jovial tone. We say goodbye, as we always do, at the corner of Seventy-ninth Street. Philip turns left, toward Columbus Avenue. I continue down Amsterdam to Seventieth Street and my non-Stalinist Stalinist apartment building.

Jormania

The figure of Officer Portofino came back to me as soon as I left Barney Greengrass's. The wide face, languid gaze, neatly combed hair, small hands, small feet, amiable smile. A short, frail man in a dark blue suit and blue tie.

He hastened to tell me, almost as soon as we met, that he had been a chemistry teacher in a high school before he switched to his current profession. His square-cut clothes reminded me of the Romanian Securitate officers, yet his manner was affable, respectful, with no trace of the socialist policeman's slyness or rudeness. He seemed to want to protect you rather than intimidate you or recruit you with the devious manipulations of a socialist cop.

In fact, he did not offer me protection, no bulletproof vest or plainclothes man, not even the instantly blinding spray recommended to unaccompanied ladies. Instead, he gave me moderate and friendly advice, as sensible as a grandmother's. I should try to identify faces that looked familiar in the street, constantly change my walking routes and the time I went out to buy my newspaper; I should not open suspicious-looking letters. He did not even recommend that I should "lie low," the customary advice in such situations. He did give me his card with his home phone number for emergencies. My self-absorption and carelessness in social situations remained the same, however, in spite of the talisman with which he had endowed me. But my nervousness and anxiety increased.

The reason for my meeting with Officer Jimmy Portofino was my *New Republic* essay. Discussing Eliade's so-called *felix culpa*, his "happy guilt"—that is, his relations in the 1930s with the fascistic Iron Guard, which has sympathizers even today in both Romania and America—the article touched on a dangerous topic. The administration of Bard College, where I was teaching, had asked for FBI protection for its own Romanian professor.

About a year after the cessation of the FBI protection, I received an anonymous letter from Canada. The handwriting on the envelope was unfamiliar, but graphology is not my specialty. Inside, I found a picture postcard with no message. I discarded the envelope but kept the postcard—a reproduction of Marc Chagall's *The Martyr*, in the collection of the Kunsthaus in Zurich, a Judaic variant of the Crucifixion, it would seem. Instead of being nailed to a cross, the martyr's arms and feet are bound to a stake, in the center of a burned-out market town, with the supporting players in the drama—the mother, the fiddler, the rabbi, and his disciples—in the foreground. The face of the young Jewish Christ, with beard and side curls, bespeaks the image of a pogrom—not the Holocaust, whose unspeakable horrors are fast being turned into cliché. The East European pogroms had their own terrors. I did not know how to decode the message. I kept the postcard on my desk.

Six years went by. I had not been threatened or assassinated, but I saw a continuity rather than a contradiction between the invectives—"antiparty," "extraterritorial," "cosmopolitan"—with which the Romanian Communist press had honored me prior to 1989 and the post-Communist epithets—"traitor," "the dwarf from Jerusalem," "American agent." Could this be the reason I did not deem myself capable of returning to the motherland, even for a visit?

After saying goodbye to Philip, I returned to the bench in front of Ottomanelli's where, one hour earlier, the past had come for me. Would it have been easier to explain things to the American policeman? At least he would not have had difficulties with the Culianu story: the bullet fired at close range from the adjacent toilet stall; the gun, a small Beretta .25, held in the gloveless left hand of the killer, probably not an American. The lethal wound, "occipital area of the head, four and a half inches below the top of the head and one-half of an inch to the right of the external occipital tubical." Professional killer, execution-style killing; location, toilet stall; time, the Eastern Orthodox feast of Saints Constantine and Helena, the name day of Ioan Petru Culianu's mother. Would Jimmy Portofino remember the murdered man's face, instantly rendered older, as if death had suddenly added twenty years to his actual age? The American police were familiar with the Chicago-based Romanian sympathizers of the notorious Iron Guard. They knew that the granddaughter of its charismatic leader, "Captain" Corneliu Zelea Codreanu, had sought refuge there at some point and that the old Alexander Ronett, Eliade's doctor and a fervent Legionnaire, also lived there. Suspicions had focused on the Romanian Securitate and its connections with the Chicago Legionnaires. The police were equally familiar with Culianu's biography. His dossier probably also contained the letter in which he expressed his regret that his veneration for Mircea Eliade had turned him into an uncritical disciple. Was Culianu the novice ready to commit parricide? He had admitted that the mentor "was closer to the Iron Guard than I liked to think." His appearance by the side of the former King Michael had certainly not endeared him to the Romanian agents of the Securitate, nor did his plans for marrying a Jewish woman and converting to Judaism. In the year before his death, Culianu had condemned the "terrorist fundamentalism" of the Iron Guard, as well as vilifying the Communist secret police, Romanian Communism in general, and the nationalistic trends in Romanian culture.

What did the American police know about the murdered professor's delvings into magic, premonition, ecstatic experiences, parapsychology? What did they know of the reaction to his assassination among the nationalists in Romania? "The worst crime, in the case of that refugee in the gangster megalopolis of Chicago, was the nauseating apologia dedicated to that piece of excrement over whom not enough water was flushed in the fatal toilet prepared for him as if by destiny," wrote *Romania Mare*. This was a weekly paper that had not hesitated to heap abuse on me after 1989, but also before, under the Communist regime, when, under the name *Săptămîna*, it had acted as a kind of cultural mouthpiece of the Securitate. Was Officer Portofino aware that unsolicited issues of *Romania Mare* carrying praise for Culianu's murder had been received by most American institutions and organizations dealing with Eastern Europe? Sent by the same Securitate, perhaps?

Should I describe for Officer Portofino, now, before returning to the motherland, the postcard with Chagall's *Martyr*, that son of the ghetto, his body wrapped in the devotional prayer shawl, white with black stripes? Neither the arms nor the feet were bound with rope, as I had initially thought, but rather with the thin straps of the phylacteries. Outlined against the sky of smoke and fire were the purple goat and the golden cock; by the side of the pyre stood the mother or the betrothed, the fiddler, the old man with the book. Was the postcard a threat or a sign of solidarity? I am no renegade, Mr. Portofino, nor a convert, and therefore, I cannot disappoint those who, in any case, expect nothing from someone like me.

Would Officer Portofino be interested in the fears Culianu and I shared about returning to the motherland? Yes, Culianu had apprehensions over the idea of returning to the country that had become his homeland two hundred and fifty years earlier, when his Greek ancestors had found refuge there from Ottoman persecution. The Romania he had loved, in whose language he had been educated, had gradually become Jormania. He had described it thus in two quasi-fantastic short tales vaguely influenced by Borges. In the first tale, the Maculist Empire of the Soviet Union collaborated with the spies of Jormania to assassinate the local dictator and his wife, Comrade Mortu—Comrade Death—thus founding a banana republic–style "democracy" of pornography and execution squads.

The second tale was a reading of post-1989 realities disguised as a fictional review of a fictional book of memoirs by a fictional author, which described the false revolution, followed by the false transition to a false democracy, the get-rich-quick schemes of the former Securitate agents, the shady murders, the corruption, the demagoguery, the alliance of the former Communists with the Wooden Guard, the new extreme-right movement. The fictional memoirs of the fictional witness also describe the false trial and rapid execution of the dictator and of Madame Mortu, the coup d'état, the funerals of the false martyrs, the "cheating" of the people. The new ruler, Mister President, the murderer of his predecessor, Comrade President, commented on the situation with the traditional native sense of humor: "Well, isn't this the essential role of the people?" To be cheated, that is.

Yes, Officer Portofino. You are right. It was not any supernatural force but Jormania—the one in the Balkans or the one in Chicago—that had prevented Culianu from ever seeing his native land again. But what about friends, and books, and love; what about the shared jokes and songs, what is their place and who can afford to ignore them? And what about the mothers who gave birth to us, our real motherlands? Can all this become one day, purely and simply, the land of the Legionnaires, or Communist Jormania? Anywhere and at any time, can't they, Jimmy, can't they?

Like Culianu himself, I had grown tired of scrutinizing the homeland's contradictions. My past was different, and it was not the gun from Bucharest that I feared. I was afraid of the knot of entanglements from which I had not yet extricated myself.

None of the pedestrians passing in front of Ottomanelli's looked like my guardian angel from the FBI, and I did not miss him. No, Officer Portofino would certainly not be able to interpret Chagall's pyre for me. In fact, Officer Portofino was not the person I was waiting for on that bench where I had been sitting, petrified, for a long time.

The woman I was waiting for, my would-be interlocutor, knew more about me than I did. She would not need any explanations. Would she remember the slim volume from my grandfather's bookstore of sixty-two years ago?

Her cousin, the young Ariel, the bohemian rebel, with his hair dyed red and his jet-black gaze, would read to those assembled around the counter from that booklet, with its pink covers, *How I Became a Hooligan*, as if it were a handbook for hypnosis. His cousin, the bookseller's daughter, was turning the pages feverishly. The same comment recurred, a single word: Departure! Insistent, vehement, firmly articulated, it sounded like Revolution, or Salvation, or Rebirth. "Now, immediately, while we can: Departure!" From time to time, Ariel turned the book over, staring with a mocking expression at the author's name on the cover: "Sebastian! Mr. Hechter, alias Sebastian!" No, the premise of my journey was not Culianu but another dead man, another friend of Mircea Eliade, from a different period: Mihail Sebastian, the writer I mentioned over breakfast at Barney Greengrass's, whose *Journal: 1935–1944*, written more than half a century earlier, had just been published in Bucharest. But this posthumous book could not be placed alongside the former ones on those bookshelves of the past. The bookstore was no longer there, and neither was my grandfather or his nephew Ariel. But my mother, no longer there either, would surely remember the "Sebastian Affair." My mother had a perfect memory; she must have it still wherever she is now, I have no doubt about that.

That old, boring, and everlasting anti-Semitism, of which pre-fascist Jormania was a textbook case, seemed to Sebastian to be located merely "on the periphery of suffering." He condescended to register "outer adversity" as rudimentary and minor, compared to the ardent "inner adversity" that, so he said, assails a Jew's soul. "No people has more ruthlessly confessed to its real or imagined sins; no one has kept stricter watch on himself more severely. The biblical prophets are the fieriest voices on earth." These words were written in 1935, when outer adversities had already begun to announce the devastation to follow. "The periphery of our suffering!" Ariel, my mother's cousin and my grandfather's nephew, shouted indignantly, in that small bookstore in Jormania in 1935, the year before my birth. "Is this Mr. Sebastian's teaching? The periphery of our suffering? He should speak for himself! He'll soon see what this 'periphery' is about!"

One year earlier in 1934, Sebastian had had to face the scandal that followed the publication of his novel *De două mii de ani* (*Two Thousand Years*), with a preface written by Nae Ionescu, his tutor and friend, who had become the ideologue of the Iron Guard. The author of the preface regarded the Jew as the irreducible enemy of the Christian world and, as such, one that had to be eliminated.

Attacked from all sides by Christians, Jews, liberals, and extremists alike, Sebastian had responded with a sparkling essay, *How I Became a Hooligan*. In a sober and precise tone, he candidly reaffirmed the "spiritual autonomy" of Jewish suffering, its "tragic nerve," the dispute between a "tumultuous sensibility" and a "merciless critical spirit," between "intelligence at its coolest and passion at its most unbridled." A hooligan? Did that mean marginal, nonaligned, excluded? "A Jew from the Danube," as he called himself with some delight. He defined himself clearly: "I am not a partisan, I am always a dissident. I can trust only the individual man, but my trust in him is complete." What does being a "dissident" mean? Someone dissenting even from dissidents?

As my mother knew only too well, such childish mind games were part of my nature. It was the same when I indulged in the urgent need to leave the ghetto. Did I expect to find on the other side friends with extended arms rather than the comedy of more ghettos? One becomes tired of oneself, as Sebastian said. My mother felt no need to define her "belonging." She lived it purely and simply, with that fatalistic faith that does not exclude anguish or depression. "We are we and they are they," she would say. "We have no reason to feel enmity toward them, or to expect gifts from them. Neither can we forget their horrors, can we?"

The hysterical reaction with which I responded to such clichés, at the ages of thirteen, twenty-three, thirty-three, and ever since, never moderated her tenacity. Character is fate, the ancient Greeks said, and I was witness to this daily, in the neurotic matriarchy of my immediate surroundings, as well as in the collective "identity."

The departure, yes, Ariel had been right. Time would eventually convince me as well. This is what you kept repeating, Mother, time would force me to admit my error and pack up to leave, but that would not be until much later. "It will be late and it will be evening," as the poet said, "and you will leave this place, you'll see."

Are poets more prescient than prophets? Sebastian's *Journal*, published in 1997, half a century after its author's death, describes the "adversities" that come from friends turned foes. "An anguished evening . . .

obscure threats: as if the door isn't shut properly, as if the walls themselves are becoming translucent. Everywhere, at any moment, it is possible that some unspecified dangers will pounce from outside."

I had finally left, feeling guilty for not having done so earlier, feeling guilty for having finally done it. In 1934, Sebastian's alter ego declared: "I would like to know what anti-Semitic laws could cancel the fact that I was born on the Danube and love this land . . . Against my Jewish taste for inner catastrophe, the river asserted the example of its regal indifference." In 1943, the writer wondered: "Will I ever come back among these people? Will the war have passed without breaking anything, without bringing about anything irrevocable, anything irreducible?" At the end of the war, Hechter-Sebastian was finally getting ready to leave "eternal Romania, where nothing ever changes." The Judaic taste for catastrophe seemed easier to cure on the shores of the Hudson than on the banks of the Danube.

Death had prevented Culianu from returning to Romania and Sebastian from leaving it. With me, death, that nymphomaniac, had adopted a different game: she offered me the privilege of a voyage to my own posterity.

It was not only the Danube that provided the setting for the biography that had to be left behind; Bukovina, my native province, could serve equally well. Language, landscapes, stages of life are not automatically annulled by outer adversities. The love for Bukovina, however, does not annul Jormania. Where exactly was the borderline that united and divided Jormania and Romania? "Nothing is serious, nothing grave, nothing is true in this culture of smiling lampoonists. Above all, *nothing is incompatible*"—these are Sebastian's statements to which Ioan Petru Culianu himself would have subscribed. "Here is a concept that is totally absent in our public life at all levels: incompatibility," Ariel, my mother's young and fervent cousin, used to say a long time ago. "Incompatibility is unknown in the lands of the Danube." I could have said this myself, entrapped as I was, like so many others, by the dilemmas of the old-new impasses. Outer adversities? I had received my initiation into such banalities at a very early age. As for the hostile campaigns of more recent years, when one is under siege, it is not easy to avoid narcissistic suspicions, or pathetic masochism. Again, a victim? The idea exasperated me, I must admit. Oh, not again, the whinings and jeremiads of the victim, especially now, when all and sundry are claiming their own threadbare badge of victimhood—men, women, bisexuals, Buddhists, the obese, cyclists . . .

But the mask was now glued to my face—the classic public enemy, the Other. I had always been an "other," consciously or not, unmasked or not, even when I could not identify with my mother's ghetto or any other ghetto of identity. Outer adversities can overlap with inner adversities, and with the fatigue of being oneself. Without shadow or identity, should I go out only after dark? If I did that, it would be easier to engage in the dialogue with the dead who are claiming me.

The Circus Arena of
Augustus the Fool

What is the loneliness of the poet?" the young Paul Celan, my fellow Bukovinan, was asked more than a century ago, just after the war. "A circus routine that has not yet been announced," he answered.

Circus clowns—this is how I saw myself and my writer friends, as we engaged in the skirmishes of daily existence. Our situation could be described as that of Augustus the Fool, as old Hartung nicknamed his painter son Hans. He was alluding to the inner nature of the artist, ill equipped for everyday life, a bungler who dreams of other rules and rewards, and looks for solitary compensations for the role he has been saddled with whether he likes it or not. Inevitably, Augustus the Fool comes up against his opposite, the White Clown, the representative of power and authority. These two prototypes in the history of the circus may personify the two sides of History; all human tragedy may be seen in this encounter in the history of the circus as History.

Augustus the Fool, a clown whose sarcasms turned on himself rather than on others, was always suspiciously lying in wait for the moment when he would be offered, yet again, the role of the victim, which the audience always wanted him to have.

Leaving socialist Jormania behind in 1986 gave birth to a kind of symbol-laden symmetry: my exile, which had begun at the age of five because of a dictator and his ideology, came full circle at the age of fifty, because of another dictator and an ideology that claimed to be the opposite of its predecessor. Emphatic laments over this duplication were nothing to be proud of and irritated me again and again. I would simply prevaricate in the hope that, suddenly, a moment of enlightenment would stop Augustus the Fool's amorphous monologue.

"I came out relatively clean from the dictatorship. I didn't get my hands dirty. And this is not something that's easily forgiven. Do you remember Bassani's Ferrara stories?" My interlocutor remained silent, unwilling to interrupt me. He knew I was straining to come up with arguments as to why I should not go back to Romania, precisely because at that point the trip had become inevitable.

"Bassani," I continued, "is known here for the film based on his work, *The Garden of the Finzi-Contini*. Among his Ferrara stories there is a novella entitled *Una lapide in via Mazzini*. The Italian sounds beautiful, doesn't it? *U-na la-pi-de in vi-a Maz-zi-ni*, a commemorative plaque on Mazzini Street."

My listener seemed happy to listen patiently for as long as that kept me pacified.

After the war, Geo Iosz returns unexpectedly from Buchenwald to his native town, Ferrara, the only survivor of all those sent to hell in 1943. His former neighbors look away in embarrassment, wishing to forget the past and the old sense of guilt. In the end, the unwelcome witness, now even more of an alien than he was on the night of his deportation, chooses, of his own free will, to leave his native town forever. Should I mention, by way of contrast, the joy Primo Levi felt, upon his return from Auschwitz, of being able to live in the same house in Turin where his parents, grandparents, great-grandparents had lived before him?"

Unimpressed with my musings, my listener kept smiling benignly.

"As I said, I escaped from the dictatorship relatively clean, I managed to keep myself apart. But I found that guilt, compromise, and even heroic resistance are easier to forgive than apartness."

My friend didn't seem bored and had failed to notice that I was. I was tired of myself.

"I was neither a Communist nor a dissident. Isn't that a bit arrogant? Anyway, I wasn't too visible in the Balkan world of Bucharest. More arrogance, of course. And then, emigration . . . as far away as possible . . . supreme arrogance."

The slim blond waitress appeared, with her miniskirt and the name tag *Marianne* on her right breast—a French girl from Israel, studying in New York and working part-time as a waitress at the Café Mozart, on Seventieth Street, on the Upper West Side, not far from the apartment where I was busy experimenting with my afterlife. She had brought the two bowls of gazpacho, the spoons, the bread, all that was needed.

My grandiose country—this was what I had tried to describe to my listener, the grandiosity of Dadaland, which I had not wished to forsake and to which I did not wish to return. The ineffable charm and the ineffable feces. It probably wasn't too different from anywhere else, but what happened in other places didn't really interest me.

"Over the last few years, I've suffered from a particular sickness. The Jormania Syndrome."

The pianist of the Café Mozart hadn't turned up yet, and neither had the lunchtime habitués. The newspapers were in their place, arrayed in their specially designed rack, trying to impersonate old Vienna. Wolfgang Amadeus was gazing skeptically from the gilded frame of his portrait at the two bespectacled diners at the table in the back.

"Self-hatred masquerading as 'Come, let me embrace you, mister.' The Romanians have this saying, as untranslatable as their soul—*Pupat Piaţa Independenţei*, general embracing in Independence Square. It's a quotation from our great writer Caragiale, impossible to translate, just like that world full of charm and feces that is equally lost in translation. It's not the embrace of Cain and Abel but a wallowing in the national mud-bath after a bitter fight, the same muddy pond where, before a new assault, the swan-whore and the ass-scholar and the hyena-minister and the innocent kid are locked in drunken embrace. No, believe me, the Romanians did not have to wait for Sartre to discover that hell is other people. Hell can be as sweet and soft as that stagnant quagmire."

I stopped, exhausted after this lengthy speech, to readjust my syndrome. "Have you heard how much mutual hostility there is these days between East and West Germans? You would need someone like Céline or Cioran, rather than myself, to describe such bilious hatred."

"Oh, stop moaning. After all, you've written about clowns and the circus. You've got a good story to tell. God has sent you one. He hasn't passed you by."

"The story is too complicated, it can be told only in aphorisms."

"Well, on this trip, your boss is coming with you. He'll be well received as the superstar of the superpower. The powerful White Clown, as you say. As for you . . . you know all the dodges, you've got everything in your head. What more could you wish for?"

"The imperial White Clown from imperialist America? And next to him, Augustus the Fool, the exile. In fact, God has sent me too many interesting stories to tell, and I haven't been able to do them justice."

"The Almighty can't do everything."

"Do you remember what Flaubert said? If you keep preaching the good for too long, you end up an idiot. Flaubert, the idiot of the family, knew what he was talking about. Can sermons change the world? No, I know that, idiot that I am. I'm preaching not to change others but so that I can stay unchanged, a rabbi once said. And yet I have changed. Look at me, I have changed."

I took a short break, just to draw breath. After all, I knew that speech by heart, I had been hatching it for a long time. I did not really need a break.

"A hooligan? What is a hooligan? A rootless, nonaligned, nondefined vagabond? An exile? Or is it what the *Oxford Dictionary of the English Language* says it is: 'The name of an Irish family in South East London conspicuous for ruffianism'? In the Romanian novel *The Hooligans*, by Mircea

Eliade, one character says that 'there is one single productive start in life—hooliganism,' meaning rebellion unto death, 'militia and assault battalions, legions and armies linked together by . . . togetherness in death, perfectly and evenly aligned regiments within a collective myth.' Did Eliade overcome his Romanian frustrations in exile once he became famous as a scholar? His was the revenge of the periphery against the metropolis. What about his Jewish friend Sebastian? The Jews had isolated him as an enemy, his Christian friends-turned-Legionnaires considered him a Jew and a pariah. Rootless, exiled, and a dissident, was this the archetypal Jewish hooligan? And the homeless cosmopolitan talking to you now, what sort of hooligan would he make?"

I took out of my pocket a letter from Romania, an undated letter, like a long-festering wound. "Disorientation, confusion, sadness," wrote my woman friend from the motherland. "You should come over, twice a year, and humbly salute the intellectuals, lend yourself to photo opportunities, participate in talk shows, frequent the taverns, replace the caricature they have made of you. I would like to know what this final outcome means: the poisonous motherland's attitude toward you."

Could it have been otherwise? Would it have been better had it been otherwise? Don't let yourself be bought with sympathy—this was Gombrowicz's advice. Remain a foreigner forever! In his Argentine exile, he used to relish sticking out his tongue at himself in an ever-present mirror.

The listener's response was an amused smile. Before we went our separate ways, he brought our conversation to a close: "You'll fax me daily from Bucharest. Just two words, to let me know that everything is okay. And if you can't cope, leave immediately. Go to Vienna, Budapest, Sophia, and from there, back to New York."

The old-new questions had been haunting me well before we reached the corner of Broadway and Seventieth. I did not need to be at the Café Mozart or at Barney Greengrass's to become their target.

"You shouldn't go back there," Saul B. had told me over the phone. We had met twenty years before in Bucharest and then renewed our acquaintance in America. "It's not right that you should return, not because you're going to be in danger, but because you're going to feel miserable. I was reading the other day the biography of another famous Romanian.

All well-educated, clever hypocrites, as you know, old-fashioned, fine manners, kissing ladies' hands, but . . ." The former friend of Eliade and former husband of a well-known Romanian mathematician was not discouraged by my silence. "You shouldn't have agreed to make this trip, you just don't need it."

I explained that what was at stake was the "tyranny of affections"; I had been won over by the insistence of Leon Botstein, the president of Bard College. I heard Saul's delicate laughter at the other end of the line. Instantly, I could see his friendly, wrinkled face, his lively eyes. "You shouldn't have been. I know that country. Just cancel everything, protect your peace of mind. You have enough difficulties here, but here you have the advantage of distance. Don't waste it."

Addresses from the Past (I)

July 19, 1986, an evening of celebration. My invited guests had been treated to Russian vodka, Bulgarian wine, Greek olives, and Romanian cheeses, all purchased well in advance and with great difficulty.

> Here come the artists, watch out!
> The artists go from door to door, the monkeys, the mimics,
> The fake one-armed, the fake one-legged, the fake kings and ministers.
> Here they come, drunk with glamour and heat
> The sons of Emperor Augustus.

Among the guests, limping and sweating, my friend, the poet, the lonely, shy, half-disabled poet, thought he recognized himself in a character from an old Romanian fairy tale, Half-Man-Riding, Half-One-Legged-Hare. Short and stumpy, with a blond beard, swaying, limping, he walked always slightly inclined toward the left, gentle and fearful, terrified by his own duplicities, and ready to admit and pay for them, if that was the price of survival. He suffered for every word that he wrote, for everything written about him or his friends. As an editor in a publishing house, exasperated by the endless negotiations between censors and authors, he masterminded complicated transactions of flattery and emotional blackmail in order to promote the books in which he believed.

The pain of writing that he underwent, and on behalf of writing, was equaled only by his devotion to his wife. Julia submitted to dialysis every second day, in a socialist hospital, with ancient equipment and frequent power cuts. In addition to his poetry and the neurosis that was calibrated by the number of pills he swallowed in a day, Julia had also become the daily measure of his heroism.

As usual, he was sweating profusely. He wiped his face and forehead with a big white handkerchief he clutched in his large and powerful fist. However, he had not taken off his best jacket, or his best tie. He had withdrawn with Julia to a side of the room, by the wall-length bookshelves, overcome at finding himself surrounded by so many close friends—poets, critics, novelists—the monkeys, the mimics, the false kings, the false one-armed men, all the friends of Emperor Augustus the Fool. We were united by our books and our readings, made brothers by the competitive guild of vanity. Party members and nonmembers, the privileged and the merely tolerated, all had become suspect—the false kings, the false one-armed, the false apes—in the socialism of generalized suspicion.

That July evening in 1986, in Bucharest, in apartment 15 at no. 2 Calea Victoriei, was the celebration of the end of an era. Very few of my guests knew it, but the month before, on Bloomsday, the day set aside to honor James Joyce's exiled hero, I had applied for a visa to the West. Little did I know where that trip would finally take me.

Exile rapidly swallowed up the decades that unrolled from that summer evening. It was as if I inhabited a set of Russian dolls, one figure retracting into another and then another and again into another, with each new time identical to the time before yet also different.

Infantilism is what feeds the TV talk shows in which fifty-year-old children claim that their unhappiness stems from God knows what unfortunate event that happened to them at the age of five or fifteen, misunderstood children, misunderstood women or men, to say nothing of age abuse, sex abuse, religion abuse, and race abuse. Victimization, the whole repertoire of planetary complaints. The trauma that happened at the age of five explains the compulsion that manifests itself at the age of fifty? Or sixty, or six hundred? Wouldn't a real grown-up, by that time, have developed a thick rhinoceros hide of insensitivity?

I was racked by the guilt of not having left my motherland in time, by the guilt of not having stayed there to the very end. In that land, the chimera of hieroglyphs first appeared to me. In that land, I concluded the pact that did not promise anything but demanded everything instead. Lady Art had remained as intangible as ever, a specter here and there, on random pages of the obituary.

In the weeks before my return, I looked back on the bends in the road of time. I remembered the taste of food and jokes, the wine and song, the mountains and the sea, the loves, the books. And, of course, the friendships that had lit up so many impasses. Yes, even someone like me, born under the sign of the intruder, was permitted to enjoy the delights of Gomorrah.

The charm of the place and its inhabitants was no illusion, I could testify to that. Paul Celan, too, had experienced it, when he lived in Bucharest after the war, the time of "puns on words," as he later called it with amused nostalgia. Tolstoy had known it, too, in 1854, in the seven months or so that he spent in Bucharest and Kishinev, in Buzău and other places. The mix of charm and sadness had not escaped his youthful gaze, hungry as he was for reading, but also for carnal adventure, obsessed as he was with perfecting his character and his writing, yet also keen to accost the barefoot young peasant girl or enjoy an evening in a whorehouse.

Yes, the intensity of a whole lifetime within one moment . . .

V-Day, Victory, this is what we were celebrating on that evening of July 19, 1986, in the apartment on Calea Victoriei. Decades after the first exile, I was facing real exile. That celebration was—although many of the guests, myself included, were unaware of this at the time—a rehearsal for the separation to come.

In April 1945, I was a boy of nine, reborn and repatriated, returning from the Transnistria labor camp. I rediscovered food, clothes, school, furniture, books, games—bliss. I had obliterated the horror of the past, that ghetto disease. I was healed, or so I thought, and determined to share with my fellow countrymen in all the splendors of the present, which the Communist motherland served in equal portions to each of its citizens. The chimera of writing subsequently took me under her wings. In the early 1980s, her tattered garb could no longer conceal the wretchedness of that circus world. The new horror had not only replaced the old one but had coopted it: they now worked together, in tandem. When I made this discovery public, I found myself thrown into the center of the ring. The loudspeakers barked repeatedly—foreigner, foreigner, anti-this and anti-that. Once again, I had proven myself unworthy of the motherland of which, truth be told, my ancestors had been equally unworthy.

In the summer of 1986, I was leaving behind, terrified, the horror of Communism and its twin horror, nationalism. Was I again being infected with the "ghetto disease" from which I had persuaded myself I was immune?

Ten years later, many things had changed, and so had I. One thing remained unchanged, and that was my obstinate refusal to again be a victim. Liberation from belonging had not in fact freed me. A true fighter would have returned to Jormania confident in himself and his new identity, a victor, through absence, over the place he had left behind, proud of having become what he had always been accused of being, honored to embody futility itself.

Ten dearly beloved people represented for me the real motherland. Could these be the friends—nay, more than ten—who had been celebrating the victory of my fifty-year war in July 1986?

The first to die was Julia. Because of Communist censorship, the letters that her husband, the poet Mugur, had been sending me after my departure had been signed "Julia" and addressed to Cella, my own wife. "I think of you with great love and lonely longing. I can hear kids playing in the street. Shall we ever play together again? Poetry, too, has grown old and can no longer write itself. We hope the days ahead will be uneventful." There was a shortage of gas and also taxis in socialist Jormania. Mugur was paying a truck driver to shuttle back and forth from the White Palace that the Carpathians' White Clown was building for himself. He took Julia to the overcrowded, grim hospital in the morning and brought her back home in the evening. They drove through unlit streets, past empty shops and pharmacies. "However, there is love. Love is not just an abstract term," the poet wrote. "Just as in the sciences we have Ohm's Law, let us imagine that we also have a Loi de l'Homme, a Law of Humanity: a man is someone who leaves behind a vacuum greater than the space he previously occupied. Absence is a prolonged spasm— once a day, once a week, several times a week. The heart grows older, and no man can bear more than a man can bear. Oh, what a playful, bashful friendship we had! If only we could start anew. Now we stand by the window like kids and wave to each other across the road, except that in the middle of the street lies the ocean."

Mugur rushed in a sweat from doctors to nurses to orderlies, distributing bribes and smiles, kowtowing to superiors, dedicating his books to Bruno Schulz and to Half-Man-Riding, Half-One-Legged-Hare. His was the blind stubbornness of life, living in order to prolong the life of one's beloved. The poet survived purely on his drive to keep his other half going. The cost had kept rising, while life itself was being continuously devalued.

What once had been the painful "destiny" of the poet had now become the collective destiny. However, a burden shared did not mean a burdened halved.

I am lame. I am trembling . . . The trembling man feels he is multiplying; the man that wants to grasp, to clutch, to smash—or to caress— has a long way to go to reach his objective, a zigzagging path. He feels he is alone, but at the same time he feels that around him there is a plaza full of people trying to reach an apple on a branch. The trembling comes from beyond my own volition, which demands that I be much; hence my idea, which I once expressed in my writing, that, before it is this or that in terms of quality, life is "much."

I often thought of that "much." Mugur had told me the parable of the fat Jew who eats voraciously and becomes grossly obese. When questioned about it, the Jew says: "When they come to burn me, I want to burn a lot, I want the burning to last."

So the poet Mugur had grown fat, too, from his neurosis and his anguish. The trembling got worse, and so did the panic and the cold and the gloom and the terror around him. The messages became rarer, constrained, fearful, and ever conscious of eavesdroppers: "We have no particular reason for complaint." The word "particular" was laden with meaning: the inevitable had not yet happened. "Thank God, we have no particular reason for complaint." This is how Mugur had codified the whole situation in a letter addressed to Cella and signed in his tremulous hand "Julia."

Only in 1989, once Julia had died and the Red Circus had collapsed, did I receive the first letter addressed to me personally.

> Shall we ever meet again? A few years ago, I was a whole man: I had five or six hearts, as many pairs of hands and feet, of noses and mouths— like any normal man, no? And now my hearts have been either buried or flung far away over the world. I am trying to replace them, those that can be replaced, with the random sheet of paper and a few scribbled words. Do you really believe that we are going to meet again? I would almost feel whole again. I would be, let us say, Half-Man, rather than the hundredth part of man with no hearts and no eyes and no nothing.

We did not meet again. Murgur died in February 1991, soon after his birthday, with a book in one hand and a piece of bread and salami in the other.

Meanwhile, another friend, Paul, had also died, the Flying Elephant, the Communist who had been spared the post-Communist masquerade after the Communist one in which he himself had been a player.

Also dead was Evelyne, Cella's mother, who had presided, discreetly and elegantly, over the anniversary of July 1986. In one of her last letters, she asked that we no longer send her mail to her address but to that of a neighbor. After the publication of my essay on Mircea Eliade, when the newspapers of the new democracy were accusing me of blasphemy and treason, local patriots had chosen as their target the mailbox of the culprit's mother-in-law, which they set on fire more than once. Other guests at what proved to be my farewell celebration had, in the meantime, found refuge in France, Germany, and Israel. Those who had stayed were no longer the same, and neither the city nor the nomad I had become had remained unchanged.

The motherland had retreated deeper and deeper into the past, and deeper inside me. I no longer needed geography or history to test its contradictions.

Was the vacuum left behind indeed greater than the body that had occupied it? This had been the prediction of Half-Man before he vanished together with the half-lame chimera he was riding. Absence was indeed just a prolonged spasm in the aging heart. And the child shouting in the street, "Come on, let's play," was now far away, beyond all the oceans of this world.

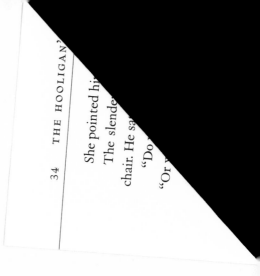

The New Calendar

It was D-Day—Decision Day—January 20, 1988. For almost two years now, I had been lingering in Transit City. Finally, after many delays, the moment had come when there was nothing left to delay. "Decision is a moment of insanity," Kierkegaard confided. So was indecision. The insanity of indecision had lasted for almost a year, after a lifetime of indecisions.

The pettiness of belonging, nothing more, its ludicrousness, nothing more, were at stake. Our hero was pale, overwhelmed by the farce that had chosen him as its protagonist in a parody of his own making. Had he not shed the tight-fitting skin in which he had previously lived? Had he not forgotten the past—he who forgot faces seen only an hour before?

"You, it's your turn to appear before the commission," gestured the lady in the blue tailored suit. He grabbed his briefcase and got up from the bench on which five other people were huddled together.

"First, you're going to talk to the French representative. When you're finished, come back and see me again."

m toward the door to the left of her desk.

r man behind the desk invited him to sit in the facing
t down, his briefcase on his lap.

ou prefer to speak German?" the Frenchman asked in German.
would you prefer French?"

"French will be fine," the applicant answered, in German.

"Good, good," the examiner continued in French. "Most Romanians speak French, don't they? My Romanian friends in Paris have no trouble adapting."

"Yes, French is easy for Romanians," he replied, in French.

He looked more closely at the man opposite him. These days, the Romanian thought, in Romanian, the examiners are all younger than the applicants.

The official had a long, narrow face, with a prominent, finely chiseled nose, dark, intelligent eyes, a thick mane of hair, and a youthful, likable smile. His tie was loosened, the collar of his blue shirt open, his dark-blue jacket unbuttoned, draped with casual elegance over his bony shoulders. His voice was pleasant.

"I was talking yesterday with a Romanian lady about you. I knew we would be having this meeting today, and I asked her whether she knew you."

The applicant said nothing. He remained silent, in French, the language that had just delivered this surprise.

The official lit a cigarette and placed both hands, palms downward, on the edge of his desk. He was leaning back slightly in the swivel leather armchair in which he appeared so comfortable.

"You seem to be quite well-known. Yesterday, reading the form you filled in, the titles of all those books you've written . . . I was struck by the coincidence."

As he said "those books," he raised the applicant's form from the desk, held it in the air for a fraction of a second, then put it back on the desk. After a long, untranslatable pause, the Frenchman resumed his melodious Gallic tones.

"I've read your novel *Captives*," he said. It sounded like the call in a fencing match: *Touché!* Had the foils engaged? No, the silence in the room was unpunctured. "In the mid-seventies, I think," the Frenchman continued. "I was taking a course in Romanian at the university in Paris. There was much talk in the class about censorship and the coded criticism of the totalitarian system—the captives' code, I believe it was called."

The applicant gripped the handle of his briefcase. "Liar!" he would have liked to shout, in all the languages he knew. Now he was certain that he was not talking to a mere civil servant. Was there no difference, then, between the East and West? The same insinuations, the same flattery, the same traps. Was the exile who had refused to cut a deal with the native devil now forced to deal with his international counterparts? Had he become a vulnerable captive, a nameless pariah, an easy target to be manipulated at the first turn in the road?

"It's quite a surprise for me, too," the applicant finally muttered, in French. "I wasn't aware . . . I didn't know that my book had made it to Paris."

"Yes, I was also surprised. Imagine, seeing your name on the application . . ." The Frenchman looked at the form again.

"I see your name, the titles of your books . . . You should settle in France, not Germany."

You should settle in France. Was that a piece of advice, a promise, the code for the deal that was being suggested? But no, the man's affability was for real, he was treating the applicant with courtesy and respect. If these were tricks, they were tricks of a different sort than those reserved for the run-of-the-mill populace.

"You must surely know that France is the easiest place for a Romanian. You would make friends very quickly. You could write in French, like so many of your illustrious countrymen . . ."

Indeed, the examiner knew not only about his novel *Captives*, he also knew about the famous trio of Ionesco, Cioran, and Eliade, also about Princess Bibesco and Princess de Noailles and Princess Vacaresco, and *la grande princesse* and *la petite princesse*. He had even heard of Benjamin Fondane. Yes, he had done his homework.

The conversation continued in much the same vein. At the end, the examiner got up from his side of the desk and stood next to the examinee, offering further proofs of his cordiality—his business card, with both his Berlin and Paris addresses; an invitation to a soirée; assurances of support, "of any kind," should there be a need, either here, in West Berlin or, even more so, in Paris. As he shook hands with the refugee, *Monsieur le grand ami* murmured, "It would be nice, meanwhile, to spend an evening together here in the place where destiny has so brought us together."

He saw the applicant not only to the door but to the antechamber, where the lady in the dark tailored suit reigned. He announced that his friend Mr. So-and-so had completed his interview with the French authorities and could now be referred to the other two Allied powers governing West Berlin. The German secretary remained completely composed in the face of this Latin complicity. She waited impassively for the two Francophones to take their leave.

The Frenchman's office door closed and the applicant was again left waiting. He looked at his watch, ten minutes to noon. When the secretary finally looked up, she said in her brisk German, "That's all! You're finished for today. Come back tomorrow morning at eight. Go to the front gate to have your name checked. Come back here at nine. Room 135."

It was a cold, sunny day. He took a bus, then a tram. Around two o'clock, he finally got home.

A year had gone by since his arrival in Transit City. On this island of freedom, he had felt at ease from the very start. The colorful billboards, the glittering shop windows, the relaxed air with which people of the city went about their business—all this gradually became routine for the foreigner who, until very recently, had known only cold and darkness, informers and falsifiers. Freedom delighted and terrified him at the same time. He could not go back, but he did not seem ready for a rebirth either. There were still too many doubts. Back there, in that matchbox where he had lived with all the frustrations and illusions, he somehow felt important and unique. Was he about to lose the language that, at every stage in his life, had left its deep imprint? This was suicide, not much different from a return to the murderous motherland, or so it seemed to him.

The night before the morning he was to appear before the Special Commission had been more difficult than the long nights of indecision he had endured for the many months since he had alighted on the island of freedom. No matter the many joys the Afterlife was ready to bestow on him, he was afraid he would always remain a senile toddler, learning sign language in his second childhood and babbling incomprehensible sounds of gratitude.

Through the night's white fog, he could make out the elegant outlines of Transit City's buildings and boulevards. He could hear music drifting from afar. The citadel was peopled with artists and spies, all enjoying a pulsating night life. He thought he could make out the Great Wall, which protected the enclave of freedom from the outside world of the captives, while also providing a barrier against the virus of liberty for the prison beyond. And it was evening and it was morning, and on the day after, there were two more steps to be taken. January 21, 1988. On this fateful day, the fifty-year-old would be reborn into the Afterlife, renamed, from this day forward, the World Beyond.

Stretched out on his couch, he looked at the date on the daily calendar, circled in red. He got up and carefully wrote, in bold red letters, above the circled date: MARIANNE. He stood for a moment gazing at what he had done. No, not good enough! He crossed out what he had written; then, with the same red pen, wrote, on the bottom of the page—FRANCE. Then, smiling mischievously, like a child who has just played a prank on an old aunt, he squeezed another word into the space before the word he had already written: ANATOLE. ANATOLE FRANCE! He went back to his couch, where he remained for a long while, his right hand clutching the French official's business card.

Should he take up the Frenchman's invitation and spend an evening with him on the town? Would that cure him of the suspiciousness he had carried with him from socialist Jormania? That would take more than a single evening. Moreover, he hadn't even had a real conversation with the Frenchman who claimed to have read his book. Was that story really true—and what if it was? He had not yet even attempted a conversation on literary topics with his devoted reader. He tore the Frenchman's card into little pieces, unable to grasp yet the advantages of making deals even in the Free World.

• • •

The next day, January 21, 1988, the applicant retraced his steps from the previous day, boarding first a tram, then a bus, going from the city center along the Kurfürsterdamm to the suburban location of the sacred Tripartite Commission. He arrived at the gate, promptly at eight, as ordered, and by nine appeared at room 135. He sat down on the familiar bench and waited patiently. At a quarter past eleven, the lady wielding the controls pointed silently toward the door at the right—the American door.

The bald young man behind the desk invited him to sit down on the chair opposite.

"Do you speak English?" the American asked, in his American English.

"A little," he replied evasively, in Esperanto.

"Okay, we can speak German, then," the American continued in his American German. "Is that okay?"

The applicant nodded silently. He studied the man sitting before him, an even younger examiner than the one of the day before—a solidly built man squeezed into a brown suit with large lapels, dark, penetrating eyes, small hands, with a heavy ring on one finger, gold cufflinks on white shirt cuffs showing from the sleeves of his jacket.

"Passport, please." Army voice, army manner.

The applicant dipped into his briefcase and produced a portfolio bulging with papers, from which he extracted a green passport. The examiner examined it closely, page by page.

"This is not your first trip to the West, I see."

The applicant offered no comment. The representative of the Great Power gave him a long look, then broke the silence that had briefly hung in the room.

"You've traveled twice to Western Europe and once to Israel."

The silence deepened.

"And where did you get the money for these trips?" the American asked, breaking the silence. "There's no convertible currency in Eastern Europe. Only the authorities can make the transaction, and they'll do so only if it's in their interest."

"I didn't travel on government money," the suspect protested. "My relatives in the West sent me the money."

"Relatives? Generous people, those relatives. Where do they live?"

The applicant hurriedly listed the countries where his nomadic family had settled.

"In the United States as well?" said the American, his face brightening. "Where? What sort of relatives?"

"My wife's sister, married for over ten years to an American. A mother with two American kids, a ten-year-old daughter and a four-year-old son."

"And how did you get to Berlin? I don't suppose it was your relatives who chose this place, Berlin."

A prolonged silence followed. The American seemed pleased with himself. "I came here on a grant from the German government, as I noted in my personal file."

"Yes, you mentioned that," the civil servant admitted, picking up the file from his desk, holding it up for a moment, then putting it back and pushing it to one side, as though it were irrelevant. "The grant that the vanquished offer to the victors. Can we call it that?"

He appeared in no hurry to be done with the German issue. After all, he seemed to suggest, defeating the enemy had been no easy feat. This is what united them, the young American and the aging East European sitting across from him. An award prompted by guilt . . . Yes, the thought had crossed the mind of the awardee himself. It was an award offered by the vanquished to the survivors whom they had failed to crush, an award tendered, after its defeat, by the now prosperous Germany to the wretched of Eastern Europe, always destined to poverty, to exile, not at all strangers to defeat themselves. Even within its diminished borders, postwar Germany remained the same country of hardworking, efficient people, with the same flag and the same anthem, even in Bavaria, which the pundits had predicted would end up being ruled by the survivors of the extermination camps. They also postulated that the Jews would demand from the Germans proof of philo-Semitism for three generations before reclaiming their German citizenship, lost in the catastrophe.

Of course, a joke read backward, from right to left, like the Hebrew Bible. For it was the Jews who were in fact asked, as they came out of the camps, to offer proof by blood of belonging to the state that had sought to exterminate them. Only if they could pass this test would they be awarded the enviable status of citizenship in the new postwar Germany, generous with its disbursements to the impoverished and the lost, who no longer hoped for a share in the spoils of victory.

The applicant had no chance to say all this. His young examiner turned to other matters and was now intent on filling out the forms. A pity, for he probably would have appreciated such ironic digressions as a form of pro-American flattery intended to win the favor of the Great Power. When he raised his eyes from his briefcase again, the applicant saw that the American official had stood up, was smiling and extending his hand.

"Good luck to you, sir, the best of luck," he wished him, American-style, finally abandoning the language of their common enemy.

The next step on this fateful day was to see the British lion, no longer a lion. The lady at the controls was engrossed in a telephone conversation and failed to notice that the American examination was over. Even when she finally hung up, she appeared not to see the shadow standing in front of her.

"What happens next? The interview with the British?" the applicant asked timidly.

"Nothing happens next. It's all over. Mr. Jackson signed for the British as well."

The applicant gripped the handle of his briefcase and headed for the door.

"Don't forget, sir, tomorrow morning at nine-thirty."

He looked at the secretary, bewildered.

"Tomorrow you have the final interview with the German authorities. First floor, room 202. Remember, nine-thirty sharp."

The day was leaden and damp. He walked slowly to the bus stop, then slowly up the stairs to his third-floor apartment, took the key from his winter-coat pocket, opened the door, and remained standing on the threshold for a few moments. The apartment was warm, silent. Without taking off his coat, he picked up the thick red pen and went over to the calendar. He crumpled the page for January 20, then the page for the twenty-first. He drew two thick red circles on the page for January 22, 1988. Across it he wrote, "If I'm still alive tomorrow," adding, in brackets, "Count Tolstoy, Yasnaya Polyana."

. . .

He had survived another night. He remembered *The Report on Paradise*, by the Polish poet, and started to recite it loudly.

> In Paradise the work week is
> fixed at thirty hours
> the social system is stable and
> the rulers are wise
> really in Paradise one is better
> off than in whatever country.

It was easy to guess the place the poet had in mind. He transcribed the verse into prose. The French, American, or English officials might have understood the code: *In Paradise the work week is fixed at thirty hours, prices steadily go down, manual labor is not tiring (because of reduced gravity), chopping wood is no harder than typing. The social system is stable and the rulers are wise. Really, in Paradise one is better off than in whatever country.* He then condensed the text in his mind: *The social system is stable, the rulers are wise, in Paradise one is better off than in whatever country.* Well, this, he thought, makes a good daily prayer.

He read the poet's words over and over again, read other verses, choosing one or two lines from each, for the benefit of the German officer he was to see the next morning. *They were not able to separate exactly the soul from the flesh and so it would come here with a drop of fat, a thread of muscle.* Then: *Not many behold God. He is only for those of 100 percent pneuma. The rest listen to communiqués about miracles and floods.* At last, he sank into a dreamless sleep, until the alarm bell rang.

As he was leaving his apartment, he turned back to pick up the scrap of paper on which he had written his final version of the prayer: *In Paradise one is better off than in whatever country. The social system is stable and the rulers are wise. In Paradise one is better off than in whatever country.* He folded the paper and put it in his pocket. He felt more protected, he had survived the night, he would survive the day as well.

At nine-thirty sharp he was in the interview room, with the German civil servant, a short, stumpy man. Oddly enough, he was wearing not a suit and tie but corduroy trousers and a thick, knitted green vest over a woolen shirt, also green. He had fair hair, parted in the middle, and big hands with large discolored patches, which also showed on his forehead and throat.

After an interrogation that lasted for an hour and a half, the applicant emerged unable to remember the questions he had been asked. What he had retained, however, was a remark the bureaucrat had repeated twice: "The road you are taking is going to be long and uncertain, and the first step is just that, a first step."

Of course, Bukovina, his birthplace, had been his very first step, but, as the applicant knew, German identity is about blood, not place. "We are not French or American or British, simply because we find ourselves here, at the headquarters of the Great Allied Commission," the German bureaucrat had said, raising scandalized eyebrows and arms toward the heavens. "One is not German simply because one is born in German territory, even if it was Germany proper, not to speak of, well . . ." He bent over the application form, looking for that barbaric name. "Oh yes, Bukovina, admittedly a former Austrian province, but only for some hundred years. Austria and Germany are two very different things, you know. That madman who destroyed Germany, it's because of him the Allied Commission now sits in Berlin." The purebred German civil servant again lifted his eyebrows and arms toward God Almighty, who so unashamedly played with Germany's destiny. "Because of that madman, Germany has to pay and pay, incurring new debts and swallowing insults and suffering the invasion of tramps and beggars delivered by the Allied Commission. That madman was not German but Austrian, as everybody knows. Mad Adolf came from Linz, Austria. He never denied it. And even if one is German, if you have been away from your country for the last eight hundred years, what sort of a German are you? I watched that lady, your compatriot, on TV the other day. Being of German extraction, she said, she had now been repatriated to Germany. After eight hundred years! Eight hundred years, let us be clear, sir! It is eight hundred years since the German colonists arrived in, what do you call it . . . the . . . Banat."

That alien name *Banat*—the name of a province in southwestern Romania, where descendants of the long-ago settlers still lived—was not to be found in the application form on his desk, unlike *Bukovina*, but in his own memory. He looked very pleased with himself.

"Yes, yes, *bestimmt*, the Banat! After eight hundred years . . . One can tell the difference immediately. From the accent, the vocabulary, the attitudes, believe me, really."

So, nothing of what had happened yesterday in the American's office, or the day before, or today was decisive. This seemed to be the message that the benevolent German representative had tried to convey to him.

He boarded the bus, then the tram, thinking all the while of what the German civil servant had said. He forgot to get off at his stop and found himself at the other end of town, a suburban area with pleasant, low houses. He hailed a cab and asked the driver to take him back to the center of town, near the ruins of Gedächtnis Kirche, the Memorial Church. The streets were alive with people, especially young people. He ambled on, absentmindedly, down a side street and went into the first restaurant he saw, ready to make peace with the futility of the day, with its cryptic codes.

He returned in the evening to his apartment, and as he opened the door, he heard the usual greeting from his roommate. "Decision is a moment of insanity," Mr. Kierkegaard whispered insidiously, as he did every evening. That's true, but the insanity of indecision is not to be forgotten either, and therefore, such nocturnal debates are now meaningless.

Before he went to bed, he said his evening prayer: *In Paradise one is better off than in whatever country. God is only for those of 100 pneuma. They were not able to separate exactly the soul from the flesh and so it would come here with a drop of fat, a thread of muscle. The social system of Paradise is stable, the rulers are wise. God is only for those of 100 pneuma. In Paradise one is better off than in whatever country.*

One month later, he was in Paris, where he had numerous occasions to regret that he had not kept the business card of his French reader from the Allied Commission. Another month later, he took an even bigger step—toward the Afterlife world, the World Beyond, the giant step across the ocean that brought him, in March 1988, to the New World.

The joy of being a foreigner among other foreigners, the limitations and masks of liberty, new lands and new grammars, not only without but also within himself, the trauma of dispossession, new maladies of the soul and of the mind, the shock of dislocation, the chance to live on into one's Afterlife. He gradually accepted the new calendar, the leap years of Paradise: each year in the exile of liberty counted as four conventional years in the old existence.

One and a half years after his arrival in America, that is, six years according to the new calendar, the Berlin Wall collapsed. In socialist Jormania, the Clown of the Carpathians and his wife, Comrade Mortu, were executed. Did he now entertain hopes of repatriation, back to the olden days and to the land of yesterday? The messages coming from the Other Side discouraged such jokes. He reassessed the confusions in which he had lived, reread the *Report* of the Polish poet that served him as a prayer, remembered the pragmatic message of Paradise: DEPRESSION IS A FLAW IN CHEMISTRY NOT IN CHARACTER. Did Ovid, the ancient poet exiled from imperial Rome to the Scythian wilderness of Tomi, far away to the east, by the Black Sea—did he transcend the sadness? Now the terms had been reversed, each day added distance between himself and provincial Tomi. In his new home of New York, the new Rome, on the shores of the Hudson, where he had been shipwrecked, sadness was being treated with antidepressants and workouts in the gym. DEPRESSION IS A FLAW IN CHEMISTRY NOT IN CHARACTER. Everything can be fixed. Call 1-800-HELP.

In 1997, nine years into the new calendar, that is, thirty-six years from his D-Day in Berlin, back in the winter of 1988, he was now being offered the chance to return to the time and space of old. According to the new calendar, he was now ninety-four years old, too old for such a journey. But, at the same time, he was only eleven years old, counting by the time elapsed since his departure from the old life. Such a pilgrimage seemed premature for so young and emotional a person.

The Claw (I)

Y ou should always be allowed in," said the professor from Brooklyn. "Considering the circumstances, this is an exception, and God will always make an exception for you, believe me." I could accept such a hypothesis, but this was not about me. It concerned the person waiting there for me—and the One Above, if He existed at all, knew very well who it was. I was keen to play by His rules only because the woman waiting for me there had been playing by them.

That is why I had phoned the Hebrew Burial Free Association and the Jewish Chapel Services, as well as the local synagogue on Amsterdam Avenue and Sixty-ninth Street. Everywhere, the answer, short and abrupt, had been the same, "Call your rabbi." I was given no opportunity to say that I had no rabbi and didn't belong to a synagogue, that all I wanted to know was whether one is permitted to visit a Jewish cemetery during the Passover week. Even someone like me, who had never belonged to a synagogue or, for that matter, doesn't belong anywhere, was entitled to such information. Finally, I called the professor from Brooklyn, whom

I had introduced to the works of Cioran, and asked him whether he, an atheist in love with nihilist paradoxes, might possibly know a rabbi.

"Of course. My friend, Rabbi Solomonchik."

I explained to my listener my dilemma, suspecting he was ready to grant me the dispensation himself, standing in for the One Above, whose existence he denied.

"You're right," I reassured him. "I could scramble over the fence of the cemetery in Suceava, that hallowed bit of ground in my native town. I'm not too old for that. But I don't want to break the rules, not this time, at any rate. If access isn't allowed, I'll stay there, in front of the cemetery gates, until I die, like Kafka's hero, eyeball to eyeball with the Law. But first, I must know what the Law says. Surely there are provisions for exceptional situations, but I must know what the Law says. You understand what I mean, the Law! I need a rabbi."

"I can call Solo," my Brooklyn friend said. "I'll phone him at once. He'll know; that man knows everything, absolutely everything."

As it turned out, the rabbi did know everything, and a few other things besides. He pronounced: "Entrance into a cemetery is forbidden in the first two and last two days of the Passover week. It is allowed in the interim days." I had a calendar in front of me and noted down the dates: The first two days of Passover would fall on the twenty-second and twenty-third of April 1997, that is, 13 and 14 Nisan, 5757. The last two days would fall on the twenty-eighth and twenty-ninth of April, that is, 21 and 22 Nisan, 5757. This would leave me four permitted days, enough time for my purpose. The rabbi, however, had added something that was above and beyond the Law. Learning that I was about to depart for Romania, he felt he could allow himself a doubt. The go-between who was passing on the sage's wisdom could not hide his bewilderment.

"Can you imagine such a thing? When the rabbi heard about Romania, 'Aha,' he said. 'Romania? Romania? Then I'm no longer so sure. He'll have to ask the people in Romania.' That's what he said. Would you expect an answer like this from Alyosha Solomonchik?"

Alyosha certainly was a sage, I had to admit. The next day, a Friday, I rang up my Christian friend in Bucharest.

"Can't you find out this information in New York?" my former compatriot asked in amazement.

"I could. The rabbi explained the Law to me, but when he heard I was going to Romania . . ."

My friend Naum—Golden Brain, as he was nicknamed—laughed. I could hear him chortling at his end of the line in Bucharest. "Bravo! I wouldn't have thought you had such clever rabbis in New York."

"Of course we do. America has everything, but the American rabbi felt he could not assume any authority over the Romanian Jews. On Sunday morning—Jews go to work on Sundays, so it's all right—could you call and find out about the rules, especially Suceava, and let me know."

And indeed, on Sunday I received my answer.

"A very nice lady gave me all the necessary information," Golden Brain reported. "I asked her to repeat everything, so I could take it all down. Here goes: The cemetery is closed between the twenty-second and twenty-ninth of April, access forbidden. It reopens on the thirtieth. That would be—I'm reading carefully now—the twenty-third of—how do you pronounce it?—Nisan, which, I repeat, is April 30. So April 30 is the first day after Passover, when entry to the cemetery is permitted."

I fell silent. My friend didn't know whether this was in tribute to Rabbi Solomonchik or to the nice Jewish lady in Bucharest, or maybe it meant something completely different.

"What's the problem, say something. So, you'll have to extend your stay by two days, it's no big deal. That way, we'll be able to have a nice long talk. Anyway, what's the hurry? Think about it, we haven't seen each other for ten years, what the hell!"

In fact, it had been almost eleven years, but Naum the Golden Brain was right about one thing, the cemetery wasn't the problem. The truth was, I did not want to go on this trip at all. I would have liked someone, preferably not myself, to explain my neurosis. Better still, I would have liked to be done with both the neurosis and the trip. I needed a simple explanation, something like "You don't want to go back to a place that kicked you out," for example. I needed a coin that would fit all possible vending machines. You insert it and out comes the sandwich, the soda pop, or the tissues for wiping away the tears. But all I was offered were pathetic clichés: "At the age of five, in the autumn of 1941, you woke up in a cattle train, squeezed in with neighbors, relatives, friends. The train was taking you eastward, east of Eden." Yes, I knew all the litanies, uttered in the name of memory and served out to posterity in films, speeches, and at fund-raising dinners. What I needed was a laconic summing up by an impersonal voice: "In 1945, when the war ended and you were a boy of nine, you didn't know what to do with your newly earned title of survivor. Only at the age of fifty, in 1986, did you finally understand what survival meant. Once again, you were leaving, but this time, westward, the 'definitive departure'—the phrase then in use for such leave-takings—'to the West.'"

The impersonal voice was lagging in wit but gaining in rhetorical force: "But in the meantime, you had found a home—language."

An "interstitial" home, is that what the voice had murmured? No, just a "home"—"interstitial" would have sounded too pretentious, although it conveyed the meaning exactly. The familiar platitudes followed: "Survivor, alien, extraterritorial, anti-Party . . . After all, language was your home, wasn't it?" Yes, I recognized the recital. "At the age of five, you were dispossessed, the first time, because of a dictator and his ideology. At the age of fifty, a second time, because of another dictator and his opposing ideology. A farce, wasn't it?"

I could recognize that simplified summary, although it failed to encompass the trap of hope, the education in futility. And what of the privilege of separation? "Being excluded is the only dignity we have," the exiled Cioran said repeatedly. Exclusion, as privilege and justification? On the threshold of old age, exile offers the ultimate lesson in dispossession: preparing the uprooted for the final rootlessness. "In 1982, you were an extraterritorial and an enemy of the Party. Ten years later, now an exile, you became an actual extraterritorial, like the Party itself, now vanished into nothingness." The newspapers of socialist Jormania had continued to pay their tributes to their exiled son: "traitor," "the dwarf from Jerusalem," "Half-Man." Indeed, the motherland had not forgotten me, nor did it allow me to forget it. My friends had spent vast sums of money on postage to send me these tributes across the ocean, year after year, season after season. In 1996, new patriots were demanding *"the extermination of the moth"*—a Kafkaesque formulation indicating that the despised cockroach had somehow metamorphosed into a moth and flown away to exile, across the ocean, to Paradise. Why couldn't I compose such terms of endearment myself, why did I leave it to an intermediary? "One confronts one's homeland out of a need for despair, out of a thirst for even more unhappiness," Cioran had said in one of his monologues.

But hatred was not my métier. I would gladly leave it for somebody else to vent, anybody, including the motherland. I was content to leave that boiling lava behind me. It had not been too difficult, after 1989, to reject all invitations to visit Romania. However, now I found it difficult to refuse the invitation to go there with the president of Bard College, also a musician, who was scheduled to conduct two concerts in Bucharest. Bard College had been my host in America. It was only natural, therefore, that, at least for a few days, I should be his host in Bucharest. Such an opportunity, unhoped for ten years earlier, should have been a source of joy. It wasn't.

When I had first heard about the projected trip, in 1996, I shrugged my shoulders and gave my reasons why I couldn't consider undertaking the journey. But Leon Botstein wouldn't take "no" for an answer. In the winter of 1997, his arguments were given new impetus. "The political situation is changing, Romania is changing. If you are ever to return, you might as well do it now. You will have a friend going with you." I had left the motherland late, without really intending to leave. I was not prepared for a reunion with the self I had been, or for a translation of the one I had become. In the spring of 1990, after the collapse of the utopia, along with its buffoons, I had had a sudden and belated revelation. It happened at a cultural conference at the Salon du Livre in Paris. The Romanian delegation there was composed, for the first time, not of the usual cultural apparatchiks, but of real writers. It was an emotional reunion, laden with nostalgia. However, after a little while, I felt that morbid frisson of fear. I was sweating, without apparent reason, attacked by something deep, hidden, tortuous. I had to get out, and I left the hall in a troubled state. My former compatriots had been polite, friendly, and yet somewhat changed, as though liberated from the entanglement that had previously joined us. Living in exile as I was, outside my native habitat, I was like a snail wearing the shell of the Romanian language. Was that a scandalous imposture? Could this "extraterritorial," of all people, properly represent Romanian culture to the world? "In the struggle between yourself and the world, you must side with the world" was Kafka's advice. Had I heeded his counsel?

Leon insisted. I heard myself saying, "Perhaps," then, "We'll see," "Possibly," "I'll think about it." I could not get used to the idea, yet I was gradually coming around. Finally, I gave a timorous yet clearly audible "yes," convinced that I would soon withdraw it. I didn't. I had to break the chains finally, or so I was being told. Only a return, whether happy or unhappy, would mark the final break, liberating me. Could I really be helped by such slogans, or by some emotional reconciliation feast, a "cultural" lunch, perhaps, where I would find myself decorated with a red-and-green ribbon, awarded by the Society of Transcendental Pensioners for my services to my country's reputation abroad? After partaking of the usual spicy sausages and beer and the usual jokes and embraces, I would then faint under the lightning stroke of destiny, the final stamp of approval: accepted in the motherland. You have been accepted at last, the old scores have been settled. You don't have to prove that it's merely a matter of your country putting on one of its performances to fool the rest of the world. No, you no longer have to prove anything . . . I could almost hear Golden Brain's voice whispering in my ear, when, suddenly, I was startled from my half-sleep by the ringing of the phone.

It was six in the morning and the voice at the other end was not my old friend making jokes but someone from Suceava, the town of my childhood and teenage years, a polite, gentle voice—the director of the Commercial Bank in Suceava. He had learned about my forthcoming reappearance in Romania, and it was his duty to inform me, belatedly, that the previous winter the Bukovina Foundation had awarded me its Prize for Literature. The citizens of my native town would be honored if . . . Suceava! Bukovina! It was there that I had been reborn after my return from the labor camp, I had never forgotten it. Would it be possible for me to receive the prize without any ceremony, without television or publicity? The director assured me that the ceremony had already taken place the year before, in the absence of the American recipient. The banker from Suceava seemed ill at ease talking about literary matters, but he was doing his duty, urging me in his soft dialect, so familiar to me, to accept the "modest" award. The word "modest," as well as the name of the speaker, Cucu, won my heart. I was firm, though, in establishing iron rules—no interviews, no public appearances. After all, the justification for the trip had already been fixed—the cemetery in Suceava. Truth be told, I wasn't prepared for even that consolation.

In the autumn of 1986, before I left Romania, I took an eight-hour journey by train from Bucharest to Suceava, into the very heart of Bukovina, to say my final goodbyes. As I entered the train compartment, I had no difficulty in identifying my fellow passenger, a stocky man dressed in a suit and tie, an attaché case on his lap, engrossed in the Party paper. Unmistakably, he was the "shadow" who would accompany me to my destination and possibly stay with me the whole time I was there, and see me safely back. It was a cold, gray November day. In the end-of-world atmosphere that was Romania in those years, it was obvious that the once bustling little town of my youth had also fallen on hard times. The people looked diminished, muted. One could read the sadness and bitterness, the smoldering anger, in their dry, wrinkled faces, in their tense greetings, even in the most commonplace exchanges. It mattered little where or under what mask my "shadow," or perhaps his replacement, was lurking. Those under surveillance and those doing the surveillance appeared equally condemned to the slow poisoning of their dead-end world. I expected no pleasant surprises, the situation was the same all over the country. Suceava, however, seemed permeated with a funereal sadness, which only added to the burden of my pending separation. I would have liked somehow to have been able to lessen that burden. I tried to focus on the amusing aspects, to convert the dour details of the daily routine into the stuff of jokes, but to no avail. All conversations kept coming back, not to the conditions of squalor and terror that were everywhere, but to the reason for my visit. I failed to convince my old parents, listening to me with depressed skepticism, that my going away was only a temporary separation.

The day before my return to Bucharest, I received the rebuttal to my naïve attempts at consolation. In the morning, while I was still lying in bed, my mother was led to my room. Her condition had worsened in the past year. She was blind and could walk only with support.

Their small apartment, in a socialist-style block, consisted of two rooms, a living room and a bedroom. My mother slept on a couch in the living room; the woman who looked after the house slept nearby on a cot. My father had the bedroom, where we both slept in the same bed during the short time of my visit. In the morning, we all shared breakfast, Bukovina-style, *Kaffee mit Milch*, in the living room, where all the other daytime activities took place, meals, visits, chats.

She had not waited, as usual, to speak to me at breakfast, but wanted to see me earlier, while my father was away at the market or the synagogue. She wanted to talk to me alone, without witnesses. She knocked on the door, then walked, hesitatingly, supported by her helper. Her heart condition had obviously drained her frail body. She was wearing a bathrobe over her nightclothes, her feet were in the slippers I had brought her as a gift from Belgrade. The thick robe was a surprise. All her life, she had complained of being hot. Now it seemed she was always cold and concerned with staying warm.

Supporting herself on her attendant's arm, she came over to my bed. I signaled to the woman to help her sit on the edge of the bed. As soon as the woman withdrew, the torrent of words began to flow, unchecked.

"I want you to promise me something. I want you to attend my funeral."

I did not want this conversation, but there was so little time, I could not afford to make a fuss.

"This time, your going away feels different. You're not coming back. You're leaving me here, on my own."

She had been staying with me in Bucharest in 1982, when an official mass-circulation newspaper proclaimed that I was an "extraterritorial." She knew that was no compliment. She also knew that the terms "enemy of the party," and "cosmopolitan" were not expressions of praise either.

She was with me when a friend phoned to ask whether my windows had been smashed. She used to read such signs better than I did. We knew, tacitly, what sort of memories were revived in both of us by those warnings.

I interrupted her, and told her again what I had told her repeatedly over the previous days. She listened attentively, but without curiosity. She had heard it all before.

"I would like you to promise me that, in case I die and you're not here, you'll come back for the funeral."

"You're not going to die, there's no point talking about it."

"There is for me."

"You're not going to die, we shouldn't talk about this."

"We must. I want you to be at the funeral. Promise me."

I could only give her the same answer: "I don't know about my return, I haven't made any decision yet. If I get the grant for Berlin, then I'll stay there for six months or a year, whatever the terms of the grant. I haven't heard from the Germans yet. Who knows, the letter may be lying in some censor's drawer. But I've heard rumors that I got the grant. Nothing certain, just rumors."

She repeated her solemn request. Finally, I told her firmly but without real strength, "I cannot promise."

She suddenly seemed diminished, shrunken. "This means that you are not going to come?"

"It doesn't mean anything. It means that you are not going to die, and that it's pointless to talk about it."

"Nobody knows when and how."

"Precisely."

"That's why we have to talk about it."

"No one knows what will happen to them. I don't know what might happen to me."

"I just want you to promise. Please, promise me, I want you to be here at my funeral."

"I can't promise. I just can't." I then added, without even meaning to, "And it's not important."

"It is for me."

The conversation reached its end, there was nothing left to say. But I went on anyway: "Even if I didn't actually attend the funeral, I would still be there, wherever I was. You must know that. Just remember that."

I could not begin to guess whether that answer had satisfied her, and I would never find out. After November 1986 I never saw her again. She died in July 1988, when I was already in America. Father informed me of her death one month later—not because he had wished to release me from the obligation to attend the funeral, but because he knew that if I came back, I would never again be allowed to leave. He also wanted to spare me from the transgression of not observing the seven days of ritual mourning, the traditional shiva, which, in any case, he doubted that his son, however pained, would observe.

Before he himself left Romania for Israel, in the summer of 1989, at the age of eighty-one, my father described to me in a letter my mother's final months. For as long as I remained in Germany, she seemed to be clinging to life for one reason only, so that she might get news about me. Neither the letters, the frequent phone calls, nor the parcels with food and medicine were able to calm her. In fact, they only confirmed the inevitability of the separation, as she saw it. The news of my departure for America finally shattered her illusion that I might yet return. She had nobody or nothing left to struggle against, nothing to hope for. Soon after, her mind began to wander. Helping her became difficult, even for the few steps needed to go to the bathroom. One day she fell, and it was only with great difficulty that one could lift her frail, inert body. The vivacious speaker she had always been turned deaf and mute, oblivious to her surroundings. When she did speak, it was in a sort of trance, about her father and about me, often confusing the two. She believed we were there, in the immediate vicinity, and was worried that we were late coming home or that we hadn't told her where we had gone. Sometimes she would say she had been murdered—Marcu and Maria were the names of the murderers, and somehow that didn't seem strange. She had brief spasms of resistance, but soon tired and fell back into her thin-layered peace of sleep, interrupted only by the same worries: Where is my son, where is Father Avram? The delirium followed the same pattern, and came on without warning, followed by the same gentle slipping into the healing peace of unreality that was to be her real home now. "Are they back? Is the boy back? Where's Father? Still in town, still in town? It's late . . ." She could not let go of these two phantoms, even when she seemed to have given up on most other people and things.

After her death, she began to visit me in strange, haunting dreams. I could sometimes feel her presence, too, in the anonymous rooms where I found rest in my nomadic life. The atmosphere would suddenly become charged, and I felt a strange and tender embrace; the gentle spirit of the past fluttered its wings over my tired eyelids and forehead and alighted in a soft embrace over my shoulders.

I saw her again in the week before my return to Romania. We were walking together in the streets of Bucharest. She was talking to me about Mihai Eminescu, the national poet, and telling me how dearly he would have liked to be with me again. She was animated, focusing on matters that seemed to give her pleasure, but that were mainly intended to please me, when suddenly she fell into a deep trench along the edge of the sidewalk, a kind of shaft where workers were repairing the sewage system. It happened in an instant, leaving me no time to catch her. But she had held on to my arm, and her old, heavy body was hanging suspended over the pit, while I lay flat on the sidewalk, gripping her with my left hand, so that she would not drop into the abyss. With my right hand I clutched the edge of the sidewalk, while my left hand gripped her bony fingers. I could feel myself slipping, I couldn't hold on to the burden of her body swinging desperately above the void, her thin, pale legs thrashing helplessly in the air.

There were men working in the bottom of the hole below. I could see their white helmets, but they could not see me or hear my vain cries for help. I was screaming as loud as I could, but I didn't produce a single sound. I was suffocating, I could feel my strength draining. I was being pulled down by the bony clasp of the old hand into the black void. I was slipping toward the edge of the sidewalk, ready either to let go of the burden or to let myself be dragged into the bottomless depth, over which my mother was writhing. I had just found her again, I had been talking to her, and I could not bear to lose her again.

No, I could not surrender that familiar touch. The thought sent a pain shooting through my mind, but it failed to give me the strength I needed. On the contrary, I almost fainted, my last reserve of energy drained. Still, I was not beaten, it was not over yet, I was still struggling, although I knew it was hopeless.

I held tight to the hand clutching mine, but I could feel the grip loosening with every second that passed. We were slipping, together, into the abyss. But no, it was not over yet, I could not let go . . . Whimpering, exhausted, I kept slipping, inch by inch, deeper and deeper. The fingers of my left hand were already numb, defeated, while my right hand, almost useless, could barely keep its grip. It was over, I was letting go, helplessly, guiltily. It was over, finis. So be it, the end, I could resist no longer, I surrendered. As we were falling, I felt a sharp pain in my chest, as if I had been stabbed repeatedly by a stiletto.

I woke in a sweat, spent, defeated, in my familiar bed on the Upper West Side. I was in bed, next to the window bright with morning sun. It was Wednesday, the sixteenth of April 1997, four days before I was due to return to the motherland.

The First Return
(The Past as Fiction)

The Beginning before the Beginning

A torrid summer day in July. Standing in line to buy bus tickets, the would-be travelers fan themselves with newspapers and wipe away the sweat with their handkerchiefs.

The newcomer, with his cropped light-brown hair, full lips, and bushy eyebrows, did not seem troubled by the slowness of the queue or by the scorching heat. His look was friendly. His nose, although quite prominent and somewhat hawkish, was not unattractively so. He wore a pale-gray lightweight suit, double-breasted, with wide lapels, complemented by a white shirt, a stiff collar, a dark-blue tie with white polka dots, and shoes with pointed toes. The tip of a blue-checked handkerchief poked out from the right upper pocket of his jacket. The very picture of an impeccably dressed young gentleman, around twenty-five years of age, intent on respectability.

Propped against a wall, and secured by one of the young gentleman's feet, was a small leather suitcase, about the size of a largish briefcase, and a leather cylinder that looked almost like an umbrella, over which he had placed his straw hat.

The young man took a shiny brown leather billfold out of his breast pocket and extracted two banknotes, crisp new bills, folded in two. As he unfolded them, they made a pleasant rustling sound. He handed the banknotes to the mustachioed clerk behind the counter, leaned forward, gave the name of his destination, then straightened up. His voice was hard to make out, for all that had been spoken was a brief request, addressed to the ticket seller. The young man took the ticket handed him and put it inside his left trouser pocket. He then folded the crumpled bill he had received as change and slipped it among the others in his fine leather wallet. He then bent down and picked up his suitcase, his leather cylinder, and his hat. He looked at the rectangular Anker watch on his left wrist. He still had half an hour before his bus was due to depart. He turned toward the park. The only vacant bench was in full sunshine. The bus stood waiting a little way off. He sat down and took a newspaper from an inside pocket of his jacket. The front page of the *Universul* carried the date in bold letters: July 21, 1933. The editorial was warning, in two columns of feverish text, that the world was "laden with dynamite" and could ignite sooner than the skeptics might expect. However, the earnest, concentrated expression of the newspaper reader had not changed since he had bought his ticket. The printed words did little to intensify the moderate attention with which he viewed his surroundings, or quicken the slow-rising yeast of that sluggish afternoon hour. He seemed pleased with himself, content with the world in which he lived, with the day he inhabited. The park, the lake, the sky, even the garrulous bustle of passengers were a sort of confirmation: he was part of the world, part of society. Only those who had never had to work hard enough to find their place in the world could fail to grasp exactly what such an idyllic day had to offer.

Soon the noise around him increased. People were hurrying toward the ticket booth and the bus. Quite a throng—women, children—a summery bustle. Remaining on the bench, he observed the commotion. Reluctantly, he got up. As usual, the bus was packed. This happened every year after St. Elias Day, the day of the famous fair in Fǎlticeni—

iarmarok, as the local Ukrainians called it. The crowds came from near and far. He tried to push forward down the aisle of the bus, then stopped. The bus was due to depart any minute now, he had to settle down. He carefully opened the leather roll, which turned out to be a tripod chair. He carefully extended the three legs of the chair and positioned it next to the small suitcase, on top of which he had placed his hat.

He sensed he was being watched by the young woman sitting to his left. He had noticed her in the park, as he was eyeing the passengers heading to the bus. She was dark-haired, Spanish-looking, with dark, deep-set eyes, a slender waist, and delicate ankles, in a white short-sleeved dress with a flowery print pattern, high-heeled suede sandals, a fancy leather handbag shaped like a basket. Slim and graceful, she seemed eager to see and be seen.

The handsome elegant gentleman had no trouble engaging the beautiful elegant lady in conversation. His young tenor led off in even, measured tones, her young alto vibrated in a quick rhythm, but avoided the higher notes.

"Are you by any chance related to Mrs. Riemer?"

This was the question that had occurred to him as he watched her hurrying toward the bus earlier.

Startled, she turned her delicate face to him, scrutinizing him intently.

"Yes, Mrs. Riemer is my aunt. My father's sister."

After only a few remarks, they felt like old acquaintances. The tripod seat lent a comic yet engaging touch to the young man's otherwise impeccable appearance. Clearly, he was mindful both of his place in the crowd of society and on the equally crowded bus.

The conversation passed from Leah Riemer to her husband, Kiva, the upholsterer, and also chess partner of the writer Sadoveanu during the latter's summer vacations in Fălticeni; then it moved on to the Riemers' academically gifted children, and proceeded to mutual acquaintances who lived in the town where the July fair was to be held, a town that, as they now discovered, they both visited frequently.

Neither of the pair got off at Suceava, as each thought the other would, but at the adjacent market towns—the gentleman at Ițcani, the first stop after Suceava, and the lady at Burdujeni, the first stop after Iţcani.

Engrossed in conversation, they were oblivious to the contours of a strange gestation forming in the air, though perhaps they did sense something. For in spite of the conversation, animated as it was by the young woman's Mediterranean vivacity, they had observed each other attentively all the time. When they parted, the feeling that they had indeed been on a journey, not homeward, but into the unknown, sought an appropriate means of expression in each.

They saw each other again, as agreed, the following week. The young man showed up, on his shiny bicycle, in front of Librăria Noastră—Our Bookstore—a medium-sized house-cum-shop halfway up the sloping main street of Burdujeni, with yellow walls and narrow shuttered windows. Only three kilometers separated the sugar factory in Iţcani, where the young gentleman worked as an accountant, from the other little town, where the bookstore, owned by the parents of the young woman, was located. An easy, pleasant ride, especially on a sunny Sunday morning.

My earliest memory is linked to this trip. A memory preceding my birth, a memory of the being I was before I came into being—the legend of a past before the past.

When the ancient Chinese sage asks me, as he has so many of his readers, "What did you look like before your father and mother met?" I conjure up the strip of road between two neighboring towns in northeast Romania in the mid-1930s, a narrow expanse of cobblestones between two slender columns of trees under a homely, sleepy sky. A ribbon of golden space made time, the necessary length of time to go from somewhere to somewhere else, from something to something else. Fairy tales call this love, the comedy of errors that we all seem to need.

After that first Sunday meeting, the accountant from the sugar factory of Iţcani continued his visits to the neighboring town. That strip of cobblestones, earth, and dust gradually turned into a magnetic tape of illusions making that forgotten corner of the world into its very center. Destiny's Chinese brushstrokes were chasing each other chaotically all over that bucolic sky, offering no vision of the future but the incandescent nebulae of the moment.

However, the young gentleman was to discover, over the next few months, what I discovered only half a century later, in the early 1980s, on the train taking me and my mother, by then almost blind, to an ophthalmologist in a town situated more than two hours away from those old places.

During my first trip to the West, a few years earlier, I had met in Paris my mother's famous cousin Ariel, the subject of some exotic family legends. By then, he had stopped dyeing his hair green, or red, or blue, as he had done in his youth, and it was not clear whether he still dealt in arms sales, as in the days of De Gaulle, or whether he still wrote for *Le Monde*, as he had claimed. The heavy, bald gentleman, almost blind himself, like many in the family, owned a dazzling personal library where you were hard-pressed to choose one book over another. When I asked about the early years of my mother, the daughter of Ariel's adored Uncle Avram—the bookseller—what she was like in her youth, all I got for an answer was an ambiguous smile. He refused to go into the matter, in spite of my insistence.

Had there been an unsettling episode in her youth, from the time before she married my father? Did the young woman, when my father met her on the bus, have a past that had scandalized the provincial society of her small hometown? Not scandalous enough, it would seem, to deter her distinguished suitor from persevering for three years through all the phases of courtship. What was I like before they met? I am not Chinese enough to remember the past before the past, but I can see the beginning before the beginning, that interval between July 1933 and July 1936, from the meeting on the bus to the arrival, more dead than alive, of their only offspring.

It was in my maternal grandfather's house, where the family's culinary and diplomatic talents were always on display, that the potentialities that were to culminate in my birth were accumulating—at the sumptuous Austrian-style balls organized in Iţcani and Suceava; during those rare trips to Czernowitz, Bukovina's end-of-the-world Vienna, at the holy days of the old-style calendar in Burdujeni; at the Dom-Polski theater in Suceava and in the old movie house where the screen flashed before the lovers the name of that American or English or Australian actor, my namesake Norman; on the bus route between Fălticeni and Suceava. The air was heavy with the smell of conifers and speeches about Titulescu and Jabotinsky, Hitler, Trotsky, and the Baal Shem Tov; the smoky rooms, redolent with the vapors of hot frying pans, the buzz of gossip and rumors. The darkness was electrically charged and the newspapers filled with alarms of planetary passions.

Nothing, however, could be more important than the hypnosis that had suddenly placed a man and a woman at the very center of the world: a sober and lonely young man, who had risen through his own efforts from an obscure family of country bakers, discreet and hardworking, keen on preserving his dignity and the respect of his fellow citizens, and an ardent young woman, avidly searching for the signs of the destiny that would embrace her panic and her passion, inherited from the neurotic Talmudic scholars and booksellers who were her ancestors. The coming together, you might say, of bread and the book.

The very differences between the two seemed to have cemented their relationship in the early stages of the marriage and possibly even later, though they were both to remain their own selves up to the very end. Engagement versus aloofness, an almost theatrical yet genuine pathos on one side and solitude, discretion, moderation on the other. Alertness versus apathy, panic versus prudence, risk-taking versus reticence and dignity. The end result of their union—not necessarily a perfect dialectical synthesis of thesis and antithesis—had new contradictions added to it, naturally; otherwise the comedy would have been utterly humorless. Was there some impatience in the contradictions that had fused in the newborn? Paradoxically enough, the premature birth of their only child, in July 1936, on the eve of St. Elias Day—the day of the Fălticeni fair—was no indication of impatience but rather of reluctance. The unborn refused in fact to be born, refused to activate his innate and acquired contradictions. He remained stuck in the placenta, and this lingering endangered his emergence, which only looked like a birth, a wounding that was dangerous for both mother and child, as they struggled for life, day after day.

Everybody sighed with relief upon learning that the young mother, she being more important than the fetus, would live. As for the child, only when his fate was no longer so closely dependent on his mother's did the grandfather, old Avram, ask, "Has he got fingernails?" Told that I had, he calmed down: I would survive. Over the short time that I knew him, and later, during the years in the labor camp in Transnistria, he should have taught me that in the real world it was not just fingernails that one needed for survival but claws.

Premature birth indeed, followed by a time of solar blankness, without contours or memories. An idyllic time out of which the mind picks up only a flash of a sloping street and the entrance to my grandfather's bookstore. Memory does not say much about the way I was before the true birth, which was still to come. Much later, fiction was perhaps more eloquent: a scene from the Tarkovsky film *Ivan's Childhood*, which I watched endlessly, many years later. The blond child, the laughing mother, happiness. Suddenly the arm of the water well swinging madly. The mirror of the lake shattered by the thundering explosion: war.

The thunder of October 1941. Thunder and lightning in one stroke split the floor of the stage set. Expulsion, the exiles' convoy, the train, the dark emptiness. The hole into which we had been hurled was no baby's cot. Behind us, only the desperate scream of the Good Fairy Maria, who had not wanted to relinquish me from her arms and was pleading with the guards to let her come with us into the abyss, she, the Christian, the Holy Virgin, together with the sinners whom she could not possibly abandon. Night, shots, screams, plunder, the bayonets, the dead, the river, the bridge, cold hunger, fear, the bodies—the long night of the Initiation. Only there and then was the comedy about to begin. Transnistria, beyond the Dniester . . . Transtristia, beyond sadness. The prebirth Initiation had begun.

Yes, I know what I looked like before I was born. And I know the way I looked afterward, in April 1945, when the surviving expatriates had been repatriated to the *patria*, the motherland that had banished them and that had not, after all, managed to get rid of them. Though it did get rid of some—old Avram the bookseller; his wife, Haia, and so many others. A diaphanous spring day was embracing the town, in 1945 still called Fălticeni, as it had been in 1933, the same departure point of destiny's bus.

66 THE HOOLIGAN'S RETURN

The truck bringing us in 1945 back "home" to Fălticeni, to the relatives who had not been taken away, did not, however, stop near the park or the booth where bus tickets to Paradise used to be sold. It stopped next to the market, on the corner of Beldiceanu Street.

A bell sounded. The wooden screen at the rear of the truck was removed. From Beldiceanu Street the crowd came running toward us, bit players whose role was to celebrate the return. A melodrama as sweet and delicate as the placenta of the newly born swelled the concertina bag's rainbow in honor of the victors—us.

I watched them cry, embrace, recognize each other. I hung back on the platform of the truck, biting my fingernails. The street was the stage and I was a bewildered spectator. Finally, they came back for the one left behind, left behind in the past.

Before I allowed myself to be lowered back into the world, I managed to bite my fingernails deeply once more. I had acquired this bad habit. I bit my fingernails.

The Hooligan Year

The premarital idyll of the baker's son and the bookseller's daughter lasted from 1933 to 1935. Mrs. Waslowitz, the Polish dressmaker who catered to all the ladies of Suceava and environs, could barely cope with the orders issuing from the bookseller's household. Elegant and serious, the future bride's knight insisted on escorting her in a different dress to each of the town's charity balls. The slim, nervous brunette had blossomed. Her vivacious black eyes sparkled, the intensity of her face was transfigured by a magic aura whose origins were easy to ascertain. Always rushed and pressed for time, she worked, as before, from morning till night, but now she also devoted more time to her dresses, shoes, bags, hats, gloves, face powder, hairdos, and lace trimmings.

One can imagine embraces in the carriage and car, visits to Suceava, Fălticeni, and Botoşani, perhaps also to Czernowitz. Balls, walks in the moonlight, gatherings at the synagogue, and festivities at the home of the future bride's family. Cinema and theater and summer gardens, skating rinks and jingling sleigh bells, trips to Bukovina's resorts. Perhaps they even stopped by the bachelor's rooms. The scenario is easy enough to imagine, the quick pulse of love throbbing with the rhythm of the times, the last idyllic holiday before the catastrophe.

The year 1934 could be called, then, a happy year. The few kilometers of road between Burdujeni and Ițcani became the Milky Way for the love story that had begun one year earlier in the hot, crowded bus bringing the pair back from the St. Elias fair in Fălticeni. The people in Ițcani, and especially the inhabitants of Burdujeni—the shtetl metropolis, as it were—were keen to comment on events as they unfolded: political debate and female gossip enjoyed an equal share in that particular corner of the world theater; small events and grand utopian discourses, the clamor of the planet as heard in the Romanian, Yiddish, French, and German newspapers jostled with workaday noises. Friends and relatives all partook in this feast, the brother and the sister and the father and his ailing and pestering wife, my grandmother Haia, nicknamed Tzura, "the affliction." A keen participant in all this was the beautiful Maria, the orphaned peasant girl adopted by the family, eager to accompany the bookseller's youngest daughter to her new household.

A happy year, then, 1934. The young Ariel, the well-educated Zionist rebel, always up-to-date with the latest news, had, however, decreed that it was the Hooligan Year. The future bride and groom were among those who gathered in old Avram's bookshop, turning the pages of the day's newspapers and the latest books. They were therefore probably not in the least surprised by Ariel's announcement: the novel *De două mii de ani* (*Two Thousand Years*), published the year before, was enjoying a *succès de scandale* in Bucharest. The author's name, inscribed on the gray-blue cover, was Mihail Sebastian, the pen name of Joseph Hechter, and the incendiary preface was by the Iron Guard ideologue Nae Ionescu. Incredibly, this extreme right-wing national was poor Hechter's mentor! In the introduction, Legionnaire Ionescu claimed that his admirer and disciple was not purely and simply a *man* from the Danubian area of Brăila, as he had assumed, but a *Jew* from Danubian Brăila.

Apparently, this fact could not be ignored or altered: Hechter-Sebastian and his co-religionists, even when they were atheists or assimilated, could not be considered Romanians. Romanians are Romanian because they belong to the Eastern Orthodox Church, and they are such because they are Romanians, Legionnaire Ionescu explained. As simple as that!

By 1935 the bookshop already stocked another volume by Sebastian, *Cum am devenit huligan* (*How I Became a Hooligan*), in which the author pronounced that 1934, a year of such happiness for the future bride and groom, was a Hooligan Year. "Why should we care?" bookseller Avram asked out loud, just to provoke his rebellious nephew. Ariel, with fanatic zeal, persisted in selling old news. Mr. Nae Ionescu claimed there was no solution for the damn situation! Shaking his wildly tousled hair, dyed blue, he would recite the verdict passed by the Legionnaire: "Judas is suffering because he gave birth to Christ, because he saw him but did not believe in him. This in itself wouldn't have been so bad. The trouble is, we Christians did believe in him. Judas is suffering because he is Judas, and he will continue to suffer until the end of time."

Sebastian's former friend Nae Ionescu had become an Iron Guard philosopher, a militant advocate for an Eastern Orthodox state. In the next Hooligan Year of 1935, Ionescu's message was even more unmistakable and Ariel's frenzied concern was hard to challenge. "Joseph Hechter," Ionescu had written threateningly, "dost thou not feel that thou art seized by the cold and the darkness?" "He's talking about us," Ariel whispered dramatically. "Our Legionnaire friend is pointing at us."

But if neither assimilation nor conversion afforded a solution to the so-called Jewish question, what could? This dilemma, Ariel helpfully supplied, was addressed in a contemporary guide, titled *Mein Kampf.* Whatever Ariel's audience's feelings, the Legionnaire had made his point. The darkness and chill of the Final Solution were not the invention of the Romanian Eastern Orthodox *legionari*. All of his forebears, from time immemorial, had endowed Judas with a gene that enabled him to sense hidden danger. Not so the family of bookseller Avram.

But what was it that distinguished the dark years of 1934 and 1935 from all the others? Ariel would reply to this question in the same way that Joseph Hechter had: they were Hooligan Years. Delighted with the word "hooligan," he waved Hechter-Sebastian's pocket-sized booklet at his audience, showing off the pink cover with black lettering, presided over by an owl, the logo of the Cultura Națională Publishers, Bucharest,

Macca Arcade 2. Of course, Librăria Noastră in Burdujeni had ordered several copies of *How I Became a Hooligan*, more copies than it had ordered of the notorious novel by the same author the previous year. "In general," the author had written, "Romanian anti-Semitism is a fact rather than an idea, which it occasionally becomes." But what about love for his motherland? "Show me the anti-Semitic law that will eradicate the undeniable fact that I was born on the banks of the Danube and love this land," the author bravely declared.

"Is it true, then, that anti-Semitic legislation will not shake your love for your native land?" our unstoppable cousin Ariel, sweating profusely, asked the unseen author. "Remember, we Jews have moved continually from one rocky precipice to another, all over this world!" His own family, now listening attentively, should have been rolling with laughter—or so he thought—at that Joseph Hechter–Mihail Sebastian. But they were not laughing at all. They merely smiled at what they regarded as the youthful musings of the young orator. They knew Mr. Hechter-Sebastian had left the ghetto and moved freely around on the wide and colorful Bucharest stage, but their small town—eternal as the blue heavens—did not understand what it meant to walk away from one's kin and still claim kinship.

"The dictionaries in your bookshop are wrong!" the all-knowing Ariel shouted, pointing at the bookshelves. What he meant was that Hechter-Sebastian had not used the word "hooligan" in its English sense, or in the sense used by the Hindus for their spring festival, or in the Slavic sense of the word, meaning "blasphemer." What Ariel intended was the French *troublion*, or, as the American put it, "troublemaker."

What the author of the 1935 booklet had in mind, in fact, was the new hooliganism: a mixture of scandal-mongering, buffoonery, and lampooning, all united by the sense of a new mission, as formulated by another of Joseph Hechter's friends, Mircea Eliade, in his novel *The Hooligans*, published in the same year and displayed in the bookshop's window. Was rebellion a rite of passage on the way toward the Great Ecstasy, Death? "There is only one promising path in life: hooliganism." Youth itself is a vehicle for the hooligan hero. "The human species will gain its freedom only when organized in regiments, perfectly and uniformly intoxicated with a collective myth"—militias and assault battalions, the legions of the present-day world, youthful crowds joined by the same destiny, collective death.

"The Legionnaires have even claimed the national poet Mihai Eminescu as the great hooligan of the nation, as a sacred forerunner of the martyrs in green shirts, chanting the glory of the Cross and the Captain Codreanu!" Ariel ranted on, oblivious to the fact that his audience had stopped paying attention once he had abandoned Judas for his more complicated ramblings.

"Collective death!" Ariel shouted. "Whatever he chooses to become, whether an atheist, a converted Jew, even an anti-Semite, Mr. Hechter cannot avoid the darkness threatened by the hooligans. 'Inner adversity,' he says. Now, while his friends are applauding assault and collective death, this is what's on the mind of Yosele Hechter from Brăila. Admittedly, we can be excessive, suspicious, agitated. But these ancestral maladies are enough, we don't need new enemies, we've got ourselves to cope with. Is anybody asking us whether we prefer the 'inner adversity' of Mr. Sebastian or the adversity of the *legionari?*" It was hard to tell whether they were still listening to him, the relatives and the relatives' relatives gathered in old Avram's bookshop. Then, as later in life, Ariel was talking more to himself. They were probably still listening, but without much pleasure, irritated by the prodigy who believed they were all half-asleep morons.

Sebastian's novel *Two Thousand Years*, with Nae Ionescu's preface, published in 1934, and the booklet *How I Became a Hooligan*, published in 1935 at the same time as the two-volume *The Hooligans* by Mircea Eliade—these publications were all on display on the shelves of the Librăria Noastră in Burdujeni. Indeed, all the major periodicals and books reached that shtetl metropolis. Avram even ordered French and German publications, if any of his customers were interested. Ariel, the son of his sister Fanny, took care to alert him to special titles and was the first to read the exotic acquisitions.

The book *Two Thousand Years* had left no one indifferent. It was no accident that I came across the volume in 1950, when the hooligans' war was over and the hooligans' peace was in force. It was one of only three

or four books I found in the house of my aunt—my mother's older sister—a simple woman of little education. I was about thirteen or fourteen years old and paying a short visit to relatives in Tîrgu Frumos,
when I found, where least expected, a first edition of the novel, with its
blue-gray covers and diagonal lettering. No socialist publishers or public library would have dared promote such a title and such themes. But
there was the book, in the home of the other daughter of the bookseller
from Burdujeni, a relic of the old times and a guide to the new. My aunt
Rebecca was one of those who had listened to cousin Ariel's tirades
against Hechter-Sebastian, who himself had used the term "hooligan"
against everybody, including those of his fellow Jews who had attacked
him. "He has the right to say what he wants. But death—how could he
traffic with death?" Ariel would shout. "The delicate Hechter-Sebastian,
unwilling to offend his mentor, accepted the Legionnaire's preface and,
with it, his death sentence. And, delicate as ever, he responded to the
hooligans by declaring himself a hooligan, too. Mere irony? Well, that's
his business. But death . . . the cult of death? The ecstasy of death, the
chill and darkness of death? These are no jokes, and Hechter-Sebastian
should know better. This is where irony itself ceases to operate. What
shall we do with the Legionnaire hooligan, with death's hero, sanctified
by the magic of death? Mr. Sebastian, the atheist, the assimilated citizen
of Romania, should have been aware of all this." Indeed, Aunt Rebecca
explained, for the benefit of the freshly minted thirteen-year-old Communist I had become, "we cultivate life, not death. Life as proclaimed by
the Torah, again and again, unique, nonrepeatable, invaluable." The urgency of this refrain was exasperating, and its reverse was no less mad-
dening. We knew only too well what the cult of death had led to, Aunt
Rebecca reminded me. The far-seeing Ariel was right. My grandfather's
family—the Braunsteins—and all the other families in that market
town, vibrating with the whirlwinds and the turmoil and the buzzing of
the beehive called life, did not seem at all interested in the "transformation of anti-Semitism into idea," as quoted by Ariel from the wisdom of
Hechter-Sebastian. But the chill and darkness of death . . . Such words
were not to be taken lightly.

In the small market towns relations with neighbors and authorities were friendly. The peasants would come to old Avram for advice on legal and even religious matters, or to borrow small sums of money. The family loved Maria like a daughter, the orphan girl whom the bookseller had taken off the streets and brought into his home as a member of the family, where she happily remained. Maria was beyond suspicion, but all around them, in books, newspapers, in the eyes of customers, suspicions were arising. One had to be vigilant, extremely vigilant.

Avram the bookseller maintained a good-humored and skeptical detachment from these ancestral obsessions, as if decency and piety could ward off evil. However, his youngest daughter, my mother, reacted promptly to any dubious sign. Aunt Rebecca reminded me of the details, already familiar to me from family lore.

Marcu, the accountant from Iţcani, my future father, remained unperturbed, friendly, and prudent in his relations with everybody. He did not have many friends, but he had no enemies either. He was easy in his dealings with colleagues of any sort, although he felt more comfortable among his own kin. He was always baffled by his happy-go-lucky non-Jewish friend Zaharia, the party-loving, womanizing, hunting, and horse-riding local Don Juan, who went through life with a smile on his lips and his hat tipped at a rakish angle. They had always been firm friends. He could not imagine Zaharia taking any interest in frenzied slogans and parades of chanting Legionnaires.

In 1935, old Avram paid no attention to Ariel's fiery calls for caution. Hostility and danger were, to him, part of the natural order of things. Since they could not be avoided, they were not worth worrying about. One had to get through the day's work and accept the surrounding stupidity and suffering, that was all; people always remembered a kind, decent man—there was no other way. Ariel, after all, had won a dubious notoriety for himself with his extravagant dress and exaggerated language. The family had other concerns apart from Sebastian's scandal, or theorizing about the confrontation between inner and outer adversity. Engrossed as they were in their wedding plans, their daily lives were dominated by other thoughts. In fact, the bustle of the preparations served as a reminder that they were at ease in the place where they had been living for as many generations as they could remember. True, they had not been born on the banks of the Danube, like Joseph Hechter, but then, the hills of Bukovina were not to be sneezed at, either. They loved their native land no less than Joseph Hechter–Mihail Sebastian, and did not have the inclination or the time to philosophize about such matters as—the *diminutive*, for example, Ariel's latest obsession.

Normally, diminutives may be thought of as agreeable things; they have a charming sweetness and naïveté about them. Only zany Ariel, the bookseller's nephew and cousin of the bride, could argue that they were bad omens. They distill poisons, poisons that could only be temporarily domesticated. Diminutives can spell disaster when you least expect it! "Here, anything can happen, nothing is incompatible," the young man recited, quoting from Sebastian. Ariel devoured everything, memorized everything, twisted words in any way he chose. "Evasiveness," that's what he called it. *Evasiveness!* The term found an audience, it inspired trust. Fatalism, a sense of humor, hedonism and melancholy, corruption and lyricism, all played their part, the excited Ariel claimed, in this, the supreme technique of survival: *evasiveness.* This is what he kept repeating, with his usual contempt and arrogance. But who was listening? Rejoicing in the preparations for the wedding, his audience felt they had no reason to reject pleasure, or lyricism, or confidence in their destiny, all denounced by the youthful Ariel.

The so-called Hooligan Year of 1934 had been a happy one, so why should the next be any different? The bookseller's favorite daughter had blossomed, joy had entered the household, the heightened emotions were a reminder that the place where they had been living for so many generations was no worse than any other. The landscape and the people, the climate and the language—all belonged to them. They lived in harmony with their neighbors. Adversity? There was no particular reason to be suspicious of the way people looked at you or to bridle at the odd world; after all, their co-religionists were no saints either. Occasionally, they even wondered whether the evil might not, after all, be in themselves, as they seemed to attract hostility wherever they went.

Did life necessarily need the galvanizing force of poison? Often diluted and almost absent, it was always ready, nevertheless, to erupt in sudden, terrible outbreaks, smashing the sweet little nothings—yesterday's tender diminutives—and heralding disaster. That was precisely what zany Ariel did, throwing names and quotations at them that were designed to alert them to the traps they themselves no longer heeded. "Even Tolstoy allowed himself to be fooled. He liked it here during his brief Romanian sojourn. The charm of the place and its inhabitants . . . the old sage was young and naïve," young Ariel pontificated. Ariel, the bookseller's nephew, son of his sister from Buhuşi, madcap Ariel, with his blue-dyed hair, reciting Rimbaud and capable of walking twenty-five kilometers every other week to play chess with his uncle, Kiva Riemer, making impassioned speeches on Jabotinsky and on the forthcoming Jewish state in the Mediterranean—this was a man who believed himself to be in a better position than Hechter-Sebastian. "Assimilation? Assimilation for what?" the young man fulminated. "To become like everybody else? Everything compatible with everything else? Do we live in the country of all compatibilities, as the author from Bucharest claims?" He did not seem to care that Uncle Avram smiled in amusement, or that Avram's daughter listened too attentively to be actually listening.

"Would we have been able to survive for so long if we had been just like these, or like those, or like the others? Five thousand years! Not two thousand, as the gentleman from Bucharest believes! Let's see how compatible Mr. Hooligan will prove to be with his hooligan friends!" Old Avram and his daughter, the speaker himself, and even the wretched Nathan, the Communist tailor who could not decide in favor of Stalin or Trotsky—they all seemed to be in a better situation than the assimilated Sebastian. And, of course, Rabbi Yossel Wijnitzer, too, the town's spiritual leader, was in a clearer and better situation than Hechter-Sebastian. Their home was illusion! The illusion of home was what Mr. Sebastian no longer had.

The Braunstein family was happy in that Hooligan Year of 1934, and happy, too, in 1935, when the wedding was to take place, and in 1936, when their heir was expected. In the town of Burdujeni, these were not Hooligan Years, as Sebastian, his critic Ariel, and newspapers proclaimed worldwide. The hooligan times are upon us, or rather, they're already here, declared the Romanian, Yiddish, German, and French newspapers that old Avram carried on his back from the station to his bookstore in

Burdujeni. Everywhere there was the morbid delight in blaspheming, but in that small East European market town, the bookseller's family lived their happy lives.

Had I been able to ask the old Chinese sage, half a century after the Hooligan Year, about what I looked like in the year before I was born, he probably would have answered with a cliché. He would probably have told me what I already knew and what time subsequently confirmed: as a mere hypothesis, as nonreality, one can have only the face that one will have later on, in actual life. I could not, for instance, become the Jewish-Romanian Anna Pauker, the star of world Communism, who left the ghetto and went straight through the red gates of proletarian internationalism; nor could I have become the worldly Jewish-Romanian Nicu Steinhardt, convert to Eastern Orthodoxy, even Legionnairism; I could not even have become Avram or his daughter Janeta Braunstein, and least of all Rabbi Yossel, their wise adviser. Likewise, I could not have been their rebellious relative, the Zionist Ariel. Rather, in 1935, the year before I was born, I was the hooligan Sebastian—and so I would be fifty years after and then ten more years after that and another ten and all the years between.

But I was unaware of all this on that Saturday in 1950 when, as a young Stalinist-Leninist pioneer, sitting in that small room in my aunt's dark house in Tîrgu Frumos, near Iaşi, I, in my turn, opened the volume *Two Thousand Years*.

My grandfather and my future parents were equally unaware, in 1935, of the Chinese brushstrokes painting themselves on that illegible sky, slumbering over Burdujeni in the calm before the storm. They were all gripped—and who could have blamed them—by the joy of the wedding preparations. They were busy drawing up lists of names and menus and clothes and addresses, checking and double-checking complex calculations. Grand plans were being discussed in detail: how to rent the house of the pharmacist in Iţcani, next to the sugar factory, for the young couple to live in, with room for Maria, the good fairy of the Braunstein household; what new furniture to buy; how to settle the debts incurred in a recent lawsuit, following which the bookseller had lost his house. Bookseller Avram Braunstein was not wealthy—although he worked hard from morning till night—but a wedding, after all, was a wedding and it would be celebrated by the book. The guest list grew in number: the brothers and sisters of Avram and his wife, from Botoşani and Fălticeni and Iaşi, all with their children and grandchildren; the parents, sisters, and brothers of the groom, from Fălticeni and Roman and Focşani, with their own children and grandchildren; neighbors and friends and officials—the mayor, the police chief, Judge Boşcoianu, the veterinarian Manoliu; the notary Dumitrescu; and even the insufferable Wechsler, the rival bookseller, who never lost an opportunity to stab his competitor in the back. There were endless consultations, conducted by the bride herself, with Surah the cook—an expert on weddings—with the Bartfeld photographer, and with the invaluable Wanda Waslowitz, the seamstress. Indeed, the bride took charge of everything, displaying unequaled energy and proving hard to please. Mrs. Waslowitz had already made and remade the bridal dress three times. A large woman, with a determined air, the Polish seamstress had not yet acquired the bulk and the short temper of her later years, when only her steely blue eyes, delicate fingers, and hoarse voice recalled her younger self. She was annoyed then, as later, by unreasonable demands. She could not, however, refuse an old and faithful customer, with whom she had had so many successes and who, she had to admit, won her admiration many times over with her novel suggestions for new designs, for which she had found inspiration, goodness knows where, perhaps in her own perpetually restless and inquisitive imagination. She had even managed to acquire a copy of the fashion magazine *Modisch*, ordered from Czernowitz. The color of the dress, the fabric, the accessories, all these had to be more special than usual. What was called for in this instance was sober elegance, not the usual provincial outfitting.

There was no time for debates on Judas' sufferings. Life, not death, now dominated the stage. Death, however, was waiting in the wings, preparing its revenge, ready, in its turn, to offer its services.

Bukovina

No less now than in 1945, Bukovina was about an hour's journey from that dreamlike place in Moldavia—Fălticeni—where I rediscovered normality. Some 170 years earlier—or so my mother's aunt Leah Riemer would tell me in her slow drawl—the Austrian Emperor Joseph, visiting Transylvania, was so taken by the grandeur of the Ţara de Sus (Upper Country), as it was known, that he sought to incorporate it into his empire. In 1777, the population of the newly acquired Austrian province of Bukovina swore an oath of allegiance to Vienna, an occasion that was celebrated with great pomp and ceremony in Czernowitz. The Romanian Prince Grigore Ghica, a fierce opponent of the acquisition, was assassinated by Turkish conspirators on the very day of the celebration.

"We are from Bukovina, young man, Bukovina," Mr. Bogen would say to me. Mr. Bogen was himself from Bukovina, and had settled in Fălticeni when love beckoned. "You'll soon go back to Bukovina," he reassured me. Apparently, Bukovina was to have been renamed Graftschaft, so said Mr. Bogen, a jovial history teacher who was married to the beautiful mathematics teacher, Otilia Riemer, daughter of Leah Riemer, sister of bookseller Avram, my grandfather. I had met Leah and her daughter and sons—hardworking children of the ghetto and recent graduates in mathematics, turned overnight into passionate champions of the revolution—as well as Mr. Bogen, in the happy months after our return from Transnistria.

"Bukovina was to be named Graftschaft, like the Austrian Tirol," Berl Bogen, my mother's new cousin, said in his German-tinged Bukovinan accent. "The name derives from the famous beeches of the Upper Country, Latin name, Silvae Faginales, *buk* in Slavonic, *bucovine* in the old Romanian chronicles." The lesson continued with recitals whose importance I could only guess at from the way Mr. Bogen punctuated the key words. "In 1872, General Enzenberg issued a decree requiring those Jews who had sneaked into, I repeat, *sneaked into*, Bukovina from 1769 onward and had not paid the annual tax of four gulden, four *gulden*, to be expelled, *expelled*. "I think our young guest"—said Mr. Bogen, turning to me—"knows what this means. By 1872, there were thirteen Jewish deputies in the Bukovina Diet, thirteen, young gentleman, *thirteen*! They all signed a protest against the expulsion order addressed to the government in Vienna."

I had already learned some strange things from Mr. Bogen. For instance, in Bukovina's Diet, in 1904, the Romanians (who, as an Austrian officer had written, spoke a "corrupt Latin") held a majority of the seats, twenty-two. "*However*," Mr. Bogen emphasized, "all the minorities were also generously represented, according to the Austrian model: seventeen Ukrainians, ten Jews, six Germans, four Poles." Why *however*?

"We are from Suceava, young man, from Suceava in Bukovina, the princely seat of Ştefan the Great!" said Mr. Bogen, wagging his finger at me. "After 1918, when Bukovina was returned to Romania, conciliation with the new Romanian administration went more smoothly in Suceava than it did in Bukovina's capital, Czernowitz. The Jews of Suceava spoke Romanian, as well as German, and enjoyed uninterrupted contact with the Romanian population. The opening of the border from Burdujeni to the Kingdom of Romania, now Greater Romania, promised to speed up trade and investment for the landowners and industrialists who retained the citizenship rights they had under the Austrians. The Jewish civil servants were kept on, but the new Romanian administration stopped appointing more," my new cousin Berl Bogen continued to inform me.

Four years previously, my father recounted, we had been expelled from "sweet Bukovina, that delightful garden," as the poets called it. "But, in fact, we're not really from Bukovina," my father said to me. "Your mother and her parents were born in the old Kingdom of Romania, in Burdujeni, near the border, it is true, but on the other side. And I was born in Lespezi, not far from here, where my parents lived."

The people of Bukovina—pedantic, calculating, proud of their German language and the customs they had borrowed from those who proved to be our most brutal enemies—had been the butts of perpetual jokes in our home. I remembered this distinctly. Although we were consumers of *Butterbrod und Kaffee mit Milch* ourselves, neither my mother nor my father was born in Bukovina. At home, we all spoke Romanian, not German. My father had been born, as I now learned, not far from Fălticeni. My mother's brother and sister had lived in that house in Burdujeni where I was born, as had my great-grandfather, his parents, and his grandparents. Burdujeni was a typical East European market town, adjoining a similar town, Ițcani, which differed from its neighbor only in the Austrian influences that could be seen there. Both gradually evolved as suburbs of the city of Suceava.

It was from Ițcani and its sugar factory that the young accountant came, the young man who, on that crowded bus returning from the St. Elias fair in July 1932, made the acquaintance of the beautiful Janeta Braunstein, the bookseller's daughter from Burdujeni. He had been struck by her resemblance to Leah Riemer, in whose house we now lived in the first postwar months. It was also in Ițcani where the young couple settled after their marriage and where we all lived before we were deported.

The two towns, Ițcani and Burdujeni, and the city of Suceava, situated at the top of a hill on the site of an ancient medieval citadel, marked the points of a triangle three kilometers long. The differences between the towns were important, however, as were those between Romanian Bukovina and Austrian Bukovina. Romanian Burdujeni had received only minor influences from its neighboring "Austrian" Bukovina, where Iţcani and Suceava were located. Iţcani's unassuming railway station, near the border, was overshadowed by the sumptuous railway station of its neighbor on the Romanian side, Burdujeni. Both stations survived all the vicissitudes of the times and stand intact to this day, witnesses of the past.

Before the war, Iţcani, unlike Burdujeni, boasted a skating rink and was host to all the philanthropic balls, held to raise money for the building of a school, a club, or a hospital. The Czech, German, and Italian "foreigners" all worked in Iţcani's sugar and oil factories. My great-grandfather from Burdujeni would walk about on the Sabbath in his festive Hasidic garb, a black satin caftan, breeches, a round fur-trimmed hat, knee-length white stockings, looking like a majestic Assyrian king to the astonished natives of Burdujeni, so my mother told me, her eyes shining with pride and tears. To the Westernized inhabitants of neighboring Iţcani, my great-grandfather must have looked like some ghost from the Polish provinces of Galicia.

Burdujeni, a typical, bustling shtetl, vibrated with all the great debates and major tragedies of the ghetto. The latest Parisian scandal, reported in the press, jostled for attention with the suicide-threatening romances of the neighboring street. The social divide between those who lived along the main street and those crammed into the narrow side streets marked a centuries-old hierarchy. Religious and political passions grouped and regrouped. Respect paid to learning and living decently competed with the chase after money. Yearning for grand adventure pulsated in every cloud drifting over the Chagallian sky of that swarming ant heap.

The German atmosphere of Iţcani was less picturesque and more formal. A major crossroads, Iţcani had opened up, like the whole empire to which it belonged, to the "foreigners," gradually assimilating them into a wider cosmopolitan community that belonged no longer to the East but to the West. Jews were not a majority in Iţcani, but it often elected Jewish mayors, as I learned from my father and from Mr. Bogen. This would have been hard to imagine in nearby Burdujeni. Frau Doktor Helmann, who, in that first terrible winter in Transnistria, demanded a lot of money from my mother for a small bottle of ordinary medicine—which proved of little help to my dying grandfather—came from a family of such mayors. Her ancestors Dische and Samuel Helmann were listed on the honor roll in the town's archives.

The deportation order of October 1941 abruptly erased the differences between Iţcani and Burdujeni. Those from Burdujeni, from the Old Romanian Kingdom, that is, my grandfather, uncle, and aunt, were placed in the same category as us, their "Germanicized" co-religionists from Iţcani. This served to cure the Bukovinans of the airs and graces of the Austrian Empire, they who, in happier times, had looked down their noses at their picturesque, noisy neighbors in Burdujeni, on the Romanian side of the frontier, who, in their turn, mistrusted the others' frosty civility.

The provisional certificate, issued by the Inspectorate of the Iaşi Police on April 18, 1945, which my father would often show to me, simply confirmed that "Mr. Marcu Manea, together with his family, comprising Janeta, Norman, and Ruti, is hereby repatriated from the U.S.S.R. through the customs point at Ungheni-Iaşi, on April 14, 1945. His destination is the commune Fălticeni, county of Baia, Cuza Vodă Street. The present document is valid until his arrival at his new address, where he will conform to the regulations established by the Population Bureau." No information was given concerning the reasons for repatriation in 1945, or for the expatriation of 1941. "We have no other documentary evidence of our expulsion," Father said tersely.

The ground for the shock of 1941 had been well prepared by the previous Hooligan Years, as I now learned, and by events that only the deaf and the blind could have ignored. In September 1940, Marshal Ion Antonescu proclaimed the National Legionnaire state. This was soon followed by the Legionnaire Rebellion. The Green Shirts marched through the streets, occupied the sugar factory in Iţcani, where my father was prevented from going to work, and hanged the musician Jacob Katz from Suceava. The people of Bukovina heard rumors about the "ritual" killings at the slaughterhouse in Bucharest, where the Legionnaires had hung the corpses of murdered Jews under signs reading KOSHER. Jews were being subject to forced labor, taken as hostages in synagogues. German officers, from the troops massed near the Soviet border, taunted Jews with threats of the Führer's Final Solution. The ordinance of the morning of October 9, 1941, required the town's Jews "to hand in immediately at the National Bank all the gold, currency, shares, diamonds, and precious stones they owned and to report on the same day in Burdujeni with their hand luggage." The concentration camp in Suceava, where 120 Jews had already been locked up, was immediately dismantled, in light of the new measures. The drums were beating out their message on that day, October 9, 1941, on the main street: "The Jewish population is to leave the town immediately. All personal belongings must be left behind. Anyone who does not comply risks penalty of death."

"This is how it all began, during the week of the Sukkot festival," my father would recount, "the march, that infamous procession familiar from so many films made after the war. Suddenly we lost all our rights and were left with just one duty, death. There we went, shivering from the cold, with our knapsacks on our backs, slowly descending the hill. Disorderly lines of people, marching along the three kilometers of that road lined with poplars." Yes, the same poplar-lined road to and from the Burdujeni railway station, along which bookseller Avram Braunstein used to carry his daily burden of newspapers.

From the Burdujeni station, the trains left for their all-too-predictable destination. The Dniester was our river Styx, across which we were ferried to such places as Ataki, Moghilev, Shargorod, Murafa, Bershad, Bug. These exotic names were often recalled in conversations in the spring and summer of 1945. In contrast, names such as Burdujeni, Iţcani, Suceava were rarely mentioned, as if they were shrouded in shame.

That unresolved conflict between nostalgia and resentment translated as silence. The oppressors had not, when all was said and done, managed to annihilate us, and furthermore, they had lost the war. Only this seemed important at the time. The new era already had its new missionaries. Among them—who would have believed it?—the new husband of our gentle Maria. "A Communist," it was whispered. The couple lived in Suceava, but for us there was no talk of returning to, or even visiting, our old haunt, which was only an hour away. Going back to the place from which we had been expelled seemed taboo. My parents did not speak about the future, and for their offspring, life in the present was a Paradise, without past or future. We were repatriated on the eighteenth of April, the day on which we registered with the Iași police and decided to go to Fălticeni. At first, we stayed with the family of my father's brother, Uncle Aron, then with the Riemers. For the next two years we lived in Rădăuți, a charming small town in Bukovina, not far from the Soviet border.

The name of Suceava was to reappear on the map of our conversations only in 1947, the year when the circle closed and we were back where we had started.

Chernobyl, 1986

April 1945. The truck stops at the intersection of two streets. The wooden tailgate is removed, to allow the passengers to get out. Another moment's wait, an endless moment of disruption. When it passes, everything begins to move again, quickly. The dead street suddenly becomes alive with a crowd of strangers, men and women running toward the truck. Within seconds, they reach the ghosts who had already alighted from the truck onto the sidewalk—into the world. Embraces follow, lamentations, tears.

Out of the void a new world has been born. The boy stares at his parents with the same bewilderment with which he gazed at the strangers. Another second or two, and it is his turn to be hugged and kissed by the possessors of unknown, freckled faces, big, rough hands, and guttural voices—uncles, aunts, cousins. The excitement of reunion! Reunion? He does not recollect ever having met these people. The world, however, has just been brought back to life, and with such people in it.

This had been the real return, the descent from the truck that had

brought us back, in April 1945, from Iași to Fălticeni, the small Moldavian town, all flowers and picture-postcard views, where my father's
older brother lived. Uncle Aron, short, stumpy, with red cheeks, an intense gaze, and quick speech, was one of those creatures shaking with
tears and laughter. He kept squeezing us, one by one, with great warmth,
in his strong arms. As they lived in Fălticeni, Moldavia, rather than in
Suceava, Bukovina, this branch of the family had not been deported.
The distance between Fălticeni and Suceava was only twenty-five kilometers, but of such trifles is the stuff of which history's farces are made.

It was almost four years since we had been driven into the wilderness,
and less than a month before the official end of the war. The curtains
were about to close on the nightmare. On that early spring afternoon the
future reappeared, a colored bubble into which I was invited to blow as
hard as I could and fill with tears and saliva and moans, thereby saving
myself from the clutch of the past. Here was this little actor, starving
for recognition and eager for new experiences. He was alive, he had survived, the surroundings themselves existed—unbelievable! There were
trees and skies, words and a variety of foods, and, above all, the joy of
the place.

In April 1945 I was an old man of nine. Forty years later, in the
spring of 1986, I found myself in the Piața Unirii Market in Bucharest. I
was watching a truck being unloaded of its cargo of apples in front of a
mansionlike white building, Manuc's Inn. The tailgate of the truck had
been removed and two swarthy young men were pushing the mountain
of apples onto the sidewalk. There was a shortage of almost everything
in Bucharest that spring of 1986, but there were plenty of apples, and
they were splendid.

In a few months' time I was to reach the young age of fifty. Over the
years I had acquired enough reasons to be skeptical about anniversaries
and coincidences. But on that spring morning in the marketplace, forty
years later, I was suddenly transfixed in front of the apple-laden truck
that seemed to have emerged out of the blue. I was staring, without
really seeing, at the truck and its load of golden apples. I lived nearby,
just a few minutes away. The nuclear accident in Chernobyl had oc-

curred only a few days previously. I rarely went out, avoided parks, stadiums, and squares. The windows of my apartment had remained shut for several days.

However, it is not Chernobyl that claims the attention of the three people in the room—my mother, sitting on the couch, myself, and Ruti, the cousin just arrived from Israel, both in facing armchairs.

"Marcu became orphaned when he was very young," the blind woman on the couch is saying. "His father died in '45, you're right. He had nine children. My grandfather, your great-grandfather, had ten children. People had lots of children in those days."

"Our fathers' father, our grandfather, was a sort of peasant," I explain to Ruti, although she has already heard this story many times. But maybe in the ten years since she settled far away, in the Holy Land, she has forgotten all these old East European tales. "He was the village baker. He owned a farmhouse, with cattle, sheep, horses. Our grandmother died when our fathers were children. She left three orphaned boys, Aron; Marcu, my father; and Nucă, the youngest, your father. Grandfather remarried and had six more children. I saw him in 1945, when we returned from the deportation."

The blind woman is waiting patiently for her turn to continue the storytelling—an old, tired voice, slowly penetrating the listeners' memory.

"He was only eighteen, my grandfather, your great-grandfather, and there he was, already a widower. He remarried, grandmother's sister, who was fourteen at the time. At fifteen, she gave birth to her first child, Adela, mother of Esther. You've probably heard of Esther, she had a son, an only son; he died in the Six-Day War. After Esther came my father—Abraham, Avram—followed by two boys and a daughter, Fanny, Ariel's mother. You met Ariel in Paris," she said, turning to me. "Then came Noah, you were named after him. Then another one, whose name I forget. He died young a long time ago. Then Aunt Leah, Leah Riemer, in whose house we lived when we came back. There was another son; he went to America and died there, of cancer, at nineteen. There was also, of course, the child by his first wife. So, there were ten of them, my grandfather's children, ten starving children. They were very poor, extremely poor, but not a week passed without some pauper or beggar joining them at table on a Friday evening."

"Eating what?"

"Well, whatever there was, nothing, something out of nothing."

"And Grandfather? Did you know him? My great-grandfather."

"No, he was before my time. Manoliu, the veterinarian, and Dumitrescu, the notary, used to tell me: Sheina—that's what they called me—it's a shame you didn't know your grandfather . . . his snow-white stockings, his immaculateness, his air of holiness. He was a religious man, very learned, very stern, that's what they all said."

"Sheina, does that come from *schön, shein* in Yiddish, beautiful?"

"Well, that's what they said . . ."

She continues to speak, but her voice never recovers its former vitality. The questions I ask do not have the hoped-for effect. The story is not new, and we who have heard it so many times before are no longer young. The ritual retelling is in honor of the guest from afar, to remind her of what she has left behind.

"What about Great-grandmother, the widow with all the children. How did she manage?"

"She had a small pension from the community. The children all worked, from a very young age, especially the boys. This was a family trait. Aunt Leah used to say, and so did her children: 'One must work, one must work hard, work hard.' Her sons started to work when they were ten. They were poor, they had no clothes. And those cold winters . . . they gave private lessons to children from rich families, the Nussgartens and the Hoffmans from Fălticeni. At five in the afternoon, these people stopped for tea and cakes, but they never offered any to the poor tutors."

"And these were your fellow Jews, all pious people? It wasn't your Uncle Marx who invented the class struggle . . . Now tell us about Grandfather, your father."

"There were no newspapers in Burdujeni in those days. You could only buy them in the big city, Suceava, a few kilometers away. Burdujeni was really just a small town then, but it was very lively, buzzing with life. All our family comes from there, from Burdujeni, my grandfather, my father, all of us. My father was the first in Burdujeni to order a news-paper by mail, *Dimineața* (*The Morning*)—one copy, just for him."

"But you said he never went to school."

"No, what I meant was that he didn't go to the Romanian-language school. How could he, on a Saturday? He was self-taught, that's what he was. All the same, many people came to him for advice, like they would to a lawyer. He was the first in Burdujeni to order *Dimineața*. The neigh-bors all came to read the paper every day. After a while, he ordered five copies. That's how he got started in his business. That's how the trouble started, too. When Wechsler—that was his name—saw that my father had ordered *Dimineața*, he ordered *Minerva*. But Wechsler had money, and for five bani he'd give you a copy of *Minerva*, and throw in a pint of beer and a cigarette as well. That's competition for you, enough to ruin us."

"When did all this happen? How old was Grandfather?"

"About seventeen at the time, when he started his first newspaper business, in Burdujeni. Eventually, he became the second biggest dis-tributor of newspapers in the country. He was decorated by Stelian Popescu, the director of *Universul*."

"*Universul*? Wasn't that a right-wing paper?"

"Of course, and anti-Semitic, too. Still, they decorated him, a Jew. Constantin Mille gave him an award as well. I've told you all this before. Mille was the director of *Adevărul* (*The Truth*), the democratic paper, and he was very fond of my father. When my sister Rebecca got married, Father sent him an invitation, and Constantin Mille sent a gift in return, an embroidered velour bedspread, and a nice telegram."

"What about Graur, Rebecca's husband? What did he do for a living?"
"Grain."

"So, one was in grain, the other in newspapers, and another in eggs. The International Conspiracy, with its headquarters in Burdujeni! Wasn't it Noah, Grandfather's brother, who used to sell eggs?"

"That's right. Noah—you have his name—he used to sell eggs when he lived in Botoşani. As you know, Jews were allowed into the country by the Romanian princes, just for this and nothing else—all we were per-mitted to do was engage in trade. So Noah exported Romanian eggs throughout Europe. He owes his death to all that dust, the dust from the packaging. All his life he had to inhale the dust from the hay. He got cancer of the throat and died at fifty. Auntie Bella, his widow, continued the business. She handled the correspondence in three languages, a first-class tradeswoman."

"Better than yourself?"

"Maybe. Yes, even better. I used to be told that I could have been a very good lawyer. That's what they said about Father, too. They all used to come to him for advice."

"You would have made a good lawyer, I'm sure. Maybe that would have calmed you down. The lawsuits would have exhausted you and helped you to relax. You told me a few years ago how much you regretted not smoking or drinking, not having any of the vices that might calm you down. That's what you told me, remember?"

"I haven't had a quiet life, that's true. I started working as a child. Father, God bless him, traveled a lot on business. I was left with all the chores. Sometimes he went beyond Suceava, into neighboring counties, to Botoşani, Dorohoi. He did business with schools, 10 percent commission on the sale of textbooks. In return, the schools made sure that all their textbooks and stationery carried our stamp."

"Librăria Noastră, Our Bookstore, wasn't that its name? Quite a socialist name, no? So, it was you people who introduced socialism to the country. The anti-Semites must be right about the Jews. Don't you remember, by the '50s and '60s all the bookstores were called Librăria Noastră? In the 1950s you used to work at a Librăria Noastră, in Suceava; all bookstores were state-owned and called Librăria Noastră. Before the war, you were all accused of being capitalist exploiters, sucking the people's blood. Then you were accused of bringing in Communism, the gravedigger of capitalism."

She is looking at us without seeing. The jokes don't seem to animate her, politics never interested her, she just wants to be allowed to re-enter the legends of the past.

"We worked hard, we lived hard. Yes, Librăria Noastră, Our Bookstore, that was the name, and it was ours, not the state's. A big difference."

"Well, yes, an essential difference."

"The schools bought only books and stationery with our stamp on them, that was the understanding. When the schools opened in September, there were endless lines, like those at the bakeries. In the evening I dropped with exhaustion. I worked hard from an early age. We all worked hard, Father and I and Şulim, my brother. After I got married, I still continued to help my parents. When they sent us to the labor camp, my parents took with them only 5,000 lei, that's all they had, but the stock left behind in the bookstore was worth a million lei."

"You carried everything, you said."

"Of course. Books by Sadoveanu, Rebreanu, Eminescu, everybody, Fundoianu, Sebastian. And newspapers, too, all the papers. Father even went to press congresses."

"And he used to carry the papers from the station himself? That's what you would tell us, all by himself, at dawn, on that poplar-lined road. I know it, I walked there recently."

There I was, manipulating nostalgia, the tricks of the past, from which my old mother could now retrieve only the odd verbal residue. Even this was going to vanish soon, I knew. Everything was going to disappear, the old tales, and this, the present moment of retelling, would soon become past. She was sliding, with her unseeing eyes, down the last bend of that toboggan run called biography. Ruti was about to return to Jerusalem, and as for me, no one knew where I would be by the autumn. All three of us were trying to ease the tension of that reunion, to sort out old conflicts. The year 1986 was a Hooligan Year, just like the ones before and after, socialist years, turned into National Socialist years. Was this the reason why I now paid attention to these tales to which I usually turned a deaf ear? Before, I was impatient with these tearful stories, just as I could not stand that exasperating refrain, *departure, departure, departure*. Was I finally acknowledging that she was right, or was I just trying to soften the blow of our imminent separation?

Mother didn't hear my last words. Recently, she had begun to fade out.

"He used to carry the newspapers back from the station himself," I repeated.

"The horse-drawn coach was only one leu. 'Only one leu, Father, why don't you take the coach?' 'I need the exercise,' he said. He walked thirteen kilometers every day. In the morning, before he set off for the station, he would have grilled beefsteak with a glass of wine. If it weren't for the deportation, he would have lived to a ripe old age; he was healthy, fit. My mornings started at seven, with black coffee, and nothing else until five or six in the afternoon."

"Did he pay you?"

"Pay me, his own daughter? I was his favorite daughter. I had everything I needed, he wouldn't have refused me anything. I worked hard, of course. I was always a fast worker."

"And the baby, your son? Were you fast with that, too?"

"You arrived before the nine months. I was almost dead when I gave birth. The doctor kept vigil by my bed from Wednesday until the following Sunday morning. He didn't know how to help, he thought I was lost. As for the baby . . . no hope. The baby will be stillborn, that's what they were saying. And then, after you were born, nobody believed you would survive. You were so tiny, under the normal weight. They put you in an incubator. Only my father remained optimistic. He asked whether you had nails. If he has nails, he'll live, that's what he said."

"I sort of lost my nails later in life. He was right, they would've come in handy, at any age, a sign of life."

The three of us laugh, Mother with her short, weak laugh. She has been out of the hospital only a few days, which is why Ruti has come all the way from Jerusalem. Ruti was like a daughter, the orphaned niece, daughter of my father's brother, who was raised in our home.

I carefully rewind the tape recorder on the coffee table. The blind woman on the couch cannot see the machine, she is not aware that she is being recorded. She is completely blind. The operation has solved nothing.

"What about your husband, the baby's father. How did he win you?"

"That's another story, a long story. I used to go to Fălticeni in the summer. It was July 20, St. Elias Day. I went from Burdujeni with my friends, young men and women. On that particular day, I was waiting for the bus home in Fălticeni, the same as I did every year. Suddenly this smartly dressed young man appeared, with a folding stool."

"A folding stool?"

"The bus was always overcrowded. He placed his small stool next to me. And after a while he asked, Are you related to Mrs. Riemer? Leah

Riemer, from Falticeni. Mrs. Riemer is my aunt, I said. I looked very much like Auntie Leah, that's what people said." The old, sagging face, ravaged by time and illness, looks older than that of old Leah Riemer, the way I had seen her for the last time, about twenty years ago, when she came—the clan's diplomatic envoy—to persuade me to break off my pagan romance with the shiksa, which had scandalized the whole family. Leah Riemer's calm, biblical face showed no signs of the traumas I now read on the blind mask before me.

"He knew Mrs. Riemer and her husband, Kiva the chess player, chess partner of the writer Mihai Sadoveanu. Kiva was quite difficult to live with, Leah had trouble with him. He was very smart, an upholsterer by trade, but he hung around at the café, gambling his money away. The young man also knew the Riemer children, brilliant, hardworking students. At that time, the Riemers spoke Hebrew at home, the only such household in town. He asked me if I knew Paulina, the lame seamstress married to a cousin of his. Then, after a while, he told me he was courting someone, Miss Landau. I knew her, Bertha, the pharmacist, a nice girl."

"So, confessions at first sight."

"Well now, how long is it from Fălticeni to Suceava? Just over an hour. He got off at the junction in Iţcani, he worked at the sugar factory there. I went on to Burdujeni. When I got home, I went over to Amalia, to tell her all about it. Amalia was my neighbor and friend. I told her I'd just met a very nice young man on the bus, a friend of Bertha's."

"Nicer fifty years ago than today, wouldn't you say?"

"The following Saturday, I got a picture postcard from him," the convalescent continued, as though she hadn't heard my question. " 'To Miss Janeta Braunstein, bookseller de luxe,' that was all that was written on it. Then, one day, I saw him pass through Burdujeni on his bicycle. He stopped and told me there was a ball in Iţcani the following Saturday and would I like to go with him. He turned up that Saturday at five, when everybody in Burdujeni was out on the porch, in patent-leather shoes and a handsome jacket. A taxi was waiting, but my parents wouldn't let me go, they didn't know who he was."

"You were so submissive? I don't believe it."

"After that, Marcu and I went to all the balls. He'd always come by on a Saturday and on Sunday afternoon, as well as on Wednesday evenings, on his bicycle. There were always balls in Ițcani, charity balls, collecting for all sorts of things, a school, a skating rink, the hunters' club. I wore a different dress to each ball. The purple dress created a sensation: purple satin, with shoes and hat to match."

"He could afford all those balls, on an accountant's salary?"

She points to her dry lips with her fingers, she is thirsty. I bring a glass of water and offer it to her, but she cannot see it. I bring her hand to the glass. The hand trembles as it holds the glass. She takes two sips, signals me to take the glass away. I put it on the table in front of her; she does not see it.

"Of course, on his salary, he had a good income at the factory. He would send me flowers, lilacs and roses, and letters. We were young, those were different times."

"And who made your dresses?"

"Mrs. Waslowitz."

"The Polish lady. The same Mrs. Waslowitz I knew ten years ago, twenty years ago? She must be two hundred years old by now."

"She charged three hundred lei per dress. She's ninety now, but she still goes to church on Sunday, I'm told, every Sunday, summer and winter, come rain or shine."

"So, she made your dresses under the King, and under the Green Legionnaires, and under the Red Stalinists? And now under our beloved Green-Red leader. What did she say when you disappeared in 1941? She must have known what was going on. And what did she say when you came back?"

"When we were taken away, the mayor would not allow me to put even my slippers in the knapsack. I left them in the corridor. Maria was clinging to us at the station, she wanted to get on the train with us, wouldn't let go of us. At the frontier, by the Dniester, at Ataki, they let us out of the train. It was a freight train for transporting cattle, we were one on top of the other, like sardines. At Ataki, the plunder began, screams, beatings, gunshots. When we recovered, we were on the other side of the bridge. My parents had been left behind. I saw a soldier. He could have been one of those who had been pushing us with their guns off the train. I am now old, poor wretched me, but then . . . then I was brave. I went to the soldier and told him: Mister, my parents were left behind at Ataki, they are old. I'll give you 1,000 lei, please bring them here."

Transnistria had not been much of a topic of conversation in our home. The Holocaust had not yet become the popular subject of later years, and suffering was not cured through public confession. Usually, these ghetto lamentations irritated me. But were we now reconciled, with the passing of time? Could the bitter, intractable conflict become the stuff of humor?

"Let's go," she would say again and again in 1945 and 1955 and all the years that followed. "And there will come an evening . . . and I will go," as the poet predicted. Had she ever read at Our Bookstore in Burdujeni that line by Fundoianu-Fondane? The Romanian poet had gone from Paris, not to Jerusalem, but to Auschwitz. Had I finally accepted the burden of this line of verse, as well as the obsessive foresight of my mother, now unseeing and unable to go anywhere? I no longer jump when I hear words such as "goy," "shiksa," "going away," I can now tolerate all the ghetto mannerisms I had previously tried to escape. She signals again that her lips are dry and she needs a drink. She takes a sip, hands the glass back to me, and is ready to return to center stage.

"'I'll give you 1,000 lei,' I told him. He could have shot me or searched me and taken all my money away. 'All right,' he said, 'I'll go back for your folks, for 1,000 lei, but I also want a jar of Nivea cream.'"

"Nivea? What did he need Nivea for? And how come you had Nivea cream with you?"

"I did, one of God's little jokes. I had squeezed two jars of Nivea into the knapsack."

"So, no slippers, but Nivea you took with you."

"I gave him the Nivea, and he brought my parents back. We took them with us, and they stayed with us until they died. When my father was dying, Frau Doktor Helmann told me she had a small bottle of medicine that might help, Dejalen drops, for the heart. She asked for 1,000 lei."

"Trading with death in the labor camp?"

"Yes, everyone did. I gave her 1,000 lei. Dr. Weismann from Dorohoi said it was useless, that it was too late. 'You'd better buy clothes or food for the children with that money,' he said. But I had to try everything, anything. My father couldn't even swallow the drops at that stage."

"You were a fighter to the bitter end."

"And how! Marcu lost his spirit right from the first, when they pushed us onto the train, and he was no better when they threw us off the train. We woke up at night to the sound of abuse, bayonets in our ribs. When he saw that his shirt was swarming with lice, he cried out, 'This is no life.' He lost hope. He was always a very clean man, so elegant and fussy, he wouldn't wear the same shirt twice, he even had his socks ironed, imagine that. 'This is not a life worth living,' he kept repeating. After the first days in Transnistria, he said this over and over again. 'It's no longer worth living, not worth it.' 'Yes,' I kept telling him. 'It is worth it, it is! If we resist, if we survive, you'll have your clean shirts again. Let's go on, just for that.' And we did. Who could have known whether we'd ever come back?"

She suddenly swings round toward the door; someone has entered.

"Celluța? Is that you, Celluța?"

Cella has made her serene and sunny entrance onstage.

"There were many times, Celluța, when I was more desperate than he was," she says, addressing her daughter-in-law.

Cella is standing in the doorway, looking at the three of us on the couch. She is being addressed as though she has been there throughout the whole conversation.

"How many times . . . I would cling to anything, to the German officer's coat, begging him to save us from the Ukrainians who wanted to murder us, bands of Ukrainians in the service of the Germans. I clung to the arm of the peasant for whom I worked. I would walk eight kilometers, in winter, dressed in sackcloth. I worked the whole week for a few potatoes, a loaf of bread, and some beans. When the Russians liberated us, in 1944, I clung to Yossele, our rabbi, begging him to perform a miracle and save Marcu. Their first action was to send Jewish men to the front to fight against the Germans. They were little more than skeletons . . ."

"But what could the rabbi do? Did he know you personally?"

"Yossele, the rabbi of Suceava? He'd been deported at the same time as us. Of course he knew me. He knew my parents, too, in Iţcani, before the war; we used to send him money, oil, and sugar regularly. I went to him and started crying: Look, Rabbi, look what we have become. I live in a derelict house with no windowpanes. The children are starving, my husband is being sent away by the Russians. I am alone and desperate. I was so thin, I weighed only 44 kilograms."

"And did he help you?"

"He did, he did. He sat there, looking at me, with his hand under his chin. And then he said, 'Go home. Go home, and tomorrow morning, there will be a real miracle.' Everybody who heard the story said so: God's miracle. 'Go home and everything will be all right. Tomorrow morning, you'll be all right,' he told me."

"And were you?"

"Marcu had escaped from the Red Army. A miracle, isn't it? He ran through the forests, for days and nights, and he managed to find us there, in the middle of Bessarabia, another miracle."

"Look, here comes the escapee. Elegant, fussy, just like you said, with his white shirt, immaculate as usual," I announce, turning off the tape recorder.

"Marcu, is Marcu back?" she asks, anxiously.

My father has just walked in, in his jaunty hat, gray summer suit, white shirt, and blue tie. Only the three-legged folding stool seems to be missing. As usual, he is his easygoing self, calm, with measured steps.

"Marcu, you went to the market? Did you get anything?"

"What could he get?" I intervene. "Do you think he can bring you lilacs and roses, as he did in the old days?"

"I bought a newspaper," Father announces dryly, "and apples. They were unloading some trucks with nice apples."

He gives me the paper, *România liberă* (*Free Romania*). The lead story reads: "An announcement of the Party and State Commission for the Control and Monitoring of the Environment. On the sixth of May, reduced radioactivity levels were recorded in most affected areas, including the municipality of Bucharest."

"Hear, hear, pollution is decreasing," I say. "Ever since Ruti arrived from the Holy Land, the press announcements have become more optimistic."

The report goes on: "In some areas, radioactivity levels increased slightly, but they pose no threat to the population." Pose no threat, yet we are advised to be increasingly cautious about our drinking water, vegetables, and fruit. Children and pregnant women are being told to avoid prolonged exposure in open spaces. Open spaces, indeed! We should consume only milk and dairy products sold within the official commercial network—wooden language, more deadly than radioactivity. So, now that the danger has lessened, caution must be heightened. Can one really believe them? Control and monitoring, that is the only credible news, control and monitoring.

We are waiting for lunch, for the afternoon nap, the moments of solitude. We are all squeezed into that small apartment, as we had been squeezed within the narrow confines of narrow-minded socialism for the last forty years.

"Listen here, a few days ago . . ." I start, pulling another newspaper from the pile on the table. "A few days ago, the comrades from Control and Monitoring were telling us: 'During the night of May 1 and 2, a rise of radioactivity well above normal levels was recorded, as a consequence of winds blowing from the northeast—the area of radioactive emission—toward the southwest.' What exactly does that mean, 'above normal levels'? Disaster?"

But I cannot get anyone interested in the matter. The whole family is placidly waiting for lunch.

I persist. "Above normal levels? What does 'normal' mean? Can we still comprehend the concept of 'normality'? And look here . . ." I pull another newspaper from the pile, on the off-chance I might trigger a reaction in my audience.

"The next day, it says, 'A relative decrease in radioactivity was recorded, but it still remains at a high level.' A relative decrease . . . but still at a high level. The Russians have announced that radioactive pollution affected only the territory of the U.S.S.R., and Radio Free Europe—broadcasting to the Un-free Europe—announced yesterday that the American Embassy in Bucharest took its own measurements, and that if they haven't yet sent their staff back to California, it may mean that everything really is okay after all. Who knows? Anyway, let's get back to Mutter Courage and her tired heart."

"My heart is not too good. But the real problem is that Mutter cannot see," the old woman whispers. "If only I could see a little, after all the pain of the operation. This morning in the hospital, at the check-up, I was with the doctor for an hour. He told me I'm going to be able to see. Well, who knows . . ."

"Can you tell the direction of the light, can you see that?"

"Yes, I can."

"Anything else? Can you see who's in the room? Or when someone moves around?"

"Just shadows. When someone comes near, I can see a shadow. Now, as you talk to me, I can just make out your shadow. I wanted to see Ruti, that's why I pressed her to come. I wanted to see her one more time, but at least I can feel her presence."

"Do you remember, Auntie . . . ?"

It is the Israeli guest's turn to take the stage.

"Do you remember when they took me off the train when we were going back to Romania?"

"Of course I do, how could I forget? They'd agreed to the repatriation of orphans from Transnistria. You were an orphan, your mother had died before we were deported. That's why we took you into our home, and that's how you came to be in the camp with the rest of us. You were on the orphans' list, for repatriation. But when they got you on the train, Moishe Kandel *hot arranzhirt az zein yingl zol nemen ir ort.*"

In recent years, especially since she lost her sight, Mother had begun to use Yiddish words more frequently—the ghetto code. Turning to Cella, I translate: "Moishe Kandel had schemed for his son to take her place," and then I resume my role as the innocent who has forgotten the story.

"How could that be possible? And did you thank Kandel for his dirty deed? He probably posed as a God-fearing man, didn't he?"

"God thanked him, not me. He emigrated to Israel, and one of his sons died there in a motorcycle accident."

"There you go again—God, rabbis, miracles. What can rabbis do when God sends you to Transnistria?"

"It was not God who sent me, He brought me back. And rabbis really performed miracles in my life."

"What about that story of the sieve?"

"Which sieve?"

"The magic sieve. Didn't you tell us the story about Şulim, your brother, how he seemed so set in his bachelor ways, until the would-be bride used a magic trick or two. Didn't she go to some woman who spun that sieve around to work magic? Isn't this how you charmed Marcu, with a sieve?"

She laughs; everybody laughs.

"Marcu had no need for sieves. And I never went to that woman. She died a long time ago, before the war."

"What about your son, to what do I owe my happy marriage? Maybe the magic sieve spun for me, too."

"I didn't recommend your wife to you. You found her yourself."

Indeed, I had. Fortune had spun the sieve in my favor.

"No, you didn't recommend her, but you stopped me from marrying somebody else once."

"Fate always decides."

The ancient conflicts have become the targets of feeble humor. Only irony retains some of its poison.

"Exactly, you protected me, you made me protect myself."

"You, protect yourself? You never protected yourself."

"When I couldn't protect myself, the sieve did it for me. You used to go to the cemetery, to visit all those rabbis buried there; maybe they'd spin the sieve the way you wanted it to turn, to change fate."

The joke is limp, and so is the moment, and our reconciliation means only that we are older, all of us, in the same small cage, within that larger cage.

"Fate, what fate? That Christian woman you wanted to marry was no fate."

"That Christian woman? Hasn't she got a name? Has she lost that, too? Isn't that what you were asking for from all the rabbis, dead and alive, for the shiksa to lose her name?"

That was the old bitterness at work, now transmuted into good-humored jokes. Is it resignation or tolerance? Tolerance in the face of imminent death? Yes, in the face of death.

"The rabbis really helped me, you know, and they helped her, too, I'm sure. If you must know, I was praying for her as well. She's doing fine, in England; she has two children now and she's doing very well."

"She may be doing well, but she isn't aware that you prayed for her."

"She knows, she knows. And even if she didn't know . . ."

"That you prayed for her? Not even God would believe this."

"Oh, but I did, I prayed that she keep out of harm's way. I don't hate her, you must know that."

"Why would you, now that she is safely out of the way? She took the danger away with her, to England. It's just too much, praying for her."

"No, it isn't. I didn't wish her any harm, you know that. I never spoke ill of her. She has two children, I've heard, Mrs. Waslowitz told me. She's always so elegant, that's what Mrs. Waslowitz says. She was always like that, but she was no beauty."

"How would you know?"

"I don't, I never met her. But this is what they say."

"If you are still in touch with Mrs. Waslowitz, why haven't you arranged to send my former lover a recent photograph so she can see my receding hairline and potbelly, so she can rejoice over what the ravages of time have done to her Romeo? You probably didn't want her to see how age has disfigured me. That sieve spins for each one of us at one time or another, doesn't it? Well, the sieve would come in handy now, with Chernobyl; it might rid us of these troubles. Have you heard what the papers say? We shouldn't stay outdoors, we can be irradiated. We have to protect pregnant women and those who could become pregnant. Boil food, if we can find any to buy. Listen to Radio Free Europe and learn from them what's happening here in our own country . . . That sieve could sort everything out, with one simple spin. If it could sort a love affair out, then I suppose a nuclear accident would be mere child's play."

She does not respond, she is tired. There are five of us around the table, for lunch—eggplant salad, roast peppers, meatballs, potatoes, pancakes. We have no reason to complain, all shall be well, in this place between good and evil . . . Lo, the dessert, the golden apple, peeled and carefully cut into thin, spiraling slices; splendid apples, unloaded from the truck straight onto the sidewalk, at the peak of the radioactive fall-out.

We lie down for the afternoon nap, the siesta which proves the superiority of placid, Eastern socialism, over the degenerate West. After sleep, we engage in diluted dialogue and two hours of TV madness, with the President Clown stammering away—another day gone, never to return. The Chernobyl accident brings incertitude to a head. Any stunted, sluggish sense of hope is bound to get the occasional slap in the face, the shock of some perverse trick. Headaches, swollen eyelids, palpitations, nausea? This is routine neurosis, not irradiation. This is the toxin that has infiltrated our bodies and minds for decades. The urgency to leap into the void has been felt by many, and for a long time, but the force of apathy is undiminished.

Within a Budding Grove

I t was the summer of 1959, and I was back in Suceava. I had left
there five years earlier to attend university and win, if not the
world, like Balzac's Rastignac, then at least the armor that would protect me from my circumstances and my own vulnerability. But here I
was, back in Suceava, back to square one, so to speak. My engineering
job offered no protection and, besides, proved wholly unsuitable for me.
Nevertheless, when one is twenty-three, the streets, the rooms, the faces
hidden behind the mysteries of the moment, the women, the books, the
friends—all served to intensify the magnetic field of my being.

Still, the terror of ending up in the trash bin of failure, that creeping
fear, expanding and contracting in turn, was with me always, asleep or
awake. As for my strategy of escape, my mistrust of political matters extended even into the area of personal relationships. I found that I functioned better, including romantically, when I had a "double solution,"
that is, an alternative possibility—in my case, Plan B, the safety hatch
of my engineering profession, useful in extreme or unpredictable situa-

tions. My youthful energy defied the ambiguities of the job and my family's modest social status, keeping the hidden fears at bay, invisible as lizards in waiting. Mrs. Albert, stunning as ever, was playing her familiar role again. Her daughter, now married and the mother of an infant son, was also back in town, the scene of our adolescent love. The families around us were unchanged, their offspring away studying, waiting for the chance to emigrate. Behind the drawing board next to my own sat a slender young blond Russian woman who would always let me know—with her inimitable lapses in grammar and her irresistible accent—when her husband was going to be away. There was ample opportunity for romantic diversion, and my professional duties were not overwhelming.

The high school that had once witnessed my fifteen minutes of fame had become coeducational, and the graduation festivities, to which I had been invited, now included a ball. The class of 1959 seemed very relaxed. After two hours in the company of my former teachers and of the new graduates, I left, with my date of the evening, to join a party of engineers with their wives and girlfriends. The graduate was only eighteen, but there was nothing immature or provincial about her. She was graceful, bold, and had a sense of humor. She was wearing a blue voile gown, with a corsage pinned to her shoulder. At dawn, dazed by too much drink and by the summer night, we climbed the hill of the old fortress of Zamca, near where she lived. She seemed at once innocent and provocatively alluring. She had a certain air about her, a mixture of Mediterranean, Slavic, and Andalusian. The flicker of her eyes was enticing, yet certain. Over the next few weeks, we conducted a steady dialogue, marked by an undiminished sense of surprise. The impatience of hands and lips intensified, the wanderings of fingers grew bolder.

We decided to spend a weekend in the nearby mountains. However, before I could do that, I had to slay the dragon from the past. I found myself on Armenian Street, standing before the house with its tall veranda that could be seen from the street. As in former days, I climbed the wooden stairs and knocked discreetly on the door. Inside, the house was wrapped in darkness; outside, as the script demanded, shone a blood-red moon. The summer night was strewn with stars, the single lamppost cast a dim glow. There I was, poised to squeeze myself through the door of the past. As it happened, the door opened after my first knock. Destiny had arranged it all very well on that July evening. Dr. and Mrs. Albert were away on holiday, their son-in-law away on business. Their daughter, my former sweetheart, welcomed me as the script prescribed. I could hear her whispering the next line of stage dialogue into my burning ear: "Slowly, slowly, to the left, slowly, let's not wake him up." I knew what was to follow, but did not know where. The beautiful daughter of the beautiful Mrs. Albert had not, after all, married the man of her choice; but marry she had, as required by the rules of the world into which she had been born. The young couple, now a trio, had not yet found a suitable house, so they lived with her parents.

We were about to commit the unlawful act in the very house where, until not so long before, I had been regarded as a desirable candidate for the daughter's hand. I did not become the son-in-law of the striking Mrs. Albert, who had once descended from her divine heights into our small and very terrestrial kitchen, with her legendary declaration "I want to meet the parents of this boy." The boy had not lived up to expectations, yet that unlikely night offered the chance of a conclusion, as well as the opportunity for revenge. Her busy hand was guiding me, delicately and patiently, through time's tunnel, toward the door at the left to the old sitting room, which I knew so well from former visits, years before, on many a pleasant Saturday night. There, in the family parlor, the sacrilege was about to be performed.

I shut the door, leaving the darkness behind. The gods had already lit the sinners' lamp, a tiny candle flickering in a corner of the room. In the family parlor, where once stood a sumptuous couch, now stood a double bed, installed there for the young couple. Next to it, the baby's crib— the crib of innocence next to the bed of sin. The air was rife with piquant connotations, but our impatience allowed no delay. I rushed into the torrid tunnel of the past, instantly recharged with every spasm of her body. Salvo after salvo, moan after moan—exhausted and drenched in sweat, the masters of the night had seen the revenge and redemption each had sought.

In the nearby crib, the baby slept unconcerned. My former lover was the same, yet also changed. She had learned new ways of giving pleasure, and she performed them with tact and passion; her long, silky legs lifted heavenward, our blood pumped furiously, the triumph of unstoppable youth.

At dawn, in a daze, I tore myself from the bed of the unfaithful wife. The baby had slept serenely throughout, oblivious to the voluptuous adultery in the bed beside his crib.

I was awakened by the elixir of the summer morning. Love was not what I felt, but the ravaged residue of possession. Everything had worked perfectly well—the mind, the feelings, the body, the moment's blindness, the subsequent detachment, the frenetic simultaneity. It was a childish sense of fulfillment, just what I needed, and received, and was taking with me. I was climbing, exhausted, to the top of Armenian Street, now deserted in the early-morning breeze. I proceeded slowly, past the old church, to the left, toward the new section of apartment blocks, and then down and left again, along Vasile Bumbac Street. On the corner, at number 18, the narrow sidewalk brought me to the door behind which, as usual, there was another servant girl sleeping.

What had happened that night was different from the teenager's clumsy gropings of ten years earlier, different from the failed attempt in the brothel on Frumoasei Street five years earlier, different from the night with the courtesan Rachèle du Gard two years earlier, and different from the more recent fling with the Russian only one month earlier. Finally, the boil of all those entanglements had burst. All that convulsive time spent under the sign of the *jeunes filles en fleur*, the maidens in their budding groves, all those days and months and years in which I had overwhelmed her with my excessive erotic-literary fumblings, had finally come, vengefully, to a gala night.

The maiden had sacrificed her virginity, not on the altar of love, but on the altar of marriage, which had given her a son. Yet her beauty was undiminished. On the contrary, the blue of her eyes had deepened, her golden hair was sunnier, her breasts fuller, her waistline miraculous, her skin a smooth copper glow. She was more beautiful than ever. Her sensuality had not lost any of its delicate ardor, but had been enriched by the gift of her now educated senses. She did not appear destined for a single husband, or a single lover. But this suspicion did not trouble me, it served only to stimulate my excitement. After that ecstatic night, I should have had the decency to phone her—that was the thing to do—but I was preoccupied not with that happy end but with a new beginning. So I kept my silence. However enthralling our night of passion, I was not tempted by the possibility of future encounters, which, I feared, might become commonplace and routine.

There were two days left before I was due to leave for the mountains with my new girlfriend, the high-school graduate. It was a period in which, as in fairy tales, time expanded. In the place where the magic comb had been tossed, mountains had sprung up. Time regained and the night that had helped me regain it were now far away, beyond that mountain range. Already, they belonged to the past.

Crossing and uncrossing her legs, the girl now sitting cheerfully beside me on the train to Cîmpulung Moldovenesc was the reason for the quick break with the past. We found unanticipated surprises—the cabin on the mountaintop that kept solemn watch over the town, the simple wooden room, the wakefulness of the starry night, the light of dawn pouring down upon the bedsheet scattered with the carnations of virgin blood. This was no parody. It was real, natural, without simulation or memories, without reproaches or plans for the future. It was simple, whole, like the forest surrounding us. I had been made new by the easeful lovemaking of a new night.

Soon, however, the traditional repertory of conventions claimed its supremacy. A fragile silence seemed to have descended over the small rooms where the Montagues and the Capulets lived, unknown to each other. Was it possible that these two lower-middle-class families from the socialist provinces should find themselves caught in a dramatic conflict more suitable to aristocratic Verona? Gossip's minions had already set the intrigue in motion. The small rooms expanded to accommodate the poisoned breath of the great drama. There were signs of imminent storm in the air, history repeated as farce. The time bomb, carefully wrapped, had revived the ghetto's eternal fear—the shiksa, the Christian siren, the honey trap of defilement, the taboo temptation.

For a few weeks after the willing surrender of her virginity, the Bukovina Juliet lived in isolation from her parents and siblings, alone in her room, studying for admission to the university. Her lover was at the seaside, wandering in solitude along the shore and going in and out of restaurants. His family had, in the meantime, received a phone call from someone who claimed that the happy couple were seen together on the Black Sea coast. Could this be the work of the adulterous wife of Armenian Street? The millennia-old anxieties had set in motion the ghetto's many tentacles, now delving everywhere for suspicious signs.

"Cousin Riemer says he has never seen a more clever girl in all his years as a teacher," the Jewish mother repeated. But she turned the tribute into caricature, not a sign of the student-enemy's scholastic excellence but an indication of her cunning. The comedy of the situation turned into melodrama racked with anxiety. It seemed as if the victims' centuries-old delirium, their fears, their demented memories had been freshly reactivated. There was no way to deal with, nor could one ignore, the tirades, the announcements of heart attacks, the threats of suicide. Mater Dolorosa was no novice in such matters and she played her prescribed role to the hilt. This time, there were no arguments, no medication that might afford relief. Her logic was unpredictable, and so were the performances. Was this the result of the damage done by the years in the labor camp, or were they evoked by earlier fears? With or without reasons, the crises escalated. At first, I could feel only compassion for this theater of despair, but compassion alone could not prevent the anger that built up in the aggrieved son. Adversity, as we have been taught by the protagonists of Verona, far from destroying passion, only served to fuel it. And so the romance continued, in idyllic groves and borrowed rooms.

In the early autumn, Juliet left her chamber for the university in Bucharest. In October, the young engineer himself journeyed from Suceava to Bucharest. On his return, Romeo moved into his own bachelor's room in a hotel in the center of town. Communication between the capital and the provinces remained intense, and the crisis seemed to have abated. However, the drama took a vaudevillian turn and produced some more surprises. One winter night, two young men, their faces hidden behind mufflers, could be seen on the platform of the Iţcani-Suceava railway station. It was after midnight. Outside, a car was waiting. The driver, one of the platform pair, was well briefed for his mission: to take the lovers to their golden cage on the first floor of Romeo's hotel. It was snowing, the wind was strong, the platform deserted. According to plan, at 1:20 a.m., the Bucharest-Suceava Nord express pulled into the station. The shivering passengers got off, one by one, and sallied forth into the Nordic night. A few short minutes after the last passenger had left the platform, it was the turn of the mystery woman, disguised as Juliet, to emerge. Wrapped in a warm white coat, she carried a small black suitcase. Without looking right or left, she hurried to the shabby automobile parked behind the station, next to a billboard. The door swung open, the driver helped her in, and off we sped. Miss Capulet stayed for a week in that happy captivity and strictly observed all the regulations of the conspiracy. She did not step out of the room, did not answer the phone, and her departure went off without incident.

The young engineer's attempts to secure a job in Bucharest always failed just when they seemed on the point of succeeding. Obscure details from his dossier got in the way every time. In the spring of 1961, during one of his trips to Bucharest, he stopped over in Ploieşti, a town fifty minutes away, for an interview with the director of the local building trust. The town center was then under construction, and building sites urgently needed engineers. The applicant received, then and there, a letter confirming his transfer from the Engineering Projects Institute in Suceava to the building trust in Ploieşti. By law, however, recent graduates were forced to stay for the first three years in the job allocated to them by the governmental commission. Upon submitting his resignation, he was warned by the Party leaders in Suceava that he would be brought back "in chains." My family's funereal silence also suggested chains, a silence far more effective than their former paranoid clamorings. But the real chains binding the rebellious son to the family's warm bosom were, of course, chains of love—an affectionate captivity, a possessive claw in a velvet glove.

One Monday morning, the engineer, still carrying his two suitcases, arrived at the office of the director in Ploieşti. Comrade Cotae had thin, frail, spiderlike legs, a consequence of polio, and had to support himself on crutches, but was otherwise a handsome, intelligent man, formerly a

top student at the Polytechnic. He was affable and firm, and it was difficult not to be won over by his directness. The newcomer was to report
the next morning to the building site in the town center.

Ploieşti was, in effect, an extension of Bucharest; the distance between them was short and the trains hourly. Juliet, for her part, proved
an intelligent listener and adept at taking risks. Extravagant, adventur-
ous, unbridled, she possessed an acute and highly intuitive mind, as
Cousin Riemer, her teacher, who kept popping in and out of the family
saga like a Friar Laurence, had already noticed.

It was a cruel April, the first spring in the new couple's life. At that
time in socialist Romania, abortions were still cheap and legal. The waiting rooms were always crowded and patients came and went like characters in a mournful soap opera. The ghetto mother would have been
appalled to know about what was happening behind those white doors—
remorse, guilt, compassion. Did the old God-fearing woman care only
about her self-absorbed trance? the guilty lover kept asking himself,
waiting for his wounded Juliet on a bench in the hospital garden. It was
a morbid wait, racked with terror and guilt. Had the beloved become the
testing ground for her lover's limitations and duplicity? Was this liaison
indeed the family's misfortune, or the ambiguity of his own wishes? Was
it the temptation of the unknown, or the delights of the forbidden fruit?

"To whom do I owe my happy marriage? Maybe the magic sieve spun
for me, too?" the former Romeo, now long married, would ask his mother
some twenty years later. "I didn't recommend your wife to you. You
found her yourself" was the reply of old Lady Montague in 1986, then
almost blind, but still able to grasp the allusion.

"No, you didn't recommend her, but you stopped me from marrying
somebody else once when it didn't suit you," her son insisted.

"Fate always decides," came the prompt answer.

"Exactly, you protected me, you made me protect myself, from what
fate had in store for me." Quips and defiance were all that remained of
the old wound. "You, protect yourself? You never protected," the old
voice, still articulating the ancient neurosis, shot back. "That Christian
woman was not your fate," she added. "Christian woman? Hasn't she got
a name? Isn't that what you were asking for, from all the rabbis, dead and

alive, that she should lose her name?" This is how he should have re-
torted in 1961 and 1962 and 1963, not only in the summer of 1986, when
the past was old, diseased, and forgotten.

Of course she had a name—Juliet, love's generic name. This is what the
tired Romeo of yore should have shouted triumphantly, that summer of
1986, before the final curtain, before the ultimate exile. Time passes,
mystifications no longer afford comfort, but the old self-justifications
linger on. "I did not wish her any harm," the old woman continued. "She
has children now, she's doing all right. In England somewhere." Of
course she's in England, where else could she be? Certainly not in Verona
or Ploieşti. She's with Bill the Bard, of course.

Love starts out as revolution, then come the chains and the ambiguities, bringing in their wake the temptation of escape, escape from love,
escape from family, escape from the chains. Let us, we pray, allow life to
complete, in its own way, the work of erosion of hope and disgrace. Tomorrow and tomorrow and tomorrow, life will usurp our illusions of perfection and erode the vanity of our sense of uniqueness. This was Wise
Will's lesson for us all. The ball, the night of union, the flight from
Verona, and then the alternate ending—the protagonists escape death
by poison only to perish by a slower poison, the passing of time. Blood
flows not in well-choreographed duels but also in miserable abortion
clinics. The poison was not simply the antagonisms of the two families,
their different traditions and social hierarchies, but life itself, with its
limitations and surprising twists.

The lover struggled with the limitations of their relationship and
with the limitations of a profession that did not suit him. The beloved,
in her turn, struggled with her neurotic possessiveness. There were
scenes of jealousy and tears. The tension to which they were now prone
was no longer prompted by the hostile world they both faced but de-
rived from their own ambiguities, the discovery of hostility, not against
the enemy, but against the beloved and against oneself.

We are inhabited by many different selves. Is the true birth marked
by the emergence of these selves? Is lying our inevitable teacher? Its oily

oozings disappear, and here we stand, the same, unscathed, as though nothing has happened, until we slip back into the tragicomedy of substitution. The lover was becoming irritated by the unannounced visits of the beloved, terrorized by her possessive claws, as she hovered above him, haunting his nightmares like a bird of prey. The beloved, fretting about being incapable of hiding or healing her wound, once appeared on his doorstep, after midnight, and discovered him with another woman. Another time, she intercepted a guilty exchange of letters. The flower of evil was blossoming, its phosphorescent petals discharging poison.

There seemed to be no escape, and yet, there was one—the lie. That filmy cloud of breath was at the ready, helping one out of trouble, by transforming reality into its many variants, a two-tongued monster, come to rescue you. Had the tale of Verona, like all tragic recurrences, become a farce? The finale was lingering, separation seemed imminent, not through tragedy and death, but through boredom. He wished for the regeneration of solitude, with its great riches and promises. The role of the tragic, purehearted lover had turned into the comic role of a man irritated by his consort and by the monotony of cohabitation. The protagonists of Verona had become consumed by exaltation, doubts, treason, and remorse. Resignation to their condition could not reignite the idyll. Their marriage had been consummated without legal confirmation, there was no barrier to their parting. Each would find, in the future, a happy marriage, a real marriage—as had been predicted by both the Gypsy woman on a street corner and the rabbis in the Suceava cemetery, and by the clouds' whisperings through their long, sleepless nights.

He revisited the image of Juliet, lying blood-smeared in the clinic, skipping along the seashore, dancing at the graduation ball. The years gradually dissipated those images, until all that remained were guilt and gratitude for that stormy apprenticeship in love. Youth had abandoned him to the lessons in imperfection.

There was one last, cryptic message, like a threat: "It's me, I will return." In the next sequence, her image fills the night screen. I see a bench, next to the stone rail of the seashore promenade. The woman is wearing a flowery dress, with brownish Oriental motifs, a silk scarf around her neck, and brown, high-heeled shoes. Visible between the shoe and the hem of her dress is a portion of white skin with bluish veins. Next to her lies an open bag with small boxes and packages, and on top of it, another thin yellow scarf. Her hair blows in the wind, she gazes intently, focused on something unseen, outside the frame of the screen. Her face bears the expression of a gentle, evasive solitude, but retains its old intensity.

I hear her saying: *The first crisis happened two years ago. I was just back from a happy trip to Spain. A good friend of mine had just died. Then I heard the news of the accident in which my youngest sister was killed, the most cherished member of my family in Romania. I was hospitalized and had to stay there for a few weeks. I went through a desperate period of rehabilitation. My true salvation came from my children. I had to look after them, to protect them from the torment that had engulfed me.*

The voice seems to come from behind the image or from nowhere. It is the same familiar voice, the same familiar face, the same appearance, and even the same self-absorbed expression of pain: *I had a terrible relapse, like an endless, dark heavy sleep. Then, having partly recovered, we went to live wherever my husband's business took us, the Far East, Africa, Latin America. He does business with Communist countries, as you probably guessed from that cheerful group picture with the Communist leader. Now I'm coming out of the hospital again. This time I'm trying traditional Eastern remedies, teas and special powders. You have probably guessed what I'm suffering from.*

The sound trails off. There is a long pause. I wait for something to move: her lips, her hands, her body, or at least the waves. *I'm trying to forgive, to forget my beggar princess's pride. I am praying that my heart may heal, that the pampered child within me may be healed. You know how intensely I sometimes resent the malevolence around us. I am too impulsive and honest, as you know. Our strange closeness still hurts me sometimes. What have I been for you, a mere source of amusement, a catalyst? That's the chemist in me speaking. But I haven't been in a chemical lab once in the last ten years. They can't allow a chemist with this sort of illness into a lab, can they? My children are now grown-up, and so am I.*

The image remains motionless, on the promenade at the edge of the sea. Behind her, equally motionless, stretches the flat expanse of water and the sky's gray horizon. The image is frozen, like a picture postcard. Only the voice animates the bizarre daydream. *Yes, the dawn of that morn-*

ing in Verona . . . those big, encompassing moments of adolescence. Nothing could have stopped me from completing my burning journey through that experience to the very end. Now here, at home, I come across all sorts of strange objects—an old cigarette pack from thirty years ago, a small mound of earth, a half-burned candle. No, I'm not frightened, the disease protects me from everything.

Her face becomes blurred, fragmented, like her voice. Maybe they will return later, but the dream was lost, memory could no longer hold it in focus. The ghost had disappeared.

Nomadic Language

Congested waiting rooms, overcrowded hospitals . . . The long lines of patients were like mystical processions, and access to health care required special connections—So-and-so knows So-and-so, a friend of one's wife, or sister, or mistress. Finding a taxi to take you to the hospital in the morning rush hour, at the other end of the city, was also a challenge to the apathy of the socialist system. To transport a patient to the clinic, you had to know an accommodating taxi driver or have a friend with a car. If successful, you finally found yourself in the anteroom of the suffering, in full possession of the right to wait, along with all the others so privileged, for the magic moment when the doctor would deign to see you.

The ophthalmologist, who only a few years earlier had been promoted from the provinces to the capital, Bucharest, had overnight become the miracle worker; to see him you had to make an appointment half a year in advance. The visit with him lasted only a moment. The miracle worker made the diagnosis and named a date for the operation.

The eighty-two-year-old patient had a heart condition, diabetes, and suffered from a nervous breakdown. Her son, no longer young himself, did not appear to have resigned himself to the inevitable, still troubled by the blind woman's slow gestures and equally slow speech.

The old woman took the much coveted referral form. It was to be a hospital admission, "with accompanying caregiver," for two days before and two days after the operation. Her daughter-in-law would have to take a week off from work to cope with all that was required, a week rather than just the four before-and-after days, because her role also involved acquiring the cartons of cigarettes, soap, deodorant, nail polish, and chocolate, all with Western labels, that were the currency of securing the goodwill of the nurses, cleaning ladies, and assorted functionaries whose assistance would be needed.

Payment for the operation itself would customarily require sealed envelopes with greasy, crumpled banknotes, the normal transaction under socialism's free medical insurance, but in this case it was a question of finding something less conventional. An autographed copy of my latest book would hardly do the trick, we had to find out what would really please the miracle doctor. A painting? Fine, we'd browse through the studios of socialist Jormania's artists. But even after the pastel drawing, in a gilded frame and paid for with a month's salary, reached the doctor's home, the coveted private room failed to materialize: the patient and her "accompanying caregiver" would have to make do with a single bed, in a shared ward with six other beds. They would sleep together in the same bed, for the two nights before and the two nights after the old woman's operation.

These were nights of moaning and spasms, of lengthy confessions, nocturnal mumblings issuing from the depths of slumber. It was hardly the calm and quiet needed to sustain the preliminary tests, the delicate surgery and convalescence. The old woman demands attention—coded laments, incomprehensible requests. Nobody can understand the bizarre language . . . Only the daughter-in-law, lying beside her, knows it is Yiddish, although she herself does not understand the meaning of the alien words.

During the day, the old woman speaks only Romanian, but the unreal night is not erased by daytime realities. The peasant women lying in the adjacent beds scrutinize her suspiciously, but are not bold enough to make inquiries from the young woman who sleeps in the same bed as the old pagan. The next night come the same ramblings, first a murmur, like water, short guttural signals, followed by an agitated, secret confession, an arcane lexicon, wailing and reproaches, lyrical, tender refrains, meant for the ears of initiates only. The daughter-in-law listens tensely. It is a sort of hypnotic release of pain, in a nomadic language, the voice of an ancient oracle in exile, wrenching from eternity a message in turn morbid and unyielding, or gentle and forgiving, enhanced by the bizarre sounds of a barbaric, sectarian phonetics, electrifying the darkness. It sounds like a mix of German or Dutch dialect, mellowed by age and by a passionate delivery, Slavic and Spanish inflections, biblical sonorities, oozing forth like some linguistic alluvial mud, carrying with it all the debris gathered along the way. The old woman is telling a tale of wanderings to her ancestors and her neighbors, and to no one in particular; her monologue is punctuated by spasmodic sounds that could be laughter or pain, one cannot tell. Is this a soliloquy about the nomads' Odyssey, the urgency of love, the call of divinity, the fears of today? The night is broken only by moans uttered in code by the incomprehensible spasms of the unknown.

In the morning, as if nothing has happened, the patient returns to the daily, communal language. Her daughter-in-law washes her, dresses her, combs her hair, feeds her, takes her to the toilet, lowers her underwear, helps her onto the toilet seat, wipes her skin clean, brings her back into the ward, helps her onto the bed. "God will reward you for what you are doing," says the slow, weak voice from the bed near the window.

Darkness, however, invariably delivers her to her past. As night comes, she continues her old cryptic monologue, addressed to an even older and more cryptic deity, and accidentally overheard by that audience of strangers, unfamiliar with the nocturnal code. She tells tales of the son and the father and the husband and the daughter-in-law, and of God, who gave them their faces and their peculiarities. The tales speak of the sunny, idyllic years of youth and the Hooligan Years of yesterday and tomorrow, modulated by those old lips, dry with thirst and exhaustion. Here is the language of the ghetto, moaning, murmuring, demanding, living, surviving. The nights in the hospital are laden with untranslatable memories. The normal routine of family life, the earlier visits to ophthalmologists and heart surgeons, retreat from her mind. The biological collapse she suffered revives, with increased intensity, old traumas, to add to the burden of the new—a final rebellion, a swooping flight, before the beginning of the end.

The Stranger

M emory finds focus in that regret which binds us to those we can no longer bring back. It is the early 1980s, an autumn afternoon, in the small Bukovinan railway station. The serenity of that moment lingers in the minds of the two travelers, even after they have boarded the train. They sit down in silence, facing each other, in opposite window seats. An ineffable melancholy has washed over them. Their first words, and especially their tone, express an acceptance of the peace which has descended on them after lunchtime that autumn afternoon. The old woman does not seem to like the question that has been put to her, but she obviously delights in the harmony of the moment, in the opportunity for closeness and the interest her traveling companion takes in her.

After a short hesitation, she begins her story. She talks about her youth, about the pace of daily events in her small market town, where normally one would have expected the stasis of the province to stifle occurrences before they could happen. On the contrary, as it turned out, events happened at hurricane speed. So-and-so became secretly engaged and eloped to Paris, scandalizing the girl's poor churchgoing parents, to say nothing of the community. The bride was forced into flight at gunpoint—imagine that. A teenager walked a distance of over twenty kilometers weekly—imagine that—to play chess with Riemer the upholsterer. The confectioner, Nathan, has started another lawsuit against his neighbor, the sixth within a year—can you imagine?—for trespassing on the sidewalk in front of his shop. His son—also Nathan, and also a confectioner—talks interminably about Trotsky and Stalin. The grand dramas of a small market town of yesteryear . . .

What about the bookstore, I ask. Peasants from neighboring villages would come not only to buy textbooks and school supplies for their children but also to talk about their legal troubles or to find out who won the elections, the Liberal or the Christian-Peasant Party, for Avram the bookseller knew everything.

"Father would get up early in the morning and walk to the station, to fetch the newspaper parcels, come winter or summer, sunshine or rain. He used to tell jokes all the time, and was kind to everybody; he never lost faith. But Mother was sickly, poor thing."

What about the troubles and the suffering? That question remains unanswered. "Did you have any troubles at the time?" I ask softly. "Ariel mentioned some scandal, some troubles."

"What sort of troubles—when did he tell you that? In Paris, in 1979?"

Instantly we have turned into protector and protected. The question has unwittingly raised the irritation the son has always felt at the mother's wish to protect him. She went on protecting him even when it became suffocating. But now the situation is reversed and he is protecting her. This doesn't seem to bother her; actually she seems touched, even flattered. In his insistence she sensed not only curiosity but also tenderness, in harmony with the serenity of the afternoon, which affects them both. She is being pulled back to the past and is being asked questions that should have been left far behind, but this time she doesn't seem to mind.

"Yes, there were troubles then about the divorce."

"Which divorce, whose divorce?" is the unuttered question. The story has barely begun, it needs room to breathe.

"We lost a house, with that divorce, the house given to me as a dowry. My brother, as a male, had priority, but even though I was the youngest, and also a female, I was the favorite."

I am no longer looking out the window, but now give my full attention to the storyteller.

"Had you been married before?"

"Yes, to a swindler. He lost everything gambling. He'd disappear for long periods of time. It was a disaster, it lasted less than a year."

"And you never said anything about this?"

She does not seem troubled by the son's naïve bewilderment, nor is she in a hurry to answer.

No one in the family had ever mentioned the episode, not the slightest allusion. The silence had been tightly maintained all these years and was only now being broken, in the train carriage where mother and son sat once more in silence. Not even Ariel, her cousin, had mentioned the divorce, that day in Paris, on the only occasion we met. He had just smiled, suggesting something questionable in his cousin's past, but had never mentioned another marriage. Ariel had quickly switched to the core topic of our meeting—the *departure*. "How," he asked, "can you live in that cul-de-sac? How can you put up with the petty local pleasures, the delicate diminutives, the charm and the feces?"

I used to bristle at such arrogant aggression; I had been its target so many times, both in Romania and abroad, but in the late 1970s, when the disaster of dictatorship had run its course, I had no counter-arguments left. My mother, Ariel's cousin, was prey to the same obsession, the *departure*, but she had learned not to press me with questions. She knew why I could not leave and had stopped asking. Ariel himself now learned why I chose to stay in the cul-de-sac he had left a long time before—I was a writer, and I had to write in my own language. After all, he too had flirted with the idea of writing in his youth and had remained an avid reader, as testified by the shelves laden with books and the chairs covered with books, and the tables and the couches and the floors all invisible under the piles of books.

"What was that man's name," Ariel asked, "the writer who created such a furor in the 1930s? Inner and outer adversities, that's what he used to talk about, didn't he?" He was lost in thought, he knew no cure for the madness of writing, but turned to me after a few seconds, staring at me with wide, opaque eyes, like a blind man's, and then grabbed me by the left arm with his powerful grip. "There's no cure for that, for writing. Not even women; even less, money; and even less, freedom or democracy," he said, laughing.

However, he did know a cure. He kept my arm firmly in his clutch and transfixed me with the stare of his large, dead eyes, ready to impart his revelation. "Only a belief in God can cure the writer's disease, or at least faith."

"Maybe. But I . . ."

"I know, I know, I really didn't mean it. You are not a believer, and you don't see the attraction of the Land of Canaan, where I shall soon retire to live out my last days. Of course, you could not be a taxi driver or an ice-cream vendor, or an accountant, like that decent man, your father, I can see that. But then again, why not a yeshiva in Jerusalem, where you can engage in passionate study."

I managed to free myself from his clutches, and stared, wide-eyed, at the blind man, who looked back at me with his unseeing eyes.

"A yeshiva? What sort of yeshiva? At my age, and with my lack of faith?"

So here I was, engaged in dialogue. Was this a sign that the absurd idea could after all compete with the absurd chimera that kept me chained among those Danubian diminutives? The rebellious Ariel had no hair left, or eyes, but the devil's fire was still raging in his goblin-infested mind.

"A special yeshiva, a theological seminary for intellectuals who have never had an opportunity to study such topics but who need to ask questions about religion, even though they may have doubts. I can fix it for you. I've got good Zionist connections. Believe me, this is the only solution. This is a true inspiration, and I haven't had one in a long time. But inspiration comes when you need it most."

It would have been useless telling my mother about all this, it would only have fed her meaningless hopes and illusions. After my return to Bucharest, the inspired Ariel would ring me up at the oddest times of night, not only to repeat his yeshiva proposal, but also to pour scorn on the country he had left behind. "Diminutives, sweet terms of endearment, are these the things that keep you all there?" he whispered in his Frenchified tones, while the Securitate agents on duty were assiduously eavesdropping. "I'm warning you of the horrors to come, as I warned your mother half a century ago. Such endearments, even about your stammering President. I've heard that the people call him Puiu, baby chick, can you believe it, Puiu! So, Puiu goes abroad and gets hugs from the planet's crowned apes and presidents and general secretaries and zoo directors . . ."

Surely this was meant for the Securitate eavesdroppers, to make life difficult for me, and have me arrested perhaps, or at least force me to leave the cul-de-sac and go, by remote control, straight to the theological seminary in that capital of capitals, where he was about to settle his final accounts. Not once did he ask about his cousin, my mother. As for the matter of that bizarre divorce, destiny was reserving that for the train trip of several years later, in that resplendent Romanian autumn that was now embracing mother and son with the softness of a diminutive term of endearment.

Ariel had simply smiled as he made insinuations about his cousin's tempestuous youth, he never mentioned another marriage. The reason for the divorce may not even have been the one the old woman was disclosing now. It was one of those non-issues, a topic on which everybody had always observed total silence. One knows next to nothing about the people one has lived with for a whole lifetime.

The mother was now over seventy-five years old, the son turned forty-five. They were traveling to Bacău—some two hours away from Suceava—to see an ophthalmologist. Her eyesight had deteriorated markedly, in phase with the general weakening in the last few years of her whole body, assaulted by disease and pain. The son had come all the way from Bucharest to accompany her to the doctor. They had no luggage, only a small case containing their night things and some frozen provisions; the hotel room had been booked in advance. He carefully helped her off the train. They walked slowly away from the station, the old woman supporting herself on her son's arm. The hotel was nearby; the room, on the third floor, was clean. She then took the food out of the bag and placed it in the small refrigerator. She took out her slippers and nightgown and housecoat from the bag as well. She took off her dress and stood there, barefoot, in her camisole. It was a humbling moment of awkward complicity: the frail body, sagging, old, with disproportionately big hands and feet—her usual lack of modesty. Long-forgotten memories were instantly unlocked, the doubts and confusion of puberty, the guilty moments—the prenatal home, the placenta. The woman would have offered herself, any part of her body, anytime, as a sacrifice, if it would be for her son's good.

He turned away in embarrassment, as he had done so many times before. He went to the window and cast his eyes far beyond the street. He could hear her slow movements, the rustle of the dressing gown. She slowly pulled her nightgown over her sad, humble body, one sleeve, then the other. Then silence . . . she must be fastening her dressing gown. Then she bent down to put on her slippers, first the left, then the right. The sun was setting in the window's narrow frame. The echoes of her surprising confession on the train lingered in the air. However, the day's harmony had not been broken. She took out her knitting; he went out into town, but quickly returned. He found her still knitting away, calmly, even happily. Our short reconciliation with the world still prevailed. Where had the son gone, to the bookstore? She knew his habits. Was he hungry? She had already taken the food out of the refrigerator and put it on a plate, to let it thaw. She sat at the table, facing him; he watched her, in silence. He had brought with him another surprise, apart from the question he had asked her on the train, in that improbably empty carriage.

He had discovered a few years earlier, in the archives of the Jewish community in Bucharest, documents about Burdujeni, the market town where his great-grandparents, grandparents, uncle, and aunt had lived, where the old woman now sitting opposite him had spent her youth, had got married, not once to his father, but twice, as she had now disclosed; the place where she had been divorced, remarried, and borne the son with whom she was now sharing this autumn idyll. He was about to take from his pocket the sheets of paper that, he was certain, she would find amusing. But that sensational confession, made in a flat, matter-of-fact tone, as if the news were some commonplace comment, had somehow stopped him in his tracks. Everything else paled compared to that moment of shock that revealed to him how easily the long-time secret had been kept and how casually it was revealed. Could the chronicle of the past, enclosed in those typewritten pages, surpass the secret he had just learned that afternoon?

"Are you interested, shall I read it to you?" he should have asked. Yes, most certainly, how could she not be interested? After all, she must have known all about the people mentioned in the documents, she must know about all the places and dates, the people and their families, professions, ages, appearances, circumstances. But he said nothing. The papers remained in his pocket.

At that time, in the early 1980s, I was not yet used to irreversible loss. Wasteful of moments, I was also skeptical about the possibility of storing them in archives. Therefore, I had no tape recorder, I did not transcribe events, I did not preserve the voice and the words of the woman who was still of this world, alive, there in front of me.

Bloomsday

On May 6, 1986, Ruti returned to Jerusalem. Two days later, my parents went back to Suceava, in Bukovina, after my mother's operation, which was unlikely to prove successful.

The days that ensued were days that Leopold Bloom would probably have sauntered through with greater detachment than myself. But if Dublin was less than an ideal place for living one's true life, as the exiled James Joyce seemed to be saying, Bucharest, in the spring of 1986, had reached levels of degradation for which even sarcasm was no longer sufficient. Not even the chimeras could survive in the underground labyrinth of Byzantine socialism. Everything seemed about to fall into decrepitude and die, including the chimeras. Facing the inevitable, a writer could either become a character in fiction or disappear altogether.

I was still supposed to be a writer. According to the rumors circulating at that time among the German-speaking literati of Bucharest, I had been awarded some kind of grant in West Germany. However, the letter of invitation to Berlin never materialized. Was all this a figment of the

Bucharest intellectuals' gossip? What had happened to the proverbial punctuality of the German authorities, even though, in this case, they were only cultural authorities? Surely they would not have neglected to inform me of the award, had it been true. Thus, skepticism and hope played out their counterpoint for months on end. Finally, I decided to take action.

On June 16, the day when James Joyce sent his hero Leopold Bloom, the new Ulysses, roaming through Dublin, I arrived at the police station to fill out an application for a passport, for a one-month trip to the decadent West. I left the mystique of numbers and names for destiny to decipher.

I had in my pocket the credo I had learned by heart a long time before: "I will not serve that in which I no longer believe, whether it call itself my home, my fatherland, or my church." I was finally leaving, I refused to become a mere fictional character in the place where I had hoped to be counted as a writer, and I had accepted the fact that I was not going to die in the place where I had been born. And yet, in exile, what else was I about to become but a character in fiction—a Ulysses without country and language? However, there were no other alternatives, I had run out of excuses for delay.

I had read and reread the Irishman's text dozens of times, I knew it by heart, but on this particular day it was important to write it down and carry it in my pocket, like some kind of identity card. "I will not serve that in which I no longer believe," I repeated silently, as I slowly moved up the appropriate line, "whether it call itself my home, my fatherland, or my church; and I will try to express myself in some mode of life or art as freely as I can." The credo deserved repeating: ". . . as freely as I can and as wholly as I can." Next followed the words that legitimated that anniversary day for me and the way I had chosen to celebrate it: ". . . using for my defense the only arms I allow myself to use." Yes, ". . . using for my defense the only arms I allow myself to use— silence, exile, and cunning." The word "exile" had revealed its true meaning on that anniversary day—Bloomsday.

The Escape

The hesitation to leave Romania was mostly due to the question of how much of me was going to die with departure. I was wondering if exile was the equivalent of suicide for a writer, yet I had in fact no doubt about that. But what about the death lurking here at home? The rapid deterioration of living conditions and the increasing dangers rendered irrelevant any doubts about a rebirth in my mature years in another language and another country. Still, I was gripped by such uncertainties even after the celebration of Bloomsday at the passport section of the police department.

This was probably what was going on in my mind as I walked along the street, unaware of the passersby. Raising my eyes, I looked straight into the serene face of Joanna, a poet friend, just back from a trip to Paris. She promptly started to tell me about the frivolousness of the French, about the decline of French literature. Most of the East European writers, myself included, were experiencing provincial frustration and were also subject to a kind of megalomania. Our Western colleagues, sheltered from socialist suffering and dilemmas, were incapable—so we chose to believe—of producing work that was in any way comparable to our grand, complicated, tragic, obscure writings, which had remained faithful to what we supposed was *genuine* literature.

"There's nothing we can do, we have to stay here," said Joanna. "We are writers, we have no alternative." I had repeated the same words to myself many times before.

"Is there really no alternative?" I asked, smiling. The young, tall, blond poet, with her good Scandinavian looks, was smiling, too. It was hard to believe that we were engaged in such a grave dialogue.

"We have to stay here, within our language, until the very end, whatever may happen," Joanna repeated. A short silence followed, quite different from those silences I normally used to signal my confusion.

"But to write, we must be alive in the first place," I heard myself saying. "Cemeteries are full of writers who no longer write. They stayed here, in their graves and don't write anymore. This is my latest discovery," I added, cheered by my belated banalities.

My young colleague stared at me and stopped smiling. "Maybe you're right. I've only been back one day. I'm happy to be back home, but I can feel death all around me."

Indeed, the terms of the options had changed. Poverty and danger had been the staple diet, delivered to us in abundance by glorious socialism. However, the last years of that hysterical dictatorship had had a catastrophic impact on our capacity to cope. Departure did not mean only dying a little, as we say when trying to mythicize lovers' separations. Departure could also mean suicide, the ultimate voyage. On the other hand, it promised at least a partial, temporary salvation, a fire escape, an emergency exit, a quick solution. Uncertain as to whether the roof of your house will hold, you get out as fast as you can to escape the blaze. The only thing you can do is save yourself from death, not a metaphoric death but a real, imminent, irremediable death. The urgency had its own challenges and confusions. Was it the survival instinct? My contemplated departure was more bewildering. I simply did not know where I wanted to be.

In the prehistory of my biography, in another life and another world, the unborn that I had been had previously attempted the experiment. The prehistoric time was that time before the Initiation of Transnistria—a world without contours or motion, happiness without history, the infinite peace of the unremembered unconscious of the time before I was five years old. There was one moment, however, that helped in the mythmaking—the Escape.

The period photographs help to reconstruct the details. After returning from the labor camp, we retrieved family photographs from relatives to whom the boy's parents, over the years, had been sending regular visual reports marking the progress of their blessed progeny.

"With much love to my cousins," my mother had written, signing her son's name on a photograph showing a young woman, with dark hair, in a flowery dress and white strapped shoes. Standing next to a stroller, in front of a wall covered in advertisements, she is holding a blond, chubby infant. The poster on the left says: "Read about it today, May 12, in *Curentul*. The tenth of May celebrated at home and abroad. Loyalty and homage." This fixes the day of the snapshot, two days after May 10, King's Day, the anniversary of the Hohenzollern ascent to the throne of Romania. The year could well be 1937, when the baby was less than one year old. The woman's body partly covers the second poster. One can see only the paper's name, *Timpul*, and the text below: "Be on the lookout for your trusted daily paper, *Timpul*. Director: Grigore Gafencu." To the right, the front page of *Dimineaţa*, on which only one headline is visible: THE NEW YORK DISASTER.

"A photo taken on the occasion of my conscription," wrote the soldier-father on the back of another snapshot showing the little two-year-old, which he kept in the pocket of his military tunic. The little cherub, with a small nose, chubby cheeks, and dressed in white, is looking straight at the photographer, rather than at liberty's distant horizon. Even in the later photograph, in which he no longer wears a ribbon in his hair and has his arm around the shoulders of the orphan cousin–turned sister, his rebellious intentions are masked under the false, familiar smile.

When I was four years old I ran away from home. After the punishment that followed, my face remained the same, inscrutable, with no signs of trauma, visibly plumper perhaps, after resuming the normal routine and comfortably resettled in respectability. In this photograph, a studio portrait taken not long after the escape, the boy is wearing a heavy winter coat with large buttons and a brown fur collar. His hair is long, like a boyar's, an Oriental mane, topped by a huge cone-shaped hat. His hands are folded behind his back, his stomach thrust forward in an arrogant pose. His feet are turned outward. Puffy breeches complete his costume, along with tumbled-down socks and solid boots. He has a double chin, a large mouth, and small teeth ruined by too much chocolate, the result of furious gorging after his recapture.

The four-year-old boy, hungry for freedom, does not seem to belong to quite the same world as the prematurely aged upstart of only six months later. The photographer, Sisi Bartfeld, to whose studio he was coaxed every few months to have his picture taken, treated him like a star in order to win the attention of his chaperone. He was unaware—stupid as he was—that Maria would never have betrayed her beloved charge for anything in the world. The photograph was stamped on the back: *Film-Photo, Lumière, Josef Bartfeld, Iţcani, Suceava, October 1940*, one year before the hour of destiny, the deportation to Transnistria—the Initiation.

The images retrieved after our return from the camp are again to be lost, over forty years later. The Initiation does not end at nine, or at nineteen, or even at forty-nine. You escape from the burning house without loading your pockets with the decades-old juvenile portraits by the photographer Sisi Bartfeld. The picture of the runaway, in the autumn of 1940, appears to be full of promise, even after four decades. His eyes are vivid and intense, his mouth contorted halfway between smile and grimace, as if the captive can no longer put up with the allurements of his jailers, who force-feed him every morning the poison of soft-boiled eggs and *Kaffee mit Milch*. There were other things he could not stomach—the alluvial, alluring, endless boredom, the comedy played out by the grown-ups, their daily grind of worries, their hypocritical chattering, their marionettes' gestures. Soon, the pampered, beloved son will run away without looking back. He will finally escape into the big, wide world, and take his destiny into his own hands.

The kingdom of emptiness is swallowing him up, second by second. He is counting, carefully, the blinks of the desert's eyelids, the morbid cadence of routine—three, six, nine, ten, annihilation, torpor, seventeen, seventeen, seventeen, the void is murmuring, nothing and nobody, death is slowly embracing the present moment, the age, the old man he has become. In a flash, the runaway shakes himself out of his hypnotic trance. Reborn, he finds himself out-of-doors, turns left, turns right, and then he is on the highway to freedom, bound for nowhere.

He passes the park and the railway station before stopping. He hadn't hesitated, he just stopped, time to tighten the belt of his puffy breeches, to check his boot laces, to fasten the flaps of his military-style cap under his chin and push his hands deep into his soft, woolen gloves. He knows the way, past the German church where the road stretches on and on. He is on his way, this is it, his Big Chance.

The photograph shows the child's girl-like face, with that pathos of the moment. The sudden disappearance of the renegade, at four years of age, meant estrangement, exile, the violence of rupture. In a trance, he had slipped away from the house, then into the courtyard, then into the street. Was he actually leaving the placenta, or was he just roaming through it, among the polyps and membranes that were obediently parting to let him pass? Was it merely a trancelike extension of the same old boredom, a slide downward into the belly of a huge anesthetized hippopotamus?

He recognizes the church, with its pointed roof and the metallic arrow of its belfry aimed at the sky. He sees, as through a fog, the unending highway that might lead anywhere. He doesn't stop, he doesn't hesitate. The yeast of all those slumbering days is finally doing its job. There is no time to waste. He lets himself be carried farther away, along the highway to Czernowitz, about which he has heard. The road unrolls before him, steadily taking him forward.

It is hard to say how long that rebellious adventure, in that autumn morning of 1940, lasted. The stranger who stopped the fugitive at some point did not seem threatening, merely polite. He was one of those faces he had left behind in that lazy, slumbering past, back home. The man looked on with amusement at the face and dress of the walker. Concerned, he asked him his name. Bad luck, that was all . . .

The punishment was commensurate with the scandalous misdeed. Spanking—rarely resorted to, and only on extreme occasions—did not seem sufficient. The criminal was tied to a table leg with the belt that was used to punish him. At first, his mother had demanded a punishment to fit the crime—capital punishment, if possible, for such an ungrateful son. But backing off as usual, she asked for the hooligan to be pardoned, invoking extenuating circumstances. Hooligan? In her anger and worry, she must have been searching for the appropriate word, and "hooligan" would have been apt, better than "good-for-nothing," "brat," "rascal." The next moment, however, the mother, alarmed at her own severity, turned from fury to tears, and to appeals for mercy. "He's just a child," the hapless mother kept repeating, imploring clemency, but it was too late, tears were of no avail. The paterfamilias—that Court of Final Appeal—remained adamant in his stern decisiveness. The adored offspring must receive the appropriate punishment. The verdict was not subject to appeal: the runaway was going to stay there, tied to the table leg. Who knows, it might bring him to his senses.

Was this destiny's rehearsal? A few months after that failed escape, the fugitive was to undergo the real Initiation, compared to which being tied to the leg of a harmless kitchen table—laden with food—was Paradise itself. The real captivity was to prove not only difficult and instructive but also a rite of Initiation.

For the next forty-odd years, captivity and freedom were to strive for supremacy through hypothetical negotiations, compromises, daily complicities and feints, occasionally allowing secret enclaves of rest. The Initiation continued, however, and the captive, tied to the granite pylon of the socialist system, kept on dreaming, like all captives, of liberation and escape. In the meantime, however, he tied himself, like a pathetic Ulysses, to the mast of his own writing desk.

Addresses from the Past (II)

I f ten righteous men could be found in the wicked city, would Gomorrah be saved? The friends—more than ten—celebrating, in July 1986, my fifty-year war, were embodiments of the motherland, not of departure. *Here come the artists, watch out! / The artists go from door to door, the monkeys, the mimics, / The fake one-armed, the fake one-legged, the fake kings and ministers. / Here they come, drunk with glamour and heat, / The sons of Emperor Augustus.* Among them, the poet himself, with a page of verse between his teeth, my friend Mugur, Half-Man-Riding, Half-One-Legged-Hare.

V-Day . . . The guests gathered on the evening of July 19, 1986, in the apartment on Calea Victoriei, were celebrating precisely this—V day. I had survived, they had survived; we were alive and together, lifting a glass of wine, sheltered by heaven and earth—poets, novelists, literary critics, the apes, the mimics, the false kings, the false one-armed men, all relatives of Emperor Augustus the Fool.

I was not interested in drawing up balance sheets at that particular time, but I was prepared to confront the invisible Chinese sage who was waiting, in a corner, to tell him not just what I looked like before I was born but what I was going to look like after the death that had already set in at the passport desk. Missing at the gathering were my neighbor Paul, the Flying Elephant, the Communist who reread Proust and Tolstoy every year, and Donna Alba, his artistic and ethereal wife. Also missing were the dead, the exiled, and the simply forgotten friends. However, those who were actually present could easily constitute the appropriate quorum for the symposium at hand. An intruder such as myself had no right to forget the delights and joys of Gomorrah, the intensity of the present moment, life as transient moment.

I had been born a Romanian citizen, of parents and grandparents who had been Romanian nationals themselves. The books from before my birth told of Hooligan Years. The horror could not, apparently, annul the charm. They seemed inseparable emblems of the times.

Before the Initiation I knew nothing of these things, happy as I was in a happy, sunlit world. Only at the age of five did I myself become a public enemy, the impure product of an impure placenta. It was then, in October 1941, that the Initiation began. At the final count, after four years, the numbers of the fallen came to about half of those who had been delivered to the great void. I was among the lucky who survived, and in July 1945, I was safely back in Paradise, overwhelmed by the everyday miracles of a fairy-tale normality—narrow streets dripping with green foliage and festooned with flowers, ample, kindhearted aunts, who reintroduced me to the delicious taste of milk and pies. The name of this Eden was Fălticeni, the place where the bus of destiny had left from nine years before.

It was a languid, deserted afternoon, in a shaded room. Alone in the universe, I was listening to a voice that at the same time was and was not my own. I was immersed in a book with thick green covers, a book of folktales that I had received as a gift a few days earlier, on the nineteenth of July.

It was then, probably, that it began, the disease and the therapy of words. I had already experienced the need for *something else*, an urgent, all-consuming need, when, at the age of four, I had made my first attempt at escape into nowhere. Now literature opened a dialogue with invisible friends, rescuing me from the disfiguring grip of authority. The system was doing everything in its power to liberate us from the chains of hope, but we were still imperfect and prone to hope. Only those who took a romantic and fatalistic view of art and writing as being ill-fated activities could not be scandalized by the threats against writing under the dictatorship. What was indubitably scandalous, however, was the fact that all those deprivations and dangers had become common currency, as though all the citizens had to atone for some obscure guilt. In the society of institutionalized lies the individual self could survive only in those enclaves that protected privacy, however imperfectly.

The evening of July 19, 1986, was one such enclave, perhaps our final one. But despair had already insinuated itself into each of us who was present that night. Our small isolation cell was no longer the ivory tower of olden times.

In April 1945, the charm of places that had been reborn with my own rebirth seemed not only irresistible but also inexhaustible. Horror had receded into the past. I had banished it, not without irritation, shrugging it off as the "disease of the ghetto." External adversity seemed to disappear, but the internal one, of which Sebastian had been so proud, remained as its residue. The decades that followed were filled with daily attempts to negotiate the strange compatibility between horror and charm, the inexhaustible combustion of confusion. By 1986, what should have been clear forty years earlier, when I had taken shelter between the green covers of the book of folktales, finally became obvious. Communist horror under the tyrant clown not only replaced the previous horror but coopted it.

Must I remain in the place where, at the age of nine, the magic of words had enfolded me, moored in the language in which I was born again and again, day after day? I knew by now that the process of rebirth could be abruptly halted at any time, the following morning, or even that very evening.

I had postponed the decision of departure to that limit of limits, the fiftieth anniversary of Bloomsday. Did departure actually mean a return to the "disease of the ghetto," from which I had always tried to protect myself? Perhaps not, for no return is ever possible, not even a return to the ghetto.

The evening of celebration had become one last exercise in separation. The relation between charm and horror had shifted again. Long after midnight, after the guests had left, I looked in bewilderment at my own hands—a child's nails, a child's fingers, a child's hands. They did not seem tough enough for the birth to come.

Maria

"One day, Mrs. Beraru offered me some potatoes and onions," Mother was saying. "They had four grown-up sons who worked hard and brought food home. But one can only take if one can give back, I told her. She answered in German: *Wenn die Not am größten, ist Gott am nächsten*, when the need is greatest, God is closest. Well, it's too late for that, I said. Then I saw Erika Heller standing in the doorway. *Sie haben Gäste*, she said, You have guests. It was Maria."

The tape recording from the spring of 1986, the time of the Chernobyl explosion, tells the story: "This was how Maria reappeared, out of the blue. At the time of our deportation, she almost got shot, she was almost arrested, but she didn't give up until she found us. One fine morning she appeared at the camp's guardhouse. She asked for a certain Jewish man, an accountant, So-and-so by name, and they brought out Marcu. When she saw him, and when he saw her . . . She had brought everything—oranges, cake, chocolate."

The orphan Maria was like a member of the family, and had acquired absolute power over all household matters, including the newborn baby. She was the Good Fairy and I adored her. In October 1941, when we were sent to the labor camp in Transnistria, the guards had a hard time getting her off the train. She tried to squeeze herself into the cattle car—it was dirty, crammed with bodies and packages—in her determination to accompany those she considered her own family. She failed, but she didn't give up and managed to reach us a few months later.

"She had money," Mother continued, "she wanted to open a tobacco shop next to the camp, to be nearby in order to help us. Of course, they wouldn't let her. The Romanian administrator of the camp offered her a job as a housemaid in his own home. She was young and pretty. In Iţcani, officers and various functionaries were always swarming around her. Bartfeld the photographer even proposed to her, several times. The camp administrator was willing to pay her twenty liters of gasoline per day; even with only five liters you could buy huge amounts of food. Maria asked us what she should do. What could we tell her? To sell herself for our sakes? Finally, the administrator persuaded her to come work for him, but he didn't keep his word. He was a mean, lying man and didn't give her the promised gasoline. Maria went back to Romania. She promised she'd come back, and she did, loaded with suitcases. She'd been collecting money from our relatives back in Romania. She knew everyone who had not been deported, and contacted every one of them. She was well-known to them and considered them relatives. She'd bought all sorts of things, she knew what we needed. Of course, they confiscated her parcels, and then they court-martialed her for helping Jews."

When we returned from the camp, in 1945, we took a detour through Fălticeni and Rădăuți, for two years, before returning to Suceava, to our point of departure. In 1947, the circle finally closed in Suceava, where we had a reunion with Maria—Comrade Maria now, wife of the Communist Party Secretary and future first lady of the city.

Long Live the King!

A bitter winter, December 1947. I was temporarily back in Fălticeni, where I would be spending the Christmas holiday. The town was in an uproar. The sudden abdication of King Michael had just been made public. For the Communists, this was hardly a surprise. Presumably the local Stalinists had been alerted even before the news came over the radio. There was no other way to explain the "spontaneous" eruption of popular enthusiasm that greeted the announcement.

Both our deportation in 1941 and our repatriation in 1945 had taken place during the reign of King Michael, who succeeded to the throne after his father, Carol II, the playboy king, had scandalized the Romanian political establishment with his dissolute behavior, to say nothing of his relationship with Elena Lupescu, his redheaded mistress, presumed to be Jewish. First crowned when he was three, Michael was crowned a second time as a teenager, in September 1941, following his father's ouster at the hands of the Legionnaires in league with Marshal Antonescu. The young king had little opportunity to prove himself. During the war, he kept to his largely ceremonial role, in the shadow of his mother and under the thumb of the *Conducător*, the country's dictator, Ion Antonescu.

In August 1944, after Antonescu's arrest and the armistice with the Allies, King Michael was decorated by Stalin. Now his portrait and that of the Queen Mother hung prominently, alongside that of Joseph Stalin, in all the country's classrooms. He had a pleasant face with an open gaze, and preferred racing cars and airplanes to the machinations of power and government. The "King's Anthem" would open all public ceremonies, while the "Internationale" would close them. The rather insipid sentiments of "Long live the King, in peace and splendor, long live the country's father and defender" paled beside the thunder of "Arise, ye prisoners of starvation."

My cousins Ţalic and Lonciu, both printers, and their father, co-owner of the printing house Tipo along with his partner Tache, were among those cheering the crowds dancing in the city streets, stomping, chanting enthusiastically, "The Republic, the Republic, the People are now king, the People are now king." The accordionist released the ample bellows of his instrument, and the dancing resumed, as did the chanting of "Long live the Republic and the People." I stood and stared, frozen on the edge of the sidewalk. Then I made my way to the marketplace, where Uncle Aron had a small tavern.

Many things had happened in the two years since I had left Fălticeni to go back to Suceava, but the event of December 30, 1947, capped them all—the King had abdicated! I was no monarchist, but I could sense danger in the air. The change celebrated by all the chanters and dancers in the town square heralded something new, good or bad—who could tell. The fairy tale can change from one perfidious disguise to another when you least expect it. The monarchy was gone; henceforth, we would be living in the People's Republic of Romania.

I arrived at Uncle Aron's tavern out of breath, and told him the shocking news. He nodded without much interest, he had more urgent business to attend to. Without stopping to take off my overcoat, I went over to inform Aunt Rachel, who would surely appreciate the enormity of the event. She must also have heard about the group of Jews who not long before had left for the Holy Land, determined to break the British blockade, then in effect, that closed the gates of Palestine to Jewish immigration. They had to steal into the land, and if caught, risked detention in Cyprus. "They went on *aliya*, they emigrated to Palestine," whispered the women watching from the sidewalk, as the masses continued to pour into the streets. But Aunt Rachel didn't raise an eyebrow at the news and, with the kindness and calm that belonged to other times, only insisted that I take off my coat, warm myself, and have something to eat.

Uncle Aron's and Aunt Rachel's indifference did not reassure me. On the contrary, I sensed that their seeming indifference masked a hidden fear. They seemed to be concealing something they could not entrust to the frightened child who had just rushed in, breathless, having witnessed a Communist demonstration. I told Uncle Aron that I wanted to return to Suceava. He gave me a long look and, to my amazement, agreed. "Fine, you can go back home," he said. "I want to go immediately," I said. Husband and wife exchanged glances, then looked with concern at their distressed nephew. A brief silence followed, while they were deciding how to deal with these hysterics. "Fine, Bernard will harness the horse," my uncle said calmly. Aunt Rachel was silent, but her hands twisted nervously. Their son Bernard, who was deaf, was sent for. He was given to understand, through expressive mouthings and gestures, that he was to harness the sleigh horse. "In half an hour," said Aron and Rachel, pointing to the clock on the wall, "everything must be ready." Bernard was as deaf as a radish, but he understood the instructions.

Only then did the unexpected guest take off his overcoat and sit down to eat as he was invited to do. He savored the meatballs, the fresh salad and bread. When he was done, Bernard, smiling, pointed to the clock. Hurriedly, he put on his overcoat again, pulled the cap well over his ears, and put on his gloves. He was ready to go. Uncle Aron embraced him, Aunt Rachel kissed him, Bernard took his hand, the sleigh was waiting in the courtyard. They swathed him in blankets, furs, and straw, and off he went on his Arctic expedition.

They rode through hissing wind, swirling snow, furious gusts. The road was a glistening white, the sky was white, the horse white, an endless expanse of white desert through which the sleigh, driven by the mighty White Knight, glided effortlessly, to the sound of fairy-tale bells jingling on the horse's strong, slender neck. It was freezing cold, the many blankets were soft, the sheepskin enormous, all covered by a heap of straw. Still, despite his thick woolen socks and solid boots, the passenger's feet were turning to icicles. The sleigh driver, well insulated by his stocky physique, drove on, unheeding, deaf to the howling around him. The white road seemed without end. The biting cold, the swirling snow, the clip-clop of the horses' hooves, their vapory snorts, the slithering of the sleigh's runners, the insanely jingling bells, the desperate wailing of the wind—an endless terror.

Home at last, the child of the snows was carefully unwrapped from his swaddling clothes and immediately set down by the hot stove. He was given a cup of hot tea sweetened with honey. He was babbling away, muttering nonsense; his mother and father couldn't understand what it was he wanted. "Leaving, leave, leave, leaving," he kept saying, with strength for only one syllable at a time. "Im-me-di-ate-ly, im-me-di-ate-ly," was all they could make out from his mewing sounds. "Leaving? You've only just got here," came Father's voice through the distance. "Tomorrow. Morning. We're leaving," the little Eskimo repeated. "Who's leaving? Where to?" Mother kept asking in complete bewilderment. "Tomorrow. Immediately. Tomorrow morning." There were no protests, no laughter. "Fine, we'll see about it tomorrow. For the time being, drink your tea. You're frozen, drink your tea."

"No, no," said the small voice again. "It's over, over." He kept staring into his cup. "You must promise me." They did not contradict him, nor did they agree. "Promise! Now, now, you must promise," he insisted, his wool-clad feet knocking furiously, rhythmically, against the wooden table leg. Someone had taken off my frozen boots and I sat there in my thick woolen socks, kicking angrily against the leg of the table where my refilled teacup had been placed. "Drink, just drink your tea for now. We'll talk about it tomorrow." I had heard it all before—the cautious, fearful message of the Old World, the archaic code, the compromises, the stagnant stasis of terrors. These things exasperated me, they suffocated me, as they always had. "All right, we promise, word of honor. Now drink your tea while it's hot," I heard their gentle, hypocritical voices, the delaying counsel of the ghetto, from which I longed to escape.

Almost forty years had passed since that winter of 1947, when my desire to leave had exploded into hysterics. In the meantime, I had learned to sing a different song. The hesitations, the refusal to swap the exile at home for a real, inevitable exile, had become my ongoing lot.

Utopia

It was now the summer of 1948, and I found myself looking forward to attending the State Primary School No. 1, a white one-story building located in the midst of the town park. Education reform had done away with private schools, and my new school meant new friends, new teachers, and perhaps a new me, immersed in geometry theorems, the laws of physics, and the history of the Middle Ages. Later in the term, the school principal solemnly informed me that I was eligible to join the Pioneers, an organization intended for only the best pupils between nine and fourteen years of age. My scholastic achievements entitled me to become the "commander" of our school's Pioneers troop, and I expressed my feelings in a poetic report in the local newspaper, *Lupta Poporului (The People's Combat)*. On Sunday, May 29, 1949, a Party activist, a former railway worker, tied the sacred red scarf around my neck and ceremonially handed me the red flag with gold lettering. The Union of Working Youth was to be our older-brother organization, and the Party, our parent. The activist, speaking to the audience gathered in the park, spelled out the mission entrusted to the youngest soldiers of the Party. "In the cause of Lenin and Stalin, onward!" he concluded. The infants' infantry responded with one voice: "Forever onward!"

Thus at age thirteen—the traditional Jewish coming-of-age—I became a partner in the task of righting the world's wrongs. The occasion was celebrated with cakes and sweets at Wagner's Confectionery. In 1949, in its narrow basement, the establishment still offered pastries and ices in the imperial tradition, of the kind that were available only in decadent, capitalist Vienna. This was the kind of "bourgeois" celebration that I would enjoy many times in my revolutionary career as a fervent partisan of the revolution.

After meeting Comrade Victor Varasciuc, Maria's husband and the leader of the local Communist organization, my father's situation also changed in a decisive way. The former accountant's cautious moderation had kept him away from politics. After the war, he avoided the Communists, the Liberals, and the Zionists alike. But this time, the suggestion for Mr. Marcu Manea to join the Party came from a most authoritative source. Mr. Manea was a man whose honesty and decency were vouched for by Comrade Varasciuc's own wife. Mr. Manea, it was suggested, should take his rightful place among those engaged in building a society of equality and justice, with no exploitation or discrimination. After all, wasn't it capitalist exploitation under which the employee of the sugar factory in Iţcani had toiled? And should Mr. Manea not bear in mind the racial discrimination he had suffered as a deportee in the camps of Transnistria? Maria, Comrade Victor's wife, had been like one of the family. More enterprising than our own relatives, she had tried during the war to help us, or even save us from the camp where we had been sent by Marshal Antonescu, Hitler's ally. The Communists had executed the Marshal and were now gradually assuming power with the support of the Red Army, which had freed us from the camps, saving our lives.

Should his honesty and common sense have prevailed to keep my father out of the clutches of the Communists? By an irony of history, Maria had returned, in a new incarnation, to the family's life. Face-to-face with the city's leading Communist, Mr. Manea tried to maintain his old reticence toward politics and politicians, but finally, he had no choice but to succumb to the pressure and become Comrade Manea. Usually a cautious man who observed and respected the norms, he now found himself an exception to the popular, if untrue, view: instead of being those who inflicted Communism on the populace by an act of will, that is, the Jews, he was a Jew being pushed into the Party by a thoroughgoing Christian woman. At ease with stereotypes, Comrade Manea did not, however, fit the stereotype that had been stamped on so many of his co-religionists. Not long after receiving his red card, the new Party member was appointed to an important leadership position in the local socialist trade system.

By this time, Mr. Manea's son had also become a Red figure of authority, but his boyish enthusiasm was, naturally, more visible than the father's more subdued responses.

The new world's principle sounded simple and just: "To each according to his work, from each according to his abilities." Comrade Stalin assured us that socialism would win everywhere, and at that point the hallowed principle would become: "To each according to his work, to each according to his needs." In the meantime, the exploiting classes were toppling daily. The industries and banks were nationalized, the collectivization of agriculture began; political parties, Zionist organizations, private schools were all banned.

The Red summer of 1949 was for me a grand affair—the Pioneers' summer camp, trips, campfires, poetry readings, meetings with former fighters of the Communist illegal underground, visits to Red factories and Red farms. And then one day, in the doorway of our tiny kitchen, stood a splendid blonde, elegantly dressed. In reality, she was probably from either Moscow or Bucharest, but no, she must have descended straight from Hollywood. She was a vision of generous cleavage, curvaceous hips, suntanned skin, blond hair, blue eyes. Her stiletto heels and chic dress were from another world. And her voice, what an incomparable voice! Instead of an ordinary "Good day," she dramatically announced: "I have come to meet the mother of this boy." From the doorway, she gazed in amusement at my mother and myself, paralyzed with amazement. We invited her in and learned that she was the wife of Dr. Albert, newly arrived in town. "We're absolutely in love with your boy," she said. This was how the gorgeous lady made her entrance into our family's home movie, as a would-be friend of the parents and as an admirer of the boy she coveted as a potential son-in-law.

The Red summer was followed by the Red autumn, the new Red academic year, and the rally of the Revolution, under a podium erected in the town square. Standing with the Party secretary, the colonel of the town garrison, and the representative of the Union of Democratic Women, the Pioneers' commander addressed the masses from the rostrum and, on the evening of the same day, spoke in the Dom-Polski hall. A new red scarf, of pure silk, a gift from the Soviet Pioneers, was wound around his neck. Next came the preparations for the great Red anniversary, the birthday of Joseph Vissarionovich Stalin.

In the grip of pubescent confusion, his hair was disheveled. The boy's hands and lips were groping and probing the object of his desire, there, in the dim light of the teachers' room. One moment I was on top of the world, the next I became a child again, knocking on the frosted-up window for my father to come and open the front door for me.

The young revolutionary found himself alienated not only from the paltriness of the family house but also from the narrow-mindedness of his lower-middle-class family—a restricted world, trapped by its own fears and frustrations, a ghetto suffering from the disease of its past, suffocated by suspicion and rumor. He felt comfortable only outside this confinement; he was secure only within the simple, clear logic of his new allegiance, under the bright rainbow in the Red sky: PROLETARIANS OF THE WORLD, UNITE. Those beings called parents, relatives, family? Their little lies that knotted the hours one to the other? Even their names, their bizarre pronunciations were something to be ashamed of, and so were their minor dramas, their fears, their desire to be with only their own, obsessed with their burdens and their illusions, feeling forever persecuted, held together by the injustice done to them two thousand years ago and seven years ago and yesterday afternoon.

"In a few years' time, this boy will get us all killed," whispered Sheina, daughter of Avram the bookseller, one night to her husband,

Comrade Marcu, also father of the commander. He did not respond to the challenge, he had enough to think about: socialist commerce was more socialist than commerce. Life, however, could not be stopped in its tracks by such bourgeois concerns. The class struggle was becoming ever more acute, Comrade Stalin warned, the enemy's agents were everywhere, even in the old Habsburg boys' lycée which I now attended, in the company of rigid, imperialist teachers and reactionary fellow pupils, sons of nouveau riche farmers, lawyers, merchants, priests, rabbis, and politicians of the former regime.

I was at an age when I was filled with, nay intoxicated by, urgent desires. Touching a female schoolmate in the darkness of the movie house was only a substitute for the real sexual initiation, for which there was no available partner, except perhaps the servant girl who slept in the kitchen and whose movements I spied upon at night, breathlessly.

There was another reason for feeling guilty. I had a new classmate, from Giurgiu, in the country's south, who had applied to join the Union of Working Youth. He was tall, quick-thinking, good with words, and I liked him. His parents' shady situation—nobody really knew why they were transferred to Bukovina—should have made me authorize a deeper investigation; nevertheless, I accepted his request and he received the red card. Was this the poison of compromise and treason?

Meanwhile, the ubiquitous Party posters, with their bold red letters laying down the Party line on every conceivable issue, remained irresistible—Party Day, the agrarian problem, the international situation, the Korean War, the Tito menace, vigilance. At all times there were deviations, excommunications, reorientations, new directives, *coups de théâtre*. The people's best sons and daughters would suddenly turn into deviationists, traitors, and agents of the bourgeoisie or of American imperialism. "The cadres are the Party's golden treasury," proclaimed the inscription at Red headquarters, adorned with portraits framed in red. Missionaries drawn from factories, farm fields, institutions and schools were the "professional revolutionaries," linked by a code of secrecy. At the top, the Political Bureau ruled, then came the Party Central Committee, below them the Central Committees of the Youth Union, the trade unions, the Women's Union. The whole system branched out downward into regional, borough, and town committees. At the bottom were the organizations in towns, villages, factories, collective farms, militia and Securitate units, and schools. At the very bottom of the heap were the public assemblies, the masses who formed the final link of the operative chain.

It is Thursday, 4 p.m., in the high-school auditorium. The year is 1952, autumn. The table on the platform is covered with a red cloth, four large portraits of the Marxist-Leninist fathers, framed in red, look down from the stage. The Secretary of the Union of Working Youth— for that indeed is the position to which I have risen—comes to the ros- trum, followed by a delegate from the regional committee, followed by the high-school director. The director advances obediently to his seat on the front bench, alongside other members of the staff. The comrade Party activist opens his briefcase, takes out the day's newspaper, and reads the communiqué of the Political Bureau, dealing with deviations among Party members on both the right and the left. He comments solemnly on this resolute text. Next on the agenda is a set of carefully prepared speeches. The Comrade Activist intervenes, interrupts, asks questions, reprimands those who still hesitate to deliver the names of the enemy.

The final item on the agenda is meting out punishment to miscre- ants, enemies of the people, and traitors to the revolution. These hap- less creatures are the son of a nouveau riche farmer, the son of a butcher, the son of a former Liberal Party lawyer. "These are dangerous times for the country, which demand closing ranks around the Party, its Central Committee, and its Secretary-General," Comrade Activist intones. "We must strengthen our vigilance and eliminate dubious elements." His voice rises: "We cannot go below three! Three!"

The first defendant remains silent, while the audience waits. The farmer's son cannot summon the courage to tell them that his father was not exactly a kulak, a peasant landowner who employed hired labor, he had simply refused to join the collective farm. The eighth-grader, new to the town, is almost ready to faint with emotion and remains foolishly tongue-tied. The vote is taken. It is unanimous: expulsion.

Next in the dock is Fatty Hetzel, son of a butcher and cattle trader. A mediocre student, the assembly is informed, the only things he is good at are fighting and cows, just like his father. Worse, the father has applied to emigrate to Israel! The son of Zionist exploiter Isidor Hetzel mutters something, but fails to find the right words. The verdict, again unanimous, is expulsion. Young Herman Hetzel, now no longer Comrade Hetzel, advances toward the red table of the Red committee and hands back his red Party card.

Next up is Dinu Moga, from the top class, the lawyer's son. The expulsion verdict comes easy. Tall, impassive, handsome, he hands in his red card to the Red secretary and walks with composure to the exit, looking as though he had no connection whatsoever with either the kulak, the butcher, or the tribunal.

This was an ordinary procedure, like so many others of the times, and yet this occasion was somehow different. Truth to tell, the Secretary of the Union of Working Youth was not at all happy with his revolutionary deed. Embarrassment was eating away at him. I was no longer a boy of twelve, thirteen, or fourteen, no longer proud of my privileged function. Lost in the glamour of the show's magic, that solemn, glacial farce, I was busily trying to cover up my doubts and embarrassment by stammering the routine inquisitorial slogans. An up-and-coming actor, I was imitating other, more senior actors, performing on bigger stages, to grander scripts, and unfurling, over all those red stages, huge red flags and banners, with the gold-and-red hammer and sickle and the gold-and-red five-pointed star. Could revolutionary consciousness separate itself from moral consciousness? Was my initial elan still buzzing under the apathetic, aping gesturing? What did it all add up to, the *Communist Manifesto*, *Anti-Dühring*, *Questions of Leninism*, that verse by Mayakovsky, that phrase of Marx's, Danton's laughter?

At the close of that memorable meeting, did the Secretary-orator distance himself from the dirty revolutionary deed? I was sixteen. The occasion had not yet revealed to me the full horror of what was going on, but I sensed that something had gone wrong under the weakened surface.

Was I so privileged that in such a short time and at such a tender age

I had undergone experiences others extended well into old age? I had
taken part in meetings, expulsions, informing, and assorted rituals,
which, I must admit, had an enormous effect on the ego, to the point
where it believed itself capable of ruling the world. Appointments to
positions, the techniques of secrecy, the vanity of honors—others, to be
sure, had experienced these on a much grander scale, reaching heights of
glory and depths of tragedy beyond my range. My moment in the spot-
light, in that auditorium, over which I presided from the red-covered
table, was something that all players of that utopian-turned-inquisitorial
game knew only too well. It is the moment when you are forced to choose,
from all the selves who inhabit and claim you, not only the one required
by the moment's ultimatum, but also the one who genuinely represents
you. It is not only during childhood, puberty, and the teenage years that
we experience our potential multiplicity. I was not the head of a family,
I did not have a profession, I did not have to face the real risks of a political renegade. However, my dilemmas were hardly frivolous, to say nothing of the fact that for adolescents there are no frivolous dilemmas.

Fortunately, there are actors who lack the gift for power, even when
they are attracted to utopian constructs and theatrical games. On that
autumn afternoon of 1952, I fell back, without anyone noticing it, to the
humble level of the anonymous crowd. It was a major turning point, a
moment when the wound has turned gangrenous and something must be
done. Was it the face of that young man, Dinu Moga, as he left the school
auditorium in silence, stripped of the precious red card? I did not reveal
my personal feelings in front of that audience, transfixed as it was with
fear and curiosity, nor would I ever tell anyone. Subsequently, I took
pains to learn the destiny of the young man expelled that afternoon. The
bright and capable Dinu Moga was admitted, the following year, to the
Polytechnic Institute in Iaşi, where he did not do so well. A few years
later, he came back to Suceava, where I was to find him in 1959, when I
returned home as a newly graduated engineer. It was only then that
we became friends. With his books, records, and strings of casual affairs,
the young man was building an enclave for himself in which he could
agreeably spend the passing years—snug in his bachelor's apartment,
untouched by Party or public trivialities, discreet in his liaisons, laconi-

cally polite, a comforting symbol of failure, invariable and permanent, like a monument.

"Joseph Vissarionovich Stalin, Secretary of the Communist Party of the Soviet Union, fellow fighter and heir of Comrade Lenin, great leader of the Soviet people, died on the fifth of March 1953 at . . ." A medical verdict without appeal. The supreme leader of peoples, the great ideologue, strategist, and army commander, promoter of the sciences, bastion of the peace, revered father of children throughout the world, the one deemed immortal, was, after all, mortal like the rest of us. His office in the Kremlin, where the lights were never turned off, was now in darkness.

The column of students and teachers was advancing toward the city's central square. I followed along, outside the marching ranks. Large loudspeakers fitted on trees and power poles were broadcasting the funeral live from Red Square in Moscow. The sonorities of funeral dirges filled the air. Party leaders, as well as delegates of all the organizations—youth groups, trade unions, women's leagues, sports associations, the disabled, stamp collectors, hunters—all marched, wearing red armbands with a black stripe in the middle. I was wearing one, too, on my left arm, at the very place where my ancestors would wind one of the two phylacteries, the very thing that might have reconnected me to the Chosen People.

The square was packed, but I had a reserved place, between the girls' lycée and the mechanics' school. I saw the Secretary of the Union of Working Youth of the girls' school sobbing helplessly into the arms of two of her schoolmates. Other schoolgirls were crying, too, and even a few of the teachers. The boys were manfully controlling their sorrow.

The Great Leader's death had sent shock waves into the African jungle and the Mediterranean, and as far as the Chinese Wall and the Wild West. The whole earth was in mourning. The Romanian People's Republic was also holding its breath. Bukovina, too, was grieved. Suceava was draped in black banners, including the boys' lycée.

At the start of the new academic year, I was seeking to be replaced as Secretary of the Union of Working Youth. I had begged off serving another term because I needed time to prepare for the university entrance exams. I had already nominated my successor and had been assiduously training the peasant's son from the eighth grade for his important new mission. He was now standing on my right, eyeing me with the shyness and respect due to a veteran militant about to retire.

In Red Square, the funeral cortège wound its sorrowful way. The Romanian delegation was led by Comrade Gheorghiu Dej, alongside Comrade Maurice Thorez and Comrade Palmiro Togliati and Comrade Dolores Ibarruri and Comrade Ho Chi Minh and Comrade Frédéric Joliot-Curie and so many other comrades from around the world, all known to us by name and face. The absence of television rendered the radio broadcast even more powerful. The funeral march, the graveside speeches, the sense of loss that had overwhelmed the world, the country, Bukovina, the city, the school, and my own tenth-grade class, all were evidence of the huge uncertainty that now surrounded us. What next, we thought, what was going to happen in a few hours, tomorrow morning, next week? The red-and-black armbands felt alien to me. I was no longer the same person I had been. The Dinu Moga episode had signaled the beginning of my break.

In July 1945, Fălticeni held its annual fair. That month, too, my formal education began, home schooling in the Riemers' living room. There were books, notebooks, little classmates parroting declensions. There was a book with hard green covers, a book of miracles, the most amazing of which were the words themselves. No one had ever told me stories when I was a small child, and nobody now was patient enough to do so. I had gradually become familiar with the only story I knew—the one I was actually living.

The green book, however, was an object of instant fascination. It contained a topsy-turvy world, colorful, irresistible. Its picturesque language was flavored with wonderful spices and herbs and rare lexical condiments. A tale of traps, pranks, and delusions, it revealed to me the world as miracle, at once narcotic and illuminating. Other books soon followed, books about adventure, love, and travel. The words, the sentences, page after page, and book after book were clearing the ground and uncovering the unreal reality of the self. Books became my world, the vehicle through which the ego was discovering and inventing itself. The inner discourse was evolving slowly, imperceptibly.

In my first year of high school, I attempted to win the heart of my homonymous schoolmate, Bronya Normann, with an amorous speech that amazed not only the object of my juvenile love but also the schoolmates invited for the occasion. The power of words, their curious radiating force, expanded into caricature. On and on I kept reading: Engels's: *Anti-Dühring*, Pushkin's *The Captain's Daughter*, Turgenev's *Fathers and Sons*, Goncharov's *Oblomov*, the tales of Maupassant. The churnings were searching for a language of their own.

Then there was the language of the newspapers. The speeches of Comrade Dej, Comrade Suslov, Comrade Thorez, and Comrade Mao jostled alongside the more lyrical words of the poets Mayakovsky, Aragon, and Neruda. Was the word wedded to the Revolution? The gap between the language of the mind and the public language was growing. The language of the newspapers, the speeches, the Party communiqués, and socialist legislation operated on the basis of regimental simplification. The "struggle" demanded simplicity, determination, a restricted language, devoid of surprises. The single Party imposed a single language, official, canonic, without nuance, promoting an impersonal, remote style lacking warmth or wit.

Simple and clear though it was, the Party's language remained encoded. Reading between the lines became the normal practice. The weight of adjectives, the violence of verbs, the length of the argument gave the measure of how serious the situation really was and how stringent the remedy was going to be. The terse communiqués about our leader's meetings with East or West European politicians, or with the Soviet ambassador to Bucharest, allowed lovers of crossword puzzles to scrutinize the cabalistic meanings of the terms and determine their distinctions—"cordial," "comradely," or "warm friendship"; "mutual esteem and agreement" or "full agreement and cooperation." These were the Aesopian formulas that expressed the tension within alliances and marked the opening or the closing of domestic and foreign political strategies. The regimentation of the language mirrored the regimentation of the social fabric. It was a language of encoded terminology, charades, a restricted, monotonous language that only served to undermine people's confidence in words, encouraging their suspicion of words. The practical professions seemed the only safe haven from this language's idiocy.

"What do you mean you're not going to study medicine?" This was the question put to me at the graduation banquet by my amazed teacher of natural sciences, a discipline rebaptized as "foundations of Darwinism." I had decided that medicine was not for me and that, instead, I would take advantage of my high marks in mathematics and go on to study engineering; more precisely, hydroelectric engineering. The press was awash with reports on dams and socialist hydroelectric power stations. In 1954, high-school students who graduated with distinction, that is, with a straight run of 5's (modeled on the Soviet 1 to 5 scale), did not need to pass the entrance examination for the university. I was only vaguely aware of the nature of my choice. I could sense, however, that I was giving up the world of "words," with all that this implied. Was I choosing "reality," against my own better nature? Was I choosing the "masculine" over the "feminine," taking a strong, manly stand against the more ambiguous, fluid, doubtful, childlike side of my nature? That masculine choice was supposed to protect me not only from the traps of the system but also from my own chimeras—the adventure of language.

The state was all-powerful. It was the absolute owner of persons, goods, initiatives, justice and transport, stamp collecting and sport, cinemas, restaurants, bookstores, the circus and the orphanages and the sheep pastures. All now belonged to the state, including trade, tourism, industry, publishing, radio, television, mines, forests, public toilets, electricity, dairy farming, cigarette and wine production. This was the central tenet of the dictatorship of the left, state ownership, and marked the basic difference from the dictatorships of the right, where private property at least allows one last opportunity for independence.

After state ownership of space came the most extraordinary of all so-cialist innovations—state ownership of time, a decisive step toward state ownership of human beings themselves, given that time was virtually their sole remaining possession. A new word was now added to the lexi-con of the new age and the new reality: *şedinţa*, "the meeting." "We keep meeting at meetings," ran a satirical verse of the time, a banal formula-tion that encapsulated a banal reality. The individual's time had been transferred over to the community: the *şedinţa*, a linguistic derivative from "to sit," now signified a major new condition, the theft of time.

"If only 5 percent of the criticism leveled against you is correct, you have to internalize it" was the mantra repeated in the meetings of the early years of socialism. The rule had been enunciated by the great Stalin himself, and nobody would have mustered 5 percent of their cour-age to challenge it; implicitly, by accepting 95 percent to be untrue, the principle established the supremacy of imposture and false denunci-ation. It consecrated the intimidation of the individual and the exorcism of the community; it was distinguished by demagogy, routine, surveil-lance, intimidation, but also stage performance. Did this ritual of obedi-ence also imply a subversive solidarity, in the act of submission itself and in spite of it? Whenever, with amused apathy, he voted "unani-mously" in favor of ready-made decisions ("in the name of the people"), the anonymous individual became a part of the masquerade in which his consent was solicited as a token gesture. Alongside and together with others, the "dazed and confused citizen" joined the collective farce, which helped him dispense with his own individuality and personal re-sponsibility, and be free of electoral dilemmas and political choices. Whether he laughed up his sleeve or was bullied into silence, the mem-ber of the "laughing popular chorus," as Mikhail Bakhtin called it, was always part of a fake confraternity, a humorous subterfuge.

What about the actors, those on stage? The child-actor was no differ-ent from the orators of the *nomenklatura*, the socialist establishment. Both the smaller and the greater pulpits of the agit prop festivities were part of the same general hypnosis of the *mise-en-scène*. The young guinea pig went through all the stages of the rise, the decline, and the fall.

It was now my turn to taste the miseries of the renegade. It happened in the autumn of 1954, my first year at the university. At last I was in Bucharest, captivated by the choruses of "Gaudeamus Igitur," the academic anthem that greeted the entrance of the professors into the auditorium. A few days later I was informed that, on the basis of my activities and academic achievements in high school, I had been nominated to be a member of the executive committee of the Union of Working Youth.

This time, I declined the honor. I justified my desertion by saying that I now wished to devote myself fully to my studies. The court-martial was promptly convened, and this time I found myself the defendant, much like Dinu Moga a few years before, my flimsy justification being nothing less than an excuse to evade my duties. However, unlike Dinu Moga, I was spared expulsion.

Freshly arrived from the provinces, I was relatively unknown to my peers. The few colleagues who took a stand at the official meeting attempted to minimize my sin out of a sheer sense of skeptical decency— "If he doesn't want it, let him be, we'll find someone else." The aborted expulsion infuriated the puppeteers working behind the scenes. Comrade Ştefan Andrei, "number two" in the student political hierarchy, took the initiative of sending me to a higher political court. At the headquarters of the Bucharest University Center, I had to submit to the appropriate reprimands and threats.

I was to meet Ştefan Andrei again, one month after the start of the academic year, at Medgidia, in the country's south, on the site of a cement factory, where our entire student body found itself unexpectedly dispatched for "voluntary work." Coming from "up north" to see his son—so precipitously snatched from his academic cloister—my father was shocked to see my huge rubber boots, duffel coat, and Russian-style cap. When he arrived, I was wading through the building site's endless quagmire. We looked at each other, and in that quick glance swapped memories of the war and the labor camp. That, of course, was an exaggeration. The workers' sheds were improvised and the food dreadful, but the atmosphere was pleasant enough, not unlike that of an adventure film. In the evenings, someone would play the guitar or the accordion; there were attempts at conversation, even romance.

I did not feel at ease with the man in the bed next to mine and tried to ignore him. However, Ștefan Andrei, a fourth-year student, soon started to initiate nonpolitical chats. He enjoyed talking about books, a rarity among the polytechnic students. I reacted with cautious reserve. During one of our talks, he mentioned the book he was just rereading, *How the Steel Was Tempered*, by the Soviet writer Nikolai Ostrovsky. The plot concerned a writer who was both paralyzed and blind, and it demonstrated how adversity could strengthen human character. Had I read it? Yes, I had read the book, which at the time of its publication, had been hugely promoted. "And what did you think of it?" asked Comrade Andrei. "A book for children and Pioneers," I replied honestly. "I read it myself when I was a Pioneer." My companion remained silent, gave me a long stare, and inquired about my recent reading. I did not know which titles to name. I casually mentioned Romain Rolland's *L'Âme enchantée*. My companion fell silent again and changed the subject.

This cultural interlude was no compensation for the misery of the "voluntary work." The reward came, however, when I least expected it—a weekend trip, just one hour away from Medgidia, to Constanța, the Black Sea port. Bukovina-born, raised among forests and hillsides, I would be seeing the sea for the first time in my life. That historic encounter was to be the first in a series, over the next decades, of annual pilgrimages to the shores of the Black Sea. During that time, my former classmate, Ștefan Andrei, Nikolai Ostrovsky's admirer, was climbing spectacularly to the top and into the charmed circle of the new leader, Nicolae Ceaușescu, whose Foreign Minister he would eventually become. He also became a serious book collector, the owner of rare books and early newspapers, as well as valuable foreign volumes, gifts from his foreign colleagues. Comrade Minister Andrei enjoyed a reputation as a literate and benevolent man, the understanding husband of a beautiful and talentless actress, whose amorous adventures were spied upon by the agents of the priceless consort of our priceless President. The Foreign Minister indulged his refined tastes during visits abroad and meetings with his opposite numbers across the world and, back home, conformed to the standards embodied by the dictator. I did not enjoy his privileges, nor did I crave them. Fidelity to the Party had conferred its advantages in his case, infidelity had conferred its own advantages in mine. I made no attempt to cross the path of the now famous admirer of Nikolai Ostrovsky and of Nicolae Ceauşescu, nor did I exult when he mouthed the customary official ineptitudes in his East European French at the annual sessions of the UN.

However, thirty years after our literary discussion, the Foreign Minister surprised me. It was during his visit to the Laboratory of Book Pathology of the Central State Library in Bucharest, where old books and prints were restored. Welcoming him, the head of laboratory, who happened to be my wife, was taken aback at the familiarity with which the distinguished visitor greeted her: "And how is your husband doing these days?" Diffidently, Cella replied with a brief "Fine." It seemed clear that the visitor had studied the couple's dossier and knew everything about her and her husband. Later, he acknowledged his former acquaintance with her husband, with whom he had attended the university a few decades earlier, and for whom he had the highest regard. He asked her to kindly pass on his greetings, as well as his request for two copies of her husband's latest book. The book could be purchased—as many copies as one wanted—directly from the publishers or bookstores, property of the state and Party, as were the books themselves, as were the authors, as was everything else produced in socialist Jormania at the time. Why two copies? It was sheer lunacy, and that cryptic request would stay with me in my faraway exile, where it seems even more absurd.

Could engineering really protect me from political pressure and the idiocy of the "wooden tongue"? The slogans, the clichés, the threats, the duplicity, the conventions, the lies big and small, smooth and rough, colored and colorless, odorless, insipid lies, everywhere, in the streets, at home, on trains, on stadiums, in hospitals, at the tailor's, in tribunals. Imbecility reigned everywhere supreme, it was difficult to remain immune.

Was our inner life the only treasure that could be saved? Was this oh-so-vague inner life all that important? Did it not also have its own sources of conformity and complacency?

Hydroelectric engineering studies were difficult, I could tell that immediately, although I did not know at the time that, out of one hundred and twenty students registered in the course, only twenty-seven of us would finally graduate. The starry-eyed enthusiasm of my debut into the academic unknown received a shock at the outset—lunch in the students' canteen. "Eggplant casserole" and "cucumber casserole" were the names of socialism's gastronomic innovations. After only a few mouthfuls, I blacked out, poisoned, and fell into serene nothingness. My stomach, used to the delicacies of Bukovinan cuisine, was registering a protest against the garbage of the metropolis. However, the first lectures offered some compensation for that early setback. Everything seemed new and interesting, especially mathematics and applied mathematics, but I would soon have to grapple with technical descriptive disciplines, which held me back.

I lodged with an old lady who slept in a folding bed she managed to squeeze into the narrow space between the table and the couch. I had discovered, however, more welcoming hosts: the Central University Library, the Arlus Library, and the Library of the Institute for Foreign Cultural Exchange. Late into the night, I would escape into reading that took me far away from hydraulics, building structure, and reinforced concrete.

The results were predictable, and I was slipping down the academic ranks. Should I jump off the university bandwagon and give up my studies altogether? Mother declared in a pained voice, "The disease must be stopped in its track"—the aria of absolute devotion. But devotion, I knew only too well, went hand in hand with emotional blackmail. Psychoanalysis has taught us that one's parents are to blame for the ruin of one's life, but perhaps my life was ruined by my own conflicting emotions, and in any case, life destroys itself moment by moment, no matter what opportunities we miss. Would a degree in the humanities offer me an alternative under the dictatorship? My family counseled against it and I complied. The Ten Commandments were an attempt to tame my fractious ancestors, exile and the ghetto reinforced the rules of prudence, vitality and courage seemed provocative and risky. Had my over-involved mother and father ruined my life? Formation through deformation, however, is not to be despised. Even within an authoritarian political system, there are imponderables.

I graduated in hydroelectrical studies in 1959. Then the conveyer belt of the profession started—probationary engineer, project leader, site engineer, chief project leader, principal researcher. Duplicity was recycled daily, time after time. After fourteen years, four months, and sixteen days, I was finally able to abandon the role of this character.

Had the Initiation of the deportation taught me as a child to reject the outer world, to resist being born, to delay the escape from the nurturing placenta? As a result, later in life, if you accepted all the scenarios that were available to you, did this lead to a multiplicity of selves, only one of which represented your real self? And should you ever be lucky enough to find this real self, should you ever renege on it? You have managed to be drugged and tortured by ambiguity. Churches and bureaucracies, careers and marriages only add, daily, to the archive of multiple identities.

Destiny thumbs its nose at us to keep things lively. In my last year at the university I bumped into Ştefan Andrei, now promoted to assistant lecturer in the Department of Geology. It was a modest interim job; he was pretending to be a "scientific" researcher before re-entering the political arena. Socialist residence regulations allowed a work permit in Bucharest only to those with long-term domicile there, and nobody was allowed to move to the capital city. I didn't have the political connections of Comrade Andrei, who, like me, came from the provinces, and so, unlike him, I could not have this handicap overlooked. "You seemed to be in line for a great career, yet you chose to return to mediocrity," I had been told in my high-school years after my withdrawal from politics. The same could have been said of me upon my return, in 1959, to my hometown in Bukovina.

I was to return to Bucharest six years later, after the "liberalization" eased the rules, having successfully passed a qualification test for an engineering post in the capital. On this occasion, I only had to produce evidence that I had a minimal residential space of eight square meters, the legal requirement for resident status in socialist Jormania. The Jewish community in Bucharest issued me a certificate testifying that I resided in a room in the ritual bathhouse of the former Jewish quarter, of all places.

Destiny was celebrating my residential victory, for no sooner was I settled than I learned about the publication, in Romanian translation, of Kafka's *The Trial*. The news came to me from a former high-school friend, Liviu Obreja, now mixing in the capital's obscure circles of cultural consumers. Booksellers in the city kept him regularly informed of such important developments. The line at the Academy Bookshop, next to the institute where I had just taken up my job, started to form on that spring day at around seven o'clock in the morning, an hour before the shop was due to open. I saw the first customers lining up as I went to work. I signed in, asked for a two-hour leave of absence, without divulging the reason, so as not to add to the suspicion already aroused by the bizarre newspapers, magazines, and books that my engineer colleagues, themselves readers of *The Sport*, had already caught me perusing. Those were the years of the great "thaw," and new publications and translations would appear regularly, in small print runs, so that one always had to be in the right place on the precise day and early enough to join the line of avid readers, waiting to be lucky purchasers of a hot-off-the-press work by Proust, Faulkner, Lautréamont, Malraux. In this endeavor, Liviu Obreja, with his pallid face and shy conspiratorial amiability, was joined by a fanatic band of like-minded devotees, I among them, who, when the signal was given, showed up at the right bookstore at the right time.

At that same time, my own first book of fiction was being published. Concomitantly—fortune was still smiling on me—I got a new job at a top engineering institution, the hydro laboratory of Ciurel, where my job applications had been rejected for years because of my unfortunate dossier. At that point, in 1969, I became the youngest principal scientific researcher in a genuinely academic institution. In order to justify my new title, I was supposed to begin studies for a doctorate. Had I actually done so, the imposture would have reached its apogee. Instead—now my fortunes took a dip—I was admitted, albeit briefly, into, of all places, a mental hospital. Somehow, after some reflection, this seems the most appropriate crowning of my dubious professional achievements.

So here I was, in the mid-seventies, confined in a mental ward, twenty years after I had first attempted, in my third year, to drop out of the university. I had tried to keep up appearances for far too long, and this performance was now duly recorded in the psychiatrist's notes. How did this compare with the duplicity and political imposture of my fellow citizens? "Professional maladjustment" appeared less serious than the alienation produced by the great political masquerade from which we all suffered, the schizophrenia of false self-representation in a false world where your substitute is not yourself yet exists within yourself. Was this not like the twisted posture of a Modigliani portrait or a caricature by Grosz or Dix?

Suddenly, when you least expect it, there you are, you have lost control, or you think you have, or you perfectly mime the condition. Now you can finally get the medical certificate that will send you home to your room, your cell, the coffin where you are quarantined from the environment—all paid for by the benevolent state. Did becoming an engineer protect me from the depredations of my society, as I had hoped? If so, it was a costly protection. Nevertheless, when all was said and done, my troubles, I concluded, were not just the result of interrogations, imprisonments, labor camps, and penitentiary colonies for "re-education" that were the hallmarks of socialist Jormenia, but were simply the outcome of the wear and tear of everyday somnambulism. The perversity penetrated everywhere, nobody was immune from the toxins of idiotization, nothing could provide a perfect shield against the insidious disease. On the other hand, a number of writers and artists and anonymous ordinary people had taken the risk of living in poverty and uncertainty, outside the reach of the brain-mincing machine. Maybe one did not have to become an engineer after all.

Had engineering, at least, cured my uncertainties and anxieties, my inclination to sloth and the scattering of my energies? Did it help me conquer my vice of hair-splitting and excessive nuance? Engineering introduced me to situations that otherwise would have remained inaccessible to me and to people whom I would otherwise not have met. These were gains, to be sure, but how positive was another matter. Such gains had been paid for with that priceless currency, time. However, no error deserves to be overestimated. Would life lived otherwise have matched our idealized blueprint for it? Was engineering slavery? What about the slavery of commitments to family, to friends, lovers, and children, or the slavery of hatred toward one's enemies?

Among the hopes I had pinned, at eighteen, on that modest profession had been the need to protect myself from myself. Such hope remained unfulfilled. Engineering had not cured me, thank God, of myself.

Periprava, 1958

I didn't recognize him at first in his prison uniform as he suddenly materialized before me, pale, head shaven, cap in hand, eyes lowered. He sat quietly across from me on the opposite side of the long, narrow table, among the other prisoners. Guards kept alert watch on each side of the table. We had ten minutes, and the parcel I had brought was to be opened only under a guard's scrutiny, at the end of the visit.

He was waiting with bowed head for the words he needed to hear. They failed to come. He looked up, smiling childishly, eyes red, swollen, scared, with deep, purplish bags under them, blotched, scorched lips. He assured me he was in good health and was coping. The work was hard, naturally, all heat and dust, but he was coping. He continued to smile, with the gratitude of orphans happy to find their parents again.

Father was fifty years old, but the desolate circumstances made him look older. I was in my fourth year at the university in that spring of 1958. I was twenty-two. Weakling that I was, I was struck dumb by the enormity of the moment, helpless to disregard the rules and cross over to the other side of the table, hug my father, and comfort him, as you would a child. I was unable even to utter the few words allowed.

I did not immediately answer his inquiries about Mother. It was better that he should not know that, because of his conviction, she had been fired from her position and finally had had to take a job as an unskilled laborer in a canning factory. She slaved for ten hours a day, stooped over the huge troughs of peppers, potatoes, and cucumbers that she was required to slice by hand. I reassured him that Mother would come to see him next month, and I also gave him the news he had been waiting for: the lawyer claimed that political tensions were easing, that the campaign of arrests had slowed down, and that somewhere "at the top" there had been acknowledgment that abuses had been committed. I leaned across the table, when the guard wasn't looking, and whispered, "The lawyer's brother is a Supreme Court prosecutor." That meant the appeal was going to be successful, probably, and the injustice removed.

His freshly shaven face was in contrast to the miserable uniform. Normally, his clothes assumed something of his own fussy, tidy nature. Now the uniform clothed a mere louse, as in the early weeks in Transnistria, when he had noticed in horror a louse on the collar of his once white shirt. "This is not a life worth living," he had said at the time, defeated, overwhelmed by shame, ready to give up. Mother, the great spokesperson for hope, had then assured him he would be wearing white starched shirts again, but she was unable to shake him out of his despair. Nonetheless, he had survived, only to find himself back again what he had been in that long night of deportation, a louse. Now, here, it was I, the young louse, son of a louse, promising rebirth, the hope of a clean white shirt again.

A few years before his arrest, he had been dismissed, without explanation, from his position as director of OCL Metalul, Suceava's metal and chemicals state trade. He had always been disciplined and honest in his work; even those who didn't like him had to admit that. With no other choice, he took a job as an accountant at OCL Alimentara, the local food-distribution organization. "Socialist commerce" was a contradiction in terms, just like "socialist philosophy." The ancient trade that kept people and goods moving implied individual will, initiative, and intelligence. State commerce, on the other hand, since all businesses belonged to the state and operated on a strictly planned basis, required only bureaucracy, regular replenishments, fresh victims.

My father had neither the vocation nor the experience for commerce. Its psychology, strategies, risks, and subtleties had always eluded him. He simply became a conscientious state functionary, just as, before the war, he had been an exemplary functionary in the private economic system.

"When we moved to Suceava," he once told us, "in 1947, I worked in marketing for the Cooperative Association. I was in charge of supplies for the newly set up cooperative farms. One day, someone came to us with an offer to sell us wood for heating. The director asked my opinion. I said it was a good deal and we immediately agreed on terms. However, we did not have enough cash to pay the man. So I contacted a few families I knew, offering them wood for heating over the winter. Most households at that time were still heated by woodstoves, and wood was hard to get. Many were ready to pay in advance, so we collected the money and paid the man who brought us the deal. The Cooperative Association made a handsome profit from this transaction. When the top people in Bucharest learned about it, I was promoted to head of supplies, which meant I had the power to sign bank drafts as a member of the association's management team. All this stopped in September 1948, when the socialist state took over all businesses and I was appointed director of the local trade association for metals, chemicals, and construction materials."

What happened, in fact, in September 1948, was that trade as such ceased to exist. Having joined the Party at the insistence of Comrade Varasciuc, Maria's husband and the city's leading Communist, my father was brought into the ranks of the new stars of that great aberration named state commerce. Disciplined and persevering, with the zeal of an old-fashioned white-collar worker, Father seemed oblivious to the absurdity he was serving. By 1953, after Stalin's death, both I—the high school's secretary of the Union of Working Youth—and Father—the director of Metalul—came to the crossroads: I disengaged myself from the political militancy, and Father was demoted from his management position.

This is what Father told us some years after: "When, some time later,

I asked an activist from the regional Party committee why I had been let go, he answered with a sort of parable: During Hitler's time, a Jew who was frantically running down the street was stopped by another Jew, who asked why he was running. Haven't you heard? Hitler has just ordered every Jew with three testicles to have one cut off, the panting runner answered. But have you got three testicles? asked the other. Well, they cut first and count later, shouted the runner, as he ran off. This is exactly what happened to you. An anonymous letter claimed that you gave someone a bicycle for free . . . How could I give away bicycles? I wasn't in charge of supplies, I was the director. You're right, nobody bothered to verify the charge. Only later did they find out that it had all been a lie. What could one do?"

In 1958, when he was head of financial services of Alimentara, Father was suddenly placed under arrest. Was it bad luck, the outcome of a curse? Plenary sessions of the Party regularly pointed to rivalries at the top; there were unexpected tactical shifts that scrambled the ranks of the *nomenklatura*, sending shock waves through the vast network of the anthill, whose apathy needed to be shaken with capricious prods of terror. The mist of socialist daily reality was quickly becoming a blood-tainted darkness. Distinct "minorities" were singled out for attention.

As he did almost every day after work, Comrade Manea stopped by the butcher's. He didn't notice anything unusual, the puppets were all going through their regular routines. Father went over to the counter, where the butcher was standing, ready to hand him his usual package. Like other workers of OCL Alimentara, Comrade Manea had an arrangement with the butcher, who in a way was his subordinate: he bought on credit and paid his debts twice a month when he received his salary installments. That day, however, without warning, the puppeteer's strings swung as though electrified and coiled around the unsuspecting victim's throat.

The scene that followed played according to the prepared script. The butcher handed Comrade Manea his package, Comrade Manea not suspecting that it was a decoy. The witnesses, masquerading as customers, were at their assigned posts, ready to confirm what they had been instructed to do, to testify that the culprit had indeed taken the ticking

bomb. Backstage, the puppeteer tugged on the strings, the helpless puppet fell on his nose, and the curtain dropped on Act One of the drama.
Arrested right on the spot, the accused found himself right in Act Two—
the trial.

Under emergency powers, the trial began the very next morning.
The overnight respite was not for the benefit of the defendant but to allow the drummers to parade through the deserted marketplace, beating
out the latest official measures—the strengthening of socialist vigilance, the unmasking of any and all attempts to undermine the great socialist achievements.

The lawyer, court-appointed and therefore reluctant to challenge authority, mumbled the word "clemency," invoking the defendant's sinless
past, his lack of criminal record, his devotion to the principles of socialist morality, socialist economy, and socialist justice. The defendant insisted on offering his own explanations to the court. This was allowed
and he, firmly but politely, denied any intention of fraud. But then—in
what was considered an impudence on the part of the hook-nosed upstart—he went on to say that the deed of which he was being accused,
of not having paid on the spot for the two kilograms of meat, did not, in
his opinion, constitute fraud and was too minor an infraction to warrant
penalty. The People's Tribunal erupted in commotion. The prosecutor,
sitting to the left of the judge, interrupted the perpetrator of the impertinence with visible irritation. Was he the defendant trying to claim
that delayed payment did not constitute grounds for prosecution? Was
he claiming that the amount of money owed warranted only a fine? This
was "legal trickery," of the old bourgeois kind. In tense silence, the
court heard the former director of OCL Metalul and current department head of OCL Alimentara sentenced to five years in prison. The
farce was quickly over and the condemned man was dispatched to Act
Three—the Expiation.

A dense, poisonous dust fills the extended stage. The setting is a labor camp, whose entrance proclaims, in glaring red letters, PERIPRAVA
LABOR COLONY. Shadowy figures in dun-colored uniforms move about.
They carry picks and spades, they push carts filled with debris. Under
the merciless sun and the howling winds, burly guards jab at the necks of

the slaves with the barrels of their guns. A sense of injustice doesn't necessarily make the injustice easier to bear. It wasn't only the butcher shops that delivered hostages to the regime's labor camps, all other socialist institutions sent their regular tribute, as well. For my father, imprisonment in Periprava meant not only confinement and humiliation but also the wreckage of his life. The accountant-turned-socialist-turned-prisoner did not have the philosopher's detachment or the merchant's pragmatism that might see him through the ordeal.

My father was no Hermann Kafka, that brutal owner of the world before whom son Franz quaked, nor was he the Great Magician and Improviser, Bruno Schultz's father, also known as Jakub the Demiurge. I knew him too well. For him, harder than the forced labor, harder than the pain of this reunion, was the humiliation he was now suffering. He had never managed to free himself from the conventions of dignity. Dignity, the guiding rule of his life, was his eleventh commandment, which for him confirmed the other ten. He could neither ignore an offense nor shrug it off with a laugh. His reputation for honesty, built up through a lifetime, reinforced his unshakable sense of dignity, which had often irritated me and as often touched me. The Communist regime made a habit of staging show trials with stock defendants—anti-Communists, landowners, bankers, Zionists, saboteurs, clerics, generals, or lapsed Communists accused of being American spies. Not as well known, but no less painful, were those accusations that fell into a "gray area," apparently nonpolitical in nature, but ultimately, and inevitably, political. The horror could fall on the head of the helpless victims, at any time and any place.

Although he had accepted the red Party membership card, my father was totally devoid of political fervor. Like all "ordinary people," among whom he proudly included himself, he disliked backstage maneuverings. He maintained his dignity only in the anonymity of traditional life, defined by common sense and decency, a man who belonged to that vast category of innocents ignored by the chroniclers. These were some of the thoughts that passed through my mind in those minutes of awkward dialogue with the prisoner of Periprava. I could not communicate my real thoughts, and not only because we were under surveillance. What we really felt remained unexpressed, as it had so many times before in our relationship. He was a man trapped in his own solitude, a man whose main defenses were silence and secrecy. Had he been able to express his shame and defiance, he would have probably found some relief, but complaint was not part of his nature; that belonged to the other conjugal partner. About suffering, as about joy, he would speak only rarely. Unlike my mother, he never mentioned Transnistria; it had been very difficult to get him to tell the story of how he had been beaten over the head with a bullwhip by an officer who, previously, had seemed friendly. He hadn't forgotten one single detail, but once, when I asked about it, I immediately regretted my error. Telling the story of that humiliation had hurt and shamed him almost as much as the experience itself.

Humiliation was something to be ashamed of. I knew I was not supposed to see what I now saw—the emaciated face, the shaking hands, the uniform, the prison cap. Just as he would never talk about the Fascist labor camp in Transnistria, he was never going to talk about the socialist labor camp of Periprava. As for me, I knew I would never be able to describe this meeting until after his death.

Then and there, I should have told him, "It's all over, we're leaving. You'll be out of here soon, and we're leaving." *"Departure, departure, we have nothing to stay here for."* Ariel's battle cry had once sounded, unheeded, in my grandfather's bookstore. I had shouted that cry myself, as I rode in the sleigh through the snow in the winter of 1947 and nobody had heard me.

I arrived in Periprava, that Gehenna of dust between the Bărăgan and the Dobroudja, the previous afternoon, by train from Bucharest. It was a scorching spring day; dust filled my nostrils, covered my hands, my eyes, my clothes. In the distance, I could see the busy anthill, the inmates at their labor, miniature insects in dun-colored uniforms, digging away. They heaved the debris onto carts and dollies and unloaded it at the foot of the dikes, then compressed it with wooden battens. Armed guards looked down from the wooden watchtowers. This was nothing less than a Pharaonic project, socialist-style, for the irrigation of arid fields, each divided into small plots, being worked, as in ancient Egyptian times, by the most primitive methods. Beyond the horizon, there

were more slaves, waist-deep in the filthy, murky waters, cutting bul-
rushes and tying them into bundles.

It was getting dark when I stepped off the train, and I had to reach
the nearby village before nightfall to look for a place to sleep. Through
the dust, I could just make out the villagers on their porches, looking,
without much interest, at the cluster of strangers gathered down the
streets. These were people like myself who had come to visit the prisoners. It seems that such spontaneous gatherings took place regularly, to
exchange information and rumors. I got closer and stopped a small distance away. I could hear what they were talking about, but felt unable to
participate. After a while, a woman, dressed in a shabby coat, broke away
from the group and came over to me. Had I unintentionally given her
some sort of signal? The young, freckle-faced woman immediately asked
me where I had come from and whom I came to see. The next day she
would be visiting her brother, she told me, who was convicted, along
with other employees of the Ministry of Foreign Trade, on trumped-up
charges in a politically motivated trial, the collective nature of the verdict making individual appeals impossible. The personal disaster that
had brought her here to the edge of the world seemed to have shattered
any reserve she might have had. She told her story simply, directly, in
her deep, guttural voice.

We left the small cluster of people and walked along the narrow,
winding streets of the village. Her nervousness was evident in the way
she occasionally shook her large head and hunched her coat around her
shoulders, despite the heat of the day. When she adjusted her scarf, I
could see her tangle of abundant hair, like a wiry crown. She was speaking about the brother she was going to meet, and about the other
brother back home, and her mother, who, upon hearing of the sentence,
suffered a stroke and was now nearly paralyzed. I asked her again what
she knew about the camp. "Sinister, sinister!" she repeated. Had I heard
of the Communist prison at Pitești, she asked, where each prisoner, in
turn, was forced to torture his fellow prisoner, the tortured becoming
the torturer? And had I heard about that Stalinist project, the Danube–
Black Sea canal, where the prisoners—those who had not been brutally
murdered—had died in the thousands? Periprava was certainly the

worst of the post-Stalinist camps, she continued to inform me, small portions of pig swill for food and labor performed by blind slaves, from dawn till night, with the perpetual barking of the guards in their ears, filthy, overcrowded barracks, and the daily quota of square meters to dig—barbaric! Those unaccustomed to physical work, or those no longer young enough, collapsed on the spot. In addition, from spring till autumn, there was scorching heat to contend with, and in the winter, merciless winds.

Obviously, she needed to unburden herself, but I no longer heard her, preoccupied as I was with the meeting of the following morning. What did he look like now, the man who undoubtedly, at that very moment, was thinking of the next morning's reunion? What was I supposed to say to him? That he was going to survive this tribulation, as he had so many others? He had survived the camp in Transnistria and would survive this one, too. What should I say to him—that these were hard times, that innocent people were being dragged through absurd espionage trials, that they were being beaten in brutal interrogations about their relatives in the capitalist world? Or should I tell him about the Yankee or Zionist or Catholic conspiracies against Communism? Could such idiocies serve as consolation?

My companion had stopped talking, perhaps because of my prolonged silence. Then she told me that the villagers were renting rooms for the night, that I had to wake up at dawn in order to make it on time to the penal colony's barracks. Then she quickly walked away. I had not listened to everything she had been telling me. The thought of seeing, next morning, the prisoner I had come to visit overwhelmed me. The minutes started ticking away, my thoughts wandered aimlessly.

The next morning, when I saw that weather-beaten face, creased by the winds and the dust of the hard labor, I still could not find words for my unspoken thoughts. What could I tell him, how could I overcome the awkwardness that had always stood in the way of our communication? Should I offer the slogans of hope, the clichés of common sense that were a mockery in the face of his lice-ridden uniform? I shook myself, determined to find my voice, to let emotion speak directly, but my mind kept repeating the same commonplaces: "The case will be reopened, I shall be graduating soon, you'll be coming out of this hell and we'll be leaving; we'll leave and be out of here, like all our relatives, like so many of our friends." But the soothing words couldn't come out. Some obscure and powerful force inhibited me. Why?

Months before, I might have said to him, "I am going to tie myself to the table leg to which you once tied me. Only now can I understand what you thought I should have understood then, the price of freedom and price of captivity. You have no idea how I inverted these terms." These were the thoughts that were going through my mind months before I knew of the disaster that was about to fall on us. In my vanity, I had thought I could define my captivity as freedom, and imagine myself the inhabitant of a language rather than a country. Now, of course, I could not burden him with my selfish, naïve obsessions, neither did I find the strength to conjure up the prospect of departure. Feeling guilty as I did, I could not promise him, even now, the break with the past called Transnistria and with the present called Periprava. I remained silent, ashamed, unworthy of the miracle of seeing him, with my own eyes, still alive.

We were both silent, our eyes lowered, after the short conversation in which he kept asking questions, like a child trying to encourage a parent, while I answered in a parental voice, bewildered with emotion, as my father, like a shadow, emaciated, pale, humbled, sat there before me. His small accountant's hands were on the table. His palms were bruised from the spade handle and full of blisters. The blond hairs on the back of his hands and on his fingers were interspersed, I could see, with white hair. His nails were cut, as always, but unevenly this time, who knows how, in the absence of scissors.

A bark from the guard and he was out of his seat in a second, propelled toward the columns of uniforms suddenly springing out of nowhere. I caught a last glimpse of him, with my parcel under his arm, walking leadenly with his comrades, each with his own parcel under the arm, all perfectly enslaved by fear of committing the slightest error. Their terror, the rapidity with which they all got in line like robots ready to move on command, shattered my hopes of ever seeing him again.

However, I did see him again. Unlike so many other terrible socialist legal masquerades never or belatedly set right, my father's more modest case was reopened and the sentence reduced from the original five years to the ten months he had already spent in the Periprava camp. A reduction rather than a revocation of the penalty enabled the socialist state to cover up its "judicial error" and avoid paying damages to the prisoner, who, in any event, remained state property.

The Functionary

Father was strict and authoritarian as a director and as a parent. His fits of rage were implacable, his moments of tenderness rare and understated. He was not unjust and never lied even when that would have been the easier solution.

Mother, shifty, fearful, was of a subtler order. She advised him, even on professional matters. She possessed intuition and instinct to spare, but she couldn't say no and couldn't resist appeals. Prone to shifting emotions and black fits of depression, she would veer quickly from reproach to remorse. She had retained strong ties to family and people in her past, from the time she had been her father's favorite. Hungry for affection and recognition, anxious, enterprising, passionate, fatalistic, sociable, she believed in miracles, kindness, and gratitude, but suffered frequently from despair. The interdictions and punishments she tried to mete out to her son seemed slightly ridiculous, because she always appealed to her husband to administer the correction and was ready to retract when the latter, as so often happened, was too severe. Life together had brought no changes in either of the partners nor did it until the very end.

Formed and deformed by his childhood as an orphan and then by his struggle to achieve a respectable social position, Father was close to the typical "Bukovinan" type, although he was born not in Bukovina but in Moldavia, near Fălticeni. He was rational, solitary, prudent, taciturn, undemonstrative, dignified, fussy, modest, with a constant, sad reserve of shyness that translated into a reluctance to engage in or condone aggression. Quite happy to be left to his own devices, careful not to intrude, he valued and embodied decency, discretion, and dignity, even in extreme circumstances. Discretion, no doubt, implied a secret life, and indeed, here and there, there were small signs of secrets, which his wife discovered with astonished indignation. Assailed by the enormity of her reproaches and incriminations, he neither protested nor denied, but simply wished the incident to be forgotten and to recede into the obscurity it deserved.

The laconic and precise style of his writing expressed the same discretion: no lyrical effusions, no outbursts of feeling. "I was born on June 28, 1908, in the small market town of Lespezi, then in the county of Baia"—so begins his terse autobiography, a document of just a few pages, written not in 1949 for the dossier that was required of every citizen of the People's Republic of Romania but four decades later, at his son's request. In the 1990s, my father was no longer a director, the son no longer a commander in the Pioneers, and we were both far from the town where we used to live and far from each other.

At the age of five I started attending cheder, the beginning Hebrew school, where I was taught the rudiments of the Jewish alphabet. At seven, I started at the Jewish school in Lespezi. I learned Yiddish and Romanian. In 1916, my brother Aron was sent to the front, my father was conscripted. In 1917, there was an outbreak of typhus. My mother passed away in that year. I was left an orphan with my brother Nucǎ, three years my junior. I was only nine at the time, but I had to look after him as well, for about a year. Then an aunt of mine, a sister of my mother's, came from Ruginoasa, county of Iași, and took us both to live with her. Nucă started as a young, too young salesman in a food store, where he also received room and board, and I went to school. When my father came back from the army, he remarried, a young girl, Rebecca, from Liteni, in the county of Suceava. I stayed in Ruginoasa for a year to finish primary school. There was a cheder there as well, and I excelled because I already knew quite a lot from Lespezi.

The narrative continues:

At the end of that year in Ruginoasa, I returned to Lespezi to find I had a stepmother. I studied privately at the gymnasium in Pașcani, which meant that I did not attend classes, only sat for the examinations. Then I went on to high school in Fălticeni. I gave private lessons to primary-school children, in order to support myself. Afterward, I got a job at the glass factory in Lespezi. When the chief accountant moved on to the sugar factory in Ițcani, he took me along. So I started a more civilized life, among engineers, technicians, and economists. The factory had a canteen run by those who ate there. When my turn came, I arranged for sweets and pickles to be served, in addition to the more traditional fare, as I had learned to cook as a young man. In 1930, I was conscripted for military service. I first served with Infantry Regiment 16, in Fălticeni; then I returned to Ițcani, and to the factory, where I had a very good income. I could afford most things and was very contented. I worked at the sugar factory in Ițcani until the deportation, and was appreciated as a good organizer and accountant. At that time, each summer in Fălticeni there was a great annual fair, on St. Elias Day. The whole of Moldavia went. I would go every summer, and spend a whole Sunday there. In 1932, as I was returning from the fair, I spoke to the young woman sitting next to me on the bus. She looked like Mrs. Riemer, from Fălticeni. She told me she lived with her parents in Burdujeni, where her father, Mrs. Riemer's brother, ran a bookstore. Our idyll lasted three years. I used to go to Burdujeni on Sunday and would return to Ițcani in the evening by horse-drawn carriage. In 1935, we got married. I worked in the bookstore, and the book business seemed to go well, but after a while, the expenses started to exceed the revenue, so I returned to the factory. We moved to Iţcani, leaving my wife's parents to run the store. Maria came with us . . . you were born in 1936 . . . Our normal life ended in October 1941, when we were deported.

From among many family events, only a handful are mentioned:

In 1939, Anuţa, my brother Nucă's wife, died of a heart attack. She just collapsed suddenly, with her little girl in her arms. I arranged to be sent, along with a delegation, to the sugar factory in Roman in order to attend the funeral. My wife, Janeta, was in Botoşani and I did not tell her anything about it at the time. In 1939, the Legionnaires were already in power. Janeta wanted us to cross the border over into the Soviet Union, to save ourselves, but I didn't agree. When I returned from Roman, I told Janeta everything. We decided to take Ruti, my brother's little girl, until Nucă could remarry. When I came back to Roman, I found Ruti in very poor condition, malnourished, unwashed, and neglected. Her grandmother was decrepit, and Nucă had never been much of a housekeeper. I brought Ruti back with me to Iţcani. Maria, who had worked for my in-laws in Burdujeni, was there with us in Iţcani, and so was Clara, my sister. At the dinner table, I used to feed you, and Clara fed Ruti. Maria took good care of her and Ruti blossomed. Maria looked after her as lovingly as she did you. But our normal life ended in October 1941, when we were deported.

So, in 1939, Mother wanted to save us from the Romanian Legionnaires by crossing over to the Soviet Communists. That initiative would have assured us, probably, free travel to somewhere well beyond Transnistria, where we were sent, not long afterward, by the former ally of the Legionnaires, the self-appointed "General" Antonescu. We would have gone, like so many others, to that renowned tourist spot, Siberia, where we would have become acquainted, sooner than we actually did, with the benefits of Communism. Instead, the Red utopia came to us as the dictatorship of the proletariat, traveling west from Soviet Russia to Romania. We were unsure of its benefits in 1949, but we responded to its signals. Father, who in 1939 had been skeptical of the Red promises, became, albeit halfheartedly, a functionary of the Communist regime, and his son, the Pioneer with the red neckerchief, believed himself to be the embodiment of the new world's luminous future.

However, we had not forgotten the perilous lessons of the 1930s, and the memories of the deportation lasted longer than ten years, longer than fifty. Even my father's terse narrative acknowledges this:

> We were just collecting a few belongings in the house when the chief of gendarmerie, who knew me from the sugar factory, told me it was useless, we would have to walk a long way on foot and I would be able to carry only the two children. So we left everything in the house, we left with just a knapsack. I took you by the hand, Tătuță [his pet name for me, which persisted long beyond childhood], and carried Ruti in my arms. However, we took the 160,000 lei we had saved to buy a house. We were squeezed into cattle cars on top of each other. The train took a long time, day and night, and another day. When it stopped it was night. We were taken off in a market town called Ataki, by the Dniester River. Then the attack started. Many were robbed by the Romanian soldiers, some were thrown into the Dniester. Among these was a neighbor of ours, Rakover, the owner of the restaurant in the Ițcani railway station. In the morning, when the money exchange opened, the money had to be changed into rubles, at a rate of 40 lei to the ruble. A kind Romanian officer whispered to us, advising us not to change our money and to wait until we reached the other side of the river, where the rate was 6 lei per ruble. That tip saved us for a while. But the money did not last. Mother paid a lot to have her parents brought over to Moghilev, the day after we arrived from Ataki, by boat and on foot and in carriages. The old couple had remained in Ataki, on the other side of the Dniester. In Moghilev, there were six or more of us to one unheated room. I did all sorts of work. The pay was one German mark per day, those were the regulations. One kilogram of potatoes cost anything between two and three marks. We sold our watches, our rings, our clothes for food. Then we arrived in a village called Vindiceni, where there was

a sugar factory. Among the Romanian soldiers there was one who had worked in Ițcani, at the factory, and knew me. He would sometimes bring us bread, tea, and potatoes. That was where Maria found us. She arrived with two suitcases full of food and other things. Everything was confiscated. She stayed with us for a while, however, in all that poverty. She looked after the grandparents, both suffering from typhus, as well as after Janeta and Ruti. People would swap a gold ring just for a few aspirin or for bread. Only you and I, Tătuță, were never ill. In 1942, in the winter, old Avram, your grandfather, died. Three weeks later to the very day, the old woman, his wife, went, too. In Vindiceni, there was an extremely malicious administrator, one Rakhlisky, a brute; he would do anything to torment us, to destroy us. We moved on to Iurcăuți, to the spirits factory. Minna Graur was with us, the daughter of Rebecca, Janeta's sister.

The episode that had caused so many nervous breakdowns, and that acquainted me for the first time with the word "divorce," was narrated flatly, as if it were a minor detail: Minna Graur, Rebecca's daughter, was with us. Rebecca was Mother's older sister, and her daughter's name was taboo in our house. Minna was involved in a family scandal, and her name was never mentioned again, not until Mother went to the funeral of the guilty Minna's sister, Betty. Only then was the family reconciled to Minna and my father's adultery.

The officer in charge of the village summoned me to come to police headquarters. I knew him, he had treated us well. Without asking me anything, he took a bullwhip out of his drawer and started shouting, swearing, and hitting me savagely over the head with the whip. My head was swollen. I thought I was going to die. Finally, we ran away from the village. We arrived back in Moghilev. This happened after Stalingrad, when the German Army was retreating. When the Soviets arrived, we tried to follow them in their push toward Bessarabia and the Romanian border. However, the Russians caught me, conscripted me into the Red Army, and tried to send me to the front line. I escaped, running through the forest, keeping away from all human settlements for a few days. As if by miracle, I found you all in a small town called Briceni. It was there that, under Russian occupation, you started school.

One day, you came home and said you wanted to be in second grade with your cousins. I went to the school and talked to the teacher, and because you were a good pupil, you were allowed into the second grade. In April 1945, we were back in Fălticeni. First we lived with the Riemers. Leah Riemer was Janeta's aunt. Then we went over to Rădăuți. There I worked as an accountant at the office that coordinated the shipping of sheep and cattle to the Soviet Union, as stipulated in the armistice agreement. The animals had to be fed and looked after, so I hired veterinarians, assistants, and workers. Farming had not yet become socialist, and the Romanian exporters were present at the weighing of the animals, to make sure that everything went according to plan, as big profits were at stake. Many cattle were kept there for a while, if they were sick. Over 5,000 cattle and some 20,000 sheep were then handed over to the Russians, the new masters of Romania. The operation lasted until 1947. We then moved to Suceava.

Brevity was also noticeable in the way he talked about his reunion with Maria, after the war, and with Comrade Victor Varasciuc, her husband, as well as about his subsequent entry into the ranks of the Party. The laconic words were the mark of the man. He avoided talking about conflict, error, and failure, just as he avoided ambiguity. When asked, toward the end of his life, why he had never mentioned, not even to his own son, the fact that his wife had been married before or that she was four years older than he, he answered without hesitation, "What would have been the point?" Had I asked him about the Securitate officer who—after his release from Periprava—pressured him for a whole year into becoming an informer, and about how he had resisted, silently, calmly, stoically, until the police got tired, he would have said much the same thing: "What's the point of talking about this now? What's the point?"

The Departure

I n 1947, my father's younger sister turned up on our doorstep with the good news that she had made boat reservations not only for herself and her boyfriend but also for our family. Father's response was immediate: "I've just unpacked and have no energy left to start packing again." Of course, there was nothing to unpack after our return from Transnistria in 1945, so there wasn't much to repack in 1947. His little joke was just an attempt to cover up his reluctance to embark on adventures.

The question of departure haunted us periodically, and for good reason, but over time, I became the one reluctant to leave. The question arose again when I was at the university, in connection not only with Periprava, but also because of the emigration of a friend.

We had grown close a few weeks into the first academic year. Dark-haired, tall, slim, Rellu was a brilliant student and a music lover. He liked mathematics, basketball, and concerts, and even seemed willing to give literature a chance. He noticed my lack of enthusiasm for engineering studies, my long hours spent in Bucharest's libraries, as well as my dalliance with the beautiful daughter of the beautiful Mrs. Albert. He was aware of my discontents, my aspirations, my whims, and we became inseparable friends. His excessive, irritating sensitivity counterbalanced the equally irritating pragmatism that made him avoid anything complicated. However, none of these differences—not even his lack of interest in the opposite sex—were significant enough to stand in the way of our friendship.

In the spring of 1958, Rellu brought me some sensational news: his mother and sisters had decided to emigrate to Israel. They had filled out the forms and had included him in their plans. We had heated debates over the issue. It seemed like a millennium had passed since that cold day in December 1947 when the King's sudden abdication sent me flying home through the snow, muttering, "It's over, we're leaving now, immediately." The Zionist ideal, which had attracted me in the early postwar years, when I was drawn to the militant ideas of Vladimir Jabotinsky, had by now lost much of its appeal. Escape to the capitalist paradise beyond the Iron Curtain, with its trappings of well-being and illusions of freedom, now seemed a vulgar notion. I was skeptical of any childish attempts to alter destiny. Taking responsibility for, and understanding, our imperfect, ephemeral condition appeared to me preferable to a mere change of geographical coordinates.

Not only did my friend come to accept the idea of departure with serenity, he even adduced a few serious arguments in its favor. His father had disappeared in the Iaşi "death train" atrocity of 1941, when Jews, hunted out of their homes and dragged through the streets, found themselves packed together like sardines in the cars of a sealed freight train bound for nowhere. The train wandered the countryside aimlessly, in the summer heat, until the starved, suffocated bodies were nothing but corpses.

I was no stranger to such horrors myself. My Initiation had also begun in a freight car, sealed off and guarded by armed soldiers, but that train had a destination: its carload of captives was to be dumped onto the human garbage heap of a labor camp. Rellu's justification for departure, however, seemed to me somewhat rhetorical and "contrived." I had grown wary of attempts to intellectualize what were mere biographical circumstances. Even Periprava could not diminish the force with which my cowardice sought out the most pretentious justifications for staying.

The candidates for emigration to the Holy Land began lining up the night before, so that on the following day they would have a chance of reaching the desk where the magic application forms were being handed out. The wandering tribes were on the move again. It reminded me of our return to the land of the living, the rebirth of 1945. I recalled the voices and the colors of the fairy tale, the fairy-tale dishes and the fairy-tale book I received from my strange bookish cousins, the Riemer progeny, who were also my teachers. The blackboard covered a whole wall and was filled with formulas, tables, and puzzles. In that wondrous place I discovered the joys of normality, the colorful sideshow being put on by the relatives who had never been dislodged by war and transported to labor camps. I awoke each morning to a fresh new day, and I gamboled happily like a frisky lamb.

Yet suddenly, once again, the invisible bird of night swooped down on this sunny world of eternal youth and immortality to which I thought I had been securely transferred. Death struck like lightning, bringing down my young uncle Izu from the telegraph pole on which he was working. Father's younger brother was brought home dead, a few hours after he had left for work. Up there, on that rain-soaked electric pole, the invisible beak had struck. He had fallen in a single spasm, eyewitnesses said. He was seventeen. His face, in death, resembled the faces of those still alive: his father, Benjamin—called by his affectionate diminutive Buium—and his brothers, Aron and Marcu, who stood silent at his bier.

Not long after, the cry of the ominous bird was heard once again. This time it sounded for Grandfather Buium, struck down in the full afternoon summer light. His huge, dark figure collapsed suddenly, on the couch next to his wide-eyed grandson. I was petrified. The sudden crumpling of this Methuselah made my blood run cold. Time froze and I could no longer breathe. I remained there in a daze, until I saw, in the big mirror hanging above the sideboard, my grandmother's long, pale hand.

There had been some gossip about this statuesque old woman, whom we called Mamaia—though actually she was not so old—about the severity with which, as a young stepmother, she had treated the three orphaned sons of the widower Buium. I was shocked to see her looking at herself in the mirror, smoothing her hair! It was only a few seconds, or perhaps just one timeless second, since she had let out the scream that took account of the disaster. Her gaze met the wide-eyed stare of her grandson in the mirror. Embarrassed, she readjusted her mask of sorrow. Her moaning and gasping increased, but things would never be the same again between her and the grandson.

In an instant, Izu, the youngest of them all, and Buium, the oldest, were gone. Then Mamaia vanished, too, settling, with her daughters Luci and Anuţa, in the faraway Promised Land near the shores of the Dead Sea. Most of the family were to follow, taking with them their ancient names—Rebecca, Aron, Rachel, Ruth, David, Esther, Sarah, Eliezer, Moshe—names that had wandered for hundreds of years through foreign lands and among foreign peoples and tongues, now returning to the place and language where they thought they belonged. The echo of those names would gradually fade, and with them their famed qualities—their mercantile spirit and group solidarity, their anxiety and tenacity, their mysticism and realism, their passion and lucidity. Where did I fit in among all these stereotypes? Had I also been affected by their suspicion, by all the embarrassment and hostility that the environment had injected, insidiously, into all of us?

I no longer felt at ease among the names and reputations of my fellow clansmen, nor did I feel bound by the fluctuations of their nomadic destiny. Had I become alienated from those among whom I had been reborn ten years earlier? In truth, I felt relieved to know that they were safe in their faraway ancestral homeland—and that I was now freed from their proximity. Their vanities, their impatience, frustrations, hypocrisies, and rhetoric were not, in fact, worse than other people's, but I was happy to be able to forget about them and to no longer be associated with them. I held no grudges against their exodus, it was a proof of normality that I accepted with undisguised relief. The chimera that had claimed me seemed to have created between us a divide that was wider than any physical distance. The geographic space between us came only as a necessary, protective confirmation.

What about my friend Rellu, and what about Periprava? Rellu now strapped on his own nomad's knapsack and joined the ranks of the dreamers and the rejected. The haste of these emigrants to leave the socialist utopia, each with nothing more than a single bundle, spoke volumes about the impasse they were leaving behind. Never before, not even in the immediate aftermath of war, had so many been in such a hurry to pack up and go. The lines forming to join the exodus were different from the routine lines for food or fuel or clothes, but they were not unconnected. I was well aware of the baggage of memories, passions, and anxieties these nomads were taking with them.

A firsthand account of this moment in history, October 1958, complements my own ambiguous response:

> At first the Jews began queuing for their emigration applications to Israel around three o'clock in the morning. Now they start at two, one, and even eleven o'clock the night before. They are ruined small-tradespeople, old people who have no family left, but also Party members, directors, and directors-general in ministries, civil servants in central state institutions, cadres from the political apparatus, from the militia and the Securitate. The impact of the queues is powerful. I am a Jew myself, but even I am beginning to experience strange feelings . . .

These lines were written by a Romanian writer named Nicu Steinhardt, who continued:

> The simple gesture of taking one's passport out of one's pocket seems like sleight of hand, it has something of a cheap trickster's magic about it. Or it seems like something that an odious mama's boy might do: I'm not playing anymore, I'm going back to Mama. Or it seems like the winning gambler who gets up from his seat, grabs the money, and leaves: I'm going home. I'm not playing anymore. So, you take everybody to the dance, you urge them on, you pay the fiddlers, you get the party go-

ing, you cheer them on, you are one of them—and then you just drop
out, you leave them all standing there like idiots: So long, I'm leaving.
The trick, the scam, the treachery, the lie! Any man in his right mind
cannot help but be disgusted, others merely smile. The more simple-
minded are piqued, envious, and bear baleful grudges for an eternity to
come.

This passage is followed by a narrative on Cervantes and a tale about a traitor, one Judas, a symbol, obviously, of all that Judas and his co-religionists
have always symbolized.

The original—but maybe not so original—transfer of hatred, from
hatred of others to self-hatred and vice versa, is not difficult to read
in these lines. I was probably not immune myself at that time to such
miserable subtleties, but I managed to remain more detached than their
author, a future Orthodox monk.

Arrested in 1960 together with a group of intellectual friends, all accused of "conspiring against the social order," the writer was condemned to twelve years' hard labor, seven years of civil degradation, and
the confiscation of all personal wealth. Prison for the Jew Steinhardt was
a place of revelation, where he found Christ and converted not only to
the Christian faith but also to the "heroism" of the Legionnaires, themselves condemned for "conspiracies," albeit of a less intellectual nature.
His subsequent book, *A Diary of Happiness*, in which he narrates his experiences in prison and the bliss of religious conversion, would become
a best-seller and required reading for elite Romanian audiences of the
post-Communist period.

My own reaction to the Jews and non-Jews who were choosing to
leave Romania sprang from a more private, less grand irritation. As a
teenager I had dreams that were radically different from those of the
young Jew Nicu Steinhardt, who saw himself as the savior of his hero,
Corneliu Codreanu, the anti-Semitic Iron Guard "captain." I had a different way of assessing the consequences of the heroic "betrothal to
Death" promulgated by the Legionnaires. My own Initiation had been
nothing less than a mystical betrothal to transcendence, and I would
probably have been incapable, even in prison, of asking forgiveness from

a Legionnaire for the fact that I was a Jew, as did the new convert to Christianity, Nicu Steinhardt.

The attempt to flee the Communist cage seemed to me both justified and vulgar. I was not complaining about the mental handicap that prevented me from making this natural decision, and I would have preferred it if my friend Rellu had shared the same handicap. Was his moral argument for leaving the country prompted by the fact that this was the scene of the brutal anti-Semitic murder of his father, the same country that never offered his family the least official apology for the atrocity, just as my own family had never received one after Transnistria? I was irritated by those who invoked such reasons. My cynicism had reached such depths that I regarded those horrors as a mere step toward the great, ubiquitous, universal crime, Death, the premise of all our lives. Premature death, violent death, was just the same old, plain, unfair death, and it did not matter how and where it hunted us down—such was my insensitive logic on the matter. In the heat of debate, I did not seem to care to whom I was addressing such words.

I had a bond, naturally, with Nicu Steinhardt's anger. There was a certain connection between us, but the differences between us remained unbridgeable. Romanian citizenship did not appear to me as exalted as it did to Nicu Steinhardt, who regarded it as a certificate of membership in the gentlest and most Christian people on the planet. No, for me, being Romanian was a fact, nothing more, nothing less. I had no liking for "transfigured" people, be they Romanian, French, Paraguayan, or Cambodian. Lacking the comfort of religious faith, as well as the convert's passionate nationalism, I believed that those who chose to change their citizenship were no worse than those who changed their faith. No, I would not ask forgiveness from the Legionnaire who, on the contrary, should himself kneel and beg the Jew's pardon. Was I condescending toward my poor fellow Jews, lining up for their exodus? Did I feel contempt for their lucidity? In the same way that the Christianized Jew and litterateur Steinhardt spasmodically defended his chimeras, I, the agnostic Jew and litterateur-to-be, defended mine. It was not religion or nationalism that kept me in Romania but language and all the chimeras it offered—and not only language and its chimeras, but my whole life, of course, with its good and bad, a life of which language and its chimeras were the essence.

When my friend Rellu spoke about the adventure on which he was about to embark, he displayed none of the con man's "scam," as Steinhardt so elegantly put it. There was nothing in him of the "odious mama's boy" or of the "winning gambler who gets up from his seat, grabs the money, and leaves." This did not describe any member of my family either, all hardworking, humble people, living in privation and fear. The applicants for the perils of uprootedness are not necessarily worse than those who accept the hazards of rootedness. In the country where they had lived for so many generations, there had not been many "winners" among them, certainly not of big money. Even those who had "danced" the waltz of Communism, even those who had paid the "fiddlers" and cheered at the masquerade, had a right to admit their error and to leave for the other end of the earth, taking their guilt with them. My relatives did not, however, belong to this category either, and neither did Rellu. That accusation would have applied appropriately to me, the Red teenager, the inflexible thirteen-year-old commissar. Yet I chose to stay, not because I considered myself guilty or because I still believed in the "specter that haunted Europe." Rather, I had found another chimera that, unlike the political one, made no promises of happiness to anyone.

No, my friend Rellu embodied not "the trick, the scam, the treachery, the lie" of Steinhart's scornful litany but its very opposite, and neither was he a traitorous Judas. Far from being "disgusted," any people in their "right mind" had every reason to envy him for seizing an opportunity they wished for themselves—to leave the country. Had the gates been opened to all, irrespective of nationality and not on the basis of the deliberate campaign of discrimination aimed at the "evil" of which the country had repeatedly tried to rid itself, then the lines of people seeking to get out would have criss-crossed the land. It was not the first time that Jews were the object of such campaigns, but this time their departure confirmed the failure of Communism in Romania, the happiest place on earth, according to Father Steinhardt. Their departure was an indictment of Communism, with which Steinhardt and his partners in philosophical debate—themselves arrested for anti-state and anti-Party "conspiracy"—should have agreed as a matter of course.

Measures placing a cap on emigration were soon introduced and reprisals launched against those who applied. Rellu, immediately expelled from the university, was lucky to escape early. In the spring of 1959, I saw him to his train for Vienna, from where he would proceed to Italy, where he would board a boat for Israel. The moment of separation was charged with emotion. His mother asked me, smiling, just as the train was about to pull out, "How am I going to cope with him without you?" It was hard to tell whether she referred simply to the disruption of our friendship or whether she meant more. Awkwardly, Rellu handed me a thick notebook, which turned out to be a diary of our happy youthful friendship. Reading his tidy hand, which covered the wide pages, I soon discovered an account of an intense, even erotic affection of which neither of us had really been aware. His departure signaled the end of an era we had lost forever. On the first page of the notebook he had written: "The separation from the main character of these pages seems irreversible. It is only natural that this journal should stay with him." The world that lay ahead would be deciphered only by a cryptic code to which neither of us had the key. I did not see much chance of a reunion.

I left the station, on that soft spring evening in Bucharest, filled with questions, but I had no doubt that my decision to stay, in spite of all the servitude that would be demanded of me, and the dangers, was the right one—right for me, that is. I did not believe that changing the place from which I observed the game-play of the world, or changing the religion into which I had been born, would improve my chances for happiness. In any case, I was suspicious of such changes, and even viewed them with contempt. The "common people," I thought, can continue sucking on their dumb lollipop of hope, they can keep on believing in instant rewards. My claustrophobic survival depended on other reflexes, but it would have been unfair, I admitted, for others to adopt my strategy.

What about the prisoner of Periprava, exhausted by his forced labor and humbled by his prison uniform? What strategy for survival could I suggest to him, forever indifferent, as he was, to rewards, wishing simply to be left alone to live in peace and dignity? That question opened up an emptiness in my brain, in my stomach, in my heart. Fidelity to a chimera—a fierce selfishness—had, once again, proved stronger. I had been busy constructing my own rhetoric of self-justification. I had no wish to join the ranks of the free in all their competitions, least of all in a foreign place. I had nothing to offer on the free market, the handicap of exile would annihilate me. I was content with the local brand of discontent and could do without the complicated adventure of escape. Impoverished in my twisted socialist tunnel, I even felt, probably, a glimmer of satisfaction with the socialist attempt to "equalize" unhappiness, to diminish social divides by reducing opportunities for the greedy acquisition of money, honors, and position. This sleight of hand was by no means innocent. The crises which my parents underwent periodically— especially Mother, whose links to family and Israel were strong—failed to move me.

Unswerving fidelity to a chimera may look like a good thing, but I suspected it would lead me into trouble. Could such fidelity, by no means a mystical matter, nevertheless possess quasi-religious aspects? It sometimes seemed that only mystical faith, even in this bizarre variant, could lend meaning to life in the socialist tunnel. I could not guess at the time that, one day thirty years later, my turn to leave would come, when I would apply for a passport in honor of old Leopold Bloom.

The Night Shift

In the early 1960s, I was busy building apartment blocks in the center of Ploieşti. I suppose the nine-story edifice, the so-called Pergola Block, next to the covered market, is still standing, one of the mitigations for my sin of not having had children or for having written ephemeral books.

The quick pace of Ploieşti came as a shock to the slow-moving Bukovinan that I was, even after my years in Bucharest as a student. A more senior engineer had warned me to "keep a close eye" on people's movements at the building site. "You can wake up one morning and find that there are fifty bags of cement missing, or that you've signed for twenty loads of concrete more than you actually received, or that you've been supplied with only half the amount of brick mentioned in the invoice." What he hadn't told me, though, was how I could become a good policeman, when I was not even sure if I was a good engineer.

Before working on the Pergola Block, then the tallest building in the new town center, I had done my apprenticeship with the L-Block, which stood on the opposite side of the market and was only four stories high. As the youngest of the site's engineers, I had been assigned to the night shift. So, from six in the evening till dawn, I worked not only with the regular construction crew but also with a group of prisoners. The contract with the local penitentiary, regarding the number of workers, the skills required, the working hours and days, and the payment due by the Building Trust, had been signed by the prison's commanding officer, Major Drăghici, brother of the feared Minister of the Interior and member of the Politbureau.

If, in my early days at the university in 1954, I had practically fainted at my first encounter with the eggplant and the cucumber concoctions in the student canteen, what was I supposed to do at the sight of prisoners and guards? In fact, nothing happened. I did not faint as I saw the prisoners, in their drab uniforms, being brought in by the guards, just as I had not fainted at Periprava in 1958, seeing my father, in his dun-colored prison garb, being watched by guards. I turned pale and speechless, as I had done before, but I did not faint. In any case, contact with the inmates was to be kept to a strict minimum, and I was only allowed to deal, in the guard's presence, with their foreman, himself a former construction worker. Moreover, the inmates and their guards were restricted to specific areas of the building site. I had asked the boss if there were any political detainees among the prisoners and was assured that the crew contained only "common criminals." I knew very well, from my own family history, that this designation was as little to be believed as any other in the farcical socialist lexicon.

The inmates were given a chance to reduce their sentences by working outside the prison, and their participation in the building of the town's new center was more to their benefit than to the Building Trust's— after all, Ploieşti, even from dusk to dawn, was hardly Periprava. In actual fact, many of the inmates could well have been "common criminals." Socialist deception did not exclude a measure of truth, however perverted. The work itself was not too demanding, and it was certainly better than being locked up all the time.

For all the assurances meant to calm my apprehensions, I still went to work each evening in a state of anxiety, mindful not only of what I was supposed to sign for—the number of loads of concrete, bags of cement and bricks—but also of the tricks that the prisoners or the guards might be trying to play on me. I was never fully at ease. As soon as evening set in, the women would appear, slinking through the still-wet concrete and the exposed girders. Carrying parcels or bulging envelopes, wide-eyed with impatience, they came to meet their husbands or brothers or lovers and to give them their offerings. The measures taken to bar the women from the building site did not keep them out. One after another, they kept coming, silently, stealthily.

I tried to shut my eyes to the "network" that facilitated these nocturnal trysts. Apparently, I had been studied by the prison contingent, who concluded that I was all right and would keep my silence about these visits. You never knew, however, where the next challenge might come from, where the next trap was being set. I had been approached more than once, outside the gates of the site, or while I was working, by relatives of the inmates or go-betweens, and it was difficult to tell them apart from the agents provocateurs. At dawn, I breathed a sigh of relief. I returned to my shabby room, improvised from a hut, where, on the iron bed, my Juliet lay sleeping.

What had been the point of my Initiation between the ages of five and nine, if, at twenty-five, I was unable to set fire to myself in the public marketplace—like those protesting Buddhist monks in Vietnam—to denounce the Big Lie that encased our lives like the thin shell of an egg? As you touched it, the membrane burst, and you suddenly found yourself alone and helpless, at the mercy of a whip wielded by authority. If in a moment of madness, you shouted out, "The Party has no clothes," the eggshell would disintegrate in an instant. You were immediately pinned by your arms, like the demented criminal you indeed were, as witnesses stepped forward to confirm your malfeasance. The Big Lie, like a new placenta, prevented us from both dying and being born. One imprudent gesture and the filmy membrane exploded. You had to hold your breath and check yourself constantly, so that your mouth, choked with lies big and small, did not let out, involuntarily, the breath of air that could have shattered the protective cocoon. In fact, we were constantly wrapping the eggshell in other coverings, one inside another, like a nest of Russian dolls. So, what was this blessed Big Lie? An egg-shaped plate of armor? A gift from Mother Nature? The membrane of lies had become, for many, a thick protective coating, dense, indestructible, resistant to cracking. Inside the armor-plated egg—the penal colony of the Big Lie—the prisoners were condemned to compulsory happiness.

I did not puncture that filmy membrane. Like so many others, I had my private compensations. I ignored, as well as I could, the shell under which I went about my business. My main concern was to ignore the public sphere, remain simply the "engineer" who was paid for his work, and nothing more. The day was young, like myself, the city vivid and alive, a sanctuary of eternal summer, like my Juliet.

Juliet had just managed to avoid being expelled from the university. A fellow student had sent a "memorandum" to the dean, alluding to the dubious morality of the dark-haired maid of Verona. She had been asked to appear at the same office where, about eight years earlier, I had been summoned by the future Foreign Minister. The rector of the university had been fired only days before and this seemed a favorable moment for the "unmasking" of his niece's immoral behavior. However, a few days later, it turned out that the rector had not, in fact, been demoted, but promoted. Overnight, Juliet's uncle had become a vice minister, and the whole episode collapsed.

There I was, once more, sitting on the terrace of the Boulevard restaurant, in the center of Ploieşti, opposite my building site. I was celebrating the sixties, the time when Western Europe was staging its great youth rebellions, while Eastern Europe was learning to adapt itself, more stringently, to the ambiguity being served up in uncertain and calculated portions. The street below was vibrant with passing humanity. All I had to do, it seemed, to pull up a plump catch, was drop my fishing line. I was waiting for the revelation that reality was real, and that I was real, and that I was meant to discover its meaning, its secret, its justification. At any moment, the gods were about to grant me some encrypted privilege, as I moved on from one stage of my life to another.

I was eating grilled sturgeon, washed down with a light, slightly acidic wine. I was smoking Greek cigarettes and looking into the eyes of my Juliet—and also sneaking a peek at the other *jeunes filles en fleur*, there in the seventh-floor Boulevard restaurant, in the Romanian town of Ploieşti, close to the 45th parallel. I didn't give a damn about the Party or the Securitate. I was young, but considered myself old, knowing, justified in my ignoring of the penal colony and its assorted inmates, political prisoners or otherwise. My head was abuzz with all the political, revolutionary, counter-revolutionary, and even liberal and humanist ideas I had gained from my reading, but when all was said and done, I simply didn't give a damn about anything. World history bored me, my own history was running according to its own beat, as I ate my fish and smoked my Papastratos, alive to the day's rhythms and not concerned about Comrade Gheorghe Gheorghiu-Dej's illness, absorbed with my Juliet and all the other Juliets around me and not with the disaster of the Vietnam War. I tried to flee into the picaresque particulars of a profession that was alien to me. Eager to know more about the unknown people who crossed my path, exultant in the mountains and the sea that always received me in triumph, avid for the books that might hold the answers to my questions, I did not wish to be drawn into the world's unhappiness, not even that of my immediate world. I was old and tired, but also obscenely young, engorged with desire and confusion.

"Comrade engineer, your mother is calling, she's on the line." The secretary had run to the top of the scaffolding, where I was supervising the pouring of the cement. "Hurry up, she's waiting. She called yesterday, too, from Suceava. She says she hasn't had any news from you for the last two weeks." Two weeks . . . the boy hadn't written home for two whole weeks, horror of horrors. Now he was running along the concrete-sheathed girders, past the piles of bricks and the heaps of glass panes, rushing to assure his mother that there was nothing wrong, that nothing bad had happened, that there was no catastrophe. His tribe's sufferings no longer interested him, he was far away from Mater Dolorosa and the ghetto's claws—but it would never seem far enough.

The past was hunting me down, always one step behind, and caught up with me when least expected. The escape into books, the majesty of the mountains and the sea, erotic adventure, politics, dictatorship, the fragile egg of the Big Lie—nothing could compete with the tyranny of affections. The velvet claw was always there, ready to reassert its power, its strength, its permanence. Was this a surrogate for normality, the metabolism of duplicity? Why couldn't twenty million people join in unison to voice their discontent and self-interest, why couldn't they all explode, simultaneously, in a burst of collective revolt? Were they all protected by the membrane of the eggshell? "Protected, protected," my brain repeated, as I ran past the wet concrete and the piles of bricks. I was an old man on the run, escaped from the tribe's clutches without having really escaped. At the age of twenty-five I no longer had time, or eyes, or ears for the political cacophony, for all the speeches, threats, police, prisoners, choruses festive and mournful, the fireworks, all the tragedies and comedies of the socialist reality.

I had no time, no eyes, no ears for any of this—or did I? Perhaps I did.

The Snail's Shell

The crook who had married Avram Braunstein's daughter and squandered her dowry forced the old man to sell the house he had bought just one year before. It was always possible to buy a house, he told himself, but his beloved daughter's peace of mind was more precious. Not long after, the true, intended son-in-law appeared, charmed by the partner sent to him as a gift from St. Elias.

After the wedding, the new couple started saving for a new house. In October 1941, they had almost accumulated the necessary sum. However, in the end, the money would be used to negotiate destiny's pathways in that terrible winter of the Initiation. The return, in the spring of 1945, did not mean coming home. The houses they left had been reallocated, the personal property sequestered. The survivors had to be content with their survival. My grandparents had died, my parents had survived, and so had we, the younger survivors. The house of their dreams was gone; now the socialist state owned all the houses and all the inhabitants.

The building of Our Bookstore in Burdujeni and the living quarters behind the shop where I was born had been relegated to memory—the pale yellow walls, the door perpetually open in the summer, the colorful interior filled with books, pencils, and notebooks; the back rooms, dark, crammed. I had no recollection of the house in Iţcani, it remained in that historyless time from before the Initiation. It was shown to me, many years after we returned from the labor camp. It stood opposite the railway station, behind a park full of benches, a solid house, in the Germanic style, with a severe façade, flaking paint, a sort of ocher in color, rectangular windows aligned on the front. Entry was through the courtyard.

In the postwar years, I had frequent occasion to be in and out of the railway station, but I was never curious enough to go into the courtyard of the house across the way and walk up the two steps leading to the front door. I also have no memory of the rooms where I languished during the four years in the labor camp, windowless and doorless, with many families crammed together, which I know about mainly from hearsay. Nor do I have any recollection of the houses we lived in in Bessarabia, after the Red Army liberated us—lost spaces all, belonging to a lost time. Only after our return did time recover me, and space, too, began to acquire a shape.

In July 1945 I was restored to fairy-tale normality; the new habitation was in the house of our relatives, the Riemers, in Fălticeni. I recall a room in semidarkness, an imperial-style bed, with its iron bedstead, old-fashioned cushions, and a bedspread of yellow plush, whitewashed walls, a round black table, two chairs, a narrow window covered by heavy curtains. For the first time I felt at home. That time, too, probably marked the beginning of something different from and beyond the immediate calendar. The green book of folktales I had received for my ninth birthday opened up for me the world of the word-magicians who became my new family.

My grandfather had invested his money in a house; my parents, in the early years of their marriage, were saving up to buy a house. After the war, when the state became the sole landlord, people were no longer looking for houses to buy but for shelters. In 1947, after our return to

Suceava, we moved into a rented house, on a street that ran parallel to the main street, next to a small, pretty, triangle-shaped park. We had the last apartment on the left side of a single-story building. The entrance was around the corner, through a sort of veranda. One small room was used as a kitchen, which opened onto a shared dark corridor, from which one descended into the basement, used to store potatoes and jars of pickled vegetables. In the corridor to the right stood a basin fitted into a wooden stand, with grooves for soap and toothbrush glasses. On the opposite wall were the towel racks. Water came from a well in the courtyard and was stored in a tank next to the basin.

The first door to the right led to our rooms. The next door, also on the right, led to the apartment of Nurse Strenski, who, not long after we moved in, married an apathetic but gentle drunk. The door at the bottom of the corridor opened onto the communal lavatory, a tall, narrow room, one step wide, the toilet lacking a seat, the flush chain rusted and useless. Water was brought in a bucket from the tank in the corridor.

Our apartment consisted of two medium-sized rooms. The first, the sitting room, where we had our meals and received our guests, also served as a bedroom and workroom for the family's two schoolchildren. The next room was the parents' bedroom, with the massive family wardrobe. There were no pictures on the walls, but in the front room, over one of the beds, was a rectangular photograph in a thin black wooden frame, history's festive recording of the young Pioneer receiving his red neckerchief on Revolution Day, when the young activist made his fiery speech in the public square and saluted the red banner on which golden letters spelled out, in Russian: TO STALIN.

My student lodgings were also fine examples of socialist Jormania's residential regulations—eight square meters per person. Old Mrs. Adelman rented me her only room, at the back of the courtyard, on 27 Mihai Vodă Street, near Podul Izvor, in order to augment her meager income. There was a table, two chairs, and a bed. The lavatory was shared with the neighbors, Captain Tudor, who was always away on training exercises, and his always available wife, also occupying a single room. Proletarian equality had divided the old bourgeois house into units for several socialist families. On cold winter nights, old Mrs. Adelman would bring her folding bed from the communal kitchen, where she now slept, and install it next to her old bed, given up to her boarder.

The move to the row of townhouses off Calea Călărași marked a step up. In one of these, I rented a room from Dr. Jacobi, a pediatrician who worked mainly at the hospital but also saw the occasional illegal patient at home. The glass door of his consulting room would open when you would least expect it. Out would come fat Mrs. Jacobi, jealous of her husband, or Marian, their son, a timid grind studying to become a dentist, who squirmed under his mother's thumb, yet was always ready to tell stories about his father's mistress, a garrulous, aggressive Gypsy who lived in the basement.

As I moved from one rented room to another, my suitcase was the only space I could really call my own. But after my marriage, I finally became officially entitled to a room, all housing being administered by the state. It was a pleasant room, overlooking the street, in an apartment on Metropolitan Nifon Street, not far from Liberty Park. We shared the bathroom, kitchen, and hall with a couple of old-age pensioners who lived next door.

The next move, both into and out of the spacious apartment on Sfîntul Ion Nou Street, near Union Market, afforded a good illustration of the socialist Byzantine comedy. One of the two apartments on the third floor of the apartment house was occupied by Cella's parents, an uncle, and an aunt. In the other apartment, her grandparents occupied a room, while the other two rooms were home to a theater director and his family. When the director successfully applied to emigrate to Germany, we were given the opportunity to move into the vacated room. According to housing regulations, Cella's grandparents could exercise an option right on the space for occupation by close relatives, and we, as their granddaughter and her husband, qualified. The two rooms, of course, were more than the one room usually permitted, but the law allowed for an extra room for members of artists' and writers' unions or scientific researchers, to be used as a study. Beyond the law, there was the customary baksheesh and string-pulling. At last we were installed in a respectable middle-class home, two big rooms, high ceilings, a hall, bathroom, and kitchen.

On the fatal night of the big earthquake of March 4, 1977, Cella came home from work carrying a box of pastries she had bought in town. I was in the study, sitting on the red couch by the night table, listening to Radio Free Europe. I rose to greet her when suddenly the room began to shake, the furniture shuddered, and the wall-length bookshelves collapsed noisily onto the very spot where I had been sitting a few seconds earlier. Terrified, we took shelter inside the door frame. Then we ran down the staircase filled with debris, out into the street. We joined a crowd of frightened people, lost and wandering among the collapsed buildings, and made our way to the center of the city. By now it was nearly midnight. We looked at each other with relief and realized that only good luck had saved us, Cella from being crushed under the wreckage of the Scala pastry shop's baked goods, and me under the fallen bookshelves.

The next year, Cella's grandparents decided, in spite of their advanced age, to emigrate to Israel. We had no rights to their room and didn't qualify for the whole apartment. Accordingly, we notified the housing authorities that we would like to be allocated a new two-room apartment, as our current residence, now a three-room apartment, could be assigned only to a larger family or to a family belonging to the *nomenklatura*. If some Party bigwig had been interested in the apartment, he could probably have arranged for us to receive a suitable apartment in its place. Indeed, second-echelon Party activists and a few vice ministers did come to see the place, but weren't impressed by it. Apparently, we had underestimated the tastes and aspirations of the people's representatives. We made useless appeals for help to the Writers Union, placing our hopes in its own bigwigs and in its channels of communication with the authorities.

For two weeks after the old couple's departure, nothing happened. Then, one morning, a family of Gypsies showed up with an authorization to take occupancy of the empty room—a father, a mother, their daughter, and a fourth member of the ensemble, in prominent view, an accordion. They had no furniture, just a few bundles, which they began to unpack. They then hammered nails into the walls, from which they strung a rope, onto which they hung all their possessions. The occupancy accomplished, the father grabbed the accordion and treated us to some lively cadenzas.

Our new neighbors' cheeriness was in marked contrast to our more dour mien. Until we could find a way of solving the impasse, we ceded the entire kitchen to them, on condition that the bathroom would remain exclusively ours. For their rare ablutions, they could use the kitchen sink and the second toilet off the corridor. However, very quickly, they managed to invade the bathroom, and came and went as they pleased, as though we had never reached an agreement. The smell of roast sausages and the sounds of the accordion dominated our shared home, from dawn till late at night.

There was only one solution left—to take extreme measures. After suffering for a year, one Monday morning, at ten o'clock, I showed up at the Writers Union, to remind its vice president of our previous discussions. I also informed him that if, by 2 p.m., the issue was not resolved, I would hold a press conference in the apartment for the foreign press. I would show them how our poor working classes lived—three persons, mother, father, and daughter, sleeping on the floor in the same room and sharing a bathroom and kitchen with the couple next door, who were rather averse to the trio's incessant accordion playing. My colleague, the representative of the state, attempted to calm me down. He understood, however, that it was to no avail, and anyway, the microphones in his office had already relayed my threats to the appropriate authorities. He made a phone call and, after a brief conversation, informed me that I had an appointment at the Party's Central Committee, entrance B, floor 3, room 309, at eleven, in half an hour's time.

Once in the inner sanctum, I was invited to sit down before a panel of four comrades. They seemed equal in rank and probably came from different departments—Culture, Ethnic Minorities, Security, and, who knows, maybe even Foreign Press, given the nature of my threat. I was invited to summarize the situation, and then was questioned by each member of the panel. Finally, I was asked whether I could suggest a solution. I repeated what I had already said: one year earlier, prior to the old couple's departure, I had suggested that the apartment be allocated to someone legally entitled to occupy it and that my wife and I, in return, be given a smaller, more appropriate residence. Yes, they were aware, mistakes had been made, but did I, they asked, have a concrete proposal in mind?

Actually, I did. The numberless small ads that I had placed, seeking an apartment exchange, had finally yielded a result, which the comrades might take into consideration. A lieutenant-colonel from the Executive Command, with a wife and a son in his last year of high school, were willing to move into our three-room apartment, in exchange for their two-room apartment, at no. 2 Calea Victoriei. However, this required special approval from the army, complex formalities, as the lieutenant-colonel explained. I gave them the officer's name, and one of the members of the panel, a grumpy-looking sort, signaled to his bald colleague, who dialed the number of Comrade Lieutenant-Colonel, who confirmed what I had said.

Suddenly the Party activists relaxed and I was assured that everything would soon be sorted out. I was even presented—would you believe it—with an apology for the misunderstanding. It was a splendid day, and as I walked home, I told myself that I didn't give a damn about the pages that I was certain would now be added to my already bulging dossier. The threat of an international press conference, it seemed, had had an immediate effect. Was this a good sign, a bad sign? Was it all a farce meant to put my nerves to sleep, before the dropping of the final ax?

I was in no hurry to get home. The day was sunny and this latest development was a lift to my spirits. I arrived at no. 26 Sfîntul Ion Nou Street around one in the afternoon. I did not take the elevator but climbed the stairs to the third floor. The accordion must have been resting or wandering through town. Our neighbors' door was wide open, with no signs of life inside. I looked in—nothing, nobody, not even the rope strung from one wall to the other, no bundles on the floor, absolutely nothing. As if no one was ever there. The windows were wide open; a ghost had taken pains to air the room.

As I went out, bewildered, I bumped into the building superintendent, who was just dropping by to let me know that the Gypsy troupe had been taken away, bundled into a truck and driven off. Who had taken them? Nobody knew for sure, but it must have been on the orders of somebody higher up. The socialist circus had performed with admirable dispatch, with a magician's deftness and efficiency. Within one single hour, a whole year's tensions had evaporated.

The two rooms at no. 2 Calea Victoriei—one half of a pre-socialist apartment—would be my last residence in Romania. The hooligan had finally abandoned his high-wire act and had become what he had been reluctant to admit—a writer; a dissident writer, to boot. I had quietly published, in a provincial magazine, a few critical lines about the new Romanian National Socialism. The official attack was prompt. The stone-throwing came from every quarter: I became overnight "extraterritorial," a "traitor," an "enemy of the Party." In due course, time tore away my masks, one by one—my caution, my timidity, my sense of humor. My insomnia grew worse. I would wake up each morning deprived of yet another of my masks. Before long, I risked losing whatever had remained of my habits as a quiet, respectable citizen. I did not enjoy the new farce. The hooligan had not forgotten the hooligan war, or the years of hooligan peace.

Time passed swiftly. It seemed as if only a second had elapsed from that distant afternoon forty years ago when I had heard the voice—mine and yet not mine—coming at me from everywhere and from nowhere, assuring me that I was not alone in the universe, as I had thought. Alone in that strange room in the Riemers' house in Fălticeni, and alone in the universe, I had discovered another home, another universe, and another self. The world of books would become my new home. I lived in this world throughout my apprenticeship years, in Suceava, my fling with revolution, the years of engineering study in Bucharest, my stay in the houses of old Rebeca Adelman, and Dr. Jacobi, and all the other shelters where I dragged my baggage of illusions, my only personal possessions.

Had I really been protected, as I had hoped, by analytic geometry and the resistance of materials and the structure of building and fluid mechanics and hydroelectrics—had all these protected me from the surrounding demagogy or from the fault lines in my own mind? Duplicity, split personality, schizophrenia were teaching us how to bury collective history deep within our personal history. My need for "something else" had not diminished, however. I had taken refuge in the home that only books could promise. The double exile of the divided ego—was that a redeeming disease? Had the hope of protecting myself from myself been replaced, finally, by the hope of recapturing myself? I followed my own zigzagging route, toward and away from myself, trying to get back to myself, to replace myself and to lose myself, and then do the same all over again. The deprivations I suffered and the dangers I risked had, in the meantime, become everybody's lot, as if everyone had to atone for some obscure crime. Under the terror, my attractions to books intensified, and I acquired invisible partners in dialogue who, by offering their companionship, delayed death.

In the room on Mitropolit Nifon Street, next to Liberty Park, where I lived with Cella in the first year of our marriage, I was finally granted the privilege, in the summer of 1969, of listening to my own voice in my own book. The volume had green covers, just like the one in 1945.

I had finally found my true home. Language promised not only a rebirth but also a form of legitimization, real citizenship, and real belonging. Exile from this ultimate place of refuge would have been the most brutal form of extirpation, would have touched the very fiber of my being.

Fifty years of a hooligan century had passed since Grandfather Avram had asked whether the newborn infant had the fingernails necessary for survival. In 1986, history seemed to recycle its black farces. Did Augustus the Fool get tired of the old role of victim? The Initiation had been precocious, and its educational value relative. I had delayed leaving the motherland I had regained in 1945 out of some hypnotic illusion that I could substitute language for homeland. Now all that was left for me to do was to take language, my home, with me.

I would be carrying the snail's shell on my back. Wherever the shipwreck would toss me, the snail's shell, the juvenile refuge, was still to be my true home.

The Claw (II)

My struggle against the ghetto was, above all, a struggle against the anxieties, the exaggerations, and the panic that my mother possessed to excess, and that she also transmitted, in excess, to all those around her. I did not emerge victorious from this never-ending confrontation, I merely survived.

"The only comfort, as I went to bed, was that my mother would come and kiss me good-night," as Proust wrote, is alien to my life story. The Jewish Jeanne-Clémence Weil, married to the Catholic Dr. Achille-Adrien Proust, was quite unlike my mother, and the social, religious, geographic, and historical differences between them were considerable. Inner adversity, which Mihail Sebastian, Proust's Romanian admirer, considered inherent in a Jew, abated when external adversities were themselves diminished. The rarely resolved tension between inner and outer adversity in the world of my childhood required different conventions and different masks. The ritual of the comforting kiss before going to sleep would have jarred with the anguish of the real or imaginary conflicts in our East European family.

By the early 1940s, my mother had foreseen the catastrophe. Confronted with disaster, her energies abruptly changed direction. The neurotic exhaustion of waiting was refocused on brisk action.

After the early weeks in Transnistria, my father abandoned any illusions. He had started without many opportunities in life and he would have liked simply to live in quiet dignity. What he dreaded was not death but humiliation. The attempt at redressing the situation was assumed, as so often before, by his wife. Her inner anxiety was nourished by uncertainty and exacerbated by a need for hope. Extremes of behavior and of danger, stormy relationships, the excitement of shared news and gossip, as well as a strong sense of community—all these mobilized her vast energies. She was good at planning the transactions of survival; she would borrow here, give back there, surfacing with a bowl of cornmeal, or an aspirin, or some piece of wonderful news.

For her son—that perpetually hungry, ghostly creature—the supreme evocation was not Proust's madeleine dipped in tea but onion pie, a miracle as unknown to the Parisian Marcel as was hunger. Tea for me, as for many other East European youngsters, was the hot drink offered by the Red Cross upon our return from the labor camp.

Fragile, crumpled, invincible—this was how our traumatized savior looked as she stood on the border of the motherland in 1945. She was instantly caught up in the vortex of revival, chained, as usual, to her brothers in suffering, dependent on that association, which contrasted strongly with the dignity and silences of her husband, who preferred solitude. She gave of herself with careless generosity, and demanded devotion and gratitude in return. My father's prudence, his self-effacing awkwardness, did not depend on others. This gentle man did not demand or expect gratitude.

When we returned to Romania, all contact with the family of my aunt Rebecca Graur was broken off. The names of my mother's older sister and her daughter Minna were never uttered by my parents, not even in the heat of argument. The ban on speaking the unmentionable names was shattered by a piece of news that struck like thunder: the death of

Aunt Rebecca's other daughter. Mother took the first train to Tîrgu Frumos, home of the Graur family, and returned after the week of mourning. A year later, in our house in Suceava, we celebrated the marriage of
Minna, the "sinner," to the widowed husband of her deceased sister. The
festivities confirmed the re-established family link, and my mother
could once more share in the events, good and bad, of her sister's family;
the incident of Minna's and my father's adultery was never mentioned
again, not even in passing.

My mother's relations to the others in the family seemed to protect
her, for a while, from herself. Her son, so intimate a part of her, received
no good-night kiss in that narrow, constricted refuge of ours. I was never
read to or told bedtime stories. Mater Dolorosa had no time or patience
for that. Bound up with herself, and with an exaggerated emotionalism,
she was prey to her own contradictions; only the core of her strong, vulnerable, agitated personality remained indestructible. Her theatricality
stimulated her passion, and her panic did not undermine her spirit, her
resilience, and her devotion.

Even if the roles had been reversed and the son had been able to give
the mother what he had not been given, he still would not have been able
to re-create a Bukovina version of the Proustian childhood. Fearful and
narrow, the East European ghetto had survived, wrapped in its twisted
mysteries, secure in its peculiar sins, a shadowy space that in the course
of time had learned to adapt to all the convulsions that had come its
way. And beyond the ghetto was the packed closeness of the Orthodox
churches, so different from the majestic spectacles of the Catholic cathedrals in the West, with their soaring Gothic stage sets, a backdrop for
magnificent performances of grace and harmony—a sacred staging, to
the accompaniment of the solemn, stately chords of the organ.

When she took her lunch break from the socialist store where she
worked, Mother instantly reconnected to the ghetto. She preferred the
exchange of news and whispers with the neighbors to conversations with
her son. She had a regular route. First she would look in on the over-
weight Mrs. Abosch, who lived in the first apartment with her small
daughter, following her Zionist husband's disappearance into the Communist prisons. Then there was Mrs. Segal, the widow, with her beauti-

ful daughter, Rita, a final-year student at the high school. Then there was the family of the accountant Heller. After all those calls, there was little time left for lunch. She grabbed a quick snack, then perfunctorily asked about the two schoolchildren in her own family. But what a fuss she made when we were laid up with flu or sunstroke! Any unforeseen event in the lives of her husband or her son, or some relative from near or far, signaled an imminent catastrophe, for whose warning signs she was ever on the alert. This most devoted mother and wife seemed, in fact, totally unsuited to her role, just as her extreme involvement in the daily round of life seemed to cover some essential lack, for which she found a measure of relief in religious faith.

Food was mainly Austrian-Bukovinan cuisine, with its own specific sweet and sour flavors. Meat was not separated from milk, as the Law prescribed, but all dishes and pots and pans were thoroughly scrubbed for Passover, as was the house. In autumn, the New Year brought with it seasonal rituals and reflections, culminating in the fast of Yom Kippur. Faith had become a sort of genetic tradition, an encompassing code of rules to help one cope with all the major and minor events of daily life. Mystical, superstitious, with an unfailing faith in the workings of fate, Mother, the daughter of the ghetto, maintained a cordial suspicion of the surrounding Christian milieu, as well as a moderate curiosity about it. On the other hand, her absolute solidarity with her own people did not preclude her directing her wit at critical assessments and judgments.

Socialism did not seem to have affected her. She was aware of the new order and its myriad regulations, but she was untouched by the vision of utopian happiness that had turned the heads of so many of her co-religionists. She regarded the changes with resignation. She saw her son distancing himself day by day from the world of his ancestors. These were troubled, dangerous times. The past, for all its bleakness, was remembered as a time of color and élan, and pointed an accusing finger at the venomous drabness of the present. Like the Greek agora, the ghetto had stimulated an active trade in emotions and ideas, as well as business. Socialist propaganda may have unmasked the petit bourgeois spirit with its speculators and traders, but it also promoted corruption at a deeper level, she seemed to be saying. I myself was suffocating in the ghetto, choked by those possessive excesses and that incessant panic, but my hostility became only another face of servility and bondage. After my juvenile fling with the Communist madness, I had come to hate anything that had to do with "we," with collective identity, which seemed to me suspect, an oppressive simplification. The chasm between "me" and "us" was one I was no longer disposed to cross.

My co-religionists were disparagingly accused by the socialist tenets, as by the former nationalist tenets, of an addiction to commerce. It was not until much later in life that I untangled the complexity of this ancient occupation and came to appreciate what it required—intelligence, risk-taking, a flair for negotiation, hard work with no fixed hours, trust, a good name. Only law or psychiatry would have suited Mother equally well, had she had the chance to pursue higher education. Socialism, however, had stifled freedom of initiative and innovation, and the trade of old, under the new dispensation, had become forced, stultifying labor, "planned" bureaucracy. Salespeople, marketing experts, planners, accountants—all were under constant surveillance by the Party watchdogs or the regular police.

From the socialist Our Bookstore, Mother stumbled into another job in a socialist haberdashery, one for which she was completely unsuited. Now, instead of books, her lifelong calling, she dealt with buttons, threads, ribbons, laces, scarves, and stockings. On unsteady feet, she would climb the rickety ladder to reach the boxes of the upper shelf. She then climbed down slowly, panting, with the needed box trembling in her big, wrinkled hand. Meanwhile, the customer, usually a peasant woman, had changed her mind. However, there was no time for argument, as other customers claimed her attention. On more than one occasion, it happened that the length of embroidered lace or a roll of ribbon vanished, along with the presumed thief, possibly a young apprentice whose work ethic was minimal and who cared only about her socialist salary, equally minimal. "Thief, thief!" I could hear my mother shouting at the part-time salesgirls, always different ones with dexterous fingers that frequently dipped into the till.

The store nightmare always culminated in the hysterical days of stock-taking, when the staff worked from morning till late at night, itemizing and pricing the goods. The tension this occasioned would affect even my father, who, after his own working hours, would check the various accounting procedures at home, to correct the errors of incompetent or even downright corrupt managers. Eventually, all the black forebodings were confirmed, and in the aftermath of a disastrous accounting error, Mother escaped prison only because of her age and some discreet string-pulling. She broke down at her trial, as she had on the night train that took us back after a visit to Periprava, where Father was churning in his humiliation. Humiliation itself did not affect her, but when it touched her husband or her son, she assumed the guilt for their disgrace.

"God will help you for all you're doing," she would repeat on those mornings in Bucharest when I accompanied her to the doctor—the same words she had used on the train from Periprava and in the days of her trial. Blind, she would wait patiently on the street corner for me to return with a taxi, no mean feat at rush hour in Bucharest.

Her obsession with my estrangement and with my plans for leaving our hometown brought on devastating nervous crises, often triggered by something trifling. She had no strength to confront me directly. Incapable of hurting me verbally, she still wanted to hurt me, deeply, incurably, for the indifference with which I distanced myself from her impasses and traumas. Her tenseness, aggravated by her feeling of helplessness, turned me into an exasperated, ice-cold witness. Were her wailings and laments a performance, produced for effect? I tried to armor myself against these assaults, but was not always successful. I was unable to escape from her possessiveness, her steely, irredeemable egoism. She seemed to want to punish all those in her immediate surroundings, by torturing herself and them, only because they were unable to reward her spectacular martyrdom, her absolute devotion.

This, indeed, was the tyranny of affection, the unbearable malady of the ghetto. The claw, covered in velvet and silk, would clutch at you when you were least prepared. I could not escape, even after I had extricated myself from the ghetto. Then, unexpectedly, she would become serene again and her sense of humor and her gentleness would, miraculously, return.

Paradoxically, the calmness seemed to authenticate yesterday's anxi-

eties and hysterics. Retrospectively, serenity afforded a strange foundation to her previous lack of balance. It was a case not so much of split
personality as of a confirmation of both sides of herself. She could not be
one thing, she seemed to be saying, without also being its opposite. Neither side could assume supremacy over her troubled, turbulent personality. A mysterious ancestral strength persisted in the face of her
vulnerability. "I'm praying for them as well," she appeared to be saying,
casting a glance at the Christian society surrounding her. She thought
long and hard about that contingent world, her hands covering her eyes,
as though in prayer, as she implored protection from the unknown.

The cemetery seemed to mean more to her than the synagogue. It
was a form of natural, unmediated, but also transcendental, communication, a way of inserting herself into history. Our ancestors were once
us, now we are them; the past and the present are fused. We come out of
Egypt every year, as they did, without ever leaving it behind altogether,
we relive other Egypts again and again, their fate is ours, just as our fate
is theirs, forever and ever. This mystical connection, the identification
with all the generations, the invocation of divine potentiality, became
more frequent, of course, whenever things here on earth were not going
well.

She accepted the fact that the world had changed. One could not,
however, believe in the equality that was being offered or consider oneself a patriot, that is, someone entitled to be a critic of the country's
predicament, as I patiently attempted to explain to her. She tried to
avoid this delicate topic, just as she avoided talking about my books. But
she was always nervous when I was in the center of the storm. She sensed
the moments of crisis, and she never demanded that I admit she was
right in her apprehensions. In any case, it would have been too late. I refused to let myself be reclaimed and chained by the clan. I had trained
myself in skepticism and had learned from that great skeptic Mark
Twain that nothing could be worse than being a man. Had I wanted to
be Romanian? Did I enjoy the joke played on me? the American wit
seemed to be asking. What would it have felt like being Paraguayan or
Chinese? Or Jewish, for that matter? This particular piece of bad luck
was not less interesting than the others.

Had I really been conceived in God's likeness, did He really have my face? In that case, the Supreme Being, who had brought everything into existence, had given birth to me. Was He embodied in the nearest of my near ones, the woman who in actual fact had given birth to me? Indeed, no conflict with divinity could have been richer than the quarrels from which I had benefited as my mother's son, nor could the chains be any stronger.

My mother was no Jeanne-Clémence Proust, née Weil, and her son was no reincarnation of Marcel. I never received any good-night kiss from her, and even now, decades later, when I revisit her in memory and am assailed by nostalgia, this is not what I lie in bed waiting for. The claw of the past is no less painful. Occasionally, she forgets to put in an appearance, but when I wake up from my mindless vagrancy, I can see again, through night's red heavens, the passage of the blind woman in her wheelchair. In His celestial chair, God is dozing off. He has taken the shape of an old moribund woman. The infirm, blind, and weary form has my mother's sunken face. Among the foreigners who surround me, here and beyond and everywhere, my confusions—the exile's ultimate treasure—bring me a familiar and accessible God.

The family album is composed of very few photographs, the rest have been lost in the family's wanderings. The young woman with a hat, veil, and black fur cape gazes shyly at her new husband. With her dark, vivid eyes, finely chiseled nose, flared nostrils, high forehead, arched eyebrows, she is the very picture of a nervous Mediterranean beauty, tempered in the fire of the East European crucible. Photographs do not represent memories. There are no memories from the years prior to the Initiation, those years were obliterated by amnesia. Those isolated, unforgettable sequences from Transnistria come with no visual aids, they were lost from the archives of history and are replaced, today, by the clichés of lament. The photographer who took the picture of the straggling bands of people dressed in rags, on the streets of Iaşi, as we returned in the spring of 1945 to the motherland that had expelled us, did not, unfortunately, go on to document the images of the rebirth—the year-end festivities, the summer holidays, the park for holiday-makers in Vatra-Dornei, the scorched fields around the dams of Periprava, my father's labor-camp uniform.

She turned pale when I told her I wanted to drop out of the university. "You're right," she finally said, "if you don't like it, you mustn't continue." She had the same reaction when, as a newly graduated engineer, I told her I was renting a room in town. "Well, if you cannot take it anymore . . ." She fretted in her kitchen as she prepared a meal in honor of her new daughter-in-law. She waited impatiently at the front gate for the postman to show up. In the throes of the illnesses of old age, she accepted her lot and railed against it. She turned her bitter sarcasm on her husband: "When I was young and I gave you pleasure, it was better, wasn't it?"

Four decades after my first exile, the current one has the advantage that it allows no fantasies about return. The witnesses of my life are now scattered to all the corners and cemeteries of the world. Images from the past visit me occasionally at night, courtesy of the Chinese sage who learned about the way I looked before my parents met. I see shadows on the wall and I can distinguish my mother's silhouette outlined in the dark. I can make out the frontiers, the place where I was born, the cemetery. When they met, in 1933, my parents could not foresee that they would be buried at such great distance from their own parents, and from each other—and at an even greater distance from the likely grave of their only son, now setting down this report for posterity.

The shadows flicker on the wall and I can see the nameless, unmarked graves in the forests of Transnistria, where my maternal grandparents were left behind. I see the flower-covered grave of another grandfather, my father's father, in pastoral Fălticeni. I see also, on one of Jerusalem's hills, the slab of stone set on fire by the Judean sun under which my father rests. Only Mother, of all people, remains in the place where she had always lived and always wanted to leave. She was the only one of us to remain in the motherland to the very end and lies in the cemetery in Suceava, a beckoning motherland for her nomadic son. She had always considered herself to be in exile, and the destiny she so believed in exiled her to eternal rest in the place from which she set out. Was this done to burden her son with yet another reason to feel guilt? Guilt, always guilt—a rich substitute for the lost family albums of the lost families.

Only now, in his more mature years, does the exile appear to need the mother's adoration and her anguish. Only now can I recognize myself in that whining mama's boy in Paris. Is Marcel's East European twin, having long thirsted for liberation, in his senescence now yearning for the comfort of a reconnection with his people? Would I ever hear my mother's steps, signaled by the swish of her velvet dress, returning from the world of no return, passing through the corridor toward the bedroom of the abandoned child? "A painful moment," says Marcel, "announcing the next, the next moment when she would have already been gone." How long would this vision last? How soon will it be before I am left alone again? "The moment when I heard her climb the stairs, then her steps along the corridor . . . I had reached the point when I wished her to take as long as possible, so that the waiting could be prolonged." Marcel's words are now mine, although, unlike him, I was not raised in the world of cathedrals and organ music. I am a different sort of exile, claimed as I am by the dark fogs of Eastern Europe. "I am allowed no moment of calm, I cannot take anything for granted, everything has to be fought for, not only the present and the future, but also the past," Franz Kafka wrote. I would never have appropriated such words before, but I would certainly have recognized myself at any time in the plight of the East European exile. Yes, everything had to be fought for, nor had we been allowed a moment of calm.

Not only the ghetto had vanished, but a whole world disappeared. It was late evening. There was no way now to begin my search for those lost times, and no miracle drugs could restore them to me. Without past, without future, was I inhabiting the illusion of a rented present, an insecure trap? One late evening I asked Franz Kafka, "Are you really nostalgic for the ghetto?" "Oh, if only I had had that choice," he whispered. Then he whispered again:

> Had I ever been given the chance to be what I wanted to be, I would have been a little East European boy, in one corner of the room, standing there without a trace of anxiety. Father would be in the middle of the room, talking to other men; Mother, warmly wrapped, would be ransacking through travel bundles; my sister would be chattering away with the girls, scratching her head and that beautiful hair of hers. And then, in a few weeks' time, we would all be in America.

I had often said these words to myself before. Now I was repeating them, and I gazed at the inscrutable sky, across which my old blind mother was crossing in her wheelchair. I was holding my breath, overwhelmed by nostalgia and solitude, and then, like someone in cardiac arrest, I felt the stab of her claw tearing at my chest.

The Viennese Couch

Anamnesis

I t was raining, but hardly the Deluge as recorded in Scripture. The biblical hero's latter-day namesake, Noah, was merely playing his refugee role in the comedy of the present.

In the elegant dining room of the elegant country house in an elegant part of New York, the talkers appeared oblivious to the persistent drizzle. The shipwrecked exile found himself telling the company about Transnistria, about the Initiation, about the war, and about Maria, the young peasant woman who was determined to join the Jews on their journey to death. Responding to their interest, he went on to talk about Communism and its ambiguities, and about the ambiguities of exile. The mirrored door opened and closed, and suddenly he saw in its crystal panes the image of the memoirist he did not want to recognize. By now it was too late to stop, and he continued with his story, to wrest a fake victory from the war against the past.

The next day a letter arrived: "I don't think it was just because it rained, but I spent a good deal of time after our pleasant luncheon thinking about you, and by that I mean thinking about your story, a fascinating one, not just because it is you, but because you lived and thought and acted at the center of the worst time in history." The publisher also wrote: "You were an eyewitness, and as a writer you must react." Publicly decoding his life, writing a personal memoir? Cioran had warned about it: "A cinder bath, a good exercise in self-incineration." It would also be like peeling away one's skin, layer after layer, in competition with the tell-all confessions of television talk shows or the self-revelations of group therapy.

I pondered the typewritten lines. Public commemorations have transformed horrors into clichés, which have been worked over until they have become petrified, thus fulfilling their function, followed, of course, by fatigue and indifference.

If I committed my life to public scrutiny, would I become its pen-wielding proxy? The audience is hungry for details, not for metaphors called Initiation and Trans-tristia. The training in evasiveness I had received during "the worst time in history" was still palpable. Did I still panic at the thought that I might suddenly be picked out during an unexpected roundup of suspects? I preferred the masks of fiction. Yet the mirror is summoning, I can see there the routes followed by the deportees, the transit camps, the sorting centers, the graves planned by the Marshal.

"I am in favor of forced migration," Ion Antonescu, Marshal of Romania, army commander, and leader of the Romanian state, declared in the summer of 1941. "I do not care whether we shall go down in history as barbarians. The Roman Empire committed many barbaric acts and yet it was the greatest political establishment the world has ever seen." The noble barbarian did not want to miss the opportunity afforded him of at last eradicating the national pest. "Our nation has not known a more favorable moment in its history. If need be, shoot," Hitler's ally declared.

Sporadic massacres had begun one year earlier, the autumn of 1941 merely accelerated the campaign. On October 4, the general gave the deportation order; on October 9, the trains—with record efficiency—were already on the move. The proclamation was explicit: "Today, October 9, 1941, the trains will begin transporting the Jewish population of the communes Iţcani and Burdujeni, as well as of the city of Suceava, from Ciprian Porumbescu Street to Petru Rareş Street and down to Sf. Dumitru Street and the Jewish House, from Queen Marie Street down to the Reif drugstore on Cetăţii Street, from the first street after the American Hotel to the Industrial Gymnasium for Girls, and all of Bosancilor Street."

The operation was due to start at the military depot of the Burdujeni railway station on the designated day, at 4 p.m. The evening before, Major Botoroagă had suddenly appeared on our doorstep: "You've got two young children, you'll have to carry them in your arms. It's a long way. Don't take with you more than the basic things," he told my father in the most friendly manner. The deportation was to begin the next day, October 9, and end one day later. The rules were precise: "Each Jewish inhabitant may take overcoats, day clothes and shoes, as well as food for several days, not to exceed what can be carried. All Jewish residents will take the keys to their houses and deposit them, along with household inventories, in an envelope bearing the name and address of the Jewish inhabitant, to be handed to the commission at the railway station."

Maria was listening attentively, looking all the time at little Noah, who stared, petrified, at the messenger. He turned toward her, as if demanding an explanation. Maria smiled back and thumbed her nose at him, their secret sign, meaning "This is all nonsense."

The major continued his recitation: "Those who do not comply, or resist, or instigate protest and acts of violence against the authorities, those who attempt to flee or to destroy their own property, as well as those who fail to deposit their currency, gold coins, jewelry, and precious metals, will be shot on the spot. Those who help or hide Jews committing such acts of insubordination will also be shot dead." The major did not necessarily look at Maria as he pronounced the last words, but she must have decided, there and then, to commit a crime more serious than merely helping or hiding the lepers—she would leave with them.

The head of the police, the prefect, the deputy prefect, the local garrison's commanding colonel, and Major Botoroagă himself, as commander of the local gendarmerie, looked on in disgust as the madwoman was dragged away from the train door. Execution would have been too honorable a death, the best punishment was to allow her to live among those she had betrayed.

A few months later, Maria was at the gates of the labor camp, loaded with suitcases filled with clothes and food for her little prince Noah and his parents. The luggage, confiscated on the spot, would be used as evidence in her court-martial.

"From across the millennia, a tragic destiny has united the Babylonian captivity with the inferno of starvation, disease, and death in Transnistria," wrote Traian Popovici, the Christian mayor of Czernowitz, the capital of Bukovina. "The looting at the assembly points along the Dniester River of whatever personal possessions the deportees still had, the long marches, barefoot, in wind, rain, sleet, and mud, the hunger and thirst, could be from the pages of Dante's Inferno," the mayor continued. He had tried, until the very last moment, to halt the deportations. "In one single transport, out of sixty babies only one survived," he wrote. "Those too tired or too disabled to walk were left behind on the roadsides, a prey to vultures and dogs. Those who made it to their destinations live in appallingly unsanitary conditions, with no proper accommodations, no firewood, no food and clothes, and are exposed to the harsh weather and the torments of their guards and of the camp's administrators."

This lesson in history and geography would not be complete without mentioning the crossing point on the Dniester—Ataki. Not Ararat, as in the biblical flood, but Ataki. Little Noah was only five years old at the time, but he would never forget that name. Fifty years later he still remembered it. The president of the Jewish community in Suceava, recalling the place, wrote: "Ataki will remain a mystery, to be understood only by those of us who stumbled, as if in chains, along its winding streets. Once-strong men suddenly collapsed. Previously sane people lost their minds. Rosa Stein, the widow of the lawyer Samuel Stein, believed she was still in Suceava and kept asking, politely, 'Could you please kindly show me the way back to my house? I live in the same building as the

Weiner bookstore.'" The Weiner bookstore still survives in the memory of the exile now being lulled to sleep in his New York refuge. After the war, it became a haven for the townspeople, brimming with miracles, until the moment when the Communists suppressed private property and all other private benefactions.

In 1941, another Jewish communal official, from Rădăuți, sent a desperate message from Ataki to his equivalent in Bucharest: "On October 14 we were evacuated and brought here, where we are now waiting to be transported over the Dniester and sent to an unknown destination in the Ukraine. We live outdoors, in rain, mud, and cold. Here in Ataki, hundreds of people have already died. Many have lost their minds, others have committed suicide. If something is not done immediately to save us, none of these unfortunate beings will survive. For the time being, there are around 25,000 souls in this situation. Some are on their way to the Ukraine, others are in Moghilev, still others here in Ataki."

The name Moghilev is also one that is not easily forgotten. It was to Moghilev that the four members of the Manea family were sent. In a letter to a Zionist office in Geneva, dated January 6, 1942, a report from Moghilev mentioned "60 deaths daily." That first winter was indeed the ally of Hitler's army, Marshal Antonescu.

Transnistria did not live up to expectations and could only show a balance sheet of 50 percent dead. In that respect, it could not compete with Auschwitz. Transnistria's achievement remained ambiguous, as did most things Romanian. Could Romania be considered Europe's most anti-Semitic country, as some chronicles were claiming? The competition is difficult to assess, but the dubious Holocaust prize should still go to Nazi Germany, despite the reports that the German Army was scandalized by the random acts of barbarity committed by their Romanian allies, always ready to kill without orders and by any primitive means at hand.

Little Noah was initiated into life, as well as its opposite, in Transnistria. First death claimed my beloved grandfather Avram, then my maternal grandmother, striking twice within three weeks. The sudden magic of lifelessness: the afterlife, in a dead grave without a name.

In his mind, the boy saw himself lying, mummylike, in an eternal stupor. He could see the grave, the snow-covered earth, the frozen blades of grass, the wriggling worms. The wind was howling, the bearded men were swaying to the cadences of the ancient Kaddish prayer.

I was alive, thinking about my own death, but what I understood then was that crying and hunger, cold and fear belonged to life, not to death. Nothing was more important than survival, Mother kept saying, as she sought to sustain her husband and son. Death was extinction, which had to be fought at any cost. This was the only way in which we could be worthy of survival, she kept repeating. Gradually, the situation improved. The war was shifting westward, an Allied victory seemed imminent, and Marshal Antonescu resigned himself to keeping the insects alive, as alibi and collateral.

Former citizen Marcu Manea obtained permission to work in a factory, where he was paid the price of a loaf of bread, the daily sustenance of the four members of the family. Nobody could predict where the roulette wheel of life and death would next stop. The logic on which my father had carefully built his life was now useless. Saving one's skin through corrupt dealings and bargains with fate disgusted him, as did the supreme reward, survival. My father's views remained unchanged, despite his brutal beating by a formerly friendly officer, who now, disfigured by hatred, seemed ready to crush the insect as the insect deserved. He could accept death, but not humiliation. Risking everything, he recoiled in disgust from the grim truth of his present reality. He did not become servile and hypocritical, as was demanded of the slaves; he would not surrender his dignity. His wife didn't care about such idiocies, but he did. The black market in sentiment, not only in aspirin or bread, that prevailed in the camps, disgusted him, and so did the barbarity of victims determined to save themselves at any cost from the barbarity of the oppressors. Monster-executioners breed monster-victims, he used to repeat in his soft but determined voice.

The Führer's Final Solution did not take into account the thoughts that went through the minds of the victims condemned to extinction. Nazism defined its purpose in clear terms, kept its promises, rewarded its faithful, and annihilated its victims without hesitation, without offering them the chance to convert or to lie. In contrast, the Communism of universal happiness encouraged conversion, lying, complicity, and was not reluctant to devour even its own faithful. The thought police, so essential to the system, imposed a truth serving the Party. Between the increasingly irreconcilable promise and the reality, the field was open for suspicion, perversion, and fear.

These were the thoughts that coursed through my mind that autumn afternoon in Bucharest in the eighth decade of the mean and insatiable twentieth century. In the quiet room, reader and book were engaged in silent dialogue when, barely audible, the phone rang. I didn't feel like talking to anybody and had turned the volume down; still, I picked up the receiver.

"Do you care to go for a walk?" asked my friend.

"It's raining, where could we go? Come on over and we'll talk."

"No, I'd rather go out. The rain is stopping. Let's meet in half an hour, in Palace Square, in front of the library."

My friend was ordinarily a sedentary sort, and his sudden eagerness for a walk surprised me. The rain had indeed stopped, and the air was fresh. He led me to the small deserted park nearby. The benches were still damp.

"It finally happened. We always think that it will be just the neighbor who falls into their net. Now it's happened. They struck."

I kept silent, waiting for him to continue.

"There were two of them, a colonel and a captain. The captain took notes. The interrogation lasted about three hours."

The reason for the walk became clear. Rooms have ears, policeman's ears.

"It all had to do with you. They wanted to know everything about you, what you do, the people you see, the mail you get from abroad and send. They wanted to know if you have a mistress, or if Cella has a lover. They asked about your financial situation, your parents', your mother-in-law's. They asked if you had expressed any hostility toward the Supreme Comrade and his wife, whether you intend to emigrate."

In socialist Romania, the roster of informants came to resemble a census of the population. The strategy of self-effacement, to give the appearance of normality, no longer functioned. Isolation had proved no protection.

"You won't believe it, but I finally gave in and signed. There was no choice. They also gave me a code name, 'Alin.'"

The name the policemen had chosen for him was the very pen name their new informant used for the poetry and theater reviews he published in literary magazines. Let this be a lesson for him; both vocations, poet and informant, after all, probe the mystery in which we all hide.

"Why did you sign? You'll only get rid of them in your coffin, and perhaps not even then. Had you held out for another hour, they would've given up. This is no longer Stalin's time, they would've left you alone."

Alin did not reply, so I fell silent, too. After all, I couldn't pretend that I was such a great hero myself, it would have been condescending. Advice or reproaches would have been equally pointless. In hell, bread means everything, and it means a good deal in purgatory, too. On the gate of the labor camp, the guards used to write: "Paradise," "Hell," "Purgatory." Bread was everywhere the leverage for blackmail.

"They threatened me. You are a public employee, they told me, you have a duty to help us."

In other words, one could lose even a mediocre job. Such a threat was contrary to the law, as this public employee knew, but he also knew that law was the plaything of power. Not only Alin's bread was at stake, so was that of his old, ailing parents.

Thus my friend became Alin in life as well as in literature. His usual double-triple life as a socialist citizen was now augmented by a precise, secret, unpaid mission: to report on the double-triple life of his best friend. He would be having weekly meetings with the liaison officer, not in the latter's office, the expected venue, but in "safe" private houses that the Securitate had at their disposal. Was the humble domestic setting, a gray, constricted, socialist living space, supposed to humanize the activity? The number of police informants had grown much more rapidly than the gross national product, and the recruitment campaign had speeded up. "The traumatized survivors of the ghetto make no distinction between the police of the prewar nationalist state and the successors of the socialist regime, Comrade Commanders," I once had occasion to say.

The all-night train trip from Bucharest to Suceava—from one end of the country to the other—ended in a short visit to the old couple. There was time for a cup of coffee and an opportunity to look into their faces and read what the telephone conversations couldn't register, their look of panic, panic nurtured by millennia of terror and ever renewable. I looked at my parents once more and got up to go out, leaving my coffee half drunk. The sense of urgency that drove me onto the train was now impelling me back to the streets of the past.

The guard at the entrance of the former Austrian town hall, now the headquarters of the local Communist Party, listened attentively to what I had to say. The Writers Union membership card still carried some authority in provincial Romania of the late 1970s. Gogol's employee seemed somewhat disconcerted by my sudden appearance and was not sure how to respond. He wrote down the details and, looking at his appointment sheet, said, "I don't know when Comrade First Secretary will be available to see you, but I shall pass the message along."

"I must see him today. I have a train to catch back to Bucharest tonight," I insisted. He hesitated for a moment, then said, with the air of someone resigned to his fate, "Come back around lunchtime. I'll have an answer for you by then."

I wouldn't wait and decided, increasing my risk, to go over to the Securitate headquarters, located in a new, modern building not far from the old hospital. Again, I showed my membership card. The officer did not seem impressed. An interview? With the commander? Today? Why the rush?

"Yes, today, before lunchtime. After that, I'm seeing the First Secretary."

The guard picked up the phone and dialed a number, then he left and someone else took up his position. After a lengthy wait, the first guard reappeared.

"Comrade Commander is not in town, but the deputy commander, Comrade Vasiliu, will see you at eleven."

It was now five past ten. On every corner my idyllic native town offered flowery gardens and inviting benches. Alder Park was nearby. The spring sunshine was making me drowsy. I walked past the old trees, witnesses of ages past.

At eleven I was escorted to the first floor. Behind the massive desk was a pale man with thinning gray hair, dressed in a gray woolen vest and a white shirt with no tie. On his left sat a handsome, dark-haired man with a black mustache, in a captain's uniform. I came right to the point: "For months, pensioner Marcu Manea has been pestered by an agent who keeps accusing him of being either a spy for Israel or a crook making shady deals as Secretary of the Jewish community. If there is evidence, let him be prosecuted. If not, this campaign of terror must stop. The suspect has suffered enough, both in the past and more recently. People in the town where he has lived for the whole of his life know him as the decent man he is."

The colonel's intense gaze signaled that he was aware of the past called "Transnistria" and, more recently, "Periprava." He also knew what "decent" meant. Both the guilty and the innocent survivors of detention were subsequently pressured into becoming informants for the state. However, former comrade and former inmate Manea had declined the honor for over a year, invoking the same refrain: "I am a decent man." Repeated with idiotic monotony, the comic statement had finally vexed the policeman, and his superior was duly informed of the failed recruitment.

The colonel made some laconic comments; he was an intelligent but dangerous interlocutor. His seeming reserve was a subtle tactic to trap me, but this was no time for caution.

"An Israeli spy?" I said. "In what way?"

I did not really expect an answer; the interview followed its own dynamic.

"He is accused," I continued, "of accompanying, in his capacity as Secretary of the Jewish community, dignitaries from America and Israel on their visits to Bukovina. These were official visits, sanctioned by the Foreign Ministry and, probably, by all the relevant ministries. The surveillance agencies must have been aware of everything everybody was saying and doing."

The colonel smiled again, inscrutably, and confirmed my bold statement with a slow nod.

"Yes, yes, of course we knew," he said, without uttering a word.

I pressed on. "It is alleged that among the visitors was a certain Brill, head of an Israeli secret service. He visited the famous Jewish cemetery in Siret, near the Soviet border. Are we to suppose that he was there to gather information, to spy on the border area with his bare eyes or with the binoculars he didn't have? He didn't even take a single step outside the zone where tourists are allowed. As for my father, how could an obscure employee of the small Jewish community in tiny Suceava know the names of suspects on the Romanian secret service lists? And after all, surveillance is quite efficient, the Romanian Securitate is well appreciated around the world." The colonel was almost laughing now, the captain raised his eyes from the minutes he was typing and joined in. Yes, he was definitely laughing.

I could not be stopped. "And what if Mr., formerly Comrade, Manea suffered, let's say, a heart attack? His old body bears the scars of Marshal Antonescu's Transnistria, of postwar Stalinism, and the Stalinless Stalinism of the 1950s. The errors of the past should not be repeated in the 1970s. This is what all the papers say."

My two listeners seemed more interested in this new narrative twist than in the previous recital, so I stepped up my tempo. "The descendants of the ghetto make no distinction between the policeman of the old nationalist state, with his vile frame-ups, and the socialist militia man of today. For them it is not always clear-cut. Socialist laws proclaim the equality of all citizens, and it is true that after the war there were Jews in important, even ministerial, positions. There are still some left. But this does not heal memories, or panic. The suspects are wary, Comrade Colonel. Maybe they have a right to be."

I had come to the end of my grand aria. I had demonstrated alertness and courage, so what were my two interlocutors waiting for, standing there smiling, hands on hips? Where was the applause, the bouquets?

My fear and my spirit of revolt had joined in producing a coherent, even brave, discourse, but the drama wasn't over yet. Still, here I was, alive, with all my thoughts and accelerated emotions still alive.

The colonel, in his turn, performed his role to perfection; it was difficult not to be persuaded by his performance. He had not objected to any of my reproaches; his resigned air seemed that of a man weary of the idiocies he had to deal with daily. By accepting my argument, he almost broke down my emotional defenses. However, I managed to keep my composure until the very end, when he had his final word: "Thank you, this is very important information on the psychology of the ghetto. We do not often receive such helpful information. Our colleagues in Bucharest will ask for your cooperation, I'm sure." All I could do was to mumble feebly, "No, I'm not suitable, not I." The colonel was no longer listening. He got up and extended his hand. The interview was over.

As I was leaving, the captain assured me that the misunderstandings concerning Mr. Marcu Manea would be dealt with quickly. Comrade Colonel always kept his word; he is a very special man, as you could see for yourself. Indeed, the occasion had been special, but I was no longer paying any attention to the captain and his words drifted away.

The tension of that meeting had been excruciating. Focused on my objective, blinded by my own drive, I had ignored where I was, to whom I was speaking. Had the whole business gone on for five more minutes, I would probably have collapsed, like a rag doll, into the arms of the colonel and the captain, and then they really could have started squeezing me for information. I was exhausted from the effort and amazed at my own audacity. I made my way down the stairs of the accursed building, eager to make my escape and forget everything.

I could not forget, however, that nobody has a right to play moralist when confronted by such demented dilemmas. Alin knew of the police pressure that had been exerted on pensioner Marcu Manea after Periprava; he knew of Colonel Vasiliu's persuasive charm, as well as of the two conversations his colleagues in Bucharest had had with me, their future expert on victim psychology. He knew that the meetings had been short and that I had declined the flattering request to cooperate. Now the police were closing in again. They must have possessed more information on their suspect than that provided by the routine reports and weekly conversations with my poet friend.

Alin, good friend that he was, told me what he had written down about me for his interrogator: "An honest man, uninterested in politics. Withdrawn, melancholy, he enjoys books and solitude." But that description somehow seemed unconvincing, it lacked the gloss of Party clichés. I had become infected with suspicion myself and began to think that my friend was keeping things from me, to protect me from myself, not only from my pursuers. I was becoming increasingly dependent on my double informant.

Tall, with big hands and flaming hair like an Irishman's, exploding with vitality, with a booming voice and wide gestures like a conductor's, Alin somehow became small and big-nosed, with his mane of hair suddenly sticking, like an oily helmet, to his diminished skull. His once-resonant voice was now a screech, difficult to understand. Was he omitting details that were likely to make me worry? I kept asking to see him, no matter how briefly. Again and again, I went over details with him, no matter how minor they seemed. Had the police inquired about my medical records? Detention in psychiatric wards, of course, was a practice much favored by the socialist police.

The interrogations appeared to be routine, bureaucratic affairs. The police put off any blackmailing tactics, just as they postponed the resolutions of the thousands of dossiers that had accumulated at headquarters. To forestall accusations that they were either lazy or ineffective, they kept adding to the numbers of their collaborators, not for the minute information that might be gained, but in order to maintain the network of complicities.

As reported to me by my poet friend, the information about me that he was passing along gave no cause for alarm and even provided some amusement. The police learned nothing about me that they didn't already know. But the anxieties that I discovered buried within me revealed more about me to myself than my police dossier, uncovering old, obscure traumas.

I discovered that I was the real beneficiary of the investigation, not through what I had learned from Alin's reporting, but through the reaction it triggered in me. I saw myself as being in the privileged center of a farce that yielded fascinating insights. The description alone of the private apartments where officer and informant met each week would have merited the attention of any anthropologist, but I could focus only on my own anxiety, like a drug addict looking for a fix. Suddenly I was plunged into the terror of the 1940s and given a chance to understand, albeit belatedly, the anxieties of that time, with all its recycled incertitudes and neuroses.

How long did this strange condition last—a year, two? Alin proved that, even in the Communist police state, friendship could be affectionate and enduring.

He continued to provide his reports and keep me informed of their trivial contents until, at last, he decided he had had enough of the socialist paradise and opted for emigration to a faraway place, from which he would write me regularly. We met again years later, but never referred to the delicate subject of his informing. I was happy to know that my friend had remained one of the few from whom destiny had not separated me.

Alin's replacement was less quick to reveal himself, and I never discovered his identity. The powers above must have refined their criteria for recruitment. I kept an eye on my close contacts, one never knew who the informer might be, every face wore a mask. This apprehension, verging on paranoia, had become so generalized as to be considered the ordinary condition. Anxiety was now a collective possession.

The exploitation of man by the state had proved no more appealing than man's exploitation by man. The dismantling of private ownership had fractured the economy and gradually established the state's ownership over the citizens. Xenophobia became more refined, suspicion ruled all individual lives. Instead of the demagogic competition among parties, there was now the absolute demagogy of the single Party. The chaos of the free market and of free speech was replaced by the schizophrenia of taboos. Enforced complicity culminated in a symbolic perversion—the red card.

Were there taboo topics, even on the psychiatrist's couch? The doctor I went to see to discuss a medical discharge from my engineering job, whose dissatisfactions were becoming intolerable, was a poet, too, like my informant of a few years later, but unlike him, he was not a friend. The risk of talking openly remained difficult to assess. The anxieties confessed on the psychiatrist's couch were no longer an individual's private property.

As the new order extended its domination, the gray areas in which one could maneuver became more restricted, as did the enclaves of normality. Years passed as everybody waited for the magic thaw. Indeed, this happened periodically, but only in order to reinforce incertitude and add to the number of traps. Suspicion and duplicity gradually infiltrated the kitchens and the bedrooms, insinuated themselves into sleep, language, and posture.

Should I tell the psychiatrist-poet what he surely knew very well, that not only the schools, hospitals, publishing houses, and printing presses belonged to the state but also the forests, the air, the water, the earth, the stadiums, banks, cinemas, button and weapons factories, the army and the circus, the kindergartens and old people's homes, the music industry, pharmaceuticals, and the flocks of sheep? The doctor and his patient, too, were state property. When you bought your package of tissues, your bed, or your morning milk, your watch or shoes or dentures, you were at the mercy of apathetic and insolent state functionaries who subscribed to the code of "socialist ethics and equity," which translated as "We pretend we are working, they pretend they are paying us."

What else was the psychiatrist but another state employee—with a red card, probably. The Party was supreme. It was the Party Secretary, not the directors, themselves appointed by the Secretary, who respectively ran the high schools and the slaughterhouses and the tailor shops and, of course, the clinics.

In a country with a strong tradition of right-wing politics, the number of red cards had increased exponentially. Without a red card you were worth very little, but even with one, you did not amount to much. In the new party of the parvenus, after half a century of Communism, one would have been hard put to find many genuine Communists. The propaganda clichés served the jugglers of the totalitarian circus, but nobody believed in them anymore. Life, or what remained of it, had moved into underground tunnels filled with muted sounds and secret codes.

Would Comrade Doctor allow himself to be psychoanalyzed by a patient obsessed with the comedy of double roles? Could the poet find the
lyric correlative of duplicitous chaos, conducted on the surface by the
masked men of power and perpetuated, underground, by the venom of
resentment?

The patient's questions quickly rebounded back to himself, as though
he had borrowed the doctor's mannerisms and was able to read the theme
of the psychiatric session with closed eyes: the Initiation after the Initiation. Or should it be called *adaptation?* And what exactly did the survivor adapt to? A familiar question. Over a decade later, it would also be
asked by an American psychiatrist. The answer was familiar, too: The
patient adapted to life, as simple as that. Indeed, it is to life that all survivors adapt, whether they are survivors of black, green, or red dictatorships. They do so with that impertinence of normality which is life
itself. This was how I summarized my own biography on the eve of exile, an experiment no less educational than the preceding ones.

How can one be a writer if one has no freedom was the dilemma
posed by the American psychiatrist, an expert on the psychoses of freedom in the New World. The question would have sounded like a bad joke
if uttered by his East European counterpart, but an exchange of exper-
tise between the specialist in the pathology of constraint and the analyst
of freedom's traumas would not have been useless. The psychiatrists of
these two very different worlds would have discovered many surprising
resemblances alongside the differences.

The freedom of the New Man meant accepting necessity—this was
what doctor and patient had learned from the Marxist dialecticians of a
party that became less Marxist every day: necessity, hence adaptation;
adaptation, hence pragmatism: hence, accepted necessity. Adaptation to
life, Doctor, this was the task facing the apprentice in the banality
served pedagogically by daily life. Life, that was all. In the East, in the
West, in the cosmos.

The future promised in the Communist fairy tales became a hell for
those under interrogation and in prisons. In between, there was the burlesque of purgatory, subject to the Party's variable shifts. When the grind
of earning one's daily bread ceased to be the only purpose, the traffic in

subterfuges allowed for some delectable falsifications. This was the face of the post-Stalinist "liberalization" in Eastern Europe. The growing ambiguities even allowed us—doctor and patient, patient and informant—to make our debuts in the periodicals and publishing houses of the Party and the state.

It was a game with shifting rules: the taboo words and the taboo ideas and the taboo allusions were regulated according to the capricious canon of the Party's shifting necessity. After one book, and then another, which I managed to squeeze past the censor's detectors, did I enjoy greater social protection? To be sure; but the surveillance also increased. The Party honored artists with privileges and penalties, writing was a profession legitimated only by membership in the Writers Union, run and controlled by the Party, and a suspect with no job and no income risked being accused of "hooliganism," that is, of leading a parasitic life, as socialist legislation termed it.

Evasiveness was all that was left—is that not so, Comrade Doctor? The true face of reality was revealed not only by the condition of the fruit markets and butcher shops, but also by the condition of the hospitals. The story was told of a policeman who had been called to the capital's largest psychiatric hospital and been shocked to find the patients deliriously shouting, "Down with Communism! Down with the Leader!" He was on the point of having them arrested, but was stopped by the hospital's director, who objected: "We are in a psychiatric hospital. These people are mad, don't you understand?" The policeman replied, with perfect common sense, "Mad? What do you mean, mad? Why doesn't anybody shout 'Long live Communism, long live the Leader'?" Unwittingly, he had stumbled on the crux of the very ambiguity of the national malady.

The wrinkled face of the old poet, saved from all illusions by medical practice, looked up at you. The potbellied, balding doctor, with his guttural *r*'s, had adopted the attitude of an expert in failure.

"And what are you going to do after a year or two? The pension is small, not even half of your engineer's salary. And for how long do you think you can extend a medical pension? Endlessly, is that what you were about to say?"

A lunatic works at engineering twelve hours a day in a huge warehouse with drawing boards, telephones, and cigarette smoke, suffocating under blueprints and dazed by interminable formulas.

Why shouldn't the sleepwalker receive a cage of his own, for life? Would the remedy for the trauma be an even bigger trauma? Writing at least offers a quick way of exiting the penal colony, leaving the carnage behind. As Kafka said, "Outside the ranks of the assassins, you can observe the facts."

"So, a grade-two pension, or maybe a grade three?" the poet-doctor asked. "Grade three means subject to review every six months by a panel of specialists. Grade two is reviewed on an annual basis."

"What about grade one?" the patient asked.

"That means incurable, a serious mental condition, with no hope of recovery. I wouldn't choose such a diagnosis. Don't even think about it!"

"Why not?" the madman was on the point of protesting. Isn't a true writer beyond hope of recovery? Isn't he capable only of sitting in his cage, playing with words, like a mental patient? Reading, writing, reading, then more writing, isn't this his life, Doctor—malady, therapy, therapy, malady, and so on, until the end of ends? You practice medicine, Doctor, so you are not incurable, but what about the engineer sitting before you? I have been practicing for too long that schizophrenia of double personality and duplicity. I have been dealing with calculations, drawing boards, invoices, almost being the person I have pretended to be, living constantly with the fear that, at any moment, the impostor would be unmasked and thrown down the stairs, a mental-hospital clown, the butt of the cheers and jeers of the audience. Only evasiveness can save us, Doctor.

Should you describe your impasse to him, or should you simply use him as a starting point for the falsifications to follow? You had to persuade him that he was, in fact, participating in a friendly cooperative venture, not in a medical consultation.

"Fine, grade two, then," you muttered, halfheartedly.

The advantage of suddenly becoming the owner of your own time in a society where even time was state property came with a built-in trap: either you collaborate with the powers that be or else we isolate you as the irresponsible person that you pretend to be. Ready to risk the new Initiation, you had gone through the motions as required by protocol, and the doctor signed the necessary papers.

What if the symptoms described in the medical report were really the case? You refused to think of yourself as a patient, and you preferred the lesser role of falsifier. Was falsification itself a sign of the disease? You had come not for treatment but for a way outside the purgatory in which a diseased authority was chained to its diseased subjects.

You never trusted psychoanalysts. You would rather read them than consult with them. When Dr. Sigmund Freud asked, What remains Jewish in a Jew who is neither religious nor a nationalist and who is ignorant of the Bible's tongue, you managed to mutter the answer he had himself given: *Much*. You did not explain what that meant, since he had been careful enough not to offer explication.

Question and answer were shockingly joined by one single word—Jew. Nonreligious, non-nationalist, non–speaker of the sacred language, was Dr. Freud speaking about himself, without defining the term? Was the definition of a Jew to be found only in the triad of religion, nationalism, and language? Could it be that the founder of psychoanalysis, so concerned with sexuality and the Oedipus complex, ignored circumcision, the covenant carved in the flesh on the eighth day after the male infant's birth? Inscribed in the flesh, circumcision cannot be revoked.

With Grandfather Avram's blessing, you became, through circumcision, Noah, a biblical code name, not for public use. After all, you don't unzip your trousers in public. Isn't Dr. Freud interested in knowing more about the circumcised Noah, who carries on a dialogue with the "double" concealed in his trousers, with its hidden, parallel life? This double life, no less comic or revealing than the life of an individual with or without religion, ethnicity, or sacred language—should that not interest Herr Doktor Freud?

In the meantime, you had acquired quotation marks, just like Dr.

Freud. Jean-François Lyotard, for instance, believes that Sigmund Freud is a "Jew" rather than a Jew, and that so are his confrères Walter Benjamin, Theodor Adorno, Hannah Arendt, and Paul Celan. As there are non-German Germans, so there are non-Jewish Jews, the Frenchman helpfully explains. They are the ones who have doubts about tradition, mimesis, immanence, but also "emigration, dispersion, and the impossibility of integration"—in other words, "the double impotence of non-change and of change."

At the age of five, in Transnistria, the little Jew was known as Noah, not Norman. At the age of fifty, on the eve of the new exile, the relation between self and Jew had become a complicated knot, one that could not fail to interest Dr. Freud. The psychoanalyst should be asked, finally, to answer not only the questions he himself has asked but also the questions posed by posterity: not necessarily what is left after you have lost what you did not possess, but how you become a Jew after the Holocaust, after Communism and exile. Are these, by definition, essentially Jewish traumas? Are these initiations carved in your soul, not only your body, that make you a Jew even when you are not one? A "non-people of survivors" is the name Lyotard gives the category of non-Jewish Jews, whose sense of communion depends, according to him, on "a unique profoundness of an endless anamnesis," an endless recalling of things past.

Anamnesis in front of the mirror? Why are you frowning, Dr. Freud? Franz Kafka—not a great admirer of Freudian anamnesis—is not listed among the company in Lyotard's quotation marks. Having asked himself, "What have I got to do with the Jews?" Kafka replied, "I have got hardly anything to do with myself."

Kafka is, however, not a non-Jewish Jew but a genuine Jew, although he was not proficient in Hebrew—he did, however, make several attempts to learn the sacred tongue—did not practice religion, and was not a nationalist. There is a scene in which he tries to cram the whole of the Chosen People into a drawer. "Including myself to the very end," he had added. That was an unmistakably Jewish profession of faith, replacing religion, ethnicity, and the sacred tongue.

Only a Jew could choose this way of releasing the self-loathing and hatred that had been his fate for millennia. These echoes can be heard when Kafka describes to Milena the invectives of the "dirty mob," chanted on a street in Prague, the Jew-hatred of the street—and of the salons, too, as well as of academia. Hatred did not stop in Kafka's Prague, or in Dr. Freud's much-beloved Vienna, or in London, where hatred forced him to seek exile shortly before he died, or in less famous places. But can we also hear, as Kafka did, the echo of our own inner struggles? What is it we hear? Our own fatigue, as we stop defending ourselves? The perfection of others, who cannot accept our own imperfection?

"In the struggle between yourself and the world, take the side of the world," the unvanquished Kafka advised.

The fatigue of belonging could be excused, Dr. Freud whispers, in our own continuing dialogue. Nobody could accuse you of trying to ignore adversity, he adds. One minute you defend your destiny; another minute, forget it, then defend it again, until you tire of all the futility. So give up taking the daily farce too seriously, stop honoring it with questions, be gracefully absentminded, bewildered, in accordance with the simplicity and absurdity of indifference—this should be your therapy, to become deaf, dumb, naïve, absentminded, inattentive.

What—after the Holocaust and after Communism—has the exile to do with the Jews, when he is no longer certain he has anything to do with himself? Much, the Viennese doctor claims; whether you like it or not, you have a lot in common both with them and with yourself. When, at the age of five, you were joined to a collective destiny, Dr. Freud pronounces, you were given an accreditation which is more important than the covenant carved in the flesh.

"We Jews will never be forgiven for the Holocaust," a German Jewish writer wrote in the days when you took refuge, not from the Holocaust, but from Communism, and in Berlin of all places. Yes, there was too much evidence for the Holocaust to be denied, and that impertinence could not be forgiven. But it was not just the Holocaust, and not just

Communism; it was Jewish guilt. There were plenty of other minor, more ambiguous guilts that could not be forgiven. Dr. Freud, guilty of founding psychoanalysis, the "Jewish science," knew this only too well.

However, even if it were possible, one cannot simply renounce the honor of being suspect, outcast, decried as the embodiment of evil, from the beginning of time to its end—this is some glory! We cannot simply reject such privilege, not even when the stereotypes themselves are not easy to bear—victim, avenger, conspirator, to which the latter-day Elders of Zion have added a new protocol: "the Jewish monopoly on suffering."

The trivialization of suffering . . . mankind's endless enterprise. Only when it becomes a cliché does tragedy find a home in the collective memory. Memory must keep watch so that the horror is not repeated, we have been told over and over. We must hold on to identity, shared memory, race, ethnicity, religion, ideology. Having finally landed on the planet of pragmatism, you thought you might escape your past and your identity and become just a simple entity, as Gertrude Stein, the American in Paris, dreamed—only to find that Thursday's atrocities have become grist for the mottoes on Friday's T-shirts, an instantly marketable product for the collective memory.

Sigmund Freud would have understood the confusions of exile and its dispossessions, its discontents, you might say, as well as its freedoms. He would know the significance of an impersonal home in some anonymous hotel room, the exile's ultimate refuge, his democratic homeland-for-rent-by-the-day, hospitable and indifferent, as a homeland should be.

You are looking at a small photograph, wrinkled and yellowed with time, now serving as a mirror. It is June 1945, in the pastoral town of Fălticeni, in northern Romania, two months after the initiate's return from the Transnistria expedition and two hours after the close of the end-of-year school festivities.

The adorable little boy, in white trousers and shirt, is standing a quarter of a step ahead of the other prize winners, three little boys and three little girls. The only thing that distinguishes him from the other prize winners, who have not benefited from the privileges of the Initiation, seems to be his victorious bearing, his status as survivor now vali-dated by his winner's laurels. Immaculately groomed, left foot forward, hand on hip, a wide smile on his face, he is every inch a star, performing knowingly before the camera.

The boy seems to have forgotten everything of the apprenticeship he has served among the thousands of starving and ragged people, the play-things of death's producers and directors. Little Augustus the Fool has instantly turned into his opposite, the White Clown, the knight crowned with laurels and applauded by the melodrama's players. The years of ab-sence from the world have been annulled. He has recrossed the Styx and finds himself back on the original shore, alive, certifiably alive, back in the Eden that was his and is now regained.

The Eden finally turned into a penal colony. You crossed the Styx again, this time across an ocean. Now you are on a different shore, your hair is gray and receding, your appearance less immaculate. Lost is the juvenile candor. The aura of survival that surrounds you is now a prop in the more recent dramas staged by memory.

Would the process of anamnesis—this endless probing with the scal-pel, this fencing match with yourself—be accelerated by pondering the photograph of the little boy at age nine? Even then, you felt like with-drawing and busying yourself in a corner of the room, forever forgotten by everyone—the vast solitude of the *entity*, Gertrude Stein would say, the exalted joy of finding yourself as you lose yourself in the endless flow of that confusing I.

Over your father's immobile, abstracted face there would sometimes pass an expression of sudden aging, the paralysis of solitude. You would watch in terror but quickly resume your place on the stage of the living, where there were teachers, parents, schoolmates, friends. The end of childhood did not signal an end to these alternations of ecstasy and ter-ror, always pondering the same questions: What if you suddenly stopped functioning and crumbled into remote unconnectedness? Still, you main-tained the illusion of escape, the possibility of last-minute rescue from the danger lurking everywhere in the dark.

The unknown could at any moment become hostile. It did yesterday, on October 9, 1941, when the appearances collapsed one by one, shattering the masks of daily life. On the platform of the Burdujeni railway station, the drama could not be stopped. Often, in your sleep, you would continue to see the great cast of hungry, shivering, and frightened prisoners, entertaining their executioners sitting in their boxes. Caution was the watchword of those days. Afterward, you feared chaos, hesitant to challenge the unknown. You nestled, finally, in the fluid shelter of language, the ultimate, essential refuge. But was this all you were looking for, a refuge?

Dr. Freud could not fail but be interested in such exercises of recall. Be yourself, said Pindar, echoed by Nietzsche, and by the Viennese doctor himself. But what is this, Dr. Freud: the anamnesis of the collective tragedy or the inability of this solitary individual to don the uniform of tragedy, for sale one every street corner? And what would Dr. Freud say about those who negate the horrors that happened, who routinely ridicule them in their boredom? Could trivialization, in the final analysis, be a necessary function, like digestion and excretion, the only way of keeping the human comedy alive? Otherwise, how could the poor actors still enjoy the fruits of the earth? Bear in mind the case of Primo Levi, who became a writer because of Auschwitz and was subsequently unable to write a simple love story as serene as the Italian skies.

The humiliation of being defined by a collective act of negation and by a collective catastrophe is not negligible, Dr. Freud. However, we are not simply the sum of collective catastrophes, whatever they may be. We are more than that, and each of us is also different. Yes, different, we should be shouting, in all the languages of the earth, shouting endlessly, like a record that cannot be turned off.

Suffering does not make us better people or heroes. Suffering, like all things human, corrupts, and suffering peddled publicly corrupts absolutely.

Nevertheless, one cannot renounce the honor of being despised and mocked, nor should we discard the honor of being an exile. After all, what other possessions do we have, apart from exile? Dispossession should not be deplored, it is preparation for the final dispossession.

When all is gone, there is still Hotel Noah's Ark and the art of pragmatism.

. . .

More time has now passed. You have learned the joys and the maladies of liberty. You have accepted the honor of exile. This is what you were telling your friends, in that pleasant place in the country not far from New York. You had finally accepted your destiny, you told them, but you continued to speak about ambiguity—the ambiguities of the labor camp, of the Communist penal colony, and of exile. You are suspicious of certitudes, even when you are the one uttering them. Still, you find yourself professing a certitude: "Exile begins as soon as we leave the womb." The straightforwardness of the statement didn't seem frightening. "One's mother should be one's real homeland. Only death finally frees us from this final belonging," you continued to recite, as though from a manual. Of course, you were just trying to give yourself courage, on the eve of your return to the scenes of your former life, but the humorless tone was not a good omen.

"The return to the homeland is but a return to the mother's grave," you concluded. It seemed you had really come to believe those words as a first step toward the impossible and inevitable return.

One does not make statements about graves without a certain apprehension. Your friends continued to listen sympathetically, attentively. You were, you told yourself, in the living present, not in the ever-present past.

It was a beautiful afternoon in the country. There was a hospitable silence—no thoughts, no questions, only the splendor of the day, the here and now.

The Second Return
(Posterity)

En Route

I n the summer of 1988, a few months after my arrival in the New World, I received an unexpected phone call from Leon Botstein, the president of Bard College in upstate New York. He made some flattering comments about a book of mine, published in Germany, and wanted to know if I would be interested in teaching at the school. We finally met in the spring of 1989, when I was invited up to Bard. He turned out to be a tall, elegant man, wearing a bow tie and thick glasses, with something of the alchemist about him. He was also a well-known symphony conductor. I had expected to be offered the appointment forthwith, but instead, I was delivered to an interview panel. "Democracy," the president explained.

Eight more years had now passed. I had published books, been awarded prizes, and had become writer in residence and a professor at Bard College. Even in the motherland, my position had changed. My *New Republic* article on Mircea Eliade and the Iron Guard had promoted me to public enemy number one, international division. My return to Romania in the spring of 1997 might seem an exercise in bridge building.

At 3:45 in the afternoon I am at Kennedy Airport, in the Lufthansa terminal, waiting for Leon. He has concerts in Bucharest and I am accompanying him. It is Sunday, April 20, the birthday of Adolf Hitler, as it happens. We are traveling first class, which entitles us to free pre-flight drinks in the lounge. We go over our schedule, and I tell Leon that the big issue in Bucharest at the moment is Romania's entry into NATO.

"You might be asked to give your opinion on a TV talk show," I say to him.

"Me? I'm not from the Pentagon or the State Department."

I explain that acceptance into NATO was regarded in Romania not only as a matter of national pride but as essential to the country's viability. A week before our departure, I had received, like other Romanians in America, a bulky envelope, from one of the Romanian President's staff, containing several enclosures urging immediate action in favor of Romania's entry into NATO. "Today, not tomorrow, and not the day after tomorrow, write to the White House. Please send a copy of your letter to the Presidential Palace in Bucharest, so that we know who our real friends are," one such document read. Indeed, I had heard that the Romanian authorities had made plans to compile a list—in Bucharest such lists are no joke—of all Romanian Americans who had done their patriotic duty in this regard.

"Is this to our advantage or not?" Leon asked. "What about the fact that you are accompanying me? Or is it I accompanying you?"

In fact, NATO was not the only hot topic in Bucharest. Mihail Sebastian's *Journal 1935–1944* had just appeared and had become the subject of controversy. Leon might be asked to comment and should therefore be briefed. Perhaps a few sound bites would do it, just like on American television: "Jewish Romanian writer, died 1945. His *Journal* describes life under Fascism, a Romanian counterpart to Victor Klemperer's just-published *I Will Bear Witness*, which documents the life of a Jew in wartime Nazi Dresden. Bares the pro-Nazi sympathies and anti-Semitism of some Romanian intellectuals." The name Klemperer might stimulate

Leon to tell anecdotes about the other Klemperer, the conductor Otto, a cousin of Victor's, and about his American career.

At last we are on our way, reclining in our comfortable seats. The flight attendant is blond, tall, and slim. We learn she was born in New Jersey, but that she and her family have returned to live in Germany. Leon again tells me that he would never have decided to accept the Romanian invitation unless I was willing to go, too. Again he tells me that my return to Romania will serve finally to separate me from my old life. I have heard it all before, and though I hope that this might indeed prove to be the case, I prefer not to think about it, or what we represent as a pair.

"What do you mean?" Leon asks.

"Well, the classical pair, Augustus the Fool and the White Clown."

Leon seems uninterested in the subject.

"The White Clown is the boss, the master, the authority, the American, if you will, and," I hasten to add, "the college president, the conductor."

Leon smiles.

"Augustus the Fool is the pariah, the loser, the one who always gets kicked in the ass, to the audience's delight. Augustus the Fool is the exile."

"What do you mean, kicked in the ass? You, a respectable writer, a writer in residence, honored with prizes and with an endowed chair? Does this boss ever kick the poor artist in the ass?"

"Well," I say, "we are a pair of travelers going to Eastern Europe, to the old stamping grounds of Augustus the Fool, who will serve as a guide to the foreign maestro, reciprocating the affection with which the American welcomed him into the circus of the New World."

Leon, now looking serious, says, "In the American circus, as you put it, the exile represents the victim. In the East European circus, the clown returning from America is a victor, a star."

He is now laughing, careful not to disturb the score of the Schumann oratorio resting on his knees. Augustus has now lost his zest for speechifying, and he makes a dismissive gesture. The pair doze off, wake up, take some refreshment, engage in casual remarks.

. . .

The old tourist guide of socialist Jormania, from the 1980s, slips to the floor:

> The Socialist Republic of Romania lies between 43° 37' 07" and 48° 15'
> 06" north and 20° 15' 44" and 29° 41' 24" east. With its 237,500 square
> kilometers (91,738 square miles) the country ranks twelfth in size among
> the European nations. East and north, it borders upon the Soviet Union,
> that is, the Maculist Empire, west upon the brotherly Socialist Repub-
> lic of Hungary, southwest upon the Federal Socialist Republic of Yu-
> goslavia. Around the central plateau of the Carpathian Mountains . . .

Augustus is thinking, A beautiful country, fine intellectuals, many decent people. Also, something not quite definable, slippery, too many
diminutives, the charm mixed in with the dirt.

At seven o'clock in the morning we arrive in Frankfurt. There is a two-
hour wait for the Bucharest flight. We wander through the airport shops.
Leon buys some cigars, some ballpoint pens, and pencils, to add to his
collection. We return to the lounge, find two seats, and try to get some
rest. I hear my first exchanges in Romanian, and I panic. Near the window is a group of youngsters dressed in old sweaters and jeans, swearing
cheerfully and profusely in my native tongue. I look around. Are the
ordinary-looking passengers perhaps really agents of the new mafias or
of the old secret services, hired to keep an eye on the suspect returning
to his motherland? I can pick out the Romanian academic returning from
a conference, the old lady who has just visited her daughter in Germany,
the doctor, the politician, the businessman. In a corner, a man in a dark
suit is bent over his expensive briefcase and pile of papers. Is he a secret
agent, too?

We board the plane bound for Bucharest. The division between first
class and tourist is less clearly marked. The cabin is filled with bustle
and noise. I am now attuned to the pulse of my anxiety. Leon is watching me, intrigued; he understands that I am already at home.

We land at Otopeni Airport, provincial-looking, small, but somehow appealing in its very modesty. Passport control goes swiftly and soberly. We wait for our luggage in a restricted, crowded space, choked with passengers, passersby, policemen, porters, loiterers—the full Oriental buzz of impatience. Our luggage is late in coming down and we look for a baggage cart. Yes, there are actually carts to be had; some things have changed, after all.

At the currency exchange desk, a pretty young woman is in charge. "How much?" Leon asks me. "A hundred dollars," I reply. Leon seems to consider this too paltry a sum and exchanges two hundred dollars, receiving in return a million lei. He stares in bewilderment at the profusion of crumpled banknotes. "Look," I say, "you're a millionaire at last!" Outside, we are met by a representative of the Bucharest Symphony and a chauffeur.

We drive through Otopeni, an impoverished suburb full of potholes, lined by billboards advertising American offerings. Near the Şosea quarter, the perspective opens up, there are trees, parks, old villas. Leon seems intrigued by the area's architecture, a strange mix of East and West. I mutter some tourist-guide drivel. Yes, the area once had a certain splendor, a sort of elegance, gone to seed under the proletarian dictatorship and further degraded under the subsequent generations of parvenus. We drive along Calea Victoriei, one of Bucharest's main thoroughfares. My first disappointment. The famous avenue, remembered as elegant even under Communism, now has a shabby look. We cross the bridge over the Dîmboviţa River, not far from my last residence, turn to the left at the university, and then again to the left in the direction of the Intercontinental Hotel.

"I wonder if the Securitate still have their eavesdropping devices in the hotel," I whisper. I tell Leon the story that made the rounds of Bucharest in the early eighties. A nice old French lady staying at the Intercontinental approached the receptionist and said timidly, "Excuse me, I have a request . . ." The friendly secret police agent, disguised as a receptionist, asked her politely, in acceptable French, what her desire was. She said, "I've been told there are microphones in the rooms. Would you be so kind . . . could I have one without?" Poor *chérie*. For months she was the laughingstock of Bucharest.

Day One: Monday, April 21, 1997

Three p.m. We make our triumphal entrance into the lobby of the Intercontinental Hotel, the former branch office of the Securitate, Foreigners' Section. Now I am a foreigner myself, although the receptionist welcomes me in Romanian: *"Bine ați venit."* We check into two adjacent rooms. At 4:30 the orchestra's car will return to collect the American conductor for his first rehearsal. I enter room 1515 and am about to unpack when the telephone rings. A pleasant young female voice is on the other end, from Romanian television. She asks for an interview. I decline politely. She understands, I have just arrived and need some time to think it over, perhaps later. What would I talk about— Transnistria, Periprava, Eliade, my success as an exiled writer? No, I shall remain firm in my decision. "You have the honor of being detested," Baudelaire once told Manet, admiringly. I repeat these words to myself like a mantra, to protect me from emotion and politeness. Should I appear onstage as a public enemy or as the victim of Fascism and Communism, or as the shy, retiring writer applauded by the Americans? I am an intruder, that's all, and all I want is to be ignored.

A recent story about Milan Kundera in Prague: After a few secret visits home, after the events of 1989, he finally accepted an official invitation to receive the award that would reconcile the motherland to its famous wandering son. However, just before the ceremony, he suddenly felt that he could not participate. He locked himself, like a besieged man, in his hotel room and watched the proceedings on television, as his wife accepted the honor on his behalf.

The telephone rings again. My friend Bedros is calling to welcome me back. I am happy to hear his voice after so many years, I am happy that I can still feel happy. He is coming over in half an hour to see me. I have no time to unpack, as the phone rings again. This time it's my old friend Naum, Golden Brain. I throw my jacket on the bed, open the window, and unlock the suitcases. I notice an envelope pushed under the door, a fax from the Romanian Television Society: "We repeat our request to you to grant an interview, to be conducted by the Department of Cultural Programs of the Romanian Television Society. We hope that you will understand our wish, given that your presence in this country will not pass unnoticed. The department has a television team available on Tuesday, April 22, 1997. We would be grateful, etc., etc." I take my clothes out of the suitcase and hang them up, and wash my face and hands. Bedros arrives.

He stands in the doorway for a while. We look at each other, smiling. We see ourselves in each other's face, as if in a mirror, a sad measure of the time that has elapsed, but also a measure tinged with the kindness that time accords to such reunions. He has the same face, the same black beard, the same big eyes, small hands and feet, the same gravelly voice, as though he were one of the characters in his own *Encyclopedia of the Armenians*. He even seems to be wearing the same sweater. Short and stubby, a fast talker, he hasn't changed a bit from those latest days in the Bucharest of socialist masquerades, when we used to talk about the day's books and exchange literary gossip. Subsequently, we had corresponded for a while. Apparently he still keeps in touch, as the fax from the television people, slipped under my door, turned out to be at his behest, as head of Cultural Affairs.

"Yes, the message was my idea, I admit."

I explain why I want to keep my return discreet, why I do not want anyone to approach me, why I do not wish to trouble anyone.

"I've been thinking about you lately, especially when I was reading Sebastian's *Journal*. It's strange how the past returns."

He pauses for a moment, then continues in his brisk fashion: "A character enclosed within brackets, that's how I remember you, a character from Proust. I've been thinking about you, and talking to friends. They all agreed, definitely a character from Proust."

I seem amazed by the flattery, so he explains: "Even when we chatted about minor stuff, you had a way of always speaking in nuances, a phrase within a phrase, a bracket within a bracket."

I recall my walks with Bedros, the Proustian detours, the twists and turns of the socialist tunnel. We go out on the balcony and he points out the Telecom Palace and Calea Victoriei running as far as the bridge, the street of my last residence in Bucharest, at number 2. The city appears old, tired, apathetic. Proustian memories? Proustian exile, in one's own room? What about the genuine exile, what about the charge of "enemy" that was hurled at me by the motherland's newspapers?

Our reunion has the calm, affectionate air of an earlier one, in 1990, in Paris, at the Salon du Livre. Bedros had traveled from Bucharest; I, from New York. My book, displayed at the Albin Michel booth, bore the title, appropriate to our present conversation, *Le thé de Proust*. Bedros on this occasion was a mere extra, not part of the official delegation, the new elite, among whom I found myself an alien. Our lunch in a small restaurant confirmed the genuineness of our reunion. Now, here at the Intercontinental, I am grateful to Bedros for reminding me of my old private self and rescuing me from the caricature that has served as my substitute on the Romanian public stage.

"Would you like a drink? Beer, mineral water, Pepsi?"

Pepsi, he says, and I bring two bottles from the fridge and two glasses. After a hearty swig, he continues: "Recently, when Sebastian's

Journal was published, I reflected on the similarities of your situations. I can understand why you don't want to meet people and give interviews. These days, most Romanians returning from abroad scramble for all this attention, interviews, applause, celebrations. They bask in all the kowtowing they get in abundance here, at the Gates of the Orient. They love adulation."

Then he speaks about the country's misery, its literature, its politicians and members of the Securitate turned nouveaux riches, the stray dogs and the vagabond children. After half a century of waiting, the country deserved better. I look at his new book on the table, with the face of an Armenian priest on the cover.

The ringing telephone saves me from imminent melancholy. It's Joanna, the poet, a former cultural attaché at the Romanian Embassy in Washington, now working for the Soros Foundation. I have to go downstairs and discuss with her the schedule of Leon's visit. More than ten years have passed since our last meeting, just before my departure from socialist Jormania. It was springtime then, just like now, lunchtime. "The place of our truth is here. We are writers, we have no other solution," she had said. I was familiar with such banalities. I myself had once been a victim of misery's pride, it had often fed my despair. That time, however, I had a different answer: "You have to be alive to write. Death is keeping an eye on us, and not only from the offices of the Securitate. The unheated apartments, the pharmacies without drugs, the empty shops—these are the masks of death." Joanna had survived nicely the nightmare of those years. She had become an able cultural and diplomatic official after 1989, and she had published books. I had survived in exile, and now I had some difficulty in stopping her flow of politeness and bureaucratic detail.

I am now back on the balcony, looking at Bucharest from the hotel's fifteenth floor. Bedros points out more landmarks, the building of the television center, the Atheneum concert hall, the Lido Hotel, the university. We go back into the room and resume our chat. We have to pass over many things rapidly—too many things have happened to us, in different ways and in different places, over the last decade. He inquires about Cella. I tell him she had a difficult time adapting but now has her own restoration workshop. She works hard and has also finally come to terms with exile.

"I didn't know her very well," Bedros says. "My wife, too, only met her once, at that birthday party at your place, in 1986, in July. But she's remained very vivid in our memories. That's why I always end my letters with regards to the lady of the house."

We need to be able to spend a longer time together, unhurried and without words, in order to recapture the simpler exchanges of the past. Rushed as it is, our meeting feels more like a consolation. Is it my tense watchfulness, "Proust's wound"? We exchange whispered words and the shadow of a knowing, but subdued, smile.

It is now five o'clock, and my friend Naum appears in the doorway. With his shiny, bony skull showing through the cropped hair of a conscript, we dubbed him Golden Brain. His eyes are quick, taking everything in. We look at each other without illusions, at what we are, at what remains. He looks even bonier than before, dried up by the winds of another age. His hair is whiter, too, but his detachment, his wit are the same. His nonchalance had been the asset that, a decade earlier, when he was a member of the Central Committee of Liars, had helped him cleverly negotiate the tightrope of the circus, amused at his own performance, no less than that of others. He still has, I am pleased to note, his old smile, his laughter, his carelessness and self-confidence. "Politics never interested me," the former politician would tell me over the phone in recent years, intrigued that I, of all people, nonpolitical and isolated from public affairs, should wish to rake the "old garbage." "I don't want to understand or explain. I'm just telling a story, as simple as that," he would repeat, again and again, without ever telling, in fact, his own story in that masquerade.

We had been brought together by books, jokes, perhaps even by his pro-Semitic sympathies, in a place where such things do not earn you merit badges. We are still held together, even now, by the same things. Near or far, our sense of fidelity has held fast. The opening gambit is awkward. I show him, on the bed, the padlock I have bought for him, the one he asked for.

"This lock is very expensive," I say. "The Romanian thieves will have some trouble getting past this one. You're going to be inviolable. Not even the germs will be able to get into your house."

Our last meeting took place in the autumn of 1986. The president of the Writers Union had wanted to talk to me, out of reach of the official microphones. The message was transmitted by our mutual friend, Golden Brain. The three of us walked together. The park was brewing in autumn's cauldron. Tense and strange, the resonance of our voices disturbed the shivering vapors of the bushes. It did not seem that we had different views or different opinions: the president was complaining that nothing functioned properly anymore and deplored, for both our sakes, the official anti-Semitic hysteria. I maintained an approving silence, and Golden Brain, the go-between, was also silent. Was that a final attempt at domesticating the would-be defector? He must have been aware of the underlying reasons for that meeting. Subsequently, less than two months later, I learned, in Washington, that the Party had scrapped the prize that the union had awarded me. Was that all there was to it? Could the pretext for the conspiratorial walk have been so minor? The negotiations between the Party and the Writers Union had failed, obviously, and the president had wanted us to part on good terms. Doubtless, Golden Brain knew what was behind that mysterious walk.

Family and friends waiting at home that day were alarmed by my lateness, convinced that the Securitate had laid a trap for me. Even now, on the fifteenth floor of the Intercontinental, I hesitate to ask my friend if the purpose of that walk had been merely an attempt to tame me, before my "defection" to the West, and prefer instead to look at him and be looked at by one who had been a friend even when he played at politics, and who has remained a friend even after the Party's roulette wheel has stopped spinning and I now belong to another place. It would be futile to ask. This citizen of Bucharest would respond with a joke, as usual, bewildered by my naïveté, cutting me off with "Are you still interested in politics, old man? I was never interested then, nor am I interested now." Are these his words or are they mine? Who knows, and what is the point of questions in a place that has no answers to give.

Yet if I am not able to risk an honest dialogue with an old friend, is it surprising that I hate public rhetoric so much? Am I embarrassed by the burden of "celebrityhood," one for which I am so ill suited? "A literary celebrity in exile" is the descriptive tag employed here for those of my kind. But I am also a domestic celebrity, known in the motherland as a "traitor," and so forth. In 1986, it seemed to me that I was reliving the 1940s. Was this awareness the source of my last-minute escape? "The stigmata of trauma" was how a younger literary critic described my writing. "The neurotic nucleus of the deportation," he said, "the reticence, the refusal, the aloneness" could well be some kind of "autistic reaction," some mechanism of "introversion."

I cannot see myself taking part in some partisan debate, followed by applause. The artificiality and aggression of public performance depress me. Nor do I wish to confront those who have pushed me against the wall and now stand ready to celebrate me. But it would appear that even those I like can inhibit me. I can predict the framework of the whole journey from the start, but if, fearing the hurt, I do not go out of my shell, I cannot hope to discover what's around me.

Golden Brain has left me to my silence. He is smiling, pleased with his new padlock and with our reunion. He tells me about the difficulties of post-Communist life, about the new class of nouveaux riches and the prevailing poverty, about his wife's retirement and return to work at menial, tiresome jobs, about the regrouping of old and new literary stars. His joviality blocks lament or resentments; this is a serene, lucid summary. He marvels at the hotel room's tackiness and is stupefied at the cost.

I see him downstairs to the lobby, then go out of the hotel and walk over to the Dalles bookstore nearby. I go in with some hesitation. Thank God, I see none of the old pilgrims, that sect of readers who used to recognize each other even without knowing one another. My old friend Liviu Obreja, familiar to all the booksellers in Bucharest, is not there either, thank God, prowling in his customary hunting grounds. The shelves are well stocked with volumes, in Romanian, French, and English. There are many browsers. Suddenly I am dizzy, unsure of my movements. I remember a similar sensation back in 1979, during my first trip to Western Europe, when I ran like a madman from one shelf to another of the

FNAC bookstore in Paris, noting down titles, counting, again and again, the available cash I had to spend.

This time it will not happen; there is no reason it should. My confusion and unease, I realize, derive from the fact of seeing so many Romanian books, of being surrounded by such a plethora of Romanian print. I can still see the wall-length bookshelves in my last Bucharest apartment, the one that vanished with my departure in 1986. After that, I stopped buying books. Now my library grows only from offerings of friends or publishers. I have learned the lesson of dispossession, and not only about books. No, this is not the same kind of faintness that overcame me in Paris in 1979, it is just the emotion of being once again in a Romanian bookstore.

At seven-thirty I head to the Atheneum, for the rehearsal. Magheru Boulevard, unchanged, seems, however, somewhat altered. The façades look dirty, the pedestrians rigid, diminished, ghostlike. The atmosphere is alien, I am alien, the pedestrians alien. The street is almost deserted. Suddenly I see a familiar face. Could that really be Dr. Buceloiu? There is no room for doubt, the slow movements, the big, gloomy head—yes, Dr. Buceloiu indeed. I remember his thick, smoky voice, his tangled mane of dark, thick hair. He moves slowly, like an old man, in his short leather jacket, a thick woolen scarf round his neck, although it is late April. He has his arm lightly placed over the shoulder of an even older man, bent, short, completely white-haired. I seem unable to wrench myself from this dream sequence, and yet I move on, turning to look at the two men now walking away with small, slow steps.

I cross the boulevard over to the Scala cinema. Next to it is the Unic block of apartments where Cella's mother lived until her death. Everything is the same and yet not the same. Something indefinable but essential has skewed the stage set, something akin to an invisible cataclysm, a magnetic anomaly, the aftermath of an internal hemorrhage. Maybe it is the squalor, but if you look closer, it is not just that. There are signs of unfinished roadwork everywhere, but even this does not seem to point to real change. I stand and stare for much longer than I should. I gaze at the Unic store, then turn around to face the Scala cinema and the pastry shop of the same name, then the Lido Hotel, and the Ambassador Hotel.

The estrangement is still incomplete, the wound still not healed, the rupture still active, although now somewhat muted. There is something else at work here, of an objective nature—the traumatizing, alienated reality itself. Gloomy immutability appears as permanence when, in fact, it is just a disease, a perverted wreck.

Death has passed this way, in the footsteps of the dead man now revisiting the landscape of his life in which he can no longer find a place or a sign of himself. After my death, Death visited this place, but was it not already here, was it not that from which I had fled? In 1986, the dictatorship had become Death, owning the landscape and the streets and the pedestrians, and all else besides.

I cross over quickly to the other side of the boulevard, where the former Cina restaurant used to be. I enter a narrow, deserted street. A thin rain begins to fall. I feel something unnatural surrounding me, some unnatural sense within myself. Could this moment and this no-man's-land be the time and place of an accident, a murder, a mysterious aggression?

I step up my pace and reach the Atheneum. The façade is under repair, covered in scaffolding, the sidewalk all dug up, muddy. I enter the lobby, where I have been so many times before. Two men stand there, chatting. They could be construction workers, they could be from the management. Attracted by the sound of music coming from the auditorium, I ascend the splendid marble staircase and enter the first door on the left.

Leon is on the podium, facing the orchestra, sleeves rolled up, a bottle of Evian at his side. The disorder of both orchestra and chorus is unbelievable. Yes, Death has left its mark here, too. Gone are the orchestra members of yesteryear. Scruffy-looking types in jeans and shabby vests, chatting away, have replaced them. "Once again," comes the command. The players continue to chatter and giggle. They are hypnotized by their own hysteria, and seem to have been picked off the streets. First one, then another, score in hand, disputes the interpretation of notes, pauses, flats and sharps. Leon is overwhelmed, his interpreter can hardly keep pace with the hubbub. "Once again," the exasperated conductor orders. He signals to the first violinist, now standing, to translate the command: "Once again, from the third bar." The cacophony begins anew.

Leon gulps down another mouthful of Evian, rolls his sleeves up higher, and again raises his imperious baton. The scene has come to resemble a boxing match between orchestra and distinguished visiting conductor. Now the conductor is on the floor and the referee is counting. Dazed, the conductor rises again, with some difficulty. It is ten past eight, and the match is supposed to be over by eight-thirty. Tonight there will be no winner, not even a draw. The only possible outcome of this fight is disengagement between the two combatants.

Leon descends from the podium, exhausted. Raising his hands toward the ceiling decorated with portraits of Romanian princes, he whispers, "*Ave Maria.*" I get up to greet him. Joanna assures us that the second rehearsal will be better and that the night of the concert will produce a fine performance. The pick-up orchestra, she explains, has to work under difficult conditions, with miserable pay and humiliations of all kinds.

We go out to look for a taxi. Joanna offers to accompany us and help us find our way. I take from my pocket an envelope marked SEDER. "Dear Mr. Botstein," it reads, "We have saved two places for you and Professor Manea at the Passover Seder on April 21, 1997. The Seder will begin at around 20.00 hour and the fee is $15 per person, to be paid at the entrance to Mr. Godeanu. The Seder will take place in the Jewish community's restaurant in Bucharest, at no. 18 Popa Soare Street." The letter is signed by Alex Sivan, executive director of the Federation of Jewish Communities in Romania. The Romanian Embassy in Bucharest had arranged the invitations, as Leon wanted to be with his co-religionists for the Seder.

The streets are deserted, there is no taxi in sight. We walk toward the university and a taxi appears. The seats have no suspension and we sink into a hole in the middle. I give the driver the address; he hasn't heard of it. I try to explain, a cross street off Calea Călăraşi; the former Calea Călăraşi, as it turns out, has disappeared so that a wide road can be built to the Grand Presidential Palace. "I don't know this address," the driver repeats sullenly. We are back on the street, and the rain is getting heavier. Two empty taxis pass by without stopping; we get into the third. The driver recognizes the address, although he doesn't quite know how to get there. We reach the Rond, he turns toward the former Dimitrov Boulevard, from there to the right, then right again, then left. "When you see the lines of policemen, it means that we're there," I say helpfully, remembering the socialist Seder nights, when the street was cordoned off by militiamen around the Jewish restaurant and identifications were checked at some distance from the restaurant, to deter Arab terrorists, troublesome dissidents, anti-Semitic agents provocateurs, and Zionists demanding passports.

We drive around in circles, until the driver announces triumphantly, "I knew it, there it is, Popa Soare." Indeed, the sign on the street corner confirms the fact. We turn back to number 18 and I recognize the building. This time there are no police cordons, just one armed guard and a plainclothes man wearing the habitual leather jacket.

An old man wearing a skullcap greets us. Yes, he assures us, we are expected. He does not ask for the fifteen dollars. We are offered two white skullcaps. Leon's briefcase and raincoat, as well as my parka, are left behind in the cloakroom. We climb the staircase to the brightly lit hall, where the Jews of Bucharest will be celebrating Passover for this Hebrew year 5757.

The tables are arranged as they were ten, fifteen years ago. There is a head table, for the presiding panel of community officials, and eight other tables for the guests. We are directed to our seats at a table on the left. We can see the president, a well-known biologist, his wife, and other community dignitaries. I clutch my copy of the publication we were given, *The Jewish Reality*, the successor to the former *Review of the Mosaic Cult*. "Cult" was a term the Communists tolerated, post-Communist Jews prefer more neutral language.

There is no fuss made over the American guest, the college president and conductor, or over the former member of Romania's Jewish community. I instantly remember that time in 1982 when I made public declarations against official nationalism and anti-Semitism, and found myself cut off even by the community's officials. Such imprudent gestures, it seemed, hindered, rather than helped, relations with the authorities and were the preserve of the Chief Rabbi, Dr. Moses Rosen, a deputy in the Grand National Assembly of the Socialist Republic for two decades, who played an intricate game in which American and Israeli Jewish organizations functioned as lobbies and pressure groups. Now times have changed, the current president of the Jewish community is no longer the Chief Rabbi, and the old strategies are no longer necessary.

"Wherefore is this night different from all other nights," my former self asks. Age has plastered new masks on the faces of yesteryear. At the present gathering I cannot detect the former air of festive duplicity, the quarter-truths, wrapped in puzzling hints and gestures, as required by the secret code of the time and, equally, by attempts to undermine it. I can no longer see the servile smiles of the bosses disguised as servants and of their doubles, all decked out in their dress uniforms. Also gone are the quotations from the Book of Regulations on Conditioned Reflexes. It seems useless to try recapturing the perverted animation, the complicity, the picturesque bit players. The atmosphere of the year 5757 lacks the former air of excitement and risk it had in the time of slavery, complicity, and evasion. All that is left is a sleepy assembly of apathetic survivors, gathered to join in the ancient recital.

"Welcome back!" A hearty voice breaks my reverie. The massive gentleman sitting across the table from me extends his big, open palm. He is a stocky, bald, smartly dressed, bespectacled man. He smiles, waits for a sign of recognition from me, and then, in disappointment, says his name in a firm, imposing voice. I should have recognized him. In the time of Romania's Socialist Pharaoh, he was one of the few palatable figures on television. I turn to Leon and introduce him to Mr. Joseph Sava, who will be interviewing him on his television show, *The Musical Soirée.* Leon bows ceremoniously to the music critic and his wife, whom he promptly engages in an animated conversation, in German, on the forthcoming performance.

"You're going to be invited on the show, too, of course," Mr. Sava tells me.

"Oh, no, I regret, but I can't. It's Mr. Botstein's interview. I made that quite clear last week, from New York."

"You must be there, too. It will make the interview even more interesting, and you can do the interpreting. It's settled. I'll be expecting both of you on Friday morning at the television center, on Pangrati Street," he says confidently. Somewhat startled, unaccustomed to such a commanding tone, I turn nervously left and right.

"This discussion is pointless," the critic's wife intervenes. "Mr. Botstein speaks perfect German, and I can do the interpreting myself."

I look around. I can recognize poets, actors, functionaries of the community, all visibly aged. I identify a friend of my friend Mugur, two actors from the Jewish Theater, a famous composer of pop hits. But this night is indeed different from the similar nights of the past. What is missing is its maestro, the indefatigable Chief Rabbi Rosen, then also president of the community, the director and leading actor of so many performances on the totalitarian stage, a deputy in the Communist parliament, a consultant to the State Department, an intermediary for Israel and diplomat-at-large of the Socialist Republic of Romania, always entrusted with important missions and roles.

It was not easy to forget the various Jewish festivals that were celebrated here, in the festive hall of Rabbi Rosen's restaurant, in the latter stages of the atheist Communist state—the tables decorated with traditional foods, the imported wine, the honored guests sitting next to the Party officials, and the visitors from abroad. Such evenings stood out as the culmination of all the efforts of the great Chief Rabbi, who could have served equally well as Minister for Public Works, or Information, or Industry. The system tolerated and even encouraged such shows, not only in order to confuse the outside world, unaccustomed to these extravagant examples of Communist "freedom," but also in order to be able to record the names, faces, and words of the participants.

Those occasions were feasts of contradictions, under the surveillance of informers disguised as parishioners, or their atheist enemies. They had plenty to see, the ambiguous, mutually advantageous cooperation between the duplicitous masters and the even more duplicitous slaves, serving two or more masters at the same time. There were even informers cast as hardworking citizens, wearing their own faces and uniforms as masks.

Now Communism has expired, the Great Rabbi is dead, and with them have gone the risks and the masks. Now there are only worn-out celebrants, a shabby hall, a ritual reduced to routine performance. One cannot compare this skinny, mumbling rabbi conducting the Seder to Chief Rabbi Dr. Moses Rosen. This substitute does no honor to his role, he looks like a mere teacher in a cheder, from another century, desperately calling his flock to order, with his squeaky voice and anguished gestures. On his left, his wife, in a leek-green dress, with an enormous red wig on her head, gives him the occasional nudge to alert him to the fact that the company is nodding off.

"Who is this rabbi?" I ask the fat, silent man sitting on my left.

My neighbor turns placidly toward me. He has a wide face and drooping eyelids.

"He's been brought over from Israel," he informs me, extending his hand and introducing himself as Dr. Vinea. Next to him is his pale mate, wearing a black lace dress, whom I recognize as a fellow student from the university.

"From Israel? But he speaks Romanian."

"He comes from the Romanian Jews in Israel," his wife, who has not recognized me, interjects. "It's the American Joint Distribution Committee that pays, and they choose. What else would they choose for Romania but the cheapest rabbi available. We mustn't complain."

I turn to Leon, to translate the explanation, but I discover him engaged in animated conversation with the couple on my right, an American Jew, a representative of a New York bank in Bucharest, and his companion, a Romanian woman who speaks fluent English and doesn't seem at all embarrassed as her escort recounts in detail the history of his family in New Jersey, including a wife, daughters, sons-in-law, brothers, sisters-in-law, their children.

"I think I know you from somewhere," the doctor's wife announces, staring at me.

"From our student days. You were one year behind me."

She seems pleasantly surprised. "Really? I graduated in 1960."

"I used to associate your name with something different," Dr. Vinea says.

"Yes, some people make a different connection to my name," I manage to murmur, before my words are drowned out by the choir, now onstage.

Leon shows no interest in the choir or the rabbi, only in the American Jewish banker and the young companion who brightens his Scythian exile. I take a sip of the wine, taste the Israeli matzos, the traditional soup, and the delicious roast. Equally tasty are the bitter herbs of legend and the memories of the flight from the Egypt of socialist Jormania, on this night of memory, in which the past usurps the present and returns my self to the one I no longer am.

My former fellow student wants to know when I left the country, where I live in America, how I am doing generally. She offers to take me on a tour of the Ceauşescu White Palace—the interior is worth seeing, oh yes, especially the interior, but not with a guided tour that rushes you through. I thank her, but decline the offer; we have no time, we are here on a short and event-packed visit. No, I do not have an e-mail address, although I'm sure I'll be getting one.

I flash my watch to Leon, it's midnight. His cake lies stale on his plate, but he shows no desire to leave. Finally, we make our way out. The dignitaries at the head table do not notice our departure, capitalist guests no longer benefit from special attention, and that is as it should be.

It is raining, the darkness is medieval. On a night such as this, some forty years ago, in Stalinist-era Prague, the representative of the Jewish Agency was assassinated. But Stalinism is no longer fashionable, and Professor Culianu's Chicago assassins would have had no interest in us. In any case, Leon shows no interest in somber speculation. This Seder in Bucharest has awakened a nostalgia in him.

"This evening has been fascinating. It's reconnected me to my East European forebears. What you have in Bucharest is unique, you couldn't find anything like this anywhere else. That rabbi, his wife, the TV man, his wife—these are all shadows from the past. And the choir and that American guy with his young mistress . . . Thank God, Romania is lagging behind in the race to capitalism."

I remain silent, I am not convinced of the advantage. I simply stand in the middle of the square, with my arm extended, waving for a taxi that fails to materialize. We proceed on foot toward the city center. Somewhere around here is where I used to live as a student, in a rented room. Here it is, one of those side streets branching off into the dark, on the left, on Alexandru Sihleanu Street, at number 18. That's it, the sleepy house with the sleepy ghost of Dr. Jacobi, now long dead, and of his fat, scandal-mongering wife, also dead, and the Gypsy mistress in the basement, the object of their daily rows, certainly now dead as well. Hail to sovereign and democratic Death, working nonstop, day and night, bored, but oh! ever so efficient.

"So what was it you enjoyed so much?" I ask Leon, to chase away the phantoms.

"Everything, I liked everything. That idiotic rabbi and his pushy wife, the music critic's wife, speaking *Hochdeutsch*, and the New York guy with his mistress, the choir, the soup, the president, the biologist—everything, absolutely everything."

"It's a shame you missed the great Chief Rabbi. He was a deputy, for a quarter of a century, in Romania's Communist parliament, the *éminence grise*, the great wheeler-dealer, as you Americans say. He managed to convince the Communists of the advantages of getting rid of the Jews, by letting them emigrate."

"Wasn't he right?"

"Sure. He convinced the authorities that there were at least three major advantages in letting the Jews go: One, they would be rid of an old troublesome lot. Two, they would get capitalist money, $8,000 per head, to be more precise, for each Jew they let out. Three, by letting the Jews go, they improved their image abroad. The Jews themselves no longer needed any convincing, and so, the latter-day flight from Egypt!"

"A clever man, this Rabbi Rosen."

"Very clever, a real pragmatist, trying to be useful to all sides. As someone once said, he was for the Romanians what prescription glasses are for the myopic. He was not happy about needing them, but happy to have them. In my parents' house, they had a completely different idea about what a rabbi should be."

"But they were believers, and you aren't."

Silently, we advance through this night of questions without answers.

"A few years ago, in Israel, a taxi driver asked me whether I was Romanian. He had heard me talking to the relatives I'd just dropped off.

Yes, I was born in Romania, I said. I met Rabbi Rosen, the old taxi driver told me, in English, many years ago, on one of his visits to Israel, here, in my taxi. I didn't know who he was at first, we have lots of rabbis visiting here, but this one spoke perfect Hebrew. I took him first to the Foreign Ministry, then the Labor Party headquarters, then to their opponents, the Likud. Afterward, we went to the trade unions, then to the religious people. Then, if you can imagine, even to the Communists. At the end I asked him, 'Are you by any chance Rabbi Rosen of Romania?' 'Yes,' he replied. 'How did you guess?' 'Well, you're well-known here. Nobody else would have visited the religious people, and the Communists, and the trade unions, and Mr. Begin.'"

This anecdote about Rabbi Rosen reminds me of how Romanians, in general, used to solve the incompatibilities of daily life, a practice so acutely denounced by Sebastian. I tell this to Leon.

"You're right," Leon says. "It would have been worth meeting Rabbi Rosen, but even without him, it was a fascinating evening."

"Ah, the famous American enthusiasm, the goodwill, the openness to the world."

"Had I told anyone at that table that I had nowhere to sleep, I'm sure they would have offered to put me up. Who would do that in America?"

"Bard College."

Leon laughs, we are both laughing.

"Taxi!" A miracle, the cab stops, and off we go into the post-Communist rain and darkness, squeezed together, in a beat-up car, a relic from a museum of socialism, the conductor-president in his handsome suit and bow tie and his fellow traveler, Augustus the Fool.

"To the Intercontinental, please," I repeat for the third time, in Romanian.

The taxi has not turned left, as it should have, but has gone straight on, toward God knows what subterranean garage of the mafia. I look through the window, trying to recognize the route; no, it is not the old Calea Călăraşi, which no longer exists. We are probably coasting along the avenue formerly called the Victory of Socialism, which leads to the new Balkan Versailles, the White Palace, the residence that our beloved Supreme Leader Ceauşescu had no time to enjoy. The taxi finally turns onto Bălcescu Boulevard in the direction of the university and the hotel. There we are, at last, on the twenty-second floor, in the deserted bar. One last toast in honor of our first day together in Bucharest. Leon seems content, the Seder has regenerated him, it all looks like a promising adventure. We say good night at one o'clock, 6 p.m. in New York, twenty-four hours since our takeoff from Kennedy.

I am here and I am there, neither here nor there, a passenger in transit, claimed by several time zones, and not only by them.

The red light of the phone blinks to signal a call. It is Ken, an American friend who has come from Moscow especially to see me. On my night table a blue-covered notebook lies open, with bold white lettering reading BARD COLLEGE, the logbook to record my pilgrimage.

Day Two: Tuesday, April 22, 1997

Ken works for the Privatization Project in Eastern Europe sponsored by the Soros Foundation. I met him five years ago, after receiving an unexpected letter from him. "This is something of a shot in the dark," he wrote, and went on to describe a project he was working on, a book about the aesthetic reaction to the Holocaust as reflected in literature, music, and art. "Something you said at the conference at Rutgers/Newark last spring has troubled me ever since. The phrase of yours that haunts me is this: the commercialization of the Holocaust."

We arranged to meet in an Irish bar in Manhattan. He told me about his grandfather who, as a penniless young man, had emigrated to America, eventually to become an important scientist, winning a Nobel Prize; about his French mother, who taught at Princeton; about his brother killed in the Vietnam War; and about himself, author of several books and a forthcoming critical study of modern conservatism. Gradually, a friendship developed. I appreciated his openness of spirit and his cosmopolitanism, the result of his French and Irish origins, as well as his

Oxford education, his Catholic moral sense, and his jovial American
sense of fair play.

He had come from Moscow to see me, here, in my old haunts. "When
you were talking in Romanian to that young man at the reception desk,"
he said to me, at our reunion in the lobby of the Intercontinental, "your
face lit up. You were relaxed, even transfigured. I can see that language
remains an open wound for you."

Transfigured, talking to a state hotel employee, about whose secret
allegiance I knew nothing? However, I accepted the challenge, language
is indeed a subject worth talking about. "My country is my language"
was my answer, in 1979, responding to my American sister-in-law, who
kept trying to persuade me to leave socialist Jormania as soon as possible. I finally did leave, but I did not leave the language in which I lived,
only the country where I could no longer breathe. "I wish for you that
one morning we will all wake up speaking Romanian," Cynthia, aware of
my linguistic distress, once wrote me. An impossible dream . . . but not
in Bucharest. Maybe Ken is right. It might very well be that the language in which I was immersed is working its magic on me. Then again,
perhaps not. I have discovered that, in the years of my absence, the Romanian language has recycled all the old clichés of the socialist wooden
tongue with injections of jargon deriving from American movies and advertising. Yesterday, when I switched on the TV in my hotel room, I was
greeted by a battery of members of the Romanian Senate, all incapable
of articulating a fully formed sentence. In the waiting room of the Frankfurt airport, I was assaulted by the same mutterings, the same mutilated
words.

Ken and I are walking toward my former home. We pass the State Library, a massive, dusty building, proceed along Lipscani Street, a sort of
bazaar arcade, then past the Stavropoleos Church, a miniature jewel set
awkwardly amid the surrounding grayness and impoverishment. We encounter potholed sidewalks, decayed walls, comical shop signs, nervous,
shivering, harassed passersby. We walk past the former Comedy Theater,
cross the new bridge over the Dîmboviţa River, and find ourselves on
Calea Victoriei. The old building, at number 2, is still there. I show Ken
the balcony of apartment 15, on the third floor.

When we moved in, the balcony was enclosed with glass panels, which created a bit of extra space. The order to demolish this type of extension came from the country's First Lady, Comrade Mortu, as Culianu would say. I was bold enough to launch a legal war against the authorities, only in order to obtain written proof of this abuse, one more act of naïveté to add to the list in my Jormanian biography.

"Shall we go up to the apartment, to see who lives there now?" Ken asks.

"I know who lives there."

Ken insists, but I hold my ground, and not because I am sentimental about my former residence. After I left the country, I continued to pay rent on the apartment, in 1986, 1987, 1988, and 1989, the years of my wanderings through Germany and America. In 1989, after the collapse of the Communist regime and the hunting down of the dictator and his spouse, the building's administrator had forced open the door of the apartment and had moved in quickly. He had obviously been helped by the country's Supreme Secret Institution, for which he had been working undercover, like all his sort. The naïve transatlantic tenant sued the administrator, but the authority stood by its collaborator. The impossible proved, once more, possible: democratic Romania's democratic judicial system pronounced, both in 1990 and in 1991, in favor of the administrator and against the traitor from across the ocean. The alien was ordered to pay not only the court costs, but also, with his filthy dollars, for the expense of redecorating the apartment on which, from his exile, he had been paying rent during all those years.

Socialist law stipulated, as I tried to explain to Ken, that whenever someone left the country "for good," they had to bequeath the apartment to the state in perfect condition. But even though I had not "returned" the apartment to the state, and the socialist law no longer applied, socialism's secret police, with its informers and administrators, had survived.

We go up Calea Victoriei and walk past the Central Post Office, turned into the Museum of National History erected by Ceauşescu but, in fact, a shrine to his and Comrade Mortu's contribution to the glory of the country and the people. The impersonal street, as impersonal as pos-

terity itself, does not seem to have missed me and is not aware that I was
its faithful pedestrian for so many years. On our left, next to the Victo-
ria department store, now restored to its prewar name of Lafayette, an
ugly modern building is rising. Next to it is the building of the old militia, now restyled as the Bucharest city police headquarters. To the right,
as in the old days, is the Fashion House and the Cinemathèque.

Postmortem tourism should never be underestimated. I am aware of
the privilege I have been afforded and recognize the instant benefits of
its sadism. Having reached the intersection with the boulevard, we turn
right toward University Square, where we are assailed by a slogan
smeared on one of the walls in big black capitals: MONARHIA SALVEAZĂ
ROMÂNIA (Monarchy Saves Romania). We go through the underground
crossing, now full of small shops, then emerge on the opposite side, on
Magheru Boulevard, just in front of the hotel.

At one o'clock I meet Leon again, at the Atheneum. The rehearsal is
in full swing, Joanna is her usual helpful self. I find it difficult to super-
impose the image of the poet of a decade ago, electrifying her audience
with her rendition of Allen Ginsberg's "Howl," onto her current reincarnation as a cultural functionary. The car of the American Embassy is
waiting for us in front of the Atheneum to take us to the lunch in our
honor given by John Katzka, the consul in charge of public relations.

We—the American star and the Romanian exile, an incomparable
team—go up the stairs of the imposing building. The White Clown,
tall, relaxed, elegant, accompanied by Augustus the Fool, tense and
oblique, are welcomed by the cultural attaché, an inexpressive woman,
and by Mr. Katzka, tall, blond, voluble, who expresses an immediate interest in Bard College, in the MacArthur Prize that I had been awarded
in 1992, and in our schedule. Soon, the Romanian guests start to appear,
"academics" is how they are described on the invitation. I introduce
Andrei Pleşu to Leon, having been informed by George Soros that he is
likely to be the preferred candidate to head the Central European University in Budapest. Pleşu regrets the fact that I didn't let people know
in advance of my visit; he could have arranged a meeting with an "interesting group" from the New Europe College, of which he is presently head.
I have no chance to be self-deprecating about my talent for missing

happy opportunities, as I find myself in the arms of Laurențiu Ulici, the Writers Union's current president, older than I remember him. He, too, is full of reproaches that I gave no advance notice of my visit. He insists that I drop by the union, where he would like to "organize something" to celebrate my return, a meeting, a festivity, a colloquium. Was that "something" supposed to be an occasion for my former colleagues finally to express the indignation they had failed to express seven years before, and since, when public lies about their fellow writer were bruited? He monopolizes my attention, eager to tell me about the union's organizational and financial achievements in these "difficult times"—for instance, from the money produced by renting out buildings to foreign agencies, they were funding pensions, sick-leave support, and literary awards; an international writers' association had been founded, with holiday homes and residential accommodations for translation projects; the Rome-based Biblioteca di Romania would be the venue for major international writers' conferences; the union has also established publishing collaborative ventures with Paris. I nod my approval, relieved that he is not questioning me about my own affairs. At lunch, we are all under the spell of Leon's animated recitation of musical anecdotes. The consul is a good host, the food plentiful, the wine acceptable.

It is getting warmer outside and sunnier. Perhaps I should go out, maybe take another look at the Dalles bookstore. I allow myself a moment of relaxation instead. I take off my jacket and shoes and lie down on the hotel bed. My tiredness increases, becomes heavy; it feels as though I am being enveloped in clouds of mist as I sink into oblivion.

"Greetings, Mynheer." The voice is slightly hoarse, slightly tipsy, guttural. "Are you back in the beloved motherland?"

I recognize the voice, but cannot see the speaker. I know who used to call me "Mynheer" and why.

"Back in the beloved motherland, Mr. Nordman?"

Should he repeat the question a third time, he will surely address me as "Tank Division General." "You're shy, but also violent, Mr. Nordman," he had told me after reading a text that triggered the Manea scandal in 1982, in the socialist press. "I have clay feet, like the Golem, as you know, but here I am, standing on one leg, reading your text. I could not set my foot down, I was so excited. *Mes hommages, Général!* You are a tank division general, *mon cher* Nordman," he repeated, in his panting voice, on the telephone.

"Are you back from the capitalist paradise? What are things like over there, in the Garden of Eden, General?"

I was now fully awake, and was looking at the curtains, at the dead man who had been my friend, the Communist, the lord of nicknames and gossip. When we first met, he had promptly changed my name to Nordman. I had instantly become the man from the north, not only from northern Bukovina, but also from the North Atlantic. I met him in the mid-seventies, probably. One evening, I received a call from an unknown woman. She had read a piece of mine in a literary weekly and was inviting me to a soirée of friends at no. 24 Sfîntul Pavel Street, apartment 12. My caller had a pleasant voice and seemed to be a discerning reader. She gave her name, and it turned out she was the wife of a well-known critic and writer. It was a familiar name, even to someone earning a living outside the literary field. I had heard much about this *éminence grise* of socialist culture in the years of Stalinist dogmatism, about his legendary double life, this sophisticated lover of books and conspiracies.

On the evening of my debut in Donna Alba's circle, I was soon won over by the classical, old-fashioned elegance of my beautiful hostess. The fragile brunette pulsated with a supple, blade-like intelligence. Her famous husband was not there. The rebel used to spend his weekends with his mistress, in another, symmetrical literary salon, presided over by himself and by his younger muse.

The tale seemed Parisian, but not without a touch of Balkan flavor. The renowned Communist critic and man of letters had become an invalid as a consequence of his interrogation by Antonescu's henchman and was now obese and sedentary, unable to walk even a few steps. He traveled from the center of the city, where he lived, to the love nest he shared in a suburb with his weekend mistress, in old Khachaturian's car. The retired driver had also been a Communist in the war years, and they had known each other since those times, but instead of giving him a reduced price for that reason, Khachaturian charged him three times more, as a kind of immorality tax.

It was not possible for him to jump straight out of bed on the third floor and into the waiting taxi. Only the elevator could carry this disabled Golem to the ground floor, where Comrade Sarchiz Khachaturian's car stood at the ready. His clay feet could no longer cope with the short walk to the elevator and Donna Alba had to support him, see him into the elevator, and, with the aid of the driver, help him into the car. Then she returned to the apartment and called her rival to let her know that the transfer had been accomplished and that the roving husband would reach his destination, as usual, in about forty minutes, when the mistress would be waiting outside her apartment house in the suburb of Drumul Taberei, to extract her beloved from the car, help him to the elevator, get him to the eighth floor, and, finally, into the love nest. All this took place on Friday at lunchtime. On the following Monday morning, with the cooperation of the same Khachaturian, he was returned home, where his wife was waiting in front of no. 24 Sfîntul Pavel Street to help him into the elevator and see him safely back into the conjugal domicile. Both women obviously adored their charismatic invalid.

At the next soirée, I found myself face-to-face with the amorous commuter himself. "I don't know what you've heard about me, Mr. Nordman, that I'm a Stalinist monster, I suppose. In fact, I sided with Trotsky, I guess that makes me a Trotskyist monster, as well. You, as a liberal in the British tradition, would say it's the same thing. Well, it isn't; take it from me. It isn't."

He must have guessed my thoughts, the nickname "Nordman" being the evidence.

"I shall be remembered for my nicknames and puns," he rasped, "not for my stock editorials of the 'obsessive decade,' as you anti-Communists call the time of class struggle. And not for my so-called multivalency during the time of liberalization, as you pacifists call that trap laid by Khrushchev, the so-called peaceful coexistence. It is quite possible that my novels of this new National Socialist period will not survive. But the nicknames and plays on words that I have launched will be remembered."

Although he was not aware of it, he had a nickname himself—the "Flying Elephant"—which his doctor, himself nicknamed "the Bulgar," had given him. Such masks and amusements were all that was left to liven that carnival-like country without real carnivals. The young, slim, ardent youth from the years of the Communist underground, maimed, as it was believed, by Antonescu's interrogators, had become, after four decades of socialism, an enormous mass of diseased flesh, the disabled elephant, immobilized, hardly able to move between table, bed, and toilet. For all that, his mind was still boiling with ideas. The elephant could still lift up his trunk and let out a roar.

"So, what's Paradise like, General?"

I had dozed off again, or maybe I had just been diving into the mists of the past. I could hear that old voice, tipsy and insinuating, but I could not see him, and it was better like that. Sixteen years had gone by since he had bestowed upon me, over the phone, the title to which I did not aspire.

"I've read your interview, it's the talk of the town. Your liberals are acclaiming your liberal courage, Tank Division General. There's a tank division general inside you struggling to get out, you know. You won't believe it, I read it, standing there, one clay foot in the air, the other on the ground. You must know what this means for an invalid like myself."

"Nordman," then "General"—who knows what other sobriquets he had attached to my name in his rounds of telephone gossip. The telephone had become his sole entertainment and only social life. In the months before my departure, I had acquired a new nickname, "Mynheer," the name of the main character in the novel I had just published, not the name of the Dutch giant from *The Magic Mountain*.

"Well, Mynheer, what do you think about our sublime motherland, now that it is Communist-free? Green, bilious green, like the green uniforms of the Legionnaires. I warned you."

It was not all Green, just as it had not been all Red, I would have answered, like the old-fashioned liberal that I was, had he been able to hear me. I could hear him all right and had recognized him—he was around there somewhere, although I could not see him, and I was quite wary of actually seeing him: the overflowing belly like a badly inflated balloon; the thick, massive nose like a trunk; the deep bags under his protruding, sad eyes; the big, yellowed teeth with gaps between them; and the small, nicotine-stained hands, with sausage-like fingers. He supported himself with both hands on the edge of the table to take the burden off his dead feet. After my departure he had grown a white, wild beard. He had not climbed out of bed in the last few years and his belly and beard had grown commensurately.

He was silent now, but the past was murmuring with yesterday's voice. "So what's all this crazy talk going on in the Atlantic democracy about the Stalinist monster? We are not in England here or in Atlantis. This is our own native patch, where it's either the Reds or the Greens, there's no alternative. *Niente.* You, for instance, with your fractured biography, should fear the Greens more than the Reds. Are you lured by free Atlantis, the Garden of Monetary Happiness? You may find that it's going to be much harder for you there."

He was absent at my July party in 1986, when I celebrated half a century of life in the motherland and also paid tribute to Leopold Bloom. He was also absent at my farewell last supper. But when he later learned that I had escaped, he was furious. After my departure, he was on the phone day and night. He called all our mutual acquaintances, spreading enough nicknames and terms of abuse to make sure that some would reach me. His affliction worsened and he did not live to see the downfall of the despised dictator, or the victory of capitalism, which he had never ceased hating.

Through the mists, I hear his raspy voice again.

"How do you like our dear little homeland, our dear little fellow citizens? I'm sure they are treating you with all due respect. And they've done so, haven't they, ever since you were five years old. Do you remember, or do you refuse to remember? I've already told you, General, this is no place for democratic confusions and wishy-washiness. It's Red or Green, that's all that's available. You had Green, then Red, then Red-and-Green, and then you made your escape. Are you better off in Paradise? Do you have a rainbow now with all the colors of the spectrum? I have traveled, too, and am now in postmortem Atlantis. We all get there. Only my poor consort is late arriving. Have you seen Donna? Have you seen what the incomparable Donna looks like today?"

No, I had not seen her yet, I would be seeing her Saturday; today was only Tuesday.

Suddenly I remembered I had an appointment. I was still half-asleep, but I knew I had an appointment somewhere, though I wasn't quite sure where and when. I had been seduced by the siesta, the Oriental rest that socialism had made standard daily practice and that the novels of the former Communist critic had tried to spice up. The siesta depleted ardor, but stimulated decisive, tough action. Was this the revenge of the mind against the impotence of the body and the futility of the soul? Was the siesta the pyre of redemption, the fire of revolution, intended to shatter mediocrity, torpor, decency, sloth? *"Alles Große steht in Sturm,"* Martin Heidegger never tired of repeating, his arm raised in the Nazi salute to honor the platonic citation—everything great is to be found in tumult. The Flying Elephant himself used to repeat, with his fist in the air, "Unlimitedness! Apocalypse and rejuvenation! *Sturm, Sturm und Drang!"*

By now I am fully awake. I look at my watch. Only eight minutes had elapsed, my reunion with the Elephant lasted eight minutes. I still have some time to spare. Maybe I could stop by the bookstore, after all, and buy a map of old Bucharest, so that my friend Saul S., like me, a Romanian in New York, can assuage his anti-Wallachian anger by reading aloud, syllable by syllable, all those enchanting names: Strada Concordiei, Strada Zîmbetului, Strada Gentilă, Strada Rinocerului.

I find I cannot move, so I lie back in bed, carefully watching the hands of time ticking away. I close my eyes and I am again at the American Embassy, the same buffet table, the same cutlery, undisturbed, the same familiar faces that time has not changed. There is the poet Mutu and the poet Mugur, my old friends. They are smiling. They see me, but remain frozen, silent, like mummies.

"What do you think, Mynheer, of these dead? Mutulache and Bunny were once your friends, were they not?" the Golem is whispering again.

Mutulache and Bunny, yes, nicknames worthy of the Lord of Sobriquets.

"Bunny was my friend, too. Half-Man-Riding, Half-One-Legged-Hare, remember? All the fears and the kowtowing and the little lies of our friend, remember? And the sweating, he was perpetually sweating, remember? He was always seeing dark omens, always fretting, chasing after that bit of glory, that speck of adulation. Otherwise, he was a good poet, that Bunny. Now, after his death, it is even more obvious. Here, in the Transcendent Realm, his name lives on. After all, poets don't have to be brave, Mr. Nordman, we both know this. It's a truth that's well known in Atlantis, too." Was the microphone beginning to crackle, jamming the long-distance transmission? The Golem's voice remains distant and clear, just as I remembered it. The hoarseness belongs to the microphone.

"No, morals don't count with the iambs and the trochees, we all know this. But there is a limit, and we all know that, too."

The two poets at the table are still motionless, as if unable to hear anything of what is being said. I am motionless, too, standing on the threshold.

"The police, that's the limit! The poet is an agent of the gods, not of the police. He is not allowed to become an agent of the police. Our little Bunny was only an agent of the muse Panic. He forced her to write poetry. His lines tremble, just as he used to tremble. They can still move one, I'm told. All that anguish made him a suspect, remember? But now we know, he was no policeman."

The Golem awards himself another break, then speaks again.

"The other one, your buddy Mutulache, yes, I know, was absent from your anniversary party honoring Leopold Bloom and from the farewell supper. I was also absent. All my internal organs were hurting, and my head, too, not just my legs, which seemed to be made of clay. Maybe Mutulache thought he was protecting you by his absence. What if—who knows—he was asked to write a memo by the Holy See about the Last Supper? They found him naked and dead, no investigation was allowed. The authorities have the rights of ownership even over death and its mysteries."

Not even these last words can stir the seated mummies. Impassible, they record everything with great care, but remain frozen.

"Death, Mr. Nordman, is the genuine happy ending. The death penalty cannot be commuted. Now you know it, too. Exile ultimately justifies itself, as that liar Malraux said. Only death can turn life into destiny. Remember that, Mynheer? But have they told you how our friend Bunny died?"

I had heard that Mugur had died instantly, with a book in one hand and a piece of bread and salami in the other. What I did not know was whether the dead knew about my own postmortem misdemeanors.

"Misdemeanors, Mr. Nordman? Did you say misdemeanors? Oh, you want to explain to the two poets about the misunderstanding, is that it? You don't have to justify yourself, Mynheer! You are a skeptic in a false situation. Oh, he doesn't want to be suspected of naïveté, our Mynheer. For you, firmness and simplicity appear as one and the same thing. You are ashamed of firmness, of coherence, of naïveté, aren't you? But you don't have to justify yourself in front of these two gentlemen, or in front of other gentlemen, believe me."

Those sitting at the table do not seem to hear what he says, they have nodded off into the nether world. I want to embrace them, at least I can do this. Just then the alarm goes off, and the phone begins to ring.

"Receptionist speaking. You are expected in the lobby. Mrs. Françoise Girard."

I look at the clock. I am five minutes late for my appointment. I wash up hastily and take the elevator downstairs. I am tired, bewildered by my nonstop role-playing.

There is a young woman in the lobby, wearing a small backpack. She sees me, comes over, and extends her hand. "Françoise," she says, the new director for Eastern Europe of the Soros Foundation. I saw her in passing, yesterday at the Atheneum, during the rehearsal, in a different outfit, a different hairdo, a different face. We find two seats and immediately get down to business. I tell her that I have no intention of participating in the work of the foundation in Romania, other than a Bard-sponsored project in Cluj. That out of the way, I listen politely to what she has to say about the foundation's activities in Romania. She smiles and whispers something about "this Byzantine country." She tells me she is from Canada, and we agree to discuss the Bard project when she is next in New York. A brisk American-style meeting, as fast-moving as these first days in Bucharest.

Again I am on Magheru Boulevard, making my way to the Atheneum. Once more, I have the feeling of being in disguise, a spy, passing myself off as a tourist. Unmasked, would I engage in casual, friendly conversation with those of my fellow citizens who may recognize me but no longer claim me as one of theirs? They would probably be uncertain whether this stranger deserves their friendship or their hostility, as he would be uncertain whether or not to hurry on, without stopping.

I stop in front of the Scala pastry shop and gaze at the building across the street. On the ground floor, in the old days, there used to be a Unic store with lines of customers waiting for hours to buy chicken or cheese. I am thinking about entrance B and its row of mailboxes, particularly mailbox 84, which was set on fire, on a spring day, very much like this one, five years ago, in 1992, after my *New Republic* article on Mircea Eliade was reprinted in Romania. "Your essay was very badly received here," Cella's mother, Evelyne, living in apartment 84, entrance B, had written then. "Very badly," my mother-in-law had repeated over the phone. "Here the media's darlings are now the anti-Communist heroes— Eliade, Cioran, Nicu Steinhardt, Iorga, Nae Ionescu, even Antonescu, and even Codreanu, that old Iron Guard monster."

I had certainly not written that review-article to ingratiate myself with the Romanian media, but I had not expected the shrapnel to ricochet and threaten the life of an old woman whom I had not even had time to warn. "The hostile reaction to your article has been unanimous," she wrote. "For the last few months, our mailbox has been constantly broken into. Two padlocks were smashed, and there were signs of a fire. Now we have installed a Yale lock, which cost five hundred lei. If you want your letters to reach us, you should address them to our neighbor." Does mailbox 84 still bear the marks of its attacks? Meantime, the tenant of apartment 84 has found a new home, in the Other World. I am not tempted to visit the apartment.

I reach the Atheneum. This time, the rehearsal has finished early and was a success. I walk on with Leon toward the Casa Română, a restaurant at the end of Calea Victoriei, next to my last home in Bucharest. The headwaiter greets us in English. In love with Romanian stuffed cabbage, Leon decides to tempt fate again. As a tribute to the past, I order sole *bonne femme*. It turns out disappointing, like the mediocre wine. But Leon is delighted with his stuffed cabbage and pays little attention to my disappointed look.

At the next table, a sort of mafia scene is in progress. The boss of the group, short and stocky, looks as if he might be a building site foreman, but from what we overhear, he is running a business and certainly not in construction. His deputy is about the same age, and the younger man sitting between them seems like an apprentice in this adventure. The restaurant owner is hovering over them obsequiously. The boss makes a sign, and the burly deputy gives him a thick pile of banknotes. The three are dining heartily on a succession of dishes. Wearing jeans and leather jackets, they are the local version of what have come to be called "Americans," not only because of their dress, but also because of their easy-handed way with money. Two young women, wearing heavy makeup and laughing raucously, are sitting at the table across from the trio. As we rise to go, the two tables join forces.

From the restaurant we visit a woman writer, a friend of Golden Brain's. By now I am quite tired and the only thing that stays in my mind from the conversation is her monologue about her spouse: "My husband, an admirable man, admirable but stupid, so stupid that even now, when the Communist polenta has exploded, he still doesn't want to leave the country. Can you imagine such idiocy?" We return to the hotel around midnight. We are both tired. Tomorrow morning Leon has his last rehearsal, and in the evening, his first concert. I will be attending the second. Midnight is the time for phone calls to New York. Cella reminds me of Philip's request that I send him a daily fax to reassure him that everything is fine.

Nocturnal Language

C*rino,*" the darkness murmurs, then after a moment, "Hypocrite."
After another pause, the whisper returns, and I finally make out
"*Hypocrino, hypocrino,*" repeated by the small, insidious voice of the
night. I twist in sleep's muddy waters, I raise my left hand, heavy, soft,
and pull the covers above my cotton-filled head, then slip down again
into the underground of slumber.

My eyelids blink. The curse has already insinuated itself, there is no
escape. "*Hypocrino,*" I hear the voice once more, whispering into my ear.
The covers cannot protect me, I cannot defend myself anymore; I shall
be slowly, slowly, extracted from the black, sweet mud of oblivion, I
know that only too well. It has happened to me before, more than once,
to be invaded in my sleep by this murmuring in Esperanto, out of which,
gradually, decipherable words separate, heralding the awakening. Tiredness no longer helps, nothing can return me to sleep's depths. Lifted
slowly, not for the first time, from the therapeutic mud to the surface, I
attempt, nevertheless, to stay, as much as I can, in the blackout, with

closed lids and heavy, empty mind, the body equally heavy, burdened, weighed down like lead into the heavy night. It lasts only a few long seconds; I have failed again, of course. The window's opaqueness is now dispersed and has become purplish, translucent, as on previous occasions. The curtains are swaying to a tender, perfidious, easily recognizable whisper: *"Hypocrino."*

I put my hand out, feeling for the newspaper on the night table. There is no newspaper, of course, but I keep caressing the silky surface of the wood, for no particular reason. The chances of self-oblivious confusion have been shattered, only seconds separate me from myself. I shall soon become aware again of who and where I am. I raise my left arm, staring, bewildered, at the clock.

"First you put one box on the left arm, close to your heart. This means that you have feeling," said my Hebrew teacher, instructing me on how to fit the phylacteries. "Then you put the other box on your forehead, close to your brain. There must be no break between these two moments, no divide between idea and gesture, between feeling and action," explained the guide who ushered me into manhood, at the age of thirteen.

In my half sleep, the wall calendar shows 1949. "One thousand nine hundred forty-nine! One thousand! Nine hundred! Forty-nine!" I mutter. I have been crossing and recrossing the threshold of age thirteen, without ever really going beyond. It is now half a century since I failed to become someone other than the one I am. All the intervening stages of life collapse into that one teenage year. On my left arm, all these years, I have been wearing not the phylactery but the watch belonging to that same orphan of time, just as I did then.

I look at the profane, silent clock face of insomnia, I turn time's gilded knob: no, it is not half-past eight in the evening, as it is in New York, but half-past three in the morning, here, between the Carpathians and the Danube. Upon landing, I should have adjusted the watch hands to the new time zone, but I am stuck in the jet lag, in the confusion where I belong.

The future into which I was entering then, in 1949, is past. The space, however, has become the old one. I look at the time on the watch face, I look out the window to *terra* 1997. "Out there" no longer means, as it did until a few days ago, Romania, the "faraway country." The faraway country is now America, the homeland of all exiles, which greets me once more with the exiles' salute: *"Hypocrino!"*

The language of life after death, in this world and in the nether world, is not owned, is not one's by right, but is merely rented. *Hypocrino!* This rented language is a function of survival, among all the tests and tricks and trophies of regeneration. "To function as a citizen of the United States, one needs to be able to read, interpret, and criticize texts in a wide range of modes, genres and media" was an injunction I knew from Robert Scholes's book *The Rise and Fall of English*. The foreigners adopted by the exiles' new country must sit for the obligatory Hypocrino Test. The ancient Greek roots of the term "hypocrisy"? Automatic compliance, interjections of approval? "The roots of 'hypocrite' are to be found in the ancient Greek verb *hypocrino*, which had a set of meanings sliding from simple speech, to orating, to acting on stage, to feigning or speaking falsely." Does one learn these words and their meaning and their pronunciation as one does in nursery school? Are the natural gestures and facial expressions simply the actor's lines learned as a child emitted by the double sent to replace and represent you?

I had cut out the review of Scholes's book from the newspaper and placed it on my night table, intending to buy the book the next day. *"Hypocrino."* I was awakened by night's hypocritical whisper. I tried not to hear. I crumpled the newspaper clipping and threw it on the floor, as if hoping to avert the curse.

In the morning, the crumpled ball of paper was in the same place. I smoothed it out, cut out the sentence that had triggered my insomnia. I pasted it on the wall in front of the computer, then learned by heart the formula supposed to defend the exile that I was from the nightmares of truth: *"hypocrino* . . . meanings sliding from simple speech, to orating, to acting on stage, to feigning or speaking falsely."

It is a sunny summer morning; the year is 1993. Five years have passed since my landing in the New World. Since one year in exile counts as four sedentary years, there were already twenty years. The mail brings a postcard from Cynthia: "I wish for you that one morning we will all wake up speaking, reading, and writing Romanian; and that Romanian will be declared the American national language!" In her familiar handwriting she has added, without realizing the danger of tempting fate, "With the world doing the strange things it is doing today, there is *no reason* for this NOT to happen." The apartment building's doorman suddenly greeting me in Romanian? Bard College's president speaking to me in rapid Romanian? My accountant explaining to me the American tax regulations in Romanian? The loudspeaker in the subway announcing the next stop in, at last, an intelligible language? A sudden relaxation in my relations with my American friends, students, publishers? A joy, or a nightmare? No, the American environment in which I now live must stay as it is; the miracle imagined in Cynthia's message would only have added a new dimension to an already grotesque situation. Her wish, however, did come true, but not in the terms she had formulated it. It happened not in New York but upon my return to Bucharest, where everybody speaks Romanian.

Ken's comment about the transfiguration he noted in me when he saw me speaking Romanian had targeted the very poisoned heart of joy. At the age of forty, on the occasion of my first trip to the "free world," the relatives and friends whom I was visiting had urged me finally to leave accursed Romania. "What if I do not inhabit a country but a language?" was my response. Was this the sophistry of evasion? And now that I am in actual exile, can I continue to carry the Promised Land, language, with me? Schlemiel's nocturnal shelter? The home that I carry on my back, the snail's shell, is not completely impenetrable. New sonorities and meanings belonging to the new geography of exile manage to infiltrate the nomad's shell. Futility can no longer be ignored, however. Every second is a warning of the death one carries within oneself. Language provides only a proud emblem of failure. Failure is what legitimizes you, Mr. Hypocrino.

Suddenly, through the misty window, I see Cioran. He walks cautiously down the hospital corridors, muttering some incomprehensible words. Over half a century earlier, he had freed himself, through an infernal transplant operation, from his native language, and had settled, like a sovereign, in the realm of the Cartesian French paradoxes. At this very moment, however, he is muttering again the old words. The Romanian language, so suited to his temperament—which, in his exaltation, he had managed to "denationalize"—returned to him, in his Alzheimer's fog. He is muttering old senseless words in his old language, his countryless exaltation replaced by a gentle prenatal senility.

He would probably appreciate being addressed as Mr. Hypocrino. We might dissect the wanderings of exile, as we had done one evening in 1990, in his Paris attic. Should I now knock on eternity's window and remind him of the letter he had sent me, after I had left Romania? *"C'est de loin l'acte le plus intelligent que j'aie jamais commis,"* he had written—emigration was by far the most intelligent thing he had ever done. Was that mere post-trauma vanity, Monsieur Cioran? Why survival at any cost? Do we need the adulation of our name and nothing else? Why don't we accept the end, why do we want to become orators again?

And what do you think about hatred, Monsieur Hypocrino? Does other people's hatred of us finally cure us of confusion and illusions, does it render us more interesting in our own eyes? Does the "metaphysical Jew" Cioran have a better grasp of the ancestral articulation of hatred than the genuine Jew? Would our own beloved Bucharest be the suitable arena for such a debate?

The watch face on my left hand, near my heart, does not have three hands, as my old watch used to, one for seconds, one for minutes, and one for hours, and I no longer need to wind it in the evening before going to bed. I no longer listen to its tick-tocking to hear my time crumbling away, second by second. I would not have heard anything anyway. The seconds died out, unknown, in the new watch's tightly closed belly.

Should I go downstairs to the lobby and listen to the language of the past, listen to Cioran, listen to my own self, to the old sound, the old language, the memory of what one was before coming into being? Such opportunities should not be missed. In Turin, in 1992, at a writers' conference on Eastern Europe, the English translation of my presentation, thank God, proved useless. There were many excellent interpreters from Romanian into Italian at hand. Saved, resuscitated, happy at learning this, I found myself accosted by two fellow countrymen. The short, plump, and smartly dressed man, wearing a wide, conventional smile, introduced himself as the Romanian cultural attaché in Rome; the other, as a literary man from the Casa di Romania, also in Rome. "What language would you use?" the cultural attaché asked, looking me straight in the eye. "Romanian," I answered. "At long last, I can speak Romanian," I added cheerfully. My fellow nationals had some difficulty hiding their smiles, a mix of skepticism and suspicion. They continued to scrutinize, in silence, the face and gestures of this surprising literary representative of the motherland, so happy, would you believe it, to address the world in Romanian. Poor thing, happy to speak in Romanian, even to the officials of an officialdom which he had little reason to trust.

As we said our goodbyes and I was advancing toward the stage, I unwittingly left an eavesdropper behind. The two had not realized that, one step away, there was a witness to the scene, my wife. Her wary ear had caught their reaction. "Have you heard," one said, "he's going to speak in Romanian. Big deal! And he's pleased about it, too." His companion replied, "He can even speak in Hungarian if he wants to, for all I care"—Hungarian being, of course, worse than English.

Yes, Ken was right to question Mr. Hypocrino about language. Its nocturnal murmur wakes me up frequently, like a vagabond electric current searching for its outlet—the night's deep underground waters capturing words in gentle tumultuous wavelets, the somnambular monologues about the richness of failure and the benefits of insomnia.

The clock face now indicates past five in the morning in Bucharest, the dead of night in New York. The silence of the room and the silence of the old heart measure out the rhythm of time's childish, implacable pulsation. For time's temporary lodger, the hotel space is adequate enough.

Day Three: Wednesday, April 23, 1997

I n a 1992 interview, my friend reminded me that I had asked her ten years earlier, "Who would hide me?" A decade later, it was her turn to ask me who was hiding me there, in faraway America, land of easy disappearances and rediscoveries. Now, five years later, we are to meet again and I wonder behind which mask can I hide, the one of the man I once was in the homeland of failure or the one I have become in the land of success?

She is waiting for me in the lobby, dressed in a green tailored suit, as if for an academic conference. She is no longer the young poet I used to know in the 1980s. She is now a Ph.D. in philosophy and a university lecturer, the editor in chief of a literary review and the head of a publishing house. But her smile is the same as before, and as her letters had confirmed, her character has remained unchanged.

We look at each other, and I see her features through my memories—the face of Maria Callas, a Balkan effigy, asymmetrical, mobile, the gentleness easily turning into asperity and back again. We go upstairs to my

room and she puts down her jacket and her bag. Her thin silk blouse outlines the fragility of her shoulders and arms. There is a prolonged silence. Should I tell her about my wanderings, my thoughts about aging?
I have no idea where and how to start. The letters have not replaced the
familiar voice and the eyes now before me again. The words, however,
are welling up with a will of their own. We are not talking about the nationalist, Communist, and anti-Communist hysteria, but about something else, and we are both, at long last, laughing. The jokes do not seem
related to what we say, for I can hear her summing up an unuttered
monologue, addressed to me: "In spite of the awards, the prizes, the
translations, and the professorship, for all of which you are envied, I
sense a wound festering in you. It is not difficult to guess what it is. You
must write more books, that's the only solution to your problem."

Of course, this is the wound, and that is the solution. Have I ever
told her about my comic doppelgänger, the stereotype in which I feel I
have been imprisoned, the witch who has been found out and is set on
fire in the marketplace by the napalm of hostility and burned to a crisp
by the past? As usual, my mind fills with quotations, as if only the
rhetorical hysteria of other people's words could release me from myself.
"Should you miss your native place," I hear an alien voice saying, "you
will find in exile more and more reasons to miss it; but if you manage to
forget it and love your new residence, you will be sent back home, where,
uprooted once more, you will start a new exile." Wasn't it Maurice Blanchot who said that? Should I tell her about the straitjacket of stereotypes,
should I open the drawer into which Kafka crammed his co-religionists?
Should I mention the circus performer riding astride two horses, or the
man lying flat on his back on the ground, Kafkaesque images both, and
indeed to be found in a postcard written by Kafka in 1916?

I am not sure whether she replies to my outburst, or whether it is my
own voice I am hearing: "No, you are wrong. You are evading the issue
with all these metaphors and these quotations and all this rhetoric."
That is what she should have said. My talkativeness seems to have no
other purpose than to speak, the words pouring out in Romanian. If Ken
was looking for further evidence of my linguistic transfiguration, he
would have found it here.

The language has returned, vibrating irresistibly, returning me to myself. I can hear myself again, in the language of our past conversations and in the silences. My friend in the green suit is now looking at me and smiling: "You, a hooligan? That is sheer imposture, borrowed armor. If I now scream to my countrymen, You have replaced him with a caricature, you don't give a damn what he has to say, you only want to defile him, would the real hooligans listen?" No, she didn't really say that. These are words she had written me in a letter not long before. "You should come here twice a year," she had added, "to salute our distinguished colleagues, to let yourself be filmed, to sit in the taverns."

She is listening to me attentively, and she does not seem aware of the verbal collages that Augustus the Fool is composing in his head. During the terror of the eighties, I had asked her, "Who would hide me?"—a question from the 1940s that has orbited for forty years before returning to its point of origin. "*My Lavatories*, this should be the title of my memoirs," another exiled Romanian colleague, a Christian, told me recently. "I have traveled the world, from the Euphrates to San Francisco, and I can testify, no place can compete with the Romanian lavatories—the apocalypse of the feces." Could my poet friend understand why a Romanian Jew could never utter such words? The one who was denied a motherland had to gain it, and giving it up is not so simple. "I have not been allowed one second of tranquillity, nothing was ever given to me, I had to obtain everything," Kafka said. But this was not what we were talking about. We had not even mentioned our exchange of 1992 over an Israeli anthology, *Jewish Writers Writing in Romanian*, and about my displeasure with the title. I considered myself a Romanian writer and regarded ethnicity as a strictly personal matter. Should I now ask: Was being Romanian something to be wished for? We may want to read Cioran on the subject for an answer. What label was I wearing now, and why should I need one? To my relief we did not revisit the issue in our conversation. The verbiage, the quotations were all in my mind and in my memory.

At some point she must have taken off her glasses. For the first time, I see a different face and hear a different voice. She remains by the window, then turns to look at me, as in the old days, frozen in expectation. Was the pendulum of that hour of long ago ready to start moving again, at a first touch? What could be the hiding place, where could it be? She is looking at me, I am not looking at her, and I am not asking her anything, out of a fear that she, in turn, might ask me to hide her away from the new times and I might find out that I do not have the place and the means to do so.

"Let your books come home," she says. "Even if only one person loves them, it will be enough. Ten were enough to save Gommorah." As she starts to describe the daily warfare among our compatriots, I interrupt her and launch into my own evocation of exile, its theatricality, mimetic fission, its division of the self. The infantile stand-in is allowed to perform his new script, while the grown-up other half is bending over in the schizophrenia of ancient reflexes. This is now me, bent over in a spasm that has punctured Hypocrino's pneuma, talking to the poet about language and the dynamics of a life underground and other preciosities.

Suddenly I am tired. I take off my glasses, rub my eyes, and observe a respectful moment of silence for the funeral subject. Then she says, "Norman, we are not all the same." I nod in agreement. Of course not. Some people would have given me shelter not only in 1992 but also in 1982, and even in 1942. I quote Mark Twain, my new compatriot: "A man is a human being, he can't be any worse."

We smile and laugh and understand just how long the words have taken to find us and that, in fact, it took no time at all. I learn that after the execution of the dictator and his wife, Comrade Mortu, my poet friend had sworn never to be afraid again, never to surrender her sense as a free human being. Subsequently, she was often afraid, but behaved as though she wasn't. I nod again. I have also learned, in the meantime, a few things about the fears of free men. I manage to mutter, "Our meeting has tamed me, it's made me vulnerable," a confused synthesis of confusion itself. I might as well have believed myself in another room and in different circumstances. I might as well have thought of Prague and of Milena Jesenska, yes, Kafka's Milena, who, after the Nazi invasion of Czechoslovakia, sheltered fugitives in her home. I am troubled, I admit, by the solidarities that posterity still permits. Before we say goodbye, I promise, rather unconvincingly, to send her something for publication by the small press she runs. We exchange promises of letters and reunions, a sort of melancholy conciliation between the halves of the still-in-transit passenger I have become. Am I being disputed over, like Kafka's rider astride the two horses? No, I am flat on the ground, as I should be.

At half-past nine, Leon and Ken return from the Atheneum, delighted with the concert. We inquire about a good restaurant near the hotel. The receptionist recommends La Premiera, just behind the National Theater. Leon goes upstairs to his room to put away his briefcase with the scores and the baton. Ken reports on the success of the evening. The Schumann oratorio, *Das Paradis und die Peri*, was remarkable; he would like to buy a recording, but as the piece is rarely performed, recordings must be scarce. The restaurant is crowded, noisy, full of cigarette smoke. The Romanian traditional dishes have bizarre English translations. But Leon, after two days in Bucharest, knows what he wants, the stuffed cabbage. We follow his lead, in honor of his success at the Atheneum.

Visibly pleased with the surprise of the rousing performance by the orchestra and chorus, Leon is in an expansive mood. He needs excitement, great excitement. "Gomulka!" he suddenly explodes, finding the magic code. "Do you remember Gomulka?" He is asking us and eternity, but doesn't wait for an answer. "Gomulka! I miss Gomulka!" the conductor is claiming. Do I remember Gomulka? I cannot enter the burlesque frenzy, but being grave, solemn, pathetic as a White Clown, comforted, finally, by such a reversal of roles in our partnership. Yes, of course I remember Gomulka, the ghost summoned to entertain us and enhance our appetite. Yet I'm telling my joyful associate not about Gomulka but about the sensation created in Bucharest by the short visit in the early eighties of his aftercomer Jaruzelski, the Polish general and Party leader, with his smoked-glass spectacles, looking like a South American dictator in comparison with whom our shabby megalomaniac Ceauşescu seemed a humble Balkanic caricature. "No, not your little buffoon and not Jaruzelski. Gomulka! Here, in Bucharest, I miss Gomulka!" Leon is repeating like an old song in a renewed Broadway intermezzo before we order the traditional borscht with meatballs and proceed to the stuffed cabbage. Leon asks me whom I've been seeing.

"I met a few people," I reply. "This afternoon, for instance, I met with a poet friend of mine, a woman who came from somewhere in the provinces to see me. Time is short, it's true, but I've also been a bit wary of seeing old friends. Ken knows that. In fact, he knows that I've turned down certain meetings."

Leon looks at Ken, sensing an opportunity for a funny story, but Ken smiles and says nothing, giving me leave to say whatever I wish.

"Yes," I continue, "some Romanian intellectuals invited us both, you and me, to a meeting, a debate. I explained we were too busy."

"You did the right thing," Leon says, a bit of stuffed cabbage impaled on his fork. "There wouldn't have been time. I'm leaving on Friday at noon."

"There's been another invitation, of a personal nature," I say. "A former lady friend of mine. Ken used to know her."

My dinner companions prick up their ears.

"Well," I go on, "Ken knows a lot of people here." Ken confirms this. "He once sent me to see a famous literary person turned politician, an arrogant, shallow man. Then he sent me to a publisher who thought I was an American, so he apologized for not knowing English, only French. When I started to speak French, he called his secretary to translate. He waxed nostalgic about the time when culture was subsidized by the state and was the focus of the nation's attention and respect. People who were never guilty of any dirty deeds under the dictatorship suddenly found themselves, after 1989, disgusted with the masquerade of democracy, with the West's rhetoric, with the rush with which each and every underdog wanted to become top dog, not on the strength of the Party card, but by dint of the bank account."

"I understand very well," Leon says. "Have you met any of these guys, the new anti-capitalists? Look, I'm letting you off from your duties. Tomorrow you don't have to come with me. Meet one of these people, talk to them, find out what they believe."

"That would be a very awkward conversation."

There is a silence. I must not let the pause go on for much longer.

"As for the woman who asked Ken to let me know she wanted to see me . . ."

"Is she a democrat or a traitor?"

"I am the national traitor, and I won't give up the title so easily. It was bequeathed to me by Captain Dreyfus."

"Okay, Okay, but you must meet with at least one of these anti-capitalists, that's an order."

It is late when we return to the hotel. I ask for the key and am surprised to see that the young receptionist does not understand Romanian. He is from Denmark, working alongside a German woman. Some things have changed, I have to admit, even in the former annex of the Securitate.

The Bard logbook duly records the long, eventful day. It has reminded me of Milena Jesenka, so it deserves my gratitude. It is past midnight when, under the entry Wednesday, April 23, I write down another Milena's name. My gaze is fixed firmly on the past. I should leave my room and wander along night's potholed alleys and find Transylvania Street, Maria's last home. I would knock on the window, the ghost would emerge, and would listen to me, as she used to a long time ago, when I was her undisputed prince and she had not yet heard of Communism and universal happiness. The Communist wife of her Communist husband had fallen victim to disease and illness, slowly destroyed by the infernal machinery that had joined her to her militant spouse, himself slowly destroyed and finally left to die, senile, drunken, discarded on the ash heap of the utopia. Holy Maria would ask me, in the Yiddish she had learned from Avram the bookseller, to tell her about what it was like to be there, in the American paradise. Peace, charity, kindness? No, Maria, competition. Paradise is no longer the boring place it used to be, a new game keeps its occupants busy around the clock. It's a different game, but every bit as engrossing.

There is no longer a Transylvania Street. There is no Maria, no past, only the stray dogs of night. Their relentless howling reaches the occupant of room 1515.

Day Four: Thursday, April 24, 1997

W e are at the Composers Union, located in the former palace of Maruca Cantacuzino, wife of composer Georges Enesco. Leon makes inquiries about the archives. We discover the desperate condition of thousands of the composer's manuscripts. Our hosts mention the complex copyright issues raised by Salabert, the French publishers, and tell us about the lack of funding. We learn that there is an acute need for archival equipment, photocopying, computerization, expanding the editorial activities, and, above all, a new agreement with Salabert, since the contract of 1965 allows for the use of Enesco's scores only in the countries of the former Soviet bloc.

At this point, Leon interrupts. "It so happens," he says, "that the new owner of Salabert is my neighbor in the Hudson Valley." There are smiles all around. Then Leon goes a step further and offers to support the "relaunching" of Enesco in the world. He asks for a detailed list of requirements, which includes the restructuring and computerization of the archive, the reissuing of recordings, the international publication and distribution of the works, a new, authoritative biography.

Leon, as if waving an imaginary baton, brings the discussion to a crescendo. "If we can bring Enesco's whole body of work to the concert halls, then the history of music in this century will reserve a place for him right next to Bartók and Szymanovski. The present century, as you know, is haunted to the point of obsession by Schönberg and Stravinsky. Bartók, being Hungarian, is marginalized, and so is Enesco, as a Romanian, while the Americans are marginalized as Americans. This picture will have to change. Enesco will no longer be regarded as an exotic but as the master of syntheses, the creator of highly original musical ideas. Communist Poland adopted Chopin, the Czech Republic did the same with Smetana, though not with Dvořák, while the Hungarians had difficulties with Bartók until Kodály intervened in his favor. Enesco needs a triumphal re-entry into the world. We have a good opportunity, let's take it."

As we step out of the elegant building, we both have the feeling that, beyond the minor and the major circumstantial difficulties, something important and enduring has happened, which has revived our spirits. Was this the state of well-being of those who do good? "Enesco was a democrat, you know, somewhat of a rarity among Romanian intellectuals. He was a Western European, in the best sense of the term," Augustus the Fool recites, like a zealous tourist guide. I stop, however, annoyed with my own self-complacency. The prospect of a major international "Operation Enesco" has also taken hold of Leon. He speaks about the Bartók archive in Budapest; he is scandalized by the provincialism of Romanian Communism, by the fact that Enesco is visible only as statues. Had the Romanian Communists been put off by the fact of the composer's Parisian exile, by his having an aristocratic wife? Why is the archive in such a state of disaster? I get no chance to respond.

It is the evening of the second concert. The entrance of the Atheneum is blocked by scaffolding, the courtyard is muddy. The red plush seats are worn, the auditorium looks like the set of a period film. In the lobby, housewives, sitting behind shabby little tables, are selling concert programs, two thousand lei each. I also buy a newspaper for eight hundred lei. The woman has no change. "You know," she says, "not too many people tonight, it's Holy Week, people have gone to church." The cloak-room charge is five hundred. I give the young woman a larger bill, she thanks me, I do not wait for the change. The audience starts to arrive—pensioners modestly but neatly dressed; a few foreigners, possibly from some embassy; a couple who look like bit players in a Mafia film; a white-haired gentleman, with the appearance of a monk, the son of the famous avant-garde poet Saşa Pană, looking exactly as his father did thirty years ago; a group of students from the conservatory; another group of school-children, carrying schoolbags; elderly widows.

I find my seat, number 12, in box 18. The hall is only three-quarters full, and I am the only occupant of my box. "Good evening, ladies and gentlemen," a clear, melodious voice addresses the audience. "We wish to inform you that the next concerts will take place on May 7 and 8, Maestro Comissiona conducting. We would also like to remind you that the Dinu Lipatti Festival and Competition will open on May 5. We wish you a pleasant evening and a happy Easter." The orchestra comes on-stage, and the players tune their instruments. Leon appears to the sound of applause.

My gaze remains fixed on a youngish couple in the last row of seats, next to my box. The man is about thirty, with thick brown hair and a mustache. Under his soiled parka he is wearing a gray suit, a purple shirt, a striped tie. He has a firm profile and arched eyebrows. His com-panion, who arrives after him, smiles and sits down without saying a word. The man looks at the young Greek-Wallachian princess, hypno-tized. She has a long, finely chiseled nose, with trembling nostrils, deep-set eyes, long black eyebrows, dark lashes. She exudes an air of delicacy and mystery. A long bronze-colored scarf encircles her neck and flows down her dress and her hips. Her lips are a deep, ancient red.

You have returned from the dead to the concert hall, I'm saying to myself, where you once vibrated, childishly, as you do now, once again.

The rehearsal I had attended just a few days before had been a disas-ter. The orchestra looked like a band of juvenile delinquents and im-posters, junior hoodlums in jeans, giggling hysterically, just to annoy the teacher. But a miracle has occurred. The jeans and torn sweatshirts have been exchanged for dinner jackets and black dresses, effecting a total transformation and proving that a uniform can also perform miracles and not just bring disaster. The swelling chords of the Schumann oratorio begin to fill the hall, and we surrender to this glorious telling of a return from the netherworld. It is the reverie of childhood, the dream of a hypothetical existence.

The program informs us that *Das Paradis und die Peri* was first performed on December 4, 1883, under the composer's baton, in the Gewandhaus in Leipzig. The peris were fairies living with the gods in Paradise, according to Persian myth, feeding on the fragrance of flowers, but sometimes descending to earth to mate with mortals. Thomas More's poem, on which Schumann based his work, was about such a peri, banished from Paradise, to which she will be readmitted only if she brings back the most precious of gifts, something human. She returns with a tear of remorse shed by a sinner moved by the sight of a happy child. The simple but affecting story unfolds in a symphony of majestic sound, a perfect harmony between soloists and chorus. The concert is a great success, a triumph for Leon, confirmed when I pick up my coat in the cloakroom. I am approached by a distinguished-looking woman who says, "I was looking for you. I'd heard that you would be here this evening." I recognize a brilliant music commentator I used to listen to on the radio and later on television. She does not seem to have aged, and her voice, with its warm inflections, is as lovely as ever.

The conductor emerges, flushed with the success of the performance. We repair to a nearby bistro, joined by Ken and a lady friend of his. On our way back to the hotel, we stop at a currency exchange. The large young man in the doorway bars our entry—closed. We point to the sign on the door, OPEN NONSTOP. Yes, but there is a break between eleven-thirty and twelve. We look at our watches, eleven-forty. Again we are caught in the straits of confusion, neither order nor absolute chaos, always something in between. You never know here, with any precision, what you have to face or avoid.

"Bad luck was your good luck, Norman," Leon is telling me, as the curtain falls on another full day that the concert has made memorable. "Your dictator was your good luck. Otherwise, you would have stayed here forever." I have given up attempting to explain my more skeptical view of good luck and bad. Later, I try to formulate the matter in Romanian, in my Bard College logbook, but the words refuse to come. What is it precisely that blocks my contact with the present, while being ineffectual against the past? In my constricted, broken shell, I entertain those old omnivorous snakes, my questions. Today has already become yesterday, the future is playing at hide-and-seek.

The future would soon turn this day into a bureaucratic joke, which arrived in a letter addressed to Leon six months later, in October 1997. It was from a representative of the Soros Foundation, to which Leon had sent a memorandum regarding the Enesco project. The letter read: "As you know, I asked a distinguished French archivist to look at the Enesco archives. I just had a report of the visit. The Enesco Foundation received him with some impatience. They told him the documents were in fine shape and he was not allowed to see them. I am at a loss to explain this. Obviously it will be impossible to provide support if the organization holding the Enesco materials will not even permit an independent assessment of their condition."

A commonsense comment, that both Leon and I could have made to our hosts in Bucharest, or just for our own amusement, had we not already identified ourselves with our roles of improvised Samaritans.

Nocturnal Interlocutors

The light is turned off, it is past midnight. I have not drawn the curtains, the darkness is not total. Seeping in from the street is a vaguely luminous fog. I am surrounded by an uncertain nimbus, the face of Mr. Giuseppe Bezzetti.

"I know a few things about you. I've heard things," he says.

I know what is coming next—a long pause. I also know what will follow.

"Have you been to America before? Do you know America? You can't have any better lessons in solitude anywhere else."

We met in January 1989, when the ten-month Fulbright grant that had brought me to Washington, D.C., had just ended. I had not completely dissociated myself from my past, had not yet explored the tricks whereby one takes possession of the future.

The Buckingham section, in a suburb of Washington, was modest and quiet. I had got used to the two small, well-lit rooms, with the wooden plank on a wooden frame that served as a desk. We would have to leave soon. Cella had found a job with an art-restoration firm in New York and had already moved into a midtown hotel, at the corner of Forty-eighth Street and Eighth Avenue. I had stayed there myself for a week. It was a cheap hotel, unlike the luxury Bucharest Intercontinental, where I am now being visited by Bezzetti's ghost. The room in New York was small, only two steps from the door to the bed. The grimy windows looked down on a narrow street heavy with traffic. On the corner there was a firehouse, from where huge red mastodons would race out in a roar. The area, not far from Times Square, was infamous for its drug trade and prostitution. In the morning, on her way to work, Cella was surrounded by a cast of extras from Brecht's *Threepenny Opera*: beggars, addicts, bums, hustlers, the orphans of the metropolis.

The small white rooms of the modest suburb in Washington seemed, by comparison, idyllic. I did not want to leave the shelter to which I had finally become accustomed. However, the couple's support would now be coming from New York. We had to move by the end of January.

Despair stimulates not only schizophrenia but also extravagance. In the last week before I was due to leave my first American home, my sense of helplessness forced me to become a different person, in the hope that destiny would be different, too. A few days before leaving Washington, I was scheduled to have an interview with Mr. Giuseppe Bezzetti, the cultural attaché of the Italian Embassy in the United States.

He observed me from the top of the stairs. Before we shook hands, I also took a good look at him—dark face, distinguished, handsome features, well groomed, altogether an elegant appearance. He waited for me to sink into the huge leather armchair, then sat in its twin, both set in front of a massive, wood-carved desk. The room looked more as if it should belong to an old Italian palazzo rather than a modern embassy in the New World.

Now he is here, in room 1515 of the Bucharest Intercontinental, regarding me with the same intense gaze, the same calm, concentrated expression that he displayed eight years ago. From the folds of the curtains, he is scrutinizing me with the same courteous curiosity as before.

What if I tried to remind him of who I was and what I have asked for, as I had done in 1989 over the phone, before meeting him? He would probably cut me off with the same words. "I know about you. I've heard a thing or two," he had said then. How, from whom? In 1989, in Washington, nobody knew about me, absolutely nobody. I was living in an obscure suburb, which I didn't leave for months on end, and here, in Bucharest, I have avoided meetings and am staying in a hotel accessible only to foreign tourists. Has he obtained his information from his French counterpart, the diplomat who had interviewed me in Berlin, or perhaps from the literary Interpol?

The diplomat is waiting, as he did eight years ago, for me to continue. Then, I had no intention whatsoever to associate this man with my dubious French interlocutor. I had to be brief and precise and make a rapid summary of my naïve request. This is why I had gone to see him. I wanted to go back to Europe before it was too late. I did not wish to settle in the New World, but equally, I also could not return to socialist Jormania. A grant for a few months' stay in Italy might give me the hoped-for breather that I needed.

This was what I was hoping for in 1989—breathing space, lots of breathing spaces. "Decision-making is a moment of madness," Kierkegaard had whispered to me, but indecision, too, seemed like complete madness, as I had had occasion to find out. I had experimented for years with the madness of indecision, I had become an expert in procrastination. I was still hoping for breathing spaces.

Time, however, had lost its patience and no longer tolerated me. That was what I had to make the Italian gentleman in Washington understand. Back in Berlin, when my grant had run out, I was looking for breathing spaces, the delay of exile. In Paris, on my short investigative visit, I had searched for another opportunity for delay. I had failed, however, to mollify the gods of the old European heaven, as well as the younger gods of America, where indecisiveness is illegal, an intolerable defiance, the mark of depravity and failure, a suspicious infirmity.

But in 1989 I formulated this plea only in my mind. I offered the diplomat a brief presentation, followed by a heavy silence.

"Have you visited America before? Do you know America?" he asked me, breaking the silence.

In one single instant, my hesitant request showed itself for what it was—a ridiculous query.

"Have you visited other places here, apart from Washington and New York?" he asked me again. His restrained cordiality was winning me over. He sensed it, too.

"No," I replied, "I haven't visited America before, I have no tourist inclinations, nor the money or the curiosity to do so."

"Maybe you should wander around America a bit," he said. But that advice was followed, thank God, not by a list of places to visit but by another prolonged silence.

"You can't have any better lessons in solitude anywhere else." His words echoed in my mind.

Yes, solitude, a familiar subject I was always ready to consider, not only in an embassy palazzo but also here and now, in a hotel tomb. "Finding your own self again in the tomb of a hotel room ," this is what Kafka said. The impersonality of hotel rooms has always been a tonic for me, I was a good student in solitude. In the eight years since I last saw Mr. Bezzetti, I have learned many new things about solitude. So, I am certain, has Mr. Bezzetti, in the tomb of the silence of death after death, for he died not long after our meeting.

"I've served in this embassy for eighteen years," he told me, "an unusually long time, as you can imagine. I've always enjoyed good relations with the ambassadors. You are Latin yourself, so you know what this means, to stay in one place, for eighteen years, a lifetime."

I looked at him more carefully now, to assess how large had been the margin of error in the age I had attributed to him.

He continued: "I rarely go to Rome, just for short holidays. I can no longer stand Italy."

Did he mean by this to discourage my hoped-for escape to Italy? He hastened to explain.

"The intimacy is what I cannot stand anymore, all those questions and embraces, the chatter, the familiarity, the friends, relatives, acquaintances, always ready to suffocate you with their affection. I am exhausted after only a few days. I have to leave."

The avalanche of words continued. I was being honored with a confession. "You've seen how Americans keep their distance, between cities, between houses, between people. Have you noticed how they keep their distance in a line at the cinema, in a shop? That's fine, really fine."

I kept silent. Was he in dialogue with the impertinence of my visit?

"Should I die tomorrow, in my small apartment, nobody will know. And that's fine, too," Mr. Bezzetti said.

I must hope that the circumstances of Mr. Giuseppe Bezzetti's death in his small apartment in the American capital were up to his standards. I can only guess that the vast realms of solitude after death have not disappointed him.

His advice to me was to get to know America, to accustom myself to a different perception of distances, to inhabit solitude. No eccentricity is totally useless, and likewise, no despair, I told myself on that winter afternoon in 1989, after I had learned that Italy did not offer governmental grants to East European writers. Solitude is our only homeland, I repeated to myself as I left the handsome Italian Embassy. The words are worth repeating even now, in the tomb of the hotel room in Bucharest.

At the end of our interview, Mr. Giuseppe Bezzetti did not suggest any further meetings, as had his French counterpart back in Berlin. But he, too, gave me his business card with the address and telephone number of the small apartment where he was awaiting his liberation. I did not seek him out. Now here he is in Bucharest, risen from his intangible faraway realm, returning my visit.

Mr. Bezzetti vanishes into the mists of Bucharest's spring. I am left there, holding a piece of pale yellow paper in my hand. I recognize my own handwriting. "Should you miss your native place . . ." I know those words, transcribed, childishly, in a moment of senile jubilation. "Should you miss your native place, you will find in exile more and more reasons to miss it; but if you manage to forget it and come to love your new residence, you will be sent back home, where, uprooted once more, you will start a new exile." These are the words of Maurice Blanchot, but it is not he now standing before me. It is another, albeit a lesser, Frenchman, though of a more complex variety. It is Emile Cioran, the man from Sibiu, from Bucharest, and a long-time exile in Paris, quoting Blanchot.

He is small, fragile, with a penetrating gaze and unruly hair. He is kneeling before me, in front of the window, staring into space.

"Forgive me," he is whispering, staring into nowhere. "Forgive me, God." Is that what he is saying? Of course not, he is a heretic and would not invoke the deity. "Forgive me," the curtains keep echoing. He looks into the emptiness, at the ceiling, at the heavens. He peers into immortality. "Forgive me, *pătlăgică*, I hear, at last. *Pătlăgică*, pickled tomato, a good name for divinity! "Forgive me, *pătlăgică*, forgive me for being born a Romanian," the nihilist implores. I know this little drama, offered from time to time to his fellow Romanians, the privileged audience to a farce that was no farce.

Leaving the motherland was by far the most intelligent thing he had ever done, he had once told me. But he had not managed to heal. "Romanians" goes one of his posthumous aphorisms. "Everyone who comes into contact with them becomes shallow, even our Jews." Ah, *la nostalgie de la boue*, the sweet delights of the mud! This country has given birth not to saints but to poets . . .

"You are not Cioran," I tell myself. "A Jew cannot say that he is wiping his ass with the motherland, as Cioran's beloved Iron Legion did in 1940. Nor that the Romanian's heart is an asshole, as one of his disciples recently declared. Nor that the history of the Romanians is the history of Romanian public lavatories. You haven't been granted that sort of legitimacy. You don't have the impudence, the therapeutic impudence. It's difficult for you to give up shame. You are ashamed for their sake, for your own sake, aren't you?"

Impudence as identity, the hidden shame, swelling with infected wounds, yes, I knew all about that, the shame of not having left on time, and then of having finally left, and the shame of being brought back to square one. "I have consecrated too many thoughts, too much chagrin, to my tribe," Cioran cries out, unheard by anybody, as he kneels by the window staring at the invisible, derisory authority.

The hidden thorn, twisted in the flesh, would not allow itself to be extracted. Kafka would probably understand. "In the struggle between yourself and the world, side with the world," he had advised me. But how could one, when under siege, distinguish among the hostile faces? It is all one face, the same illegible grimace. How can you be on their side if you cannot distinguish their faces, and how can you distinguish their hostility from the enemy within, with whom you spontaneously fraternize? "Too much chagrin," Cioran mutters, his head between his knees. They could have been my own words, too many thoughts, too much chagrin. The old century is tired, this is the endgame. We are all making our own beds, to hide somewhere from the monsters of tomorrow. Pajamas are not the most appropriate costume for this. "The night's circus requires magic," the ghost whispers, "and you have never been any good at magic." That's true. I have failed again. Magic would solve everything, would turn everything upside down, inside out.

Cioran disintegrates, leaving me in the night of nothingness with the echo of his whimper in my ears. "My country," he cries out wildly, as he disappears. "I wanted to cling to it at any cost, and there was nothing I could cling to." At any cost? I could no longer afford that. I was bankrupt, not the first or the last to be so. One cannot lose what one does not possess, and there is no return. "No return, either good or bad," Cioran had repeated, as had so many others, from time immemorial. What privilege can compete with this impossibility? To belong to nobody, to be a stone, with no other legitimacy than the present moment. Nothingness, and no revenge apart from transience.

I was suddenly looking forward, impatiently, to my return to America, to be back among my fellow citizens, the exiles, the lodgers with equal rights in the motherland of all the exiles, freed from the excesses of involvement and the aspirations to ownership, reconciled to the nomad's tent and the present moment. "You have come to the right place" was how Philip welcomed me, the East European Augustus the Fool, in the spring of 1989, upon my arrival in the New World. Nothing in the wanderer's face showed that there might be any place in the world he could call his own. Stuttering, with his hand pointing to the wheel of fortune—is this what I looked like? My American interlocutor looked at me with moderate curiosity, from behind gold-rimmed glasses, and smiled encouragingly. He was leaning back in his comfortable armchair. He had put up his long feet, American-style, on the table. I could see the Italian-made shoes, soft as gloves, in which his bare feet luxuriated.

"I don't think so. America doesn't suit me," I muttered. "I did not mean to end up here, and now I can't find a hole in which to hide."

He continued to smile his encouraging smile. "Everything will be fine," he murmured, with a kind of parental resignation. "Gradually, you're going to start writing again, you will be published. You will even have your own circle of fans. Not many, naturally, but in America everything comes out well in the end. You will gradually get to understand how great this country is."

"How many generations ago did your family settle here?" I asked, just for the sake of asking something, to forget my self.

"Three," he answered.

"My family buried five generations in Romania. Then something happened, as in Germany, or in medieval Spain. My mother's parents are buried, not in Romania, but in a forest in the Ukraine, in that ethnic dumping ground called Transnistria, in an unmarked grave. My mother always wanted to leave Romania after the war, but that is where she will be buried, she is old and ill. Only my father might yet make it to the Holy Land. He will get his own privileged grave, close to his God."

Philip listened politely to my little speech. I was aware of how boring the sound of East European self-pity can be.

"In America these things cannot happen. The Constitution will not allow it, and neither will the country's diversity. There are immigrants here from all over the world."

The silence that followed confirmed that the wanderer's pathetic recital had not been to the taste of his host, a master of irony and sarcasm. I was on the point of supplying this last ingredient, but in the meantime, the conversation turned to other topics. I managed to do that years later, when we had become closer, and after I had started to make sense of America's triumphs and disasters. So free within the freedom of the country he loved and represented, he was by now himself under public siege. Under siege, one can no longer distinguish the faces on the merry-go-round. I had had similar experiences in socialist Jormania, and

I was now reliving them in the messages that reached me from the post-Communist motherland. I now had the exile's advantage of being able to contemplate the meaning of my "belonging" from a distance, even though no one can ever claim they are far enough from themselves.

Philip believed that my visit to the motherland was absolutely necessary to my healing process. Now, having arrived in the place that, until the other day, had been "home," I was thinking of those I had left behind, in America. "I have no prejudices. I can stand any society," the American Mark Twain declaimed from beyond the ocean. "All that I care to know is that a man is a human being, that is enough for me. He can't be any worse." Céline and Cioran could not compete with such sarcasm. "A man is a human being . . . He can't be any worse." Supreme toleration, supreme skepticism, that's the way to go, as the Americans say.

I continue to receive nocturnal messages from beyond, and by day, requests to confirm that everything is okay. But the fax machine at the hotel in Bucharest is not working. An American, even one endowed with a fine sense of humor, would hardly get a joke like this. Still, we had telepathy. Through the long night, the guest in room 1515 of the Intercontinental Hotel in Bucharest is transmitting, over oceans and countries and time zones, the news that the earth continues to rotate and that its insomniac passenger is okay. There is nothing suspicious lurking behind the night's curtains. Everything's okay.

Day Five: Friday, April 25, 1997

Today we are to visit the imperial compound, the White Palace of the White Clown, Jormania's Versailles. We pass through a long avenue of apartment buildings, each with a slightly different façade, designed as residences for the Party bourgeoisie. On the top of the hill, dominating the cityscape, is the White Palace, an eclectic mix of East and West, not unlike some prewar villas but grotesquely "modernized," with a strong North Korean imprint. This is the first time that I see this monument of the Byzantine Communist dictatorship, and I am reminded of the epic destruction of the old neighboring areas following the "working" visits of our President and his beloved wife to the building site not far from my last home in Bucharest. I would stop my ears to keep out the sound of the sirens heralding the cortège of black limousines bringing the imperial pair. At night, the cranes stood out against the night sky, lit by the welders' flames. By day, the sidewalk trembled under the rumble of the cement mixers. I can still hear the wail of the police sirens, the mechanical cadences of the construction workers.

Leon is intrigued by the palace; for him it is one of the much antici-
pated highlights of the trip. "In twenty years' time," he says, "when the
political context is forgotten, this building will be studied in architecture departments. Such a project would now be impossible anywhere in
the world. Only a tyrant can afford to demolish and build on such a large
scale."

I am not in a conciliatory frame of mind and do not share Leon's enthusiasm, although I am aware of the American fascination with the pre-
modern world, which America has left behind and from which it continues
to distance itself. In spite of its own difficulties and sufferings, America
remains ready to offer its support to this old world, as if hoping that it
might in this way pay for its own sins of privilege.

We have lunch nearby, at the historic Manuc Inn. It is Good Friday, a
day for semi-fasting, and all the waiter can offer is salad and beer.

Before leaving for the airport to board his plane for Scotland, where
he has a date for a recording session with the Royal Scottish Philhar-
monic, Leon tells me that he has really enjoyed this exotic adventure. He
has bought an Oriental rug for his office at Bard College and enjoyed
haggling, in English with the merchant, a former diplomat. As for me, I
benefited from his company and the American efficiency he generated,
which prevented me from staying too long in communication with my
ghosts. We had come to Romania with different objectives, but the counterpoint proved to our mutual advantage.

Just two streets over is no. 2 Calea Victoriei, where I used to live. In
a few minutes I could be standing at the door of apartment 15, under the
sign of another time, paying tribute to the Communist siesta of a decade
ago. Would the old rhythms return, would I change back into the one I
could no longer be? Only if time annulled all that had happened in the
meantime.

Not far from my old apartment is Antim Street, Saul S.'s old place.
During the months prior to my trip, he kept saying that he would like to
accompany me. He thought he was too frail to make his perpetually
postponed return on his own, but if we went together, it might help to
alleviate the trauma we had both suffered, in very different ways.

Seven American years had passed since our first meeting. I had been recommended to him as a fellow Romanian, to arouse his sympathy, but this only evoked the opposite effect. This didn't surprise me, but neither was I deterred. He reminded me of the great Romanian poet Arghezi, not only because of his silences and economy of speech, his mustache and balding head, but also because of the quick verbal snap with which he greeted the unknown as well as the too familiar. He was like a watchful feline, slow in appearance, but easily aroused to anger if necessary. He was what could be called a grumpy old man; he had certainly been a grumpy young man.

Our closeness became evident one day when he phoned to ask me how I was doing, and I gave the conventional answer to what I thought was a conventional question. "No, you can't be doing well, anything but well. I know this. We are under a curse, it's the place we come from. We carry it in ourselves, and this cannot heal easily. Maybe never."

Despite having lived happily for half a century in America, where he had found his life's work and his fame, Saul had never been able to heal his Romanian wound. "Have you read that book about Romania in the 1940s, *Athénée Palace*, I think it's called. The author is a countess, an American countess, if such a thing is possible. We are anti-Semites here, lady, the countess reports one of the local excellencies telling her, but we cannot give up our Jews, not only for economic reasons, but because Romanians do not trust other Romanians. They can only confide their dirty secrets to a Jew."

He was waiting for my comments, but I offered only a smile.

"But if they are anti-Semites," Saul persisted, "how come they can trust Jews? If they trust them and they think they are intelligent and good people, why are they anti-Semitic?"

My answer was a continuing smile.

"The charm of the place! You see, this is the magic of our native land!"

He regarded his pre-exilic past as some kind of incurable disease, a viscous mud penetrating all his pores, infecting not only the profiteers but also the victims, who were well trained to adjust to the surrounding hatred and complicities, in a continuing bargaining that had deformed their character. He would speak with embittered, venomous vehemence about that grotesque suburban metabolism that fed on minor domestic pleasures and a persistent brew of hypocrisy. Here and now, I think, standing on this Bucharest street in 1997, I could do with his energetic sarcasm, a mix of compassion and mercilessness.

His unique drawings were a concentrate of his vision of the world, which I shared. Dadaland had become an obsession with him over the last few years, not just as the "Black Country" or "Exileland," as he called it, but also as "Childhood's Land of No Return." The artist was constantly drawn to his remembered landscape, with its magical decor and buffoonery, its ecstatic fragrances. With the frenetic imagination of youth, he would abandon himself even now, past eighty, to the memories of all those past aromas—the smells of the shoe shops and spice shops, the dust and the sweat of the nearby railway station, the pickles and pies and spicy sausages, the scents of the hairdressers.

"Having placed ourselves in the immigrant's uncomfortable position, we are like children again," he wrote. Childhood is exile, too, but it is miraculous, filled with visions and magic. His famous maps, which began life in Manhattan, on his desk, never failed to include the magic circle of Palas Street and environs in Bucharest. "I am one of the few who continue to perfect the sketches we used to draw in our childhood," he confided.

I can hear him on the phone and I can see him, here and now, asking anybody who happens to be around what he used to ask me: "*Cacialma*, what do you think? It's a Turkish word, like *mahala*, like *sarma*, *nargilé*, *ciulama*, no? What about *cică* and . . . *cicăleală*? They're all Turkish. Jobs are German, flowers are French, but *rastel* comes from the Italian *rastello*. And *rău* from the Latin. *Zid* is Slavic, and so is *zîmbet*. *Dijmă* seems Slavic, like *diac* and *diacon*. What's this *diac*, a church copyist or a church singer?" He discovered strange words, their exotic phonetics would suddenly recapture the time and place that had formed and deformed us and had thrown us out into the world. "We cannot be Americans," this long-time resident of America declared, consolingly, despite being considered a national treasure of the New World. He had every reason to accompany me to Romania and every reason to avoid going back.

Now, after Leon's departure, we could have wandered around the places where, once, the Palas paradise of his childhood had existed. However, in the end, he decided to go back to Milan, the city of his youth, a "safer" substitute for his more remote past and a place with fewer surprises. As a bon voyage gift, he sent me a copy of a page from a book about Bucharest, with a map where he highlighted his enchanted domain. "Dear Norman," he wrote, "here is my magic circle: Palas Street, off Antim, and Justiţiei Street crossing Calea Rahovei. Nothing is still standing of all this? Have a look, if you've got some time."

After Leon's departure, I have plenty of time. The site of the magic circle was not far from where I am. It had been swept away by the dictator's bulldozers and is now in New York, living on only in the memory of the old artist residing on Manhattan's Upper East Side. I can hear his melodious voice as he recites the archaic names: "Palas Street, Antim, Rinocerului, Labirint, Gentilă Street. Concordiei, and right next to it, Discordiei! Here we have Trofeelor, Olimpului, Emancipata. Listen to this, Emancipata! Isn't it wonderful? And Rinocerului, Labirint, Gentilă, Gentle Street! And Cuţitul de Argint, Puţul cu apă and Cuţitul de Argint—the Water Well and the Silver Knife!"

The magic circle has disappeared, but I can buy in the bookshop near the hotel old postcards for Saul's collection, as he had asked me to do. There were also old picture postcards of Suceava and Fălticeni; here was a treasure to take back to New York.

On his first visit to us, Saul did not bring the customary bottle of wine, or the even more customary several bottles, as he did later on, but an old colored postcard of Buzău, the home of his grandparents and parents and his early childhood. He offered it to us, watching carefully to see if Cella and I were worthy of such a gift. This was the calling card of the exile who could not stand to hear the name of Romania being mentioned, but could not extract himself from the past, even after half a century of absence from the native places. "I cannot make my peace with the language," he said.

I am now standing in front of the Intercontinental, in full spring sunlight. My protective ghost has returned. I recognize the silhouette, the gait, the shopping bag on her arm. Am I following her again, as I did, not long before in New York, up Amsterdam Avenue? She is smiling, her eyes filled with joy and that intelligent gentleness I had been yearning for. Reality had made enemies of us and had divided us so many times, but then again reunited us. Her smile follows me for a fraction of a second into room 1515. I return quickly to the street, to be in the midst of the daily din, and to be on my own, completely on my own, as I deserve to be.

In the evening, I dine at the Café de Paris, a new and expensive restaurant not far from the hotel. Also in the party are the counselor and the chargé d'affaires of the American Embassy, with their wives. The atmosphere is cordial. I confirm that the week I have spent in Bucharest has been peaceful, busy but peaceful. At the official luncheon in honor of Leon and myself, we had agreed that I would report anything of a dubious nature. There was nothing to report.

Indeed, nothing that I have encountered here so far has helped me to unravel any better than I had done in New York the Chagall image of the martyr tortured on the pyre of the East European pogrom. There was nothing here that could have helped me better understand whether the postcard contained a message of hostility or sympathy. The conversation in the restaurant focuses on post-Communist Eastern Europe. The diplomats offer cautious assessments of today's Romania; question me about Mircea Eliade, the assassination of Professor Culianu in Chicago in 1991. "Soon, even here, in the East, the intellectuals' nationalist nonsense will become irrelevant," says the young chargé d'affaires. "The intellectuals here will become as irrelevant as they are in the West. The debate on nationalism will be marginalized, too. All intellectual debates end up like this, don't they?" I give up trying to inquire about the diplomatic ramifications of his missions in Eastern Europe and the former Soviet Union. I accept, serenely, the pleasant young man's optimistic pragmatism, the friendly atmosphere of the dinner table, comforting in the very limitations it presupposed.

The group insists on seeing me back to my hotel. They accompany me, all four of them, into the lobby, where we spend ten minutes chatting. Were they observing the obsolete rules of the Cold War? Was this little drama destined, as in the old days, to signal to the receptionists and their superiors that I had been in the company and under the protection of American officials?

Once in my room, I open the blue notebook. I hold the pen in my hand, but a shadow seems to envelop the room, taking possession of it. I shut my eyes and close the Bard notebook, and conclude a pact with the shades haunting me.

The Home of Being

Ken's perception that my face lit up at the sound of Romanian, even a casual exchange on Tuesday with the hotel desk clerk, was probably correct. For that one instant, the native language had become my true home. It had happened before. In Zürich, the hotel porter, having heard us speak Romanian, had addressed Cella, all smiles, *"Bună dimineața,"* good morning, and then continued on with some small talk, in which I happily joined.

Waking up was a joke. Once one had done that, one had no choice but to go out and earn one's living, with words. The days follow in succession, one on the heels of another, step by step, in the nomad's labyrinth. Then, there was the day not long ago, in New York. I had woken up without actually waking up, after a night as short as a second. My American friend, an early riser as usual, was on the phone.

The voice, the bantering tone, were the same, but the words themselves, the sound, the accent . . . this was a strange substitute, a Balkan doppelgänger. Still half asleep, on my way to the bathroom, I heard voices in the living room. Who had invaded our apartment at such an early hour?

On her way out to work, Cella had left the TV on. It was the O. J. Simpson trial, playing out in California but suddenly transmuted into another vocabulary, other phonetics. Clutching the remote control, I switched to a different channel, then another, through all the 75 channels on New York television. On each—there was no mistake—everybody spoke Romanian! I switched off the TV and went to the bathroom. The mirror told me I was in a state of jubilation; I had an idiotic smile pasted on my face. That mask of happiness contradicted what I thought I had been feeling in the minutes after the telephone rang. I lowered my eyes into the white shell of the sink, to avoid looking into a stranger's face. My hands were trembling, the soap slipped into the sink, but in spite of the anxiety, my face still wore an emblem of triumph.

I managed to get out of the bathroom without another look in the mirror, got dressed, went out into the hallway, and proceeded cautiously to the elevator. I was going to get the newspaper, as I do most mornings. At any moment, the door might open on yet another hallucination. On the ground floor, Pedro was at his accustomed place, behind the marble desk, smiling with his usual affability. "Good morning, sir," he would greet me every day, in his Spanish-accented English. This morning, nodding his head in the usual way, he said, *"Bună dimineaţa, domnule!"* The simple "Good morning," which was my usual response, didn't seem right this time. The cretinous smile of enchantment continued to light up my face. Pedro, too, was speaking Romanian. And not only Pedro but also O. J. Simpson and Johnnie Cochran and Marsha Clark and President Clinton and Magic Johnson, all of whom I had seen, only a few minutes before, on TV, along with Barbra Streisand, Diana Ross, and Ray Charles, all singing, if such a thing could be imagined, in Romanian. *"Doamne Dumnezeule,"* I found myself muttering, convinced that God spoke Romanian, too, and could understand me. The young Asian at the newsstand stared at me, stupefied, not because he could not comprehend the strange language in which I addressed the divinity, but because, actually, he, too, understood the code. Of this I was certain. I left the change on the counter and bent over to pick up a copy of *The New York Times.*

I looked at the headlines. What was I looking for? A wish, a promise, a message from an oracle? Such a message had indeed arrived the year before, from a town with the romantic name of New Rochelle. It came in the form of a handwritten card from Cynthia and again I recalled her words: "I wish for you, that one morning we will all wake up speaking, reading, and writing Romanian; and that Romanian will be declared the American national language (with the world doing the strange things it is doing today, there is *no reason* for this NOT to happen)." Words, mere words, there was no power of predestination in the way they were put together. Should I have been suspicious of the parenthesis? I am not among the fans of Jacques Derrida and of "textual ambiguity." Cynthia's words were naturally affectionate, playful, innocent, well-meaning. Had I passed too quickly over the "NOT" that Cynthia herself set in capital letters? Should I have reminded myself of the old Chinese curse about not wishing for anything too much, lest the wish come true? The wish had come true, and indeed, it had brought me not felicity or healing but total bewilderment. I felt as though I were a puppet in one of those TV children's shows, which, to my horror, suddenly began speaking in Romanian. Does a foreigner win his linguistic citizenship, like an outlaw bursting in? When the motherland orders you out, do you take the language and run? What does the "Home of Being" really mean, Herr Professor Heidegger? Is it language, disabled alienated language, insomniac language, the Greek *hypocrino*? Is language simulation, dissimulation, lies? Is it theatricality, the retarded playing at imitation? Is it masque and masquerade? All of a sudden, everything was fake, falsified. President Clinton in Romanian, Ray Charles in Romanian, Magic Johnson in Romanian—an absurdity; Romanian turned into a global language, with nobody having any difficulty understanding and speaking it. Had exile become universal exile? Was everybody now a performer in Hypocrino's circus?

The toad-turned-prince was smiling idiotically, but was feeling quite uncomfortable talking in Romanian to Pedro the Mexican and to the Asian newspaper vendor, or even to Philip. What Cynthia had in mind, when she played with the words, was something altogether different. Like so many writers, and nonwriters as well, she was oblivious to the dangers hidden in words.

My lunatic smile, my apoplectic seizure of happiness—everything had become simple, natural. Had I suddenly been cured of the hesitancy with which, in old age, I was trying to interpret my childhood, in a different vocabulary? That bewildering farce had not set things right but had just twisted them into caricature instead. Monsieur Derrida would have had reason to be pleased: language cannot pretend to be nonambiguous, this is what he claims, isn't it?

Too late, Cynthia, too late! If the miracle had happened on March 9, 1988, when I landed, as innocent as an infant, at the Washington airport, coming straight from the moon, then yes, I would have been happy to talk in Romanian to Cynthia and Philip, to Roger and Ken, to Leon, Saul B., Saul S., and so many others. Had that been the case, I would have joyfully conversed in Romanian even with Dan Quayle or George Bush. But now, everything had got mixed up. I was no longer the infant who is just learning, through gestures and babbling, its way into language. The new language to which I had exiled myself had, in the meantime, infiltrated itself into the interstices of the old. I had become *hypocrino*, a hybrid. Nothing in me remained pure or whole.

I now understood a conversation I had had, a short while before, with Louis. We talked about the bizarre similarities and differences of our personal histories, not only our traumatic childhoods, but also what happened to us subsequently. I could have imagined for myself an American destiny comparable to his—studies at a reputable university, work as a lawyer and writer—had my parents, like his, immigrated immediately after the war to the United States, and had they had the mean to finance their son's tuition. Conversely, I could see Louis—a name, I guess, as unusual in Poland as Norman was in Romania—having stayed on in his native country and following, who knows, a course of life not too different from mine, through the meanderings of Polish socialism.

There were few diners in the smart East Side restaurant where the famous lawyer and writer seemed to be a regular, judging from the attentiveness of the waiters.

"Yes, you could be right," he said. "We are very much alike without even realizing it. The only difference is that you, at least, have a language."

The quiet of the restaurant was immediately shattered, as if someone had dropped a tray full of dishes on the floor. No, the clatter was only in my mind. Louis's remark did not make me jump from my chair, but I froze. What did he mean? I had just lost a language and no other loss could equal it. What was he saying, he, an American writer, perfectly at ease in his country and language.

As if reading my thoughts, he continued: "I live comfortably in the language of my American milieu. It's a language I handle, if I may say so, to perfection. The difference is that you have your own language. This is quite obvious, believe me, even in those translations you complain about. My language, perfect as it is, may be merely a tool. Sure, I can do with it whatever I wish. But you are one with your own language; you have a coherence, a wholeness, even in exile, especially in exile."

A coherence? A wholeness? In my exotic language, Romanian, which gets lost in translation? Do I write in an easily translatable language, with a vocabulary that travels effortlessly across international borders? In the silence of that smart restaurant, I was again assaulted by a battery of questions, as I had been on that day when I went out to buy a copy of *The New York Times* on Amsterdam Avenue. One stroke and I was transfixed: the words had found their captive again, and had regained their meaning.

I stood there, suddenly transfixed in that unlikely moment. A century passed. My hand continued to reach out for *The New York Times*. I bent to pick up the newspaper. Yes, a Romanian newspaper! But now I was back in Bucharest. On a morning that felt as improbable as the one on Amsterdam Avenue in New York. I was standing at a news kiosk in Bucharest and saw the headline THE POSTHUMOUS JOURNAL OF MI-HAIL SEBASTIAN.

Whatever Monsieur Derrida might claim about the ambiguity of language, limpid words have a limpid, unequivocal meaning. No ambiguity there. Yes, Louis was right. Nobody could take away my coherence and my wholeness. Nobody and nothing, not even that dream that had suddenly turned into reality.

Day Six: Saturday, April 26, 1997

Today I am having lunch with my friends Bebe and Silvia. The street where they live is no longer called Fučik—in honor of the famous Czech Communist journalist and author of *Notes from the Gallows*—but Masaryk, a more optimistic designation. Because of neglect, the building has lost some of the prestige of its privileged location. The apartment, once comfortable and elegant, now looks shabby and modest. But my friends do not appear to have aged, they have maintained their composure despite their environment. Bebe edits an excellent cultural magazine, Silvia helps with editing the manuscripts. The conversation runs smoothly. We talk about the post-Communist transition and about nationalism, about New York and Bard College, about the visiting American conductor, about Eliade and Sebastian's *Journal*. Bebe, a former student of Sebastian's during the war, talks about the postwar life of the actress Leny Caler, Sebastian's former mistress, a central character in the *Journal*'s first part. The actress kept a diary herself—Bebe owns the manuscript—which turned out to be less interesting than her tempestuous life would lead one to expect. Her sister's life, however, was truly sensational. A refugee in Berlin, like Leny Caler herself, she formed inscrutable relations with the secret police of at least one country, or even more, whose names Bebe reels off with the rapture of an old collector of dubious narratives. It is a lengthy, Oriental-style conversation, lasting over five hours, and it seems almost to come from a previous life.

My next visit is with Donna Alba. When I rang her up to arrange the visit, the telephone instantly recaptured the voice of a decade before, but her talk now was no longer about books, a subject on which she had held forth at length and with verve.

Donna Alba, as I had nicknamed her, was, in her youth, a starry apparition. Beautiful, delicate, intelligent, she dominated literature seminars with her chimerical presence, intimidating her fellow students. They would never have dared address her in—what seemed, compared to her elegant locutions—their crass, plebeian jargon. After graduation, she survived for only a few months as an editor at a publishing house before being fired for her cosmopolitan style of dress and her silences. But the firing was not a disaster. This fragile offspring of the middle classes acquired in the meantime a new name and a new family—she got married. The godlike creature abandoned Mount Olympus and descended on terra firma as the spouse of a famous critic and feared ideologue of the new Communist elite. The apparatchik needed no permission from officialdom in his choice of spouse, and serenely accepted the incompatibility between his socialist aesthetic criteria and those of his own wife.

The famous critic, lame, myopic, sarcastic, had once been an underground Communist, tortured and condemned to death under the dictatorship of Marshal Antonescu. He bore the double scar of an invalid and of a rebel. For this admirer of Proust and Tolstoy, whom he reread every summer, the class struggle must have simply meant revenge against a corrupt Romanian society, a society that would remain corrupt under socialism, as he was to discover, himself overtaken by the speed of the turncoat disguises.

The "thaw" of the 1960s meant more for him than the loss of his official function, and the Communist fell into a delirium. It was not, however, a fear of democracy—which he considered a game for retarded children—but the nightmare of resurgent Fascism that triggered his crisis. He literally hid under his bed, terrified of imminent execution. Committed to a psychiatric clinic, he could think only of Fascism and execution. He seemed to have lost even his ability to read and write. A renowned psychiatrist, a writer himself and a friend of the patient's, finally found a way to reach him, by reciting to him famous selections from familiar literary masterpieces. It worked, and the patient's memory gradually started to regurgitate the words, the lines, the pages, helping him to regain his reading and writing abilities.

By the time I met him, the former militant had become obese and sedentary. His only link with politics now was gossip and sarcastic asides. He had not lost his literary fervor, however, and was writing excellent novels and short stories. What remained in his revolutionary arsenal were barbed shafts aimed at American imperialistic capitalism, socialism turned National Socialism, and the games of the literary world. His ailments multiplied, but his tenacity endured. Moving from one chair to another became a physical feat. When questioned about the state of his health, he invariably answered, "I'm happy, sir. Happiness is the only thing I've got left." Those were hard times for Donna Alba, too. Her incongruous fur coat could be glimpsed in the long lines waiting to buy cheese, lemons, or medicine. This woman, who had never even made a cup of tea for herself, was now heroically doing her duty in looking after her ailing spouse. Formerly aloof, never replying to people greeting her in the street, she now chatted with the elderly pensioners standing in line for hours on end to buy a bag of potatoes.

The real survival test in the unheated rooms in the old apartment building next to Cişmigiu Park where they lived was the winters. Like the besieged population of Leningrad during the blockade of World War II, the frozen couple resisted by reading. The ailing critic and his wife became partners in a bookish dialogue, her austere beauty complementing the sick man's pathos, her aesthetic detachment a foil for his frustrated militancy.

By now, however, the couple's biography had become history, and the woman I was on my way to see was, like so many others, a mere survivor, living at a different address. I decided to bring flowers, and in the flower shop the florist addressed me in English. The price of a small bouquet of roses was the same as in New York, a staggering sum for Bucharest. I did not even bother to protest that the flowers weren't fresh enough.

The street was in the cold belly of a cloud, the passersby unnaturally alive. The only thing I perceived was the fear of touching them or of being touched in turn. I suddenly felt shy, as I followed the meandering twists of the street. Donna Alba's new home was somewhere nearby. I had been walking for quite a while, uncertain of ever arriving at my destination.

The elevator creaked its way up to the top floor. The door was flung open even before the doorbell stopped ringing.

"Oh, you are finally here, dear man."

Her voice was unchanged, I knew that from the telephone. I would have liked to embrace her, but such gestures of intimacy had never been her way and she always seemed to discourage them. I kissed her hand formally, as in former times. She took the bouquet, which I was holding awkwardly, as usual.

Ten years had passed since our last meeting. In the meantime, her mother had died, and so had her husband, and she herself had attempted suicide. The post-Communist nightmare had succeeded the nightmare of the dictatorship. She could no longer afford a hairdresser, or maybe she no longer paid attention to such details. She had lost her feminine allure, her mystery, her ostentatiously cerebral manner. Her hair was now white and she was wearing an everyday sweater. Neither the early-afternoon hour nor, as it were, the time of her own heart allowed for more fashionable dress, as in the past. Before me was the pale face, the sunken Semitic eyes of old Leah Riemer, my grandfather's sister, the face that, as a child, I thought was biblical. I instantly felt older myself. She motioned for me to sit in the armchair. She did not offer to show me the apartment. The small hallway was divided by a glass door, beyond which I could see a table covered with papers and a straight chair. Somewhere at the back, probably, were the bedroom and a small kitchen. It all reeked of poverty and solitude. I did not recognize the worn furniture. Gone was the literary salon of Sfîntul Pavel Street, along with the red velvet coverings and the red silk gowns.

I remembered that autumn evening when, intrigued by the voice of the woman who had called me two weeks before, I was at her door and rang the bell. She appeared in the doorway, then as she did now, and for a moment I again beheld the romantic vision of yore. The woman came straight out of a period portrait. She had a small white porcelain face, with black eyes, her forehead encircled by a white headband. She wore a sumptuous red gown and moved with restrained, refined slowness. She had a slender waist and ample, Oriental hips under the velvet folds. Only her hands displayed something sad, unfinished. Her fingers were as thin as a child's, her elbows brittle, unlikely to bear touching. She gave off an aura of inviting, anachronistic adventure, amid all that socialist vulgarity.

"Well, you shouldn't look around too closely," she said. "Better tell me about America, but not the America we see in the movies, with all that moronic gun fighting."

I was silent, not knowing where to start.

"I heard you came with a conductor, or something like that, someone who is also a historian and speaks German, too. So, it's not all barbarians, sex, and money in America."

The prejudiced views of America do not seem too different from images that foreigners have of Romania. I responded by painting a flattering portrait of the conductor.

"So, a European, then, I see."

"Yes, American and European."

I looked at the cake on the plate in front of me. At Donna Alba's literary soirées the refreshments consisted of only light sweet drinks, liqueurs, vermouth, and a piece of cake, usually a rich chocolate cake, heavy and sweet. Each forkful would release a mass of cream and sugar. Later, when there was a shortage of basic foodstuffs, such gastronomic torture became impossible, and the lack of heating finally spelled the end of those extravagant soirées. This time, the cake was not too sweet, and I was spared the torture of the past. What I was eating was a decent-enough cake, bought from a trustworthy pastry shop in town.

Unable to ask her about the last months of her mother and husband, or to discuss old age and poverty, I gazed in bewilderment at the table covered with books, papers, and notebooks, trying to identify the dusty, dilapidated ledger that I remembered. I almost asked her about it. I was looking at the clock, not knowing what to say and secretly hoping for the miracle that often occurs when you feign indifference, that I would catch a glimpse of the mystery ledger lying somewhere about, a survivor of all the calamities.

This had been one of my accidental discoveries, during one of my visits to the great litterateur, Donna Alba's husband. I had arrived at two o'clock, as usual. The novelist went to bed at dawn and woke up late, so meetings took place after lunch. I had rung the bell and the door was opened, as usual, by the mother-in-law, an old Russian lady. She spoke only a bare minimum of words, but I knew she liked me, because she called me *ruskii pisateli, russkaia intelligentsia*, the Russian writer, the Russian intellectual. I was flattered by the error. She invited me into what she called the *salyon*, the living room. I sat in the usual chair, at the table covered in red velvet, which held a framed portrait of Donna Alba and a copy of *À la recherche du temps perdu*. I gazed at the photograph, mindful of the noises coming from the adjacent room, shuffling steps, panting breath.

Finally, the Flying Elephant emerged, limping along and supporting himself against the walls. To get from the door to the table, not too great a distance, he would grab the rope fastened to the wall for the purpose of aiding his movements. Having reached his destination, he would collapse, exhausted, into his chair.

"Hey, liberal, any news from Atlantis?"

The litterateur and retired Communist seemed, however, more interested in the latest local gossip than in any news from the North Atlantic inferno. So we chatted about books, adulterous affairs, literary conspiracies. After about a quarter of an hour, the *salyon* was honored, according to the customary protocol, by the old Russian mother-in-law bringing the cake and a glass of water. I thanked her, as usual, for the alimentary torture I was about to endure, but Matushka did not withdraw immediately.

"Paul, Paul, here is Kafika," I heard her mutter. "Brought Kafika," she repeated in her inimitable accent, with the stress on the first syllable.

"Kafka?" I asked, once alone with the maestro, and after allowing the Slavic sonorities to disperse. The old lady had left a great, thick ledger on the table, now keeping conspicuous watch. It had thick, old, black covers, with a stained school-notebook label on the front.

"Ah, the register, with all the addresses and telephone numbers. Yes, Kafka, that's the name I've given it. See here it is, written on the label, 'Kafka.' Like the writer, this register is full of mysteries," he said in an offhand manner.

I wondered under which code name I had been inscribed, but that mattered less than the fact that I had been admitted into the charmed circle. The *salyon*, over time, underwent changes, but always I was certain that somewhere, not too far away, Kafka was keeping watch.

I kept looking at the clock on Donna Alba's table, its metronomic ticking rhythmically marking time to the words that now invaded my mind.

"I am watching the clock. It was given to me by my mother, my omnipotent, immortal mother, who has been lying in the earth for an eternity, for a day, for a minute." These were words that Donna Alba had recently published. "With an effort, I watch the second clock on the chest of drawers, a solid high-quality clock, which my omnipotent, immortal father joyfully bought for himself just a few days, not more than seven, before he died."

I did not forget those mournful words.

On the bedframe—made of rosewood, blackened and stained with time—is another watch, the wristwatch of my youth, belonging to my double. It has stopped running long ago and now shows the same time in perpetuity. I am not looking at it, but I know it is there. My father gave it to me, so that I can make a gift of it to my double—an extraordinary Swiss watch, imported from Geneva. They say a gift made of a gift makes heaven, but I think it can also make a Gehenna, because now my omnipotent, immortal father is lying in his grave. And my double, my soulmate, vulnerable, strong, and immortal, is also lying in a hole dug deep in the earth and covered over with dirt, the hole in which I myself repose.

I hear the echo of those words, their metallic ring resounding in my ears, and I see again the smoky day much like this, twenty-five years ago, or maybe centuries, when the telephone brought me the voice of the woman now calling to me from the grave.

I answered Donna Alba's questions about America, but my words were mere conventional noises, not only because my return to Romania, too, seemed conventional, but because I knew how shocked she had been in 1986 when she heard of my departure, and later, when her beloved husband began to heap abuse on me. Would she be able to speak of her husband's anger?

"I am rich in losses," she says. "How shall I put it, I am an expert in this field. So I know what I am talking about. Don't ever forget what I'm telling you now: you haven't lost a thing by leaving. On the contrary."

Donna Alba also seemed to be speaking on behalf of the dead man. Was this a commutation of my sentence? She did not mean loss of language, for she knew, better than many, about the value and worth of words. She had other losses in mind that were, in fact, gains. Was she thus passing judgment on her own remaining in place? I did not have the strength to explain to her what I had learned myself, in the meantime, about gain and loss. All I could hear was the repeated refrain: "You haven't lost a thing, not a thing, dear Norman. On the contrary." To escape the obsessive metronome, I asked where the bathroom was. She showed me the way, and even accompanied me for a few steps down a narrow corridor. I switched on the light, and the minuscule bulb shed an uncertain illumination on what looked like some sort of storage room— worn-out suitcases, brooms, brushes, dusty chairs, old clothes, pock-marked basins, old hats, fur collars, old-fashioned shoes. I thought for a second that I caught a glimpse of stuffed birds perched next to chipped busts and disabled umbrellas.

There was a small sink in the corner, next to the toilet. Without looking in the mottled mirror, I turned off the tap, but no use, the thin trickle of rusty water kept on dripping. I took one last look at the cracked toilet bowl with its broken lid, at the dull gray floor and gray walls, the old window frame, the bucket and the mops. I switched off the light, and remained for a second, motionless, in the midst of eternity, among that pile of rubbish unable to summon the courage to resume the visit.

Back in the room, I listened to her tell of Securitate agents who had gotten rich and of suicidal pensioners, about vagabond children and stray dogs. Did she also say something about the Italian shoes one could buy at the corner shop, if one had the money?

After a few more minutes, I was out on the street, but I could still hear her voice. "Who am I? Who am I? I close my eyes and I can still see, but I am not allowed to see. I chase away the ghosts, I try to empty my skull, wet with the salty trickle of sweat. I wonder: Who am I now?" The metallic, slightly tired voice was familiar, the words came from the eternal void. "I thought we knew each other well, my ego and I. Now I wonder, What's left of me now? In fact, who am I?" My ego and I also know each other well, but as I walked away, I kept repeating that question in which I had lost interest a long time before.

It is only a few minutes' walk to University Square and my hotel. It is twilight and few people are in the streets. I enter the underpass at the university and emerge on the other side, where street vendors display their newspapers and books. I am close to the wall with the black painted message MONARHIA SALVEAZĂ ROMÂNIA. Across the street is the Intercontinental Hotel, where, on a table in room 1515, lies the traveler's logbook, ready to confirm that the day and the hours that have passed were indeed real and belonged to me.

The underpass joins the four corners of the intersection of Boulevard Magheru and the boulevard that used to be named Gheorghe Gheorgiu-Dej. In my previous life, streetcars used to run along the boulevards and there were the usual pedestrian crossings. Here, on this very spot, thirty years ago, destiny had crossed from one side of the street to the other and was coming toward me.

I was watching, hidden from view, on the university corner of the intersection, standing on the narrow street leading to the Institute of Architecture, in that privileged space occupied by the one who can see without being seen. Time had stopped, as it has now. I am waiting for the traffic light to change. She is waiting, too, on the opposite side. I am as invisible as if I were on the moon. She cannot see me. She does not see anyone. She is alone, ethereal, supreme lady of the moment. The traffic light blinks from red to green. Another fraction of a second passes and then she steps into the street. She is wearing a black fur coat and high-heeled ankle boots. Her face is unseen, lit by a nimbus. It is Cella, my wife-to-be. I gaze at her graceful walk, her slender figure. Her face is limpid, like lunar light. This Nordic princess, disguised as a student at the university, was walking straight into my watchful gaze. I was surprised, on that cold afternoon, to see her crossing from the shore of the opposite pavement straight toward the university clock and toward me, a secret, solitary revelation. We were married not too long after.

I am now standing, thirty years later, at that same astral spot, at the fateful intersection, a place that belongs only to me.

I decide to go over to the news stalls. Once again, I descend into the underpass and emerge facing the hotel, a pile of newspapers under my arm. Back in my room, I look at the headlines. Of course, today is the eve of the Orthodox Easter. *Curierul Naţional* announces, in bold red letters, CHRIST IS RISEN. *Ziua* proclaims, LUAŢI LUMINĂ, receive the light, above a half-page image of the Saviour, surrounded by saints and disciples. *România Liberă* carries the greeting SĂRBĂTORI FERICITE, CU HRISTOS ÎNVIAT DIN MORŢI, a happy Easter with the risen Christ, accompanied by the image of Christ and a message from His Beatitude, Father Teoctist, Patriarch of Romania. *Cotidianul* also displays Christ's image, as well as a photo of King Michael I, who is celebrating this Easter in Romania and to whom the paper extends greeting. *Adevărul*, above its name, runs a box reading: "On this holy night of rebirth in hope and love, let us all rejoice, CHRIST IS RISEN."

I spend a longer time with *Adevărul*, the Truth, a name not easy to find in the West. *Le Monde*, *The New York Times*, *Corriere della Serra*, *The* (London) *Times*, *Die Zeit*, *El País*, the *Frankfurter Allgemeine*, the *Neue Zürcher Zeitung*—none of these have the certainty of *Adevărul*, the Truth. In interwar Romania, *Adevărul* was a respected daily. Immediately after the war, the proletarian dictatorship suspended its publication. The Communists in Moscow had their own *Pravda*, another Truth, the inspiration for the daily *Scînteia*, meaning "spark," the organ of the Romanian

Communist Party, its title borrowed from Lenin's sparkling *Iskra*. After 1989, *Adevărul* was resuscitated as an "independent newspaper."

Five years ago, in its issue of March 7, 1992, *Adevărul*, listed me as subhuman. The author of this information, a former journalist from *Scînteia*, had exchanged the usual Communist revolutionary rhetoric for a new jargon, recycled to meet the debased tastes of the current readership. His article "The Romanianism of a Complete Romanian," devoted to Mircea Eliade, cited me among those "fractions, halves, quarters, of a human being" who stood in the way of the motherland's path to a better future. Half a man, a quarter of a man? It was not necessarily an insult. My friend, the poet Mugur, had made a point of calling himself Half-Man-Riding, Half-One-Legged-Hare. So much for "hope and love," as proclaimed by *Adevărul*, five years later, this holy eve of April 26, 1997.

I skim through the papers looking for reviews of Mihail Sebastian's *Journal*, the literary event of that Romanian spring, competing in importance with the debates about Romania's being accepted into NATO. Published half a century after the author's death, the volume focuses on the "rhinocerization" of the leading interwar Romanian intellectuals, Eliade, Cioran, Nae Ionescu, and so many others. "Lengthy discussion on political topics with Mircea, at his place. Impossible to summarize. He was in turn lyrical, nebulous, brimming with exclamations, interjections, apostrophes. Out of this, all I wish to select is his—finally loyal—declaration that he loves the Guard, places his hopes in it, and looks forward to its triumph," Sebastian wrote in January 1941.

The Iron Guard, the ultranationalist movement, "wiped its ass" with Romania, Cioran had declared. Indeed, even as Sebastian was writing, some Legionnaires were believed to proceed, on January 22, 1941, with the ritual killing of Jews, at the slaughterhouse in Bucharest, to the ecstatic accompaniment of Christian hymns.

Late that night, I watch on TV the church celebration of the Resurrection. I go back to the pile of newspapers. Reactions to Sebastian's *Journal* are varied. They run the gamut from emotional to bewildered to irritated. Why should I care? After all, I wasn't present when an overheated Ariel harangued his audience, in those Hooligan Years before my birth, in Grandfather Avram's bookstore in Burdujeni, nor did Sebastian have anything to do with either Transnistria or Periprava. It is true, he, too, had wanted to leave the ghetto, and he, too, had been welcomed not with flowers but, predictably, with the prospect of more ghettos. He, too, under siege, had remained a captive of inner adversity. These are similarities that cannot be easily ignored but that do not, however, annul the radical differences between us. He had lived in the world of the old codes, at a moment when they were ready to implode. I lived after the codes had already imploded. No, I am no Sebastian, but if I were to write about his *Journal*, would I be once more covered in abuse? Would I again be called "traitor," "extraterritorial," "White House agent"? I could read the future in the past, or in today's newspapers: "Augustus the Fool has come back for more! Augustus the Fool will write about that hooligan Sebastian's *Journal* and will, once more, become a hooligan himself! He has insulted the Romanian people and has prevented Romania from joining NATO!" And more. Again, I would have provoked the ire of Bucharest's intellectual elite over the Jewish "monopoly on suffering" and the Jewish "monitoring" of Romania.

It is late, I have no strength left to tackle the future's charades. I have been hard hit by an item in the newspapers, the death of the writer and scholar Petru Creția, a religious Christian. Only days before he died, the journal *Realitatea Evreiască* (*Jewish Reality*) had published an essay of his on anti-Semitism in which he excoriated the new stars of the intellectual elite—"figures who in public display flawless morality, an impeccable democratic conduct, a wise moderation, accompanied, in some cases, by a pompous solemnity, yet are capable of, privately and sometimes not so privately, foaming at the mouth against the Jews." Just as in Sebastian's Hooligan Years. Creția's voice suddenly fills the room: "I have seen the irrefutable proof of the fury triggered by Sebastian's *Journal* and of the feeling that lofty national values are being besmirched by the disclosures made, so calmly and with such forgiving pain, by this fair-minded, often angelic witness." Petru Creția's words resound: "The most monstrous thing after the Holocaust is the persistence of even a minimal anti-Semitism."

The traveler that I am can now go to sleep with these words in his ears, here in the motherland he had not wanted to leave and to which he did not want to return and where he was racked by ambiguities. A tardy therapy, sleep. One can take into the healing night everything that one has lost, as well as everything that one might lose, things one doesn't even know about yet. I think of the hooligan Sebastian, and the hooligan Jesus, mocked by the Pharisees and resurrected in thousands of faces and burned alive, under thousands of faces, in the crematoria of the hooligan century. I can no longer fight my fatigue, I am like an old child who has finally been given the anesthetic he has been asking for.

Day Seven: Sunday, April 27, 1997

The narrow streets of the old quarter are, for the most part, demolished. I am walking, cautiously, along Sfînta Vineri Street, toward the Choral Synagogue, the headquarters of the Jewish community. It is almost ten o'clock in the morning, but the street is deserted. After the long night of the Resurrection, the population of Bucharest is enjoying a late-morning sleep. The synagogue's courtyard, too, is empty. Only the Christian porter is at his post.

I ask for Mr. Blumenfeld, the secretary. The short man in a leather jacket, standing next to the porter, turns to me. "I could take you there in the car, I'm the community's driver." "You have to get authorization," says the porter, pointing to the building at the back of the courtyard and pronouncing a name I can't catch. "You have to talk to the gentleman over there, at the office."

Mr. Isaacson, or Jacobson, or Abramson, keeps his eyes glued to some file. I explain who I am, where I come from, and why I am here. I need the address or telephone number of Mr. Blumenfeld. Silence. I add that Mr.

Blumenfeld knows me. The official does not lift his eyes. Head still lowered, he barks, "What do you want?"

I will not respond until he emerges from those important papers.

Finally, he looks up. "Who are you and what do you want? Mr. Blumenfeld has a fracture or something. He's in bed, on sick leave. And I'm busy."

I bang the door shut and manage to suppress a curse, but I am silently boiling over with rage. I walk past the porter's lodge and then continue down Bălcescu Boulevard, back to my hotel. I think Sebastian mentions, somewhere in his *Journal*, the need one feels, in difficult times, to be with one's fellow believers, as well as the ensuing disappointment.

The city is deserted, except for the occasional pedestrian or stray dog, first one dog, then two, then three, then four. I have been told that hundreds, thousands, of starving dogs are loose on the streets, menacing the citizens. I hadn't encountered any packs, but then, I haven't been out that much. Now I can imagine, having seen these quartets, what it would be like to meet a whole, snarling pack.

The streets are still empty, the doors are locked, there are no signs of life at the windows, on the balconies, the terraces. There is nothing moving. Yet, after a few more steps, in front of the paint shop, there she is— the ghost. There are only the two of us on that narrow sidewalk. The old woman is familiar with the street to which I had often accompanied her. Yes, there is no doubt about who it is. I recognize the thin, pale legs, the white, short-cropped hair, the bony, bent shoulders, the sleeveless, shapeless dress, the shopping bag in one hand, the sweater in the other. She is walking slowly while I hurry on, and yet we are walking together, shoulder to shoulder. In front of the hotel, I am alone again, and the narrow, crooked streets are also behind me, in the void.

Back in my room, I manage to obtain Mr. Blumenfeld's telephone number and I call him. The convalescent man speaks in a weakened, aged voice. Yes, I can come and visit anytime. I set off again toward the Amzei market. On the way I stop at a post office—happily open—to buy postcards for my American friends. The woman at the counter scrutinizes me intently. Is she someone I know? I don't recognize her pleasant, open face. She keeps on smiling at me while I choose my cards. I admire her large, moist eyes, full lips, perfect teeth. From the very first moment, I liked her calm, pleasant manner. She recalls similar, forgotten images, the domesticity of an inhabitable past, a time when one did not need many words.

"Do you happen to speak German?" she asks.

"Yes," I reply, cheered by her friendly voice.

"Oh, you are my salvation, really."

She hands me a note with instructions in German, directions on how to use a powder for coloring Easter eggs. I translate; the lady nods in understanding and writes down the information, smiling all the while. At one time, the young man I once was would not have remained unresponsive to the hidden promise of that smile.

I go to the shop in the Amzei market where, in Communist days, one might find the rare allocation of meat. Now the shoppers are mostly Romanians from abroad, come to celebrate Easter as they used to. I buy a few bottles of expensive Romanian wine for my friend Golden Brain, and also two bottles of whiskey, one for him, the other for my planned trip to Suceava.

The apartment house where the Blumenfelds live stands in the middle of a vacant lot, the result of all the demolition work that has been going on in the neighborhood. The lady of the house opens the door and I recognize her, the petite, beautiful woman who was a striking presence at all the community festivities, usually accompanied by her tall, handsome, distinguished husband. Mr. Blumenfeld looks visibly aged and has lost his once-imposing posture. I am offered a cup of coffee, which I decline, and Mrs. Blumenfeld brings a glass of water on a small crystal saucer. Time has deposited its thin layers of rust over this old-fashioned, comfortable home.

I pull up my chair next to the convalescent's armchair and inform him of the reason for my visit. A few months ago, I had applied for a certificate showing that my family was deported in 1941 to Transnistria. The certificate is for my father, who emigrated to Israel in 1989, at the age of eighty-one, and who now lives in an old people's home in Jerusalem, suffering from Alzheimer's disease. Mr. Blumenfeld takes notes, confirms that the files of the deportees are now in the community's archives, and yes, a certificate will be issued, so that Father can receive the reparations due him—not from the Romanians, of course. He does not ask lengthy questions, his infirmity makes him irritable. The situation in post-Communist Romania, like his advanced age, is not conducive to cheerfulness.

A deputy minister for transportation in the Communist government, Mr. Blumenfeld, upon retirement, like other Jewish Communist officials, became a leader in the Jewish community, with which he had interrupted contact in the postwar years. He was always seeking to avoid harming anybody, and to offer help, if at all possible. Used to the whims of authority, he proved useful in his new position as Secretary of the Jewish community. The end of the Communist dictatorship found him, however, not among the system's adversaries, as might be expected. Now, in old age, he found adaptation to the capitalist chaos a humiliating experience.

I am expected for lunch at Naum's, my old friend Golden Brain. His destiny has not been too different from that of Mr. Blumenfeld, and as a talented writer, he has found additional career options. Then there is his wife, Felicia, the heroine who has ensured their conjugal sanity for the last thirty years. During my last decade in Bucharest, I used to celebrate all the festivities—Christmas and Easter, as well as Jewish holidays and profane observances—in their spacious home, where now the only novelty is their big, black, jumpy dog.

Lunch will be a lengthy affair, I know, a carefully planned gastronomic gradation. *Tarama salata* and spiced, chopped lamb begin the procession of dishes to stimulate the appetite, accompanied by homemade plum brandy and red and white wines to intensify the flavors. Foreigners, invited into a Romanian home in the years of the Communist dictatorship, were amazed by the culinary abundance, which contrasted so sharply with the prevailing deprivations. When I was visited by relatives or acquaintances from abroad, I always avoided any explanation regarding the ingenious tricks needed for such shows of hospitality.

We clink the first glasses. Golden Brain and Felicia toast each other with the traditional "Christ is risen." We talk about New York and Bard, about the American conductor's concerts. We pay tribute to the salads, the borscht, the roast lamb and pork, the pickles, the white and red wines. The conversation moves from Donna Alba to her husband, who died shortly before the demise of Communism, on which he had wasted so much intelligent effort. We talk about former friends who, in the meantime, had relocated to the cemetery, and about those relocated to Paris, New York, and Tel Aviv. We gossip about friends and acquaintances still active here, in the free-market post-Communist world, as they were, until recently, in the Communist netherworld.

At seven, I go back to my hotel, accompanied by my host, who wants to walk his dog. Along the way, we meet people we know, an actress, an actor, a professor. The street is tranquil, the sun is setting. It feels like the old life. We talk about the confusion and the dangers of the last days of the Communist regime, when rumors flew, changing hourly, fed not just by the omnipresent Securitate but also by obscure forces poised to gain from the people's resentments.

At eleven, I am at the Gara de Nord, the main railway station, to board the night express to Cluj. The flight that I wanted to take was canceled at the last minute because of the small number of passengers, as well as the Easter celebrations. There are only two other passengers in the sleeping car and two young attendants, who look like college students. I miss the old, colorful conductor. When I was a student, I used to travel by train several times a year, making the seven-hour night trip between Bucharest and Suceava. Later, in the Juliet years, I would travel between Ploiești and Bucharest. It was also a train that took me to the labor camp of Periprava to visit my father, and another train that carried me on my farewell journey, in 1986, to say goodbye to my parents and to Bukovina.

I am now traveling in the train of the past. My fellow passengers are the ghosts accompanying the ghost I have been and have become. The compartment seems clean enough, but there is a persistent smell of disinfectant, and the sheets, when I make up the berth, have suspicious-looking stains. The pillow, located directly over the carriage wheels, gives little promise of soothing away the exhaustion that has accumulated over the week in Bucharest. I spread the blanket over the sheets, take off my clothes, and, feeling cold, climb into bed. I draw the curtains. The darkness is shot through with moving shafts of light. The wheels are clanging under my head, and I try to cover my ears against the night's din. The iron horse, snorting and bellowing, is racing through the darkness.

Night Train

It is October 1941. Dozens of people lie piled on top of each other on the cold, damp floor of a cattle car. Everywhere, there are bundles of personal belongings, whispers, moans, the smell of urine and sweat. I am armored in my own fear, diminished, constrained, separate from the body of the collective beast which the guards managed to push onto the train and which is now writhing and struggling with its hundreds of arms and legs and hysterical mouths. I am alone, lost, as though I am not tied to the arms and the mouths and the legs of all the others. "Everybody in!" the guards had shouted. "Everybody, all of you," they had screamed, raising their shining bayonets and guns. There was no escape. "Everybody in line, everybody in, everybody."

We were shoved into the car from behind, and we huddled together, ever closer, until the car was sealed. Maria was beating with her fists against the wooden slots of our pen, begging to be allowed to go with us, her cries growing weaker. The guards gave the signal for departure and the train's wheels began to turn, clanking rhythmically. The train, a mortuary procession, moved into the dark belly of the night.

My second journey by train was the miraculous Return, in 1945. It was April, just like now. Centuries had passed since my first train trip, and by the time of the second, I was old. I did not know then that, centuries later, there would be another return. Now I am old, really old.

The wheels are beating out their nocturnal rhythm, and I am sliding along the fault lines of sleep, of darkness. Suddenly I become aware of fire. The train's cars are ablaze, the iron horse's mane is on fire. Fire and smoke are everywhere. The ghetto is burning, a pogrom is under way. A pyre has been erected in the center of the town, ready to receive the sacrificial lamb. The martyr, a young man with reddish hair and a scraggly beard, is tied to the pyre. The scene is a kind of crucifixion, but the horizontal bar of the cross is missing. There is but a single stake, to which the martyr is bound, his hands tied behind his back. The sacred straps of the phylacteries encircle his body, which is wrapped in a prayer shawl. His legs are tied to the stake with rope. His feet, his chest, his arms, one shoulder are bare. His skin is yellowed, his face pale. His tired lids are closed, his brimmed ghetto cap askew. The windows of a nearby building are flung open and one can hear screams. People are running desperately to and fro. The vertical stake dominates the scene. Death on the cross has transmuted into a burning at the stake, simple and crude. To one side of the tragic scene, a man stands poised to jump from the window of the burning house. A fiddler rushes about in the crooked street to escape the burning houses, collapsing onto one another. A woman holds an infant in her arms, a pious scholar tries to decipher the day's curse in the pages of his book. Reaching out to the martyr at his feet is his mother, or wife, or sister, her long veil touching his body. Over all looms the ominous stake.

I am walking, seemingly forever, toward the young martyr. The pyre is on the point of igniting. I cannot walk faster, I am powerless to save him, I have only a few moments to find a hiding place. I desperately want to tell him that this is no crucifixion, no resurrection, just an ordinary pyre, but the flames are getting closer and closer. I hear the train approaching. I hear the deafening sound of its clanking wheels. I see smoke and flames. The train is a moving torch, hurtling through darkness. It is getting closer, booming and rattling, ablaze, ever closer.

I wake up in terror and try to free myself from the tangled blanket. I am rolling on top of the wheels, propelled by their sharp, heavy rims. It takes some time before I realize that they have not punctured my skin, that I am not being dragged by the wheels. I am in a train compartment, in Romania, a passenger in an ordinary night train.

I remain there drenched in sweat for a long while with the lamp switched on, unable to summon the courage to reenter the present. I try to remind myself of fairy-tale journeys of the past, youthful sleigh rides in a wintry Bukovina, train trips to smart Bukovinan summer resorts, that autumn train journey in an empty compartment when my mother divulged the secret of her wounded youth. Of course, somehow, I fall asleep again and then wake up, with a sudden thought: the postcard of the Chagall painting, at which I had often stared, unable to understand who had sent it and why.

Day Eight: Monday, April 28, 1997

The train arrives on time, at seven in the morning, at Cluj. I had visited the capital of Transylvania only a very few times. The last time was in the late 1970s, for the anniversary of the excellent literary review *Echinox*, which brought together leading writers of the younger generation. I had always had good relations with the writers of Cluj. My books were always well received in Transylvania, which had never participated in any of the public campaigns launched in the media against the "traitor" and the "cosmopolitan."

I proceed to the University Hotel. I should shave, take a shower, and, especially, get some coffee. But I am exhausted and lie down, fully dressed, on the hard bed, trying to relax my body and mind. I lie there for half an hour, numbed, unable to sleep; then I leave the hotel, stumble into a nearby restaurant, and at last get the resuscitating coffee.

It is a sunny day, a light breeze is blowing. The tranquillity of the scene and the short walk have cheered me up. The hotel room is modest, the bed inhospitable. Even less pleasant is the bathroom—faulty taps, the continuous murmur of leaking water in the toilet bowl. "This was my life in Romania," I can hear the voice of one of my Romanian friends, now living in the West, saying. "The heaps of shit are a memory not easily forgotten," he had once told me. He was the descendant of an illustrious family of Romanian scholars. There are few moments more revealing, he had said, than those moments when, after a subtle conversation with a friend who overwhelms you with quotations in French and German, you go to the café's feces-infested toilet and are dazed by the mounds of refuse, felled by the stench, horrified by the swarming flies.

Before I leave for the rector's office at the university, I report the problem with the bathroom's fixtures to the hotel receptionist. She agrees, with some embarrassment. It seems that she is not unaware of the situation. At the rector's office, I meet with members of the university staff to explain the concept of a college of liberal arts and sciences. Bard is planning to embark on a fund-raising campaign for the purpose of establishing just such a college in Cluj, and is looking for the university's cooperation. The people I am talking to assure me that they are eager to join in the project. I have no reason to doubt them, since the advantages are all on the Romanian side.

I go out to lunch with the rector. It is difficult to find a restaurant open on Easter Monday. Judging from the waiters' hoverings, the rector seems to be a well-known figure, but they can offer us only a single dish, roast beef and fried potatoes. Conversation is difficult, unlike our talk of the year before, in a New York café, when the visiting rector from Cluj surprised me with his objective and critical analysis of conditions in Romania, particularly of the problems faced by intellectuals. He knew the Untied States quite well, having received a doctorate from an American university. I was relieved to be spared the anti-American clichés normally served up by so many Romanian literati, as well as by their French mentors. I had asked him whether he would agree that, there often did not seem to be much difference between the extreme language of the Romanian nationalists and the narcissistic discourse of so many Romanian scholars. He agreed, comfortable with the challenge. I accepted his invitation to come to Cluj, and so here I am, armed with a major project for the cultural improvement of his university. I cannot foresee how long it would take for the post-Communist bureaucracy to defeat us.

My friend Liviu Petrescu is now head of the Writers Association in Cluj. Our reunion in 1990 had been a real delight. Liviu was then in New York as director of the Romanian Cultural Center and we used to meet regularly, either at home or at some other place in town. He had given up inviting me to the center after I rejected his suggestion that I be the subject of the inaugural literary evening. I had never stepped into that building, dominated as it was by political functionaries who were most certainly in touch with the Romanian post-Communist media, which, like their predecessors, continued to describe me as the enemy of national values. Liviu, in his delicate way, had tried to build bridges between all the parties concerned. I was sorry when he later quit his post, disgusted with the arrogance of the Romanian diplomats who tried to manipulate him. He was sorry, too—I was soon to be told—that he had not followed my advice and endured the unpleasantness for a little while longer, since his activities in New York had led to radical improvement in the center's program.

The schedule of events prepared for me by the university did not include anything with Liviu—a sign of the rector's hostility?—and I have been wondering whether we might get together, at least briefly, the following day, in a break from the official schedule.

We meet on the street, in front of the Dacia publishing house. He has an air of British elegance, dressed in a perfectly tailored suit, with perfectly matching shirt and tie. Also present is Alexandru Vlad, the bohemian-looking writer, with his long hair and a wild beard, whom I used to see regularly in my Bucharest years and with whom I kept up a correspondence after I moved to America.

Liviu has arranged an official meeting with the Cluj Writers Association, where I am finally being offered an antidote to the public hostility. Despite the praise in Liviu's welcoming speech, I begin to feel that I am here under false colors, as a buffoon tourist, being hailed as the great star of Romanian literature. This caricature does not replace its opposite. On the contrary, it only reinforces it. Augustus the Fool is out of touch with local clichés, and the murmurs of praise sound more like the screeches of invective. It is all like an annoying case of scabies: the more you scratch, the more you suffer. There is no way to win, and I feel guilty because I am as uneasy with the bouquets as I was with the brickbats. I feel completely inadequate in this comedy of the impossible return, so my former compatriots seem justified perhaps in no longer accepting me as one of them. For them, this is what the occasion celebrates—a stranger's visit. I am no longer used to their pomposities, and I am impolite enough to put an abrupt end to this outpouring of praise, thereby unintentionally offending a friend.

Even the discussion that follows fails to deliver the simple words I have been waiting for. It feels like a meeting of local pensioners, forced to perform in some jolly farce. The only moment of real animation is triggered by a question from an athletic, smartly dressed, Kent-smoking woman: "Do you think that Mircea Eliade's Legionnaire-inspired writings undermine his literary and scholarly works?" The question is obviously addressed to the "anti-national militant," as the media continue to depict me. No one seems to care that I am also the author of anti-Communist writings. It would appear that Communism was never a serious concern of the four million or so Party members of socialist Jormania. Do the members of the Cluj audience believe that whatever fame Eliade enjoys in the West could redeem all the pain endured in yesterday's and today's Romania? Is this the reason they want to see him enshrined as a saint? These questions remain unspoken, as I give my reply: I have never made any public statements about Eliade's "literary and scholarly" work. Neither literature nor scholarship can be judged by moral criteria. My "blasphemy" against Eliade did not refer to his fiction or his scholarly achievements. The questioner ignores my answer and carries on with her plea for "conserving Mircea Eliade's world-renowned works." Before I leave, I am offered a consolation prize. "This has really been a Party meeting. The only ones here who were never Communist Party members are you and me," a distinguished academic whispers to me as we go out.

"I'll never forgive the rector for having kept me off the official schedule of events," Liviu tells me as we say our goodbyes. I leave feeling guilty for not having been more gracious about accepting his praise. (After the visit to Cluj, I was never to speak to him again. A disease he didn't know about at the time would soon carry him off.)

The charming wife of the rector presides over the evening meal. The food and wine compensate for the absence of intimacy. The road back to the hotel becomes a perilous adventure, in a car driven uncertainly by the spouse of a professor at the university. The blue notebook is patiently waiting. My thoughts wander far off, to the cemetery in Suceava.

Day Nine: Tuesday, April 29, 1997

I wake up bleary-eyed and dazed after a sleepless night. Somehow I make my way to the lobby, where I am met by a man with glasses, wearing an elegant overcoat. Politely I extend my hand. The unknown man is smiling, looking as awkward as I. Behind him, I can see Marta Petreu, looking on with a smile. Then I realize that this must be Marta's husband, Ion Vartic. I haven't seen him since the tenth anniversary of *Echinox*, in 1979, when he was one of the literary review's famous three-member editorial board. Young Ion Vartic has changed, and so have I. Only Marta looks the same, still wearing her air of perpetual student.

I learn that they have returned from a trip to Budapest just to see me. Marta is carrying a hamper containing sandwiches and coffee. We go outside and have breakfast on the lawn, then return to the lobby. The surprise of finding myself again among old friends does not lessen, even after the coffee has dispelled the daze.

Today I am to give a lecture at the university, before the faculty of language and literature and their guests, and we proceed to the campus, where we are greeted by the dean and a group of academics. We make pleasant chitchat about America, American education and literature, as well as the projected collaboration between Bard College and the University of Cluj. I recognize many faces in the audience. A TV crew asks for permission to film the proceedings, which I readily grant. I seem to feel less vulnerable in Cluj than elsewhere in the country, although I would rather be having a discussion with the assembled group than giving a lecture on "End-of-the-Century Literature." Under the circumstances, all I can do is hide my uneasiness.

Before we take our leave, Liviu gives me a recent translation of a study on Eliade by Claudio Mutti, the Italian Fascist scholar. Eliade again? The Legion? What have I to do with all this? I've hardly anything to do with myself these days. I am a refugee, hidden away in a corner of the world, that's all.

Next on the schedule is a short meeting at the modern offices of the Soros Foundation. The head of the local branch is a Magyar who, in a display of ethnic courage, was brave enough to challenge his own community. There is a refreshingly professional manner about him that makes me both pensive and melancholy. Romania, I think to myself, has always had such solitary fighters, but, alas, too few.

After lunch, I go to the Vartics', where we are to be joined by the rector and his wife. Marta takes me on a brief tour of the book-lined apartment. I am reminded of the wall-length bookshelves of my old room on Sfîntul Ion Nou Street, then my books on Calea Victoriei, then in no-man's-land. Wine and Easter cake are passed around. Ion asks me about the phrase *felix culpa*, happy guilt, which was the title of my now notorious essay on Eliade. I am among affectionate, faithful friends and I don't see the question as a threat. Still, I can't rid myself of the feeling that I am some kind of dubious character, a leper, someone with a shameful disease that everyone knows about. What have I got to do with . . . But I refrain from going into these old-new questions.

I decide to put an end to the prolonged silence and pick up the thread of conversation. Oh yes, the phrase *felix culpa*, that famous fragment from Saint Augustine. *O felix culpa, quae talem ac tantum meruit habere Redemptorem*—"O happy guilt, which merited such a great Saviour." The term *culpa*, not devoid of ambiguity, means sin, error, disease, crime, mistake. However, most encyclopedias of religion render it as guilt. The silence that follows this learned outburst seems longer than the preceding one.

The rector and his wife arrive, we clink glasses and sit down to a pleasant lunch and some easygoing conversation. Then Marta, taking fidelity to its limits, drives me to the airport, where I will catch a flight back to Bucharest. She is right, this is no ordinary departure. I came only for a brush with posterity.

The plane to Bucharest is full, narrow, cramped. The lady in the next seat is quick to engage in conversation. I had noticed her upon boarding—tall, slim, with a simple, casual elegance. She appears worried by the weather conditions, not exactly favorable for flying. She asks where I come from, where I am going, and receives my replies with no visible signs of shock. She is surprised that I speak Romanian so perfectly, without a trace of foreign accent. Even Romanians who left the country more recently, she says, come back with changed intonations. My seatmate, an engineer from Cîmpia Turzii, asks what I do. I am also an engineer, I tell her. I graduated from the Institute of Construction in Bucharest, not Cluj. Yes, I worked in design offices and on building sites and also did research. The old profession conveys an impression of normality. My parents were indeed right about engineering, a respectable profession; one has no need to apologize for it.

Emboldened by my confessions, the lady engineer asks how well I am doing in America as an engineer, but does not wait for an answer. She rushes on, eager to tell me how she had to change her job in recent years. With her husband, also an engineer, she is now running a small private timber-processing company that produces lumber for coffins, boxes, and smaller items. Nothing much, she adds, but it's lucrative. She is on her way to Bucharest for the auction of a forest, but things aren't going well: the Communist legacy is still a burden, corruption is rampant, it would be good to have a king again; yes, her family are royalists, they have always been so. Her father, she tells me, was a top pilot in an elite royal aviation unit, a monarchist who educated his daughter in the same spirit. Of course, he was persecuted by the Communists.

I ask minimal questions. The woman admits that she and her husband had been Party members. This was common practice, nobody believed in those slogans, it was all a lie. Not that things are perfect now. Although there have been free elections, young people don't care about morality anymore, all they know are American movies with their violence and sex. We're lucky to have the people from the mountain regions—the people she meets in her work. They're the only guardians of faith and decency, they're the only ones to have preserved their beliefs, they are the future. Once more she expresses her surprise at my perfect Romanian. And what are the impressions of my visit home? I remain silent for a while, finding it difficult to come up with an adequate answer. I have a friend in Bucharest, I say at last, my friend George. One spring morning, "the morning of the most beautiful spring," as the story puts it, George, a man with many amusing nicknames, finally decided to finish a letter he had started writing to his old friend who, many years before, had escaped to a faraway land, where he was "toiling to no avail among strangers."

The lady engineer is listening to the story, wide-eyed. My friend George, I go on, continued to stay where he was. His letter, therefore, was all the more important. That Sunday morning, "the morning of the most beautiful spring," seemed the right time to finish the letter he had begun a long time before. He was wondering what he should say to his friend, living in a real exile.

My listener grows more intrigued. I continue, pretending not to notice her growing bewilderment. So, George is wondering what he should say to his exiled friend. Should he advise him to return home, to take up his old life, re-establish the old connections, including their old friendship? Should he tell him, indirectly to be sure, that the experiment has failed and he should consider coming home? But if he did so, he wouldn't understand his old motherland, if he ever did. If he returned, he would remain a foreigner, as he was everywhere and always. Therefore, having lost his friends, his family, his language, he would be better off staying where he was, "among foreign people," as the story puts it.

There follows a profound silence, the lady engineer is obviously at a loss for words. She must be wondering why I answered her perfectly ordinary question in such a bizarre way.

"Why did you keep repeating 'as the story puts it'?" she asks, fidgeting nervously in her seat.

I allow myself another long silence.

"I read this story somewhere, I think it was a book of children's tales. It was called 'The Judgment,' if I'm not mistaken."

By now, the woman is staring at me, and it is clear that our chat is finished. For the rest of the flight, she doesn't even move in her seat for fear we might touch. As the plane lands, she rushes to the exit without saying goodbye.

The Balada restaurant, on the seventeenth floor of the Intercontinental, is decorated in red and gold, with red leather chairs, red tablemats with a rustic motif. The waiters wear red jackets and the waitresses, red skirts. The band is also decked out in red, each member sitting behind a little red stand with a gold emblem. It is nine in the evening, and I am the only customer. Undiscouraged, the band plays for my benefit. There is a female vocalist, also in red, singing in Italian, mimicking the passion of our Latin cousins. The dark-haired, mustachioed waiter greets me in English and brings me a massive red leather folder containing the menu and drinks list in Romanian and English. I order in English, not only to get better service, but to give the silent, morose-looking waiter the illusion that at least one customer this evening is a tourist.

Everything is pure kitsch. The waiters without diners, the band, the Italian singer, the second vocalist, singing rock and blues, the twenty-three empty tables add a Gothic touch to the scene. The food itself seems fake. The stuffed cabbage that Leon and Ken had so fancied I find tasteless. My palate fails to detect the old flavors; stuffed cabbage belongs to posterity, I should have explained to my American friends. Is my palate at fault? as Proust put it. Only a year before, after learning that I was about to go to Budapest for an academic conference, a Romanian reporter asked me why I did not go on from Budapest to Bucharest, only an hour's flight away. For me, Budapest is as far away as Sydney, I told him, while Bucharest . . . No, it was the fault not of my palate but of posterity.

The band has stopped playing, the waiters are frozen, like mummies, in the night's red vaults. Nobody pays any attention to the placid customer now wiping his glasses with a red napkin. More visions . . . the ghost walking slowly up Amsterdam Avenue. "There is a Führer in every mother, and a mother in every Führer," the Flying Elephant used to quip.

Finally, I was alone and free, as I lay there, on the edge of the sidewalk, gripping her hand and trying to stop her from falling back, once more, into the abyss of no return, into the bottomless pit. My teeth were still grinding with the effort of hanging on to that familiar touch. Her hand had stiffened round mine, and I was screaming, but nobody could hear me in the red, empty vault of the restaurant. The claw was gripping me tightly, piercing my chest. The pain was all the wealth I inherited for my wanderings in the wilderness.

The Longest Day:
Wednesday, April 30, 1997

T he secretary of the Jewish community in Suceava, an old friend of my parents, assured me on the phone that even though the cemetery is closed because of the Passover holiday, an exception will be made for me, "since you've come all the way from America," he says. "Jewish law allows for exceptional situations."

The cemetery in question is the one on the hill, just past the little woods known as the Pădurice, not the one in town. That cemetery, not far from our old home at no. 18 Vasile Bumbac Street, was closed a long time ago. In the early 1960s, when a new highway was being built whose route would cut through the cemetery, the workers, local peasants, refused to disturb the rabbis' graves where, for as long as one could remember, they had been leaving petitions addressed to the Almighty. I knew the old cemetery well, with its eerie stillness, far removed from the bustle of the town. I had never been to the cemetery on the hill.

The flight to Suceava makes a stop in Iaşi. My friend Naum, Golden Brain, is accompanying me. While we are waiting to board the plane again, I tell him about my experiences in Cluj, and he rewards me with juicy gossip from the literary scene. This is the kind of "Oriental" talk that I know so well, with its concealed narratives and inside jokes.

In Suceava, as we come out of the airport, we are greeted by a tall man with a camera slung over his shoulder, unknown to both of us. It turns out that he is a local reporter and a poet, sent by bank director Cucu to meet us and bring us to the headquarters of the Commercial Bank, where I am to receive the Bukovina Foundation Award. I tell him that first I must go to the cemetery. We get into his car.

Looking somewhat shrunken since I last saw him, but wearing the same hat and the same short winter coat, the Secretary of the Jewish community is waiting for me, as arranged, in front of the Tarom travel agency. We drive past the old Austrian town hall, turn left toward the power station and the Pădurice, scene of my adolescent adventures. We go down, then up, turn left again, toward the hill. We catch a glimpse of Stephen the Great's old citadel in the distance, turn right, and reach our destination.

I see the grave for the first time. In the top right-hand corner of the headstone, set in a gilded oval, is her picture. Underneath is the Hebrew text and the Romanian translation, four lines: JANETA MANEA / DE-VOTED WIFE AND MOTHER / born 27 MAY 1904 / died 16 JULY 1988. This is my father's terse style, an expression of the tired tone of their last years together. Had my father died first, my mother would surely have composed a more generous inscription.

The grave is surrounded by a low iron railing. I see a lamp holding a flickering candle and a glass jar containing a few wildflowers. Obviously the caretaker has been alerted to my arrival. I place my hand on the cold railing and look at the gray stone. "I want you to promise me that you will come back for my funeral," she had said. The stone feels rough and cold, but not unfriendly. "You can't leave me here alone. Promise you'll come back, it's important to me." Someone nearby is murmuring the ancient words of the Kaddish: *Yisgadal veyiskadash shemei rabbo.* The words of the prayer for the dead drift in the air. I recognize the voice of that friend of my parents, now feebler with age. He is reciting the memorial prayer in their son's name. I listen to the mournful chant, without joining in and without understanding: *Be-olmo divro chirusei veyamlich malchusei.*

The blind woman had knocked on the door and entered the room, hesitating. She was wearing a bathrobe over her nightgown and she seemed cold. "This time, you're not coming back, I can feel it. You're leaving me here alone." I knew nothing of the future. Unlike her, I was incapable of reading the invisible. "I want you to promise me that if I die and you're not here, you'll come back for my funeral. You must promise me." I had not promised, fearing the binding burden of promises. Now I am free, nobody promises me anything, nor do I have anyone left to make promises to. The God who gave birth to Augustus the Fool was a woman. I could not bear her adoring love and her crushing anxieties, and now there is nothing I can replace them with. She descended into the depths and then ascended into the ephemeral stems of the flowers and the trees and toward the opaque heavens. She is nowhere to be found now, not even in the indifferent, cold stone that I keep touching absent-mindedly.

Min kol birchoso veshiroso, the dirge continues. The chanter is bent with age, and he is swaying back and forth, as custom requires, in memory of the woman who was a friend and whom he accompanied to her grave. He is now invoking her memory on behalf of the son who has come back for the funeral, nine years too late. The prayer is over. We observe a moment of silence—I, Golden Brain, the Kaddish sayer, the poet-reporter, the peasant who tends to the graves, all of us, our heads covered by white skullcaps.

I go on ahead alone, up the hill, and am met by my mother's new neighbors—David Strominger, Max Sternberg, Ego Saldinger, Frederica Lechner, Gerson Mihailovici, Lazăr Meerovici, Jacob Kaufmann, Abraham Isaac Eiferman, Rachel Schiller, Mitzi Wagner, David Herşcovici, Leo Hörer, Leah Lerner, Leo Kinsbrunner, Sumer Ciubotaru, Lazăr Rauch, Joseph Likornik. I know them all, and she knows them even better, sociable as she was and eager to share in their gossip, rumors, and praises. This is her ideal home, I tell myself. Here there is peace, amid the trees and the stones and the neighbors. This idyllic hilltop in Bukovina should bring rest at last to my anxious, neurotic God.

On the last day, before we said goodbye, she had stopped her laments and requests. "You're right, we must not think of what lies ahead. Nobody can predict anything, and at this age, nothing really matters anymore. I may be old and ailing and feeble, but even at this point, I would be happy to leave Romania anytime you want me to, don't forget." It was not to be. She had stayed behind, among her own kin, but far from the one dearest to her. Now she resides on a hilltop in Suceava, and her husband is dying in Jerusalem. A grave for their son awaits him in the nondenominational cemetery of Bard College, where Hannah Arendt and her husband, Hans Blücher, a Bard colleague, both also escapees from the nightmares of twentieth-century Europe, lie buried.

Ever since our return from Transnistria, where she had saved us all by her resilience and devotion, Mother kept repeating that the best thing to do was for all the family to leave the motherland forever. I knew very well the reason why she and my father themselves never left—she would not leave me behind—and I know equally well that she has forgiven me. It was I who finally left her, she would never have abandoned me, but now she is ready to forgive me, even for this betrayal. "It doesn't matter where I'll be. Wherever I am, I'll be here, too," I had tried to reassure her. And so, here I am, at long last, and nothing else matters. All that matters is the grave and the woman who lies buried in it. That pretentious home called the motherland was only a transient residence, as transient as the traps it had laid for us.

I don't remember going down from the top of the hill, but there I was, next to the now extinguished candle at the side of the grave. The Secretary of the Jewish community was waiting for me.

"You know," he said, "the railing is getting a bit rusty. It should be cleaned and repainted. The gravestone, too, is chipped and should be repaired."

"Of course, I'll leave some money with the caretaker," I replied.

I inquire about the cost of the repairs. The money from the Bukovina Foundation Award should cover the cost nicely, and the arrangements are worked out on the spot. I ask for the address of the community office and promise to stop by later with the necessary sum. No. 8 Armenian Street is the address, and I remember it all. That's the street where, just a few houses away, my parents' friends Dr. Albert and his beautiful wife used to live, to say nothing of their beautiful daughter, my erstwhile partner in romantic adventures. Dr. Albert is dead now and Mrs. Albert, that vision from Hollywood, is agonizing somewhere in the Holy Land, while their spectacular daughter must by now be resigned to the routine of middle age. Farther up the hill is the Armenian cemetery, where, at night, the ghosts of Romeo and Juliet still wander. Number 17 was the house of my high-school classmate Dinu Moga, whom I am hoping to see. The Kaddish chanter gave me his telephone number and told me that my old friend is unchanged, he meets him often in the street. Armenian Street, I know it well.

"A small, modest house," the Secretary adds. "It doesn't look like a headquarters. And there's no sign, either, you see what I mean . . ."

No, I don't. The Kaddish sayer, who has known me since I was a child, realizes from my puzzled expression that I don't understand.

"Well, they broke the windows a few times . . . It's better not to have a sign."

I look at my watch. It is eleven o'clock on this splendid spring day, time to go see bank director Cucu, who is waiting to present me with Bukovina's proof of its love.

We leave the cemetery. I know what I've always known, and what these silent stones have confirmed: that nothing lasts, that this day accommodating my past is going to end soon.

In town, we stop at the Gah synagogue, where we are met by two elderly members, neatly dressed in the old Austrian fashion, who must have been notified of my visit. They approach and introduce themselves. The names do not mean much, but they tell me they were friends of my parents. I inquire about Dr. Rauch. Yes, he is still alive, over ninety years old, and said he would like to see me. Dr. Rauch lives in one of the apartment buildings nearby. He has known me from childhood and looked after my mother in the years of her illness and old age. It was he who checked her dead pulse just before lunchtime on her last Saturday. We ring the bell, wait, ring again, knock on the door, until somebody finally appears and tells us that the old man has been taken to the hospital during the night with a urinary infection.

At the Commercial Bank, the jovial Mr. Cucu welcomes us with whiskey and anecdotes about Jews. He is a big, voluble man, dressed in a dark blue suit, who speaks with a heavy Moldavian accent. We are treated to stories about the small market town of Săveni, near Dorohoi, where he was an apprentice at the shop of Moses and Sarah, from whom he learned about business and life. These affectionate memories have obviously been enhanced for tourist visits such as this. Finally, he hands me the certificate and the envelope, and apologizes for not being able to join us at lunch, as he has to go out of town.

We walk along the main street, past the old Austrian town hall, the last headquarters of the local Communist Party. The bell in the tower of the Catholic cathedral across the street announces the noon hour, to the tune of "Awake, Romanians," the new national anthem. A gentleman comes toward us and the reporter-poet stops him. We make the acquaintance of the director of the Agricultural Bank, a massive man with a steady gaze. He and the reporter engage in huddled whispers. When he leaves, I learn that the Agricultural Bank is sponsoring our lunch, at a recently opened restaurant, and that the bank's car is waiting to take us to our feast. We enter the establishment. American music is booming from two loudspeakers affixed to the wall, which is also decorated with a clutter of posters and advertisements. There are about ten small tables in the tiny room. I open the door to the toilet, only to close it immediately and rush away. I return to the table, and the reporter asks for an interview, his tape recorder at the ready. Why not, I think, after all I let myself be filmed by Cluj television, and I'm not in Bucharest but in my native town, where I have always felt at home, and still do. But first, I tell the reporter, I want to settle accounts for the repairs to my mother's grave.

On the way to the Jewish community office the driver asks, with pride in his voice, for my opinion of the restaurant. "You can eat as much as you like, this is what Mr. Director said," he assures me. "Mr. Director is paying for lunch, he told me. Eat as much as you like," he repeats.

At no. 8 Armenian Street, I enter the small room, made even smaller by the tangle of desks and tables. The office staff seems to be expecting me. Near the door an old gentleman looks at me with affection; an elderly, pale lady looks on shyly. We transact our business and I am given a receipt. We exchange thank yous and smiles. I do not know them, but they seem to know me. We shake hands. Everything is over quickly, too quickly. It has all been so decent, friendly, courteous.

I sit down in the courtyard. A few doors away is the Albert house, with its fateful bedroom. Also the Moga house, and the Armenian church, and the cemetery, and the road to the citadel of Zamca, with its pretty little houses with windows like telescopes, Juliet's house . . . The comedy of errors cannot reclaim me. I rise from the nebulas of legends, the driver waves to me, and we return to the restaurant. I give my fellow diners the message I received earlier: We can eat whatever we like. That means grilled pork and roast potatoes, the only items on the menu.

"What memories do you have of Suceava, what is the purpose of your visit?" the reporter-poet asks. I lean into the microphone, and I hear a voice that sounds like mine, but the words are those of a stranger.

"In 1941," I hear myself saying, "I left Bukovina for the first time. After the war, I became a two-bit juvenile actor in the drama of the Red utopia, whose theatrical character was bound to interest a child. In 1959 I was a junior engineer. I left Suceava again in 1961, after a poignant love affair." It all sounds false, as though I am reciting something I learned by heart. The two-bit actor, the Red farce—all these adolescent revolutionary sins, meant to baffle the former servants of the Communist myth, who now compete with each other in denouncing the dictatorship whose accomplices they were.

We are back in the center of town, not far from my parents' last home. The hardworking reporter goes off in search of a camera, reappears, and tells me that somebody, a woman architect, wants to talk to me. A woman of about fifty comes running out from the building on our left where her firm has offices. She has an attractive appearance and seems flustered by the occasion. She is at a loss for words, and simply keeps saying that she used to go for a weekly cup of coffee at a neighbor of my parents. She is nervously searching for words. She mentions my mother's intelligence, her intensity, especially the way she used to speak about her son. "She adored you, simply adored you. You must know this, of course. She would have done anything for you." Her pleasant, deep voice comes to a halt. I mutter something, we shake hands and go our separate ways.

I am now about to make another foray into the past and I tell Golden Brain about the man we are soon to see. Dinu was a high-school class-mate at the time the dictatorship of the proletariat was consolidating its power and class struggle became more acute and the weakened enemy increasingly aggressive, as Joseph Stalin taught us. Any deviation from the accepted Party line, whether to the right or to the left, was not to be tolerated, and the remnants of the old society were to be isolated. As Secretary of the school's Union of Working Youth, I was charged with the task of routing out the three ideological deviants in our midst. The last was Dinu, son of a former liberal solicitor who had done time in Communist prisons. Dinu was majestic in his indifference. "I, an enemy of the people?" he seemed to be saying, as he slowly advanced to the Red podium for his punishment. His dark, sleek hair was parted in the middle, like that of an Argentinian tango dancer. His face was pale, his gaze self-assured. He was looking straight at me, and I could read in his eyes the miserable duplicity of the proceedings over which I was presiding. Or so I remembered. In fact, Dinu returned his Party membership card without looking at, or seeing, anybody.

"I was no longer the innocent celebrity, and very soon I would cease to be a celebrity altogether, cured as I was of the illusions of the stage on which I was performing and of the subtlety of the masquerade," I said, as we were walking toward Dinu's small apartment. After that high-school event, Dinu and I met again, during one of my visits back to Suceava. Neither of us was happy with the arid profession of engineering that we had chosen to escape the confusion of the times. Dinu soon dropped out of the race after only two years of study and ended up as an obscure petty functionary. He managed to preserve his aristocratic aura by becoming a professional failure. In so doing, he avoided having to wear the equalizing uniforms and bureaucratic masks, nor did he have to worry about the mediocre trophies coveted by the parvenus.

In 1959, as a newly graduated engineer, I visited him at his old home in Suceava, at no. 17 Armenian Street. His father was now dead and Dinu lived there with his stepmother, my former history teacher. She remembered me as a pupil and overwhelmed me with praise, which, I suspect, was partly for the benefit of the stepson, who did not complete his studies and settled for a modest job in his hometown. The unflappable Dinu seemed untroubled, he was happy managing his life in his own discreet way. We shared a taste for the same books and records and, probably, a girlfriend or two. It was an easygoing camaraderie, without intimate confessions.

After I moved out of Suceava, I used to see him when I came to Bukovina to spend holidays. By then, he had moved into his own place, furnished with items he had brought from his family home—a pull-out couch, which served as his bed, two armchairs, a small table, two or three pictures, and an old carpet. The Soviet portable radio must have been purchased on his last trip to Riga or Kiev and shared space with the Czech-made tape recorder from Prague and his collection of records, acquired on his summer trips to various socialist destinations. In each of his holiday photos, he was pictured with a different girlfriend. Most of his books were not on display; they were probably in storage somewhere. The only books visible, in the old glass-fronted bookcase, were a set of the red leather-bound Classics of World Literature and a set of the brown leather-bound Classics of Romanian Literature. On top of the bookcase there was an array of wine, vodka, liqueur, and whiskey bottles. Each time I saw him, nothing seemed to have changed, while my own life underwent change after change. I abandoned engineering, got married, published books, entered new stages of exhaustion or exasperation. All these seemed emptied of meaning, as if annulled by the ultimate triviality of any change. Dinu's lack of ambition and zeal, the austere harmony of his provincial life, seemed proof of a lofty indolence compared with my own milieu, as well as with my anxieties and illusions.

As we continue walking, I tell Golden Brain the anecdote about the two Romanians, former high-school classmates, who bump into each other on a flight from New York to Paris and proceed to run through their class roll. Mihai? He practices gynecology in Milan, now on his third wife. Costea? Oil refinery in Venezuela, unmarried. Mircea? He died, poor guy, of a strange infection, in Algeria. Andrei? In Israel, a bank director. Horia? Engineering, in Basel, five children. And Gogu? Gogu Vaida? Gogu stayed home in Suceava. Are you surprised? Not at all. Gogu was always an adventurer.

We climb the stairs to the third floor and ring the bell. Within seconds, Dinu appears at the door, smiling. We go in, sit in the two armchairs, and are offered a sweetish wine he bought on a recent trip to Cyprus. But for the wear and tear, the decor seems unchanged: the same carpet, furniture, drab walls. The leather-bound red and brown volumes are in their familiar places, as are the rows of bottles. My schoolmate seems unchanged, too, apart from one or two extra wrinkles. Otherwise, the recently retired Dinu—he immediately informs me of his change in status—seems only a slightly retouched version of his old self. He tells us that no one in his family is left, they are all dead, including his brother, an engineer in Hunedoara. The brother's wife was Jewish and she and her son later left for Israel. These two, his sister-in-law and nephew, are his only living relatives. What else? He has sold the family house and has just sold off a valuable collection of old silverware for a laughable price. It was hard to find buyers because of the economic crisis and he didn't want to deal with nouveau riche former Securitate agents. He should have sold it in Germany, as advised by another of our former schoolmates, Ştefi, now a photographer in Bremen, but he had no time for the complications involved. Without extra sources of income, however meagre, he would not make it; the pension is an insult.

I ask about Liviu Obreja, "the tormented blond guy," as I used to call him, on account of all his allergies and obscure anxieties, as well as his unnaturally fair, almost white, hair, invisible eyebrows, and albino skin, so delicate and sensitive that even the air irritated it. His pale forehead was always scarred, and he was scarred, too, by the imbecilic political atmosphere and his equally imbecilic engineering job. He withdrew into books, music, and art, and had married a very blond, very shy student. They lived in Bucharest, and I might have run into them last week at the Dalles bookstore or at Leon's concert, or as I walked by the library.

"Obreja!" Dinu says, with some irritation; he had never liked him.

"That sissy! His father, the prosecutor, is dead; his uncle, too. Do you remember him, the director of our high school? His old mother lives alone here in Suceava. Instead of living with her, he prefers to move from one rented room to another, in Bucharest. He and his wife now have two dogs. How can they look after two dogs when they are incapable of looking after themselves?"

He hasn't asked me any questions and I don't know what to tell him about myself. Should I mention the teenage sweetheart who "lured" me to Bucharest, as he used to say? She has been living in England since the early 1970s. I describe the photograph of herself, with her husband and children, that she once sent me; I also inform him of her recent divorce. The subject doesn't seem to engage him, and he simply remarks that he has kept in touch with the Londoner's younger sister. Should I ask him about the political situation? His reply is prompt: "Swine, all of them." He is not referring to the present government but to their predecessors, the coalition led by the ex-Communist Iliescu. He offers us more wine, and I notice that Golden Brain has dozed off in his armchair. I rise to go to the bathroom—the decisive moment, the condition of the lavatory. The room is tiny, the ancient paint is peeling off the walls, the pipes are rusty, likewise the chain of the toilet. The razor is old, the towel crumpled. The room isn't dirty or untidy, just impoverished, the loneliness of the bachelor. I return to the room. Dinu is holding a photograph. "Do you remember the class of 1953? Here you are, in the middle."

I recognize all the faces, but can remember the names of only a few. Lăzăreanu and his accordion; Fatty Hetzel who played the violin; the butcher's son who, in the years of the left-right deviations, was called an "enemy of the people" and who later became a veterinarian in Israel. There is Shury, grown rich in Caracas. And there is Dinu Moga himself, in a white suit and checked shirt. Behind him, withdrawn and modest, the absolute prize winner, Mircea Manolovici. I spot myself in the center of the second row, with my hand on the shoulder of—I can't believe it— Fatty Hetzel, whom I had expelled from the Union of Working Youth the year before. I stand there in my checked shirt, sleeves rolled up, with my thick hair and that stupid smile of adolescence. To the right, partly obscured, is the banner with its lengthy slogan: "The great Stalin has educated us . . . serving with devotion . . . the people's interests . . . a holy cause."

"Let me take the photo to New York," I say. "I want to have an enlargement made. I'll send you back the original."

He agrees, and then says, "I have all your books. I think this would be a good time for you to inscribe them."

Surprise! He has never told me before that he has any of my books. But there they are, eight copies in good condition, which he retrieves from some niche hidden to view.

He seems less impassive than before, his disgust and bitterness are on the point of bursting. Is this the accumulated effect of all those socialist decades, or the realization that a new beginning is impossible?

In the old bookcase, the books are still displayed in the familiar order. The bottles stand in orderly rows, as always; the old carpet is the same. It would seem that the incomprehensible entity called biography is looking for an appropriate epitaph. This is an ordinary visit, as in the time when I used to come for a few days to see my parents and my hometown. We say goodbye with few words, as usual, as though I were not going back to New York and as though we were not aware of something called death.

"Quite a character, your friend," Golden Brain says as we go down the dark staircase, "a mummy, all embalmed arrogance."

Not far from the park entrance we are met by the reporter-poet, this time accompanied by another poet. We go for a short walk in the direction of Zamca, the thirteenth-century citadel whose remains are among the city's chief tourist attractions. The hill, the forest, and the ancient walls, marking some old border, are now a no-man's-land from which one recedes into one's self before venturing forth again into the city.

On both sides of the sloping street are small, neat houses, which I remember from the old days. On the right, at number 8, is the unmarked headquarters of the Jewish community. Next to it, the three-story apartment building where my cousin, the teacher Riemer, with his wife and four kids, used to live. Now they are all in Jerusalem. At number 20 is the white house with a colonnaded porch, the former home of Dr. Albert and his family. To the left, the small, elegant house of the Moga family, which Dinu has sold to who knows which inhabitant of the future century.

We are now at the top of the slope, facing the Armenian belfry and cemetery. We turn left, walking side by side, and reach the walls of the citadel and church, where the reporter takes our picture.

We return to town along a parallel street, the route, I now remember, that my Juliet and I, intoxicated by our heady words, used to take, under the hostile eyes peeping from behind the curtains. We stop in front of a rustic-style house, displaying a pink sign with yellow letters: LA MIHAI, BAR-CAFÉ. Another sign touts Pepsi-Cola. We continue down the slope. From behind a window, a skeptical-looking white cat, with the pointed nose of a gossip, stares out at us. Not far from the end of the street, just before the high school, is a massive one-story house, with elaborate ornamentation. Finally, we come to the severe Austrian lycée where I was once a student, with its heavy wooden front door, the playground, the gym, the basketball court.

Back in town, we pass the bookstore, the park, the travel agency. There is a bus at the stop waiting for its passengers. I should go back to the cemetery, to the one keeping watch over me. She would have approved of how I spent the day. Yes, I did well to seek out Dr. Rauch, a very kind man. I did well to take a bottle of whiskey to the Secretary of the Jewish community, who had arranged for me to visit the cemetery and who will oversee the repairs to the grave's iron fence. It was a good thing, too, to have given an interview to the local paper; after all, this was our hometown, and you saw, didn't you, how that woman architect hasn't forgotten you, hasn't forgotten us. People don't forget, we mustn't bear grudges against anyone. The gentle, old words of the past . . .

Has today been a calm day in her anxiety-laden life? I wanted to believe so, a peaceful day of conciliation with the world. She would have listened avidly to my stories about Dinu and the director of the Agricultural Bank and my former sweetheart, who moved to London. She would have wanted to hear about Leon's success at the Atheneum in Bucharest and about my nightmare on the train from Bucharest to Cluj.

She would have repeated all the old words of forgiveness and acceptance. Then she would have asked for news of her husband, now resettled in Jerusalem, and of my dear wife, who shares my life in New York.

But I cannot go back to the cemetery. It has receded, locked up in the darkness, its residents have withdrawn into their well-earned night. At the airport, I wait for takeoff. I look out the glass wall and see the field, the forest, on the distant horizon. A loudspeaker plays Romanian folk music, the same tunes that were played ten, twenty, thirty years ago.

Two hours later, I am back on the seventeenth floor of the Intercontinental Hotel in Bucharest. Tonight, the Balada restaurant is offering an evening of folk music, instead of the Italian and American popular songs. This time I am not the only customer, I share the golden and red space with a pilot from British Airways.

Back in my room, my eyes glued to the ceiling, I try to regain possession of the day I had left behind. The wall behind the bed is cold in the blackness of the night.

The Penultimate Day:
Thursday, May 1, 1997

May 1, International Workers' Day, is no longer celebrated in post-Communist Romania. The tiny group who have rallied in front of the hotel are a joke compared to the mass rallies of socialism's early decades. The modest, straggling assembly, the improvised banners, the cheeky rebelliousness, all belong to the country's impoverished present, not to its equally impoverished past. The Tyrant himself, in the last decade of his reign, had canceled all "internationalist" festivities. Those that remained acquired a pronounced nationalist character, focusing on the figure of the Incomparable One.

More than half a century ago, on May 1, 1945, having but recently returned from the labor camp in Transnistria, I participated, at age nine, in the celebrations of the "first May Day in freedom." After the Nazi nightmare, that spring promised resurrection and liberty. In my pocket was the Provisional Certificate that guaranteed my "repatriation" to the motherland. The Iaşi police had taken us under their wing as soon as we had crossed the border, and had endowed us with official proof: "Mr. Marcu Manea, together with his family, comprising Janeta, Norman, and Ruti, is hereby repatriated from the U.S.S.R. through the customs point at Ungheni-Iaşi, on April 14, 1945. His destination is the commune Fălticeni, county of Baia, Cuza Vodă Street." No mention, of course, of why we were "expatriated" and then "repatriated," or by whom. Two weeks after our return, I was marching with my father on the streets of Fălticeni, to honor the promises of the repatriation.

Now, more than half a century later, I have made a new return and am witness to another May Day in freedom, this time, however, after the fall of Communism and not, as then, before its imminent advent. The quartet named in the 1945 document has, in the meantime, disbanded, and estrangement from the motherland has become our new state of belonging. Only the resident of the grave in Suceava has stayed behind, and that against her will. Today, I will be observing May Day with a visit to another cemetery, not the one in Străuleşti, where I might have a short chat with the Flying Elephant, or Bellu, for a reunion with Maria. I have little time, as both the dead and the living well know. I am going to the cemetery in the Giurgiu section, to visit the graves of Cella's parents and grandparents and to pass on to them her incommunicable messages.

After ten years of separation, I would also be reunited with my friend Half-Man-Riding, Half-One-Legged-Hare. "Love is not just an abstract term . . . A man is someone who leaves behind a vacuum greater than the space he previously occupied," he had written me before he died. The poet had turned Ohm's Law into a Law of Humanity. "I think of you with great love and lonely longing. I can hear kids playing in the streets. Shall we ever play together again?" After 1986, we continued our play, albeit from a distance, and we are still playing now.

I set out for the cemetery, again accompanied by Golden Brain. The gatekeeper is the same old man of years before. We pay the entrance fee and make a "contribution" for the community. We look in the register of burials and find the location of the graves we want.

Just inside the entrance is a sculpture in the shape of a tree trunk with broken-off limbs. A plaque, with white lettering in the style of the early postwar years, reads: "During the Second World War, the Fascist armies invaded and devastated the Jewish cemeteries in the U.S.S.R., using the forced labor of the Jewish detainees. Tens of thousands of granite gravestones, genuine works of art, were destroyed or transported by the Fascists to their own countries. The gravestones on display here were saved from that destruction." The granite slabs rise from a pedestal to form a tree trunk from which emerges a body with amputated arms. On one of the slabs is inscribed in Russian: "Journalist Julia Osipovich Shakhovalev." Next to it; "Sophia Moiseeva Gold. *Mir tvoemu, dorogaia mato*"—Peace unto you, beloved mother. A marble monument, dated 1947, bears the inscription: "To the memory of the holy martyrs from Romania who perished for the Sanctification of the Holy Name, in the waters of the Black Sea, on the ship *Struma*."—commemorating the 769 fugitives from Romania seeking haven in Palestine, who met a watery death when their boat was sunk by a Soviet torpedo in the Black Sea on February 24, 1942. Their names are inscribed on three sides of the marble.

I am silent, lost in the past. I see a tall, slim man, slightly bent, moving with a kind of quick determination and totally engrossed in his tasks. I also see a neat, elegant woman, with a serene air of distinction about her. And I see another woman, lost in the fog of old age, enjoying a secret sip of cherry liqueur. They have finally found their roots here; nobody can accuse them anymore of being "rootless aliens," foreigners. Now they are all dust, the nation's soil, property of the motherland. Once they were strangers, now nobody cares. They are dust of planet Earth, which does not belong to anyone. I lay my palms on the white slab marking the grave of Cella's father, Jack, and on the stone of the grave shared by Evelyne and Toni, Cella's mother and grandmother. I place a pebble on each gravestone, as is the custom of the ancestors, now all turned to stone, to dust. I see the cemetery in Suceava and the small cemetery awaiting me at Bard College. We look for the grave of the poet Half-Man-Riding/Half-Dead-Man-Riding, Half-One-Legged-Hare/Half-One-Legged-Dead-Hare.

"*Encore un moment, monsieur le bourreau, encore un moment*"—one moment, please, Mr. Executioner, my friend had pleaded uselessly, still riding a half-lame illusion. "The fire is weaker than the book it is consuming," he is saying, as he hobbles around, frightened and sweating. "You may ruin yourself, if you wish, but you must do it with enthusiasm," the tireless one tirelessly repeats, shaking with fear at each syllable, as though it were a sword. "Where are you, student of fear? Where are your Bibles?" he asks me as he hops around on one leg, together with his lame black dog. Then he again whispers his secret into my ear, with brotherly tenderness: "Poetry, the lie detector prone to burst into tears." The shadows and the clowns take off their masks, their prostheses, leave aside their crutches, and line up into a neat row of phosphorescent letters: "Florin Mugur—Poet—1932–1991." I am alive, still alive, for yet another living moment, leaning against the gravestone of Florin Mugur, and against that other gravestone, in the cemetery of Suceava. "I hope to be the first to die," she had said. "Without Marcu, I'd be a burden for you. I'm difficult, not easy to live with. I've always been nervous, prone to exaggeration. It would be too hard on you."

Indeed, it would not have been easy. She panicked easily, she was difficult, she certainly had a tendency to exaggerate—yes, it would have been hard. "Someone you love is someone whose absence in the space he or she previously filled is greater than their presence there." Her prayer was fulfilled; she was the first to die, leaving behind a vacuum even greater than her overflowing presence had been. Yes, she fulfilled the criteria of Ohm's Law, as reformulated by the poet Florin Mugur. Her presence could be unnerving, possessive, unbearable, but the vacuum she left was even greater, even more unbearable. "You and Cella, look after Father," she had said. "He's not like me, he would never ask for anything. He's silent, unsociable, you know him. He's remote and fragile, easy to hurt." Destiny had looked after him. The widower was extricated from his native land and sent to the Holy Land, into the loneliness where, in fact, he had always lived. Recently, he had been transferred to the desert of Alzheimer's disease.

The day before, at the cemetery, we had not had a chance to speak about Father, or about Cella. Our reunion had been brief, the dead woman's questions concerned only with her son and her father. These, it would seem, had been the only important men in her life, the son now living in the Babylon of New York and the bookseller Avram lying in a nameless forest in Ukraine. Now, as I was leaving the graveyard of the past, I must speak to her of her husband.

I visit him at least once a year, I tell her. His eyes brighten whenever he sees me. He smiles happily, an even, unchanging smile on a serene face. I tell her of my last meeting with him.

It was a Sunday in June. I had arrived earlier than planned at the Beit Reuven Nursing Home in Jerusalem. I went up to the second floor. This time Father was not among the phantoms in the dining room. I went to seek him in his room. I opened the door and stood on the threshold, without making any attempt either to advance or to retreat. I looked at him. He was standing, naked, in front of the window. A tall blond young man, a towel in each hand, was cleaning him up. The young man saw me and smiled. We knew each other from previous visits and had chatted a few times. He was a young German volunteer, working at that old people's home in Jerusalem. Thin, delicate, he behaved with untiring courtesy, both in his work and outside it. He switched easily from German to French and English, as well as improvising sentences in Yiddish, to make himself understood by the old people in that Babel of senility. We had chatted in German, the language he now used to soothe my father. What I saw confirmed what I had learned from the nurses who sang his praises. He devoted himself, like no one else, to the daily tasks that made the other attendants collapse with exhaustion. He was carefully cleaning each part of Father's feces-smeared body—the bony arms, the waxen thighs, the flabby buttocks, the glassy knees. The young German was carefully wiping the old Jew clean of the dirt that the Nazi posters had once heaped on him. I looked on, motionless, then left, closing the door behind me. I returned to the dining room. Father arrived half an hour later, smiling. "You're late today," I said. "I've been sleeping late," he answered, with the same absentminded smile. He had forgotten all about the young man who had just finished cleaning him, brought him fresh clothes, dressed him, and taken him to the dining room where I was waiting.

I had to give her this last bit of important information before leaving the graveyard of the past, that Father, freed at last from solitude, was now, without any thoughts or worries, in the tender care of a young German seeking to redeem his country's honor. At last, nine years too late, I had finally showed up for my mother's funeral, and my motherland's, too.

The Last Day: Friday, May 2, 1997

The shadow is tiptoeing around the room, careful not to wake me, impatient to wake me, so that she can see me and get some meaning back into her meaningless world. No, I am not going to move, I am not going to wake up. She withdraws at last, and I get up, mindful not to look around, eager to be fully awake and start my preparations for departure.

Marta calls from Cluj to wish me a safe journey and to give me the bad news: her request to the Soros Foundation for a subsidy to publish the books I had finally agreed to let her bring out had been turned down, despite her best efforts. "I don't know how they could reject this application," she says mournfully. "I used the American promotional method: The future Nobel Prize for Romania! The Laureate's Reconciliation with his motherland! I even believe these statements, you know." I am reminded of the reporter-poet from Suceava, who had boasted of the financial support he had received from the same foundation for one of his books of poetry to be published in England. Marta's news seems like an affectionate prank, a farcical ending to my journey.

I take a seat near the window in the café off the lobby, one last hour in the bosom of the motherland. I am looking through the quotations I have jotted down on the first page of my blue notebook, to guide me on this trip—Hannah Arendt, Emmanuel Levinas, Paul Celan, Jacques Derrida, all of them with something to say about language as motherland. I needed other people's words, after having talked to myself for too long. I am seeing and unseeing at the same time. I can, however, make out the silhouettes from the past and I am sure I see them—miraculous apparitions—Liviu Obreja, my former albino classmate, and his blond wife. They are walking past the carpet store on Batiștei Street, with two big shaggy brown dogs pulling at their leashes and dragging Liviu along.

Liviu has a lot of gray hair now. He looks, and doesn't look, older, like those of us who, not having had the time or the strength to grow up, have extended adolescence into old age. He is the same as he was fifty years ago, the same ghost I have bumped into over the past fifty years in bookstores and record shops. He is the permanent symbol of this place, of any place. In a thousand years' time, I would probably find him here, unchanged.

I had been waiting for this inevitable meeting since the first day of my return. Here he was at last, on that May afternoon, dragged by his two large shaggy dogs. Here they were, the four of them—father, mother, and two huge, fretful babies. I look at them through the glass wall of the aquarium where I am having my farewell cup of coffee. I would like to get up, go out into the street, and catch up with Liviu, but time has already blinked and the moment is gone.

Dinu was right, I concede in my perplexity, about the two dogs Lache and Mache, they really exist. I saw them with my own eyes, only a moment ago, on Batiștei Street, at the corner of Magheru Boulevard, not far from the Intercontinental Hotel in Bucharest. Was that the route we had started on forty years before, the three of us—Liviu, Dinu, and myself—in the purple days of Stalinism, from which we had tried to escape, with the help of books, music, and other teenage tricks? No, at that time none of us would have guessed what purgatory lay ahead.

Augustus the Fool had been oversensitive, awkward, and remote throughout his tour of posterity. But now, at last, he has found a suitable audience. In an enlightened moment I open my blue notebook and start an epistle to Lache and Mache: "The departure did not liberate me, the return did not restore me. I am an embarrassed inhabitant of my own biography." Lache and Mache, being genuine cosmopolitans able to adapt anywhere, would understand how enriching the experience of exile has been, how intense and instructive. I have no reason to feel ashamed before such an appreciative audience, so I write feverishly, in scrambled, hurried words, all the unanswerable questions that come to my mind: Was my journey irrelevant? Did this very irrelevance justify it? Were the past and the future only good-humored winks of the great void? Is our biography located within ourselves and nowhere else? Is the nomadic motherland also within ourselves? Had I freed myself of the burden of trying to be something, anything? Was I finally free? Does the scapegoat, driven into the wilderness, really carry away with it everyone else's sins? Had I taken the side of the world in my confrontation with it?

I have finally found my audience. All those delayed thoughts now find expression, as I scribble away furiously in the hotel café and in the taxi taking me to the airport. The impossible return was not an experiment to be ignored lightly, dear Lache and Mache. Its irrelevance is part of our greater irrelevance, and therefore I bear no one a grudge. As I wait to check in at Otopeni Airport, I write down the ending of a story that, I am certain, the recipients of my epistle will understand: I will not disappear, like Kafka's cockroach, by burying my head in the earth. I will simply continue my wanderings, a snail serenely accepting its destiny.

I board the plane for the flight from nowhere to nowhere. Only graveyards are permanent. The permanence of passage, the comedy of substitution, the magic trick of the finale—Augustus the Fool could have experienced such banal revelations without ever submitting to the parody of the return from which he is now returning. Now I am certain: America offered the best possible route of transit. At the very least, I now have confirmation of this truth. I climb the stairs to the plane, to the rhythm of the prayer I had learned from the Polish poet, step by step, word by word: "In Paradise one is better off than in whatever country. The social system is stable and the rulers are wise. In Paradise one is better off than anywhere else." I mutter that refrain of the aliens as I settle into the womb of the Bird of Paradise. The emptiness increases, and so does the dizziness. Takeoff—an uncertain suspension, the privilege of feeling dispossessed of one's own self, the gliding, the void, the absorption into the void. I use the stopover in Frankfurt before my transatlantic flight to complete my letter to Lache and Mache—details from my last morning in Bucharest, the swirling vortex of the thoughts in the passenger's mind, the scapegoat, the cockroach, the snail's shell, the prayer of Paradise's aliens. My blue notebook has been good company at the Intercontinental Hotel in Bucharest, on the train to Cluj, and on the flight to Frankfurt. Over the twelve days of the journey, it filled up with nervous, twisted letters, arrows, coded questions.

The return flight is very different without Leon's cheering presence. The young Chinese man sitting next to me seems to divide his time equally between watching the in-flight movie and sleeping, with spasmodic fits of snoring and facial grimaces. I had bought *The New York Times* and the *Frankfurter Allgemeine*, and I had a book as well. I scribbled occasionally in my notebook, but time passed slowly. I would have liked to land in a bed as quickly as possible and sleep for a decade, suspended in emptiness. DEPRESSION IS A FLAW IN CHEMISTRY NOT IN CHARACTER was written in the phosphorescent sky. These seemed appropriate words of welcome as I approached my destination. I repeat the message gratefully, the password of my re-entry, as I continue to glide through the sky.

"I just wanted to know if you're safely back yet. We had a great time together in Bucharest." It is Leon's voice calling from the car taking him to Bard. Next Saul S., wearing a big white cap, swims into view. He is holding a map in his large, bony hands. His bushy white mustache has grown into a brush above his mouth. "Strada Gentilă," he reads, smiling with delight, seduced by the names. Gentle Street, Concord Street, Rhinoceros Street . . . Yes, I am on my way back, rocked in the armchair of the heavens.

Leon's voice is still floating upward. I see his long black car speeding up the Taconic Parkway. "We had a great time in Bucharest. Great time."

Suddenly the plane begins to swerve, people are startled out of their sleep, I hear moaning. I am too dazed and exhausted to try to re-establish contact with Earth. The flight resumes its motionless gliding. Leon's voice comes back, crackling with static. "We had a great time in Romania. The best things that happened to you there were the bad things." Is it Leon talking, or Saul? I am no longer certain. It might very well be Saul, who knows all about the East European child hiding in a corner of the room, listening to his father talking to the other men, looking at his mother, dressed in traveling clothes, and at his sister, with her beautiful hair . . . all of them, soon, fleeing to America.

"You're coming home, don't you forget that. Home is here. Here, not there. This is your luck, born out of your bad luck." It is Leon's voice this time, I'm sure, and I am ready to acknowledge, yes, I am returning home, in the snail's shell, ready to talk about the graveyard in Suceava, about the new course I am preparing for the fall semester, *Exile and Estrangement*, but he doesn't listen anymore, he never has time for long chats. I close the blue notebook with its stories about the Flying Elephant and Half-Man-Riding, Half-One-Legged-Hare. I put my notebook away, at the back of my seat, so that I can feel it. The plane is bouncing again and I am dizzy and shaken.

The flight attendant comes over. "Would you like a drink?"

I am offered wine, beer, soft drinks, and whiskey. I ask for a glass of mineral water. Evian, Perrier, Apollinaris, Pellegrino? I opt for Pellegrino, the pilgrim's drink.

The plane lands and I rush to the exit. The luggage comes down quickly, the Asian taxi driver speeds away, and soon we arrive back in Manhattan, on the Upper West Side. Dazed after the long trip and the lingering confusions, I have difficulty finding my way around the house. There is no place like the paradise of home.

Later that evening, after nine, my inner alarm goes off. I rush to the travel bag, unzip the first compartment, then the second, and start ransacking, in despair. I have a sinister foreboding, but refuse to accept the reality of the disaster. The notebook! The notebook is missing!

Suddenly it all comes back to me. Augustus the Fool had fallen into a fitful, delirious sleep, than drank his Pellegrino, then rushed to the exit door, eager to forget everything, to get home as quickly as possible. The blue notebook had stayed behind on the plane, nestled in my empty seat.

In a frenzy I call the airport, then Lufthansa, and learn that the plane will be flying back to Frankfurt that same evening. I am given polite assurances: whatever was found when cleaning the plane will be collected and classified during the night. The next morning, around ten, I should call back and they'll know whether the precious object has been found. Among the pile of newspapers, bags, and other assorted items left behind on the plane? Germans will be Germans, I said to myself, they're orderly and thorough. The notebook would be found. After all, I was traveling first class, and class privilege must mean something. I had reason to be confident.

My first night back in America is not a pleasant one. Fatigue, panic, rage, annoyance, impotence, regret, guilt, hysteria. The pages could not be lost, they must not be allowed to disappear! Yet somehow I felt that they would not allow themselves to be found.

The first American morning is no better. At ten my fears are confirmed. At eleven they are reconfirmed. At twelve an irritated voice explains that there is no hope of finding the lost item, but should a miracle occur, it will be sent to my home.

Home, to my home address, in New York, of course. Yes, the Upper West Side, in Manhattan.